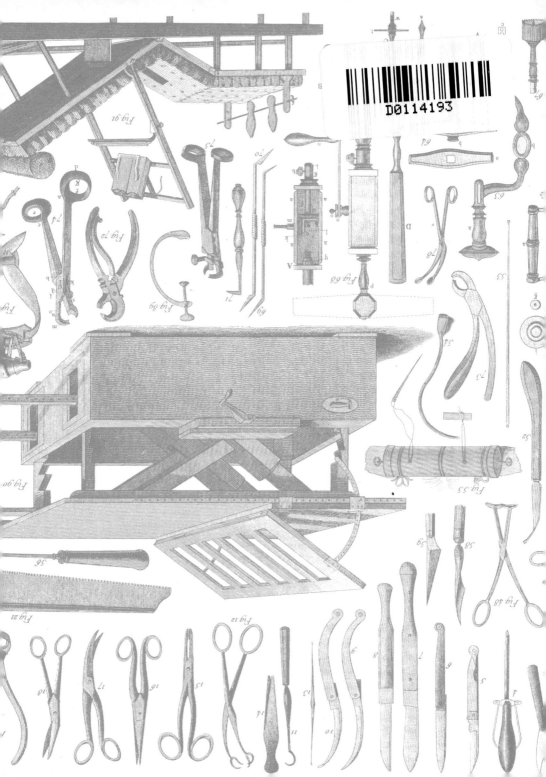

THE BODY IN THE LIBRARY

THE BODY IN THE LIBRARY

A Literary Anthology of Modern Medicine

◆

Edited by

IAIN BAMFORTH

VERSO

London • New York

First published by Verso 2003
Collection © Verso 2003
Introductory material © Iain Bamforth 2003

1 3 5 7 9 10 8 6 4 2

Verso
UK: 6 Meard Street, London W1F 0EG
USA: 180 Varick Street, New York, NY 10014−4606
www.versobooks.com

Verso is the imprint of New Left Books

ISBN 1−85984−534−7

British Library Cataloguing in Publication Data
Bamforth, Iain, 1959–
   The body in the library: a literary anthology of modern medicine
   1. Medicine–Literary collections
   2. Social medicine–Literary collections
   I. Title
   808.8′0356
   ISBN 1859845347

Library of Congress Cataloging-in-Publication Data
A catalog record for this book is available from the Library of Congress

Typeset in Bembo
Printed in the UK by Clowes

CONTENTS

INTRODUCTION

The Body in the Library

"Sapere Aude!" was Kant's clarion-call to the new age in his short essay *An Answer to the Question: What is Enlightenment?* (1784)—have the courage to know for yourself. But doctors, some of them at least, had been daring to know for quite some time.

If there is a Year Zero in the history of this medical daring it is 1543. That was the year when Andreas Vesalius, a physician from the Low Countries newly appointed to the position of dissector in Padua, published his treatise *On the Structure of the Human Body* in Basel, one of the centres of the printed book. The new medicine was a wager on the body: no longer would medicine be guided by the prestige of what had been written, most notably by Galen of Pergamon, the great Roman doctor. No longer would the *medici* be allowed to see only what they expected to see. As Vesalius wrote: "the violation of the body would be the revelation of its truth." Bodies were the thing. And there they are, throughout Vesalius' treatise, in extraordinary graceful poses in the middle of classical landscapes: men missing the tops of their heads, skeletons digging their own graves. It is easy to see why dissection was to become the rite of passage for generations of medical students: this is the frontier at which the student has to grasp a profoundly unsettling thought: violation is devotion, mutilation repair. The student has been authorized, in the name of society itself, to subvert a social taboo. And just as much as Descartes' philosophy, Galileo's physics or Bacon's experiments, Vesalius' refusal to be guided by the authority of a dead language was to wrench us all into modernity, imposing a strict dualism between humans and their bodies, and making the latter vehicles of their being in the world.

In Marguerite Yourcenar's 1968 novel *The Abyss (L'œuvre au noir)*, the central personage, the sixteenth-century physician and alchemist Zeno, recalls his student days at Montpellier:

We were short of corpses for study, public prejudice being what it is. A physician called Rondelet, as comically rotund as his name, lost a son from an attack of purpuric fever, a young student of twenty-two with whom I had often gone collecting herbs in Grau-du-Roi. He died a day after. In that room impregnated with vinegar, where we dissected this dead youth, who had ceased to be either son or friend, and was now only a fine specimen of the human machine, I had the feeling for the first time that the arts of mathematics and mechanics, on the one side, and the great art, alchemy, on the other, apply to our study of the universe only those same truths which our bodies teach us; for in our bodies is repeated the structure of the Whole.

Zeno's logic is impeccable. The body might have been an object of odium, in Christian doctrine, but the knowledge of it opened sits uncomfortably with the fact that in social life, a cadaver is never purely a thing, especially not for those who were acquainted with it in life. Besides, wasn't it the Lord's tabernacle?

This bifocal view of reality is peculiarly Western, and that only over a relatively short period of time. Yet Western medicine is ignorant of its past. Europe's medical tradition would not have survived had it not been for the physicians and scholars of Baghdad. While the first medical school on European soil, at Salerno, was set up by Muslims in the ninth century. The Chinese famously made fireworks, not weapons, out of gunpowder. Similarly, Chinese medicine retained its classical knowledge scheme, and remained resolutely traditional. The human body was a microcosm of the natural and social worlds; cosmology and psychology were in intimate connection. This made healing a philosophical problem, a matter of restoring harmony to a whole based on systematic correspondences; and in many respects Hippocratic medicine was no different. So it is all the more remarkable that a tradition which had been around for two thousand years, and which carried the prestige of ancient Athens, should give way to another kind of tradition: one that explicitly denied the claims of the past, devalued the claims of memory, and took nothing on trust. Even so, it didn't like to turn its thinking on itself, and the accusing fact, in Berz

Keizer's words, that "medicine doesn't always have to deliver the goods, but it can still send the bill." In China, doctors were paid only if they kept their patients healthy.

Signal discoveries emerged in the Renaissance period, as anatomists and doctors, equipped after 1609 with precision lenses imported from the Netherlands, opened up the world of the infinitely small. As voyagers set off to chart the globe, the human body was probed and dissected, yielding up its new found lands to its eponymous explorers: the Fallopian tubes, the Malphigian tubules, the Graafian follicles, Bartholin's duct, the circle of Willis. William Harvey's demonstration of the circulation of the blood (on a live dog) threatened to eclipse the noble organs of Galenic medicine completely, while offering in its spectacle of blood indifferently in motion a paradigm more persuasive than movable type for the commercial society rapidly developing in Europe. The Englishman Robert Hooke used the word "cell" for the first time in his *Micrographia* of 1665. A baroque age of information was under way, in which mountains of reports, treatises, monographs and letters piled up in fantastic profusion. The foundations of modern chemistry were laid, and advances were made in what would later become known as physiology. Morgagni's 1761 treatise *The Seats and Causes of Diseases Investigated by Anatomy* began to codify diseases in terms of their loci.

These discoveries, and thousands more, form part of the conventional history of medicine: the recitation of heroes and saints, experimenters and campaigners. Medicine as a profession had, until the Renaissance, been a divided one: the life of the soul was, in Christian doctrine, more important than that of the body. Surgery, and dealing with the body generally, was the remit of barber-surgeons, who were looked down on by the learned doctors. The Church abhorred blood. Hospitals, alms-houses and hospices were institutions devoted to the idea of charity. Any medical arts practised there were secondary to the essential nature of such places, which was moral: to recuperate souls before bodies gave out. Yet the body was unmistakably the seat of power: the royal body was never without its compliment of doctors, who as often as not put it through torture. Functionally, priests and doctors had a common goal; and both supped at the master's table.

Medicine was a series of rituals, teachings and practices; a theatre of healing or purgation, in which a doctor hammed it up like most people in public life. One of Pascal's *Pensées* reads: "if learned doctors did not wear square caps and robes four times too large, they would never have deceived the world, which finds such an authentic display irresistible. If they possessed true justice, and if physicians possessed the true art of healing, they would not need square caps; the majesty of such sciences would command respect in itself." Medicine was masquerade; and Molière wrote its apotheosis in a profound study of medicine, theatre and belief, his play *The Imaginary Patient*.

As for the mass of the common people—the voices never heard and faces never seen in learned medical discourse—they would have known no other medicine than folk traditions and midwifery, or the herbs that provided the pharmacopoeia for a world still reasoning in terms of cosmic analogies. Barnaby Factotum down at the market might have drawn a tooth, but knowledge was oral, and treatment took place at home rather than in an institution. Much of that knowledge was in the hands, and heads, of women; and sold in thousands when the presses came, in vernacular works like *The English Housewife* (1615).

New genres flourished with new technologies: self-help and morally uplifting reading were all the rage in the early eighteenth century. Roy Porter has brilliantly recaptured the stock figures of the doctor that featured in the rambunctious and refreshingly savage political cartoons of the era. Medicine and malady were equal tormentors, giving rise to the tenacious belief that a "physick" had to hurt to work. The title Rowlandson gave to the lecherous physician in one of his caricatures says it all: Doctor Doubledose. In *Tristram Shandy* Laurence Sterne mocks his hapless physician-hero by giving him a comic name: Dr Slop. Medicine itself was shifting from a quasi-religious moral drama to a more naturalistic ethos; along with confidence in human nature the Enlightenment brought an interest in temporal well-being. Penal reformers condemned corporal punishment as futile, and made plans for the body to be removed from the public arena to the subjugating gaze of the expert. One of the men who proposed such things, the utilitarian Jeremy Bentham, not wanting to feel idle after his death, bequeathed his carcase to University College, London, as an auto-icon. It can still be seen today. Yet already a certain irony was making itself felt: the more health was pursued as a good, the more people seemed to feel ill.

The Revolution in Paris in 1789 gave medicine another galvanic jolt. Revolutionary lawyers wrestled charity from the hands of the Church. Health councils were set up in the major French cities; university teaching was overhauled; and with Bonaparte's *coup d'état*, and the appointment of a physician, Jean-Antoine Chaptal, as Minister of the Interior, medical services were organised on the grand scale. Traditionally one of Europe's most conservative centres of medical education, Paris became a vast public endowment: its hospitals were to offer more beds than all of England, and as Orwell discovered a century later, they were not places of good cheer. A model citizen-patient was called into being, and hygiene became a respectable philosophical subject for exposing the relations between illness, social class, urban geography and occupation. Knowledge was to be applied for the public benefit. The reorganisation of Revolutionary year *an XI* gave medicine its status as a liberal profession, and the figure of the "bon docteur" appeared: morning rounds treating the indigent in the local hospital and afternoons attending to rich bourgeois clients in his well-appointed chambers.

The conflict of interests between morbid anatomy's hunger for corpses and the work of the executioner that had first emerged in the sixteenth century became downright murky. Paris would become famous in medical circles for its autopsies, and in Edinburgh, grave-robbers made a brisk trade until the Anatomy Act of 1832. *Libido sciendi*—John Donne had called it "hydroptic immoderate thirst for humane learning and languages," and De Quincey, closer to the events in question, the work of "morbidly virtuous" men. Already Xavier Bichat's *Treatise on Membranes* (1799) had largely dispensed with what the patient said about his suffering. In his often quoted words: "symptoms, corresponding to nothing, will offer but incoherent phenomena. Open a few corpses, and this obscurity, which observation alone would never have removed, will straightaway disappear."

Life was epiphenomenal to what really counted. René Laënnec discovered that a rolled-up wad of paper offered a better appreciation of internal body sounds (mediate as opposed to immediate auscultation, which required the ear to be directly applied to the patient's body): his device was to transform what happened at the bedside. Not only that, but the distracting, unreliable and perhaps even unwashed patient could be decisively rebuffed. Soon students were being drilled so as to perceive morbid signs and sounds: an education of the senses. Other instruments followed the stethoscope: thermometers, hypodermic syringes and laryngoscopes. Soon after Pierre Louis suggested measuring the outcomes of different treatments numerically, the first social statistics were elaborated. The moral condition of a nation would be worked out probabilistically, in 1840, by Adolphe Quetelet. The individual patient was on the way to becoming a case study, while the old Hippocratic notion of the medical triangle (disease, doctor, patient) gave way to a dual between doctor and disease.

Oddly enough, while the French were the leading theorists in matters of hygiene and urban planning, they were stragglers in terms of social works. In England, however, the state accepted that it had to provide medical care for the sick poor, and a Poor Law was introduced in 1834. By 1840, London was being opened up to allow the laying of pipes for the supply of fresh drinking water and the removal of sewage. These social innovations slowly transformed the colonies too. Chloroform was first used during a delivery in 1847; some twenty years later James Lister had his operating room sprayed with carbolic acid vapour, an antiseptic method against whatever it was that caused infection. Bawdy humour about doctors and bodies became unacceptable to the Victorians. As medicine became more virtuous and evangelical, and physical examination came to figure in the consultation in a way which would have struck eighteenth-century patients as odd (and perhaps even impertinent—diagnosis having commonly being made by letter, as Smollett's novels attest), it would simply not do to have brutish or lecherous practitioners. Medicine had to get its act together; and it did.

Clinical skills might have been learned at the bedside, but doctors wrote and wrote: medicine was moving back into the library. It was to be an age of noble men, and thick biographies. *The Lancet* had been founded in 1823, and its first editor, the surgeon Thomas Wakley, battled to raise standards. Medicine was slowly becoming more humane, and bloodshed, especially that of phlebotomy, no longer associated with treatment. The British Medical Association emerged; and the General Medical Council, with its public list of those eligible to practise. Although they were subject to the law of supply and demand, like retail traders, some doctors even aspired to be gentlemen. By the 1870s the first female practitioners were appearing in Britain, to much mirth; while the nursing profession, reorganised after Florence Nightingale's sterling work at Scutari, was idealized. Nurses were not a threat to doctors' professional standing.

That the French are better at theory than practice is an accusation with staying power: perhaps it has something to do with their respect for the *Maître*, the severe and dogmatic father-figure. No figure was more characteristic of the new moral tone that Jean-Martin Charcot, the great neurologist. The diarist Léon Daudet, and Axel Munthe—a young Swede who in the 1920s became a famous society doctor (and much else besides)— both portrayed Charcot as the high priest of a coldly sacerdotal medicine. His whole bearing laid emphasis on the distance between the doctor's knowledge and the patient's consciousness. Although, like many doctors of his time, Charcot allied himself with writers (in this instance, Daudet's father Alphonse, but Zola also comes to mind) against anything that smacked of religious obscurantism, it is difficult not to detect something hierophantic about him, and perhaps even a whiff of brimstone. Years later, Thomas Szasz, in his *The Myth of Mental Illness* (1961) fingered Charcot as the figure who, through his clinical knowledge of neuropathy and his social standing, made it possible for disease, through a confusion of the organic and the psychological, to become metaphorically contagious. Being sick was no longer a bane, it could bring boons and benefits. But one thing Charcot most explicitly did not offer his handsomely paying patients was salvation.

If cultural stereotypes made a high priest of Charcot, Arthur Conan Doyle, a young GP in Southsea, took to writing detective stories for want of patients, and created a self-image that was more acceptable to doctors, indeed one with sufficient staying power to define the profession for a hundred years. Although the doctor in Doyle's novels is actually Watson, bumbling sidekick to Sherlock Holmes, the character of the arch-criminologist himself was based on one of Doyle's lecturers at Edinburgh University, "the most perfect reasoning and observing machine that the world has seen." As Doyle recognised, facts are not hierarchically disposed, they are all of a kind. Medical mysteries could be solved by plotting out the various clues discerned in the patient's "history" and in the signs of the failing body, and effects linked back to causes following criminological principles. Semiotics (for that is what this is) started out as a medical skill: semiology. It is Watson, though, who keeps the novels going; like most of us, he is partial (as Holmes complains) to a good story, a bit of gossip. He has not yet acquired the master's full powers of clinical reasoning. Other fictional detectives were to feel the pull of the parallel between medicine and crime, too: among them Simenon's Maigret, who wants to be a "repairer of destinies" but has to abandon his medical studies to become a policeman.

But perhaps the analogy should have been more disturbing than it was. What was the crime exactly? Who had done it? Was the victim (patient) really innocent, or did she invite the culprit (illness) in? And how could it happen in the library?

Meanwhile, medicine was expanding its purview in other ways, and in other countries. Vienna developed, in Paris's train, as a great centre for pathological anatomy. As the rich and liberal capital of a still feudal empire, it was a magnet for the mobile. People were becoming as unpredictable as nature had once been. So Vienna became an incubator for psychoanalysis, whose attention-starvation themes were adroitly handled in the stories of the doctor-writer Arthur Schnitzler. Only Sigmund Freud dared to go one further: he recast classical myths in the shape of infantile sexual complexes. Freud saw himself as a natural scientist, and a heroic one at that; and yet his thinking reinstates an old Platonic idea of castes, in which those who are wise give their backing to the order of things, and the way things are validates their superior wisdom. Freud wanted to make of the psyche a new property-owning middle class, by reforming the narcissistic ego and educating the mob of the id in the democratic ways of the mind and the pleasures of being a citizen. It was a vision of decent class ambition that was to run and run in the United States, at least until Woody Allen started getting smarter than his analysts.

Germany gave priority to basic research very early on, and some of the first and best laboratories were set up in German universities. Living organisms were subjected to precise chemical analysis, in order to determine their physico-chemical composition. Though Claude Barnard's ideas of the "internal milieu" and "homeostasis"—or equilibrium sought by the organism—proved to be influential in physiology, many of the famous scientists of the era were German: Müller, Helmholtz, Du Bois-Reymond and Schwann. Publication of the first X-ray portrait, the hand of Wilhelm Roentgen's wife in 1895, was a world sensation: now patients could be stripped naked to the bone, and the later refinements of improved safety and contrast media made it possible to visualize soft tissues and body cavities. Justus Liebig, after inventing the German equivalent of the Oxo cube, laid the foundations of the modern pharmaceutical industry. Metabolic processes began to be understood; and the cell was hypothesized as the fundamental unit of zoological life. The energetic Rudolf Virchow did for the study of the cell what Xavier Bichat had done for the tissue: he studied and identified the principle of cancerous growth. As with so many other academic topics, there was fierce rivalry between France and Germany: Virchow's notion of disease as internal to the cell battled it out against Pasteur's outstanding work on the bacterial (and therefore external) causation of disease. Koch extended Pasteur's discoveries, and identified the bacteria which give rise to tuberculosis and cholera. One pathogen, one disease: the post-Revolutionary attitude to disease seemed to be vindicated. Like the Kaiser's army, these German manufactories of knowledge were much admired and imitated in the United States: William Carlos Williams, the American poet, was one of 15,000 American students who travelled to Germany to study before the First World War. He went to Leipzig; a generation or two earlier he might have gone to Edinburgh, Leiden or Paris.

It was not all about dead tissues. Virchow believed much illness could be prevented by medical economic welfare, and his views fed the technocratic notion that the state should undertake scientifically informed actions to improve the health of its population—this would involve social engineering and moral propaganda. Theories of socialist medicine, on the other hand, perceived the causes of morbidity essentially as relations of economics and social class and urged redistribution of power and resources. They were to battle it out in the twentieth century, but already medicine was inseparable from politics. There was a growing appreciation that the bacteriological model of disease was only part of the story, and that disease ought to be conceptualized as a social issue, involving issues of income, diet, habit and profession. In 1883, the author of the "delayed nation," Bismarck, set up what was the first state-administered medical insurance scheme. Medicine had become a social utility; a vote-puller; a profession of "singular benefi-cence" (Sir William Osler). Fatherlands were about to become maternal, a uterus for their children, rather than eating them alive, like the French Revolution. The British were as deeply suspicious of the notoriously German virtue of efficiency (Chesterton talks about "the Prussian poison")— of purely technical as opposed to practical knowledge—as they were of the French *dirigiste* version of the state; yet even the British government had to admit that recruits during the Boer War were in poor physical shape. Fitness was the thing; and doctors were the people to provide it. "I hope our competition with Germany will not be in armaments alone," thundered Lloyd George, whose 1911 National Insurance Act tacitly acknowl-edged the foresight of the Bismarckian programme. Organized medicine needed the backing of the state: even in the United States, ideologically wedded to the notion of medical care as a private transaction, the entre-preneurial "one-man medical service" was destined to become a thing of the past. Socially progressive Sweden adopted eugenic policies, which had yet to acquire a bad name. Tsarist Russia, slow to modernize in other areas, had a decently functioning rural hospital system run by the provinces or *zemstvos*. For Mikhail Bulgakov, who worked in one such clinic in 1917, the doctor was sometimes literally a beacon of light in a vast sea of darkness.

By 1900, physicians were licensed by law in most countries, but good practice was a matter for the profession. Self-policing is, after all, an essential feature of a profession—a corporation that restricts membership by other than market considerations. In fact, the medical profession in Britain acquired considerable "sovereign" control over rival professions: apothecaries ended up as pharmacists; midwives, by necessity, were allowed to be an outwork of the great medical enterprise; even dentists were subject to regulation from the General Medical Council. Medicine has been described as "the most jealous trade in the world" more than once. Anyone claiming to have specialist knowledge or pretending to a theoretical system that differed from biomedicine could expect wrath from above. It was terribly like ecclesiastical history. Aspirant groups like chiropodists could only achieve upward mobility by imitating the behaviour of the dominant caste. In France, the state had effectively instituted a medical monopoly by 1892, after a century-long campaign against midwives and barber-surgeons. The American Medical Association would enjoy hegemony from 1910. In the medical division of labour that the new health-endowed societies demanded, physicians were adroit in retaining top-dog status. Nearly all work done by doctors at the end of the nineteenth century was hands-on. By the end of the twentieth century, in the great juggernaut of industrial-style medicine (paralleling the military-industrial complex in its scale and complexity), only one in twenty doctors was a practising physician, and the number of irregular healers outstripped that of registered GPs.

Despite the self-image of the late great nineteenth century (and the tone of respect was to change dramatically after 1918, as announced by Lytton Strachey's *Victorians*), therapy had lagged a long way behind diagnosis. Jean Nicholas Corvisart's opinion that medicine was "not about the art of curing people" was still obviously true. In the early 1900s, the Canadian physician Osler, the great moderating voice of the profession, had little more to recommend than "Doctor Diet" and "Doctor Rest." In his memoir, "1933 Medicine," Lewis Thomas tells of his father, in the early years of the twentieth-century, getting up at night to go and see his patients with little more than a vial of morphine, some aspirin and his diagnostic acumen. What was known and the difference it might make were not congruent. Two industrial revolutions had been and gone, and still doctors were—*faute de mieux*—"therapeutic nihilists." Then, with the discovery in

1910 of Ehrlich's "606" (Salversan) to combat syphilis, insulin for the treatment of diabetes in 1922, the first of the sulpha drugs (Prontosil) in 1935, and penicillin in 1942, doctors could actually treat a range of infectious diseases. These were the "magic bullets" that made once common infectious diseases all but unknown to those born in the latter half of the last century. Childbirth became a much safer procedure for mother and child. The "first pharmacological revolution" in the 1950s, with the development of cortisone, plastic surgery, cardiological interventions, the puzzling out of the DNA code and the workings of the immune system, were to give doctors a technical competence to swell the social competence they had acquired in the nineteenth century.

The Second World War sped up the therapeutic age enormously, and not just at the level of basic research (with mass production of drugs and vaccines and the development of instruments from war technology) but in the organization of healthcare itself. The World Health Organization was founded in Geneva, an offshoot of the earlier work of the League of Nations, on the confident assumption that all the world's problems could be tackled with a combination of good management, military precision and fixed goals. After the moral debacle of the war, the governments of France and Germany set themselves the task of reviving democracy and committed themselves to constitutional reform. Moderation was the new virtue. State power was broadened beyond the economic sphere to include social welfare. The collectivism of the interwar period was to be avoided at all costs: "far better to join the European Club of Victims Anonymous, and to convalesce in a comforting community of fellow-sufferers," as the historian Norman Davies wrote. Being risk-averse would be another virtue of the new Europe.

Triumphant and rich at the end of the Second World War, American medicine displayed the same tendency to specialization, reliance on new and improved technology, and business ingenuity as American science generally. From its beginnings, American medicine had been aggressive and interventionist: Max Weber saw this "can do" imperative as a legacy of Protestantism. As Lynn Payer observed in *Medicine and Culture*, one of the rare books to attempt something like a comparative medicine, Rousseau's true children regard themselves as naturally healthy. "It therefore stands to reason that if [they] become ill, there must be a cause for the illness, preferably one that comes from without and can be quickly dealt with." Private health insurance, with its access to extensive laboratory services and disease palaces, was big business, and the fee-for-service system boomed until the late 1960s. Like any modern industry, labour was divided: it paid to be a specialist. The trend that had started in the 1930s, of investing in more elaborate health for the better-off, began slowly to consume all available funds. In *Medical Nemesis* Ivan Illich denounced the health industry as a system rigged for every interest but that of patients, and even a Congressional study reported in 1974 that 2.4 million unnecessary operations were performed with the putative loss of 12,000 lives. Today, 35 million Americans have no medical insurance, though the health juggernaut consumes a massive 15 per cent of the GDP. Yet everybody sings in the choir of the therapeutic gospel: therapy has become the dominant language in which government and the governed express their duties and responsibilities. Hundreds of wacky therapies, self-help groups and self-esteem boosters suggest a kind of *folie à deux* between American individualism and psychologism: above all, no negative thinking! Just coat it in science!

Writing in the earliest days of the consumer society, the philosopher Hegel spelt out the paradox of the way things were going in his *Philosophy of Right*: "What the English call 'comfort' is something inexhaustible and illimitable. Others can reveal to you that what you take to be comfort at any stage is discomfort, and these discoveries never come to an end. Hence the need for greater comfort does not exactly arise within you directly; it is suggested to you by those who hope to make a profit from its creation. A liberal economic view of society says nothing about welfare." In other words, being comfortable with what one knows, which is a definition of conservatism, would, in the future, shift to being in thrall to novelty and change. Strange conservatism! Change had become the archetypal norm for social life, and medicine would hardly escape the rising expectations fuelled by the affluent society and the media, which, by the 1960s, had replaced infectious diseases with electromagnetically contagious rumours.

The panic of "health scares" is like the plague in Albert Camus' novel of the same title: it need no longer be a physical agent. It can simply be ontological.

Entire health sectors were nationalized in eastern Europe, while in Britain and the Nordic countries, which had a strong belief in the essential benevolence of the state, the welfare system was financed through national taxation so that it would be free at the point of delivery: all citizens should have access to a basic minimum. Having won the war, the British were reluctant to abandon what they thought had made them great. Aneurin Bevan, the Labour Minister of Health, going against the wishes of the medical profession, instituted a form of organized medicine that actually made the profession stronger than before. GPs were independent contractors, paid by the state, but in such a circuitous way that their clinical autonomy was left untouched. It was a Heath Robinson approach to modernity, at a time when every other Western European society was being rationalized and brought into the jurisdiction of the specialist and expert. Yet these were the golden years of general practice, when modest British medicine managed to set the standard for practice.

If medicine is essentially theatre, as Roy Porter has suggested, Brecht was its dramaturge: illusion was shunned, and there was to be no jiggery-pokery—"*die Wahrheit ist konkret.*" Doctors were encouraged to be as objective as scientists. Indeed, they had absorbed enough of the scientific spirit (through Popper) to know that they could only be right if they tried hard enough to show why they might be wrong: such was the mark of a sceptical and honourable intelligence. Self-criticism, though not of the Soviet variety, was the best defence against bad faith. "In Utopia," wrote its chronicler, the psychiatrist Michael Balint, "specialists have long realized the advantages of relinquishing the role of superior, omniscient mentors, and have accepted the much more realistic and rewarding role of expert assistants to the general practitioner, who now remains in full charge of his patients."

One problem with Utopia ("first consideration goes to the sick, who are cared for in public hospitals," as Thomas More wrote 400 years ago) is that it has dispensed with politics. As John Berger diagnosed in his brilliant 1967 study of a country GP, *A Fortunate Man*, Britain had long suffered from the fact that its people were deprived of a sense of what a civic identity might be: "the industrialization of the British has removed their means of expression." Not only that. The island people sought to preserve unity in manners rather than ideas, and the limited social mobility experienced early in Britain was never reflected in a society that understood the deeper relationship between mobility and representative government. Empire reinforced the class system; by the time it had gone, doctors were associated with the *ancien régime* of paternalism and deference. Theirs was a role, as much as a job. "By their apostolic function doctors train the population from childhood what to expect and what not to expect when they go to the doctor's"—who could write that now?

Thatcherism, born of the unrest of the 1970s, was Britain's French Revolution—two hundred years too late. Hostile to all institutions that were not part of the state, it had no concept of social as distinct from economic behaviour, no underpinning idea of civic society. Doctors would soon lose control of the means of production and become wage-labourers under the control of the health system's owner-managers. In the old days being "accountable" carried a direct ethical charge, of doctor to patient; now it carries a contractual weight, of doctor to manager, for only the accountable may enter the new world order. Needless to say, the notion of a vocation is no longer fully understandable, and perhaps even slightly suspect. Older British GPs still talk of a golden age, a more innocent time of genuine excitement and decency that characterized much of the 1950s and 1960s. But the sad truth is that the threat of state control was always implicit in Bevan's experiment itself. Now it has come to pass. And there are no bad guys in the story, only accountants.

Nineteen eighty-nine was the end of the bifurcation of Europe, and the end of an ideology that had itself come out of the Enlightenment: the attempt to make us feel at home in the world. With the market now sovereign, in a kind of Leviathan Redux, medicine has arrived in a strange place—one, in some respects, not entirely dissimilar to that of the medieval church. Facing social conditions that are partly of its own creation, in which people generally are healthier by almost any scale of reference than ever before, the temptation is to seek to expand its mandate indefinitely: to medicalize ordinary life-events, to make diseases out of risks, to opt for total somatic control. The dazzling *heroi iatroi* (hero-physicians) of TV and humanitarian dramas are surely part of the problem, not the solution.

When Kant wrote, near the end of his life, "[Man] can *feel* well, but he can never *know* that he is healthy," he can hardly have suspected that he was describing the irony, explored by Lynn Payer in her book *Disease-Mongers*, that the healthier Western society becomes, the more medicine it arrogates: 87 per cent of international healthcare expenditure is spent on 16 per cent of the world's population. Hadn't Shakespeare's Falstaff boasted that he would "turn diseases to commodity"? Yet, lacking any kind of political compact, citizens can never be anything other than consumers. Medical consumerism condemns the citizen to consume himself. Postmodernism, the politics of the person, and the ideology of choice, intensify the sense of disillusionment and isolation. And when health attracts a moralistic overlay, as it so often does in a latently paranoid society, then seeking to be healthy clearly has nothing to do with the history of daring to know. It is part of the soteriology of safety, which is religion's concern; and the price of safety is life itself, there being no bolthole for those who live in the phenomenal world. Melville's *The Confidence Man* points out that the salesman is a parody of the preacher. What about the doctor, all too knowingly aware that he is a drug? Should he "sell" his doctrine, when medicine can't save? "By applying the methods of technology to actions and behaviour that technology cannot dominate," wrote Karl Jaspers, "scientific superstition leads to a specific, devastating activity, analogous to magic's aberrations, which have never been overcome."

The body was discreetly removed from the library long ago; it is the library in the body which is now our preoccupation. In 1943, the American physician Walter Alvarez commented: "when [people] go to see a physician they hardly think it necessary to give a history or to have a physical examination." The first anatomists, in collaboration with artists, had wagered on the body: humans would lose "the immense privilege of being at the centre of the universe" (Goethe) in return for which artefacts, machines and prostheses would come to inhabit the world. That artificial zoology is the third dimension between fallen nature and divine grace, the work of man. Technology has transformed medicine not only by making it more humane—by debrutalizing surgery and medical care generally— but also making the body transparent and readable. Millions of people now carry prosthetic joints and valves within their fleshly bodies. By 1987, there were 1400 technologically-based diagnostic tests on the market, from simple blood tests to endoscopy, CAT and PETT scans, magnetic resonance imaging, and so on. It is already possible to get a walk-in whole body scan in the USA. If the digitalized image is superior to information gained by bedside examination, by the old education of the senses, then doctors no longer require the physical presence of the patient before making a diagnosis. In the information age, the body is no longer this "all too solid thing." Equally, the success of technical medicine and analytic computer technology, with its digitalized images and total recall, could make doctors redundant, at least as diagnosticians. The new biology, too, has laid siege to conventional medicine, which assumes that the body is a unity: if the body itself is a society in the shape of an organism, then disturbances of normal microbial ecology may not signal sickness so much as the emergence of microcosmic novelties. And our statistical way of life, the taming of Fortuna—which is too much a way of life to even merit comment—it, too, firmly denies that the individual can be the fundamental unit of reality, as Dickens bitterly realized in *Hard Times*. Amid universal indifference, self is our piety. We are, whether we like it or not, subjects of a relentlessly inward polity in a most impersonal age.

Not that things ever unfold entirely as predicted. But leaving it all to machines would ironically make for a much more passive relationship than in the old doctor–patient compact. The patient hardly need be asked where it hurts, if indeed it does. Like the Victorian child, he may be (must be) seen but not heard. And what about the reality-denying field of enhancement technology: does it represent a legitimate desire to extend the boundaries of human possibility, or is it a Gnostic dissatisfaction—a feeling that being merely human is not enough? What sense is to be made of the huge rise in the numbers of patients with depressive symptoms, making it, as of 1970, the most widespread psychiatric problem in the world? The literate liberal is convinced that all values are personal and private, yet the new technology pressures him to recognize the need for total human interdependence. Equally, if we lose touch with ourselves as embodied beings, with the very corporeal source of our individuation, we are likely to end up as tourists in the Library of Babel, which, steadily expanding since Leibniz's day, now boasts splendid thoroughfares, squalid alleyways and perhaps even lonely squats and shelters. They are all likely to be cold and windy places, inimical to warmth and conviviality. Jorge Luis Borges returned to tell the tale:

> When it was proclaimed that the Library contained all books, the first impression was one of extravagant happiness. All men felt themselves to be the masters of an intact and secret treasure. There was no personal or world problem whose eloquent solution did not exist in some hexagon. The universe was justified, the universe suddenly usurped the unlimited dimensions of hope. At that time a great deal was said about the Vindications: books of apology and prophecy which vindicated for all time the acts of every man in the universe and retained prodigious arcana for his future. Thousands of the greedy abandoned their sweet native hexagons and rushed up the stairways, urged on by the vain intention of finding their Vindication. These pilgrims disputed in the narrow corridors, proffered dark curses, strangled each other on the divine stairways, flung the deceptive books into the air shafts, met their death cast down in a similar fashion by the inhabitants of remote regions. Others went mad ... The Vindications exist (I have seen two which refer to persons of the future, to persons who perhaps are not imaginary) but the searchers did not remember that the possibility of a man's finding his Vindication, or some treacherous variation thereof, can be computed as zero.

Its curators, those white-coated people with the angelic expressions, are what people used to call doctors.

★

This book has been a long time in the making, and some of my friends are probably justified in seeing it as a *Bildungsroman* by proxy. I owe a particular debt of thanks to my friend Jim Campbell, whose *Picador Book of Blues and Jazz* showed me how it might be possible to relate a social and intellectual history, even of an institution as sedate as medicine, through literature and journalism. Medicine, as the present book demonstrates, sits uncomfortably between institutional respectability and a not always domesticated or socialized horror. Throughout I have been on the lookout for the "professionally surprising," in Randall Jarrell's phrase, rather than a Whig story of medicine's rise to power and glory. I even abandoned some of the classic literature about the estate of medicine: Thomas Mann's *Der Zauberberg* has, I think, to be read in its entirety to exert its mountainously magical effect. I would dearly have loved to include something by Molière or Rabelais, or even Smollett, but faced with an embarrassment of riches I decided to limit the anthology to works produced after the event which turned medicine into a public utility—the French Revolution. Other likely contenders such as Sinclair Lewis' *Arrowsmith* have aged badly. Erudition being the modern form of the fantastic, I would also have liked to include one of the intricate essays written by the American pathologist F. Gonzalez-Crussi, but eventually decided Guido Ceronetti's lesser known work filled the same need. In general, I have avoided the burgeoning category of what might be called, in Raymond Queneau's expression, "literatorture": he even suggested there was a special kind of language "for the sick to express their sickness," though Virginia Woolf tried it out before him, and found it mute. I am sceptical about the asseveration that literature can make for better doctors. Most of the doctor-writers represented in my book, as distinct from writing doctors, are writers who just happen to have been doctors, and who have ended up in medicine for any number of reasons. Even then, the best of them have to resist a temptation to reach for "the trigger of the literary man's biggest gun" (William Empson): the reductive view, a life seen only in terms of symptoms, illness, or even death. Medicine is indeed a library, but it has to read in the right way.

What it can do, in alliance with anthropology, philosophy and some notion of medical history, is to broaden our conceptual grasp of how medicine and society aid and abet each other: a bit of comparative ethnography would do wonders for Europe's parochial physicians. As the philosopher Bernard Williams has said, medicine, along with many other modern institutions, is compelled to be reflective—"forced to understand itself as at once care, business, and applied science." Medicine contributes to the successfully unstable civilization that has made it one of its bulwarks: the doctor of the future—or Dr Futurity as Philip K. Dick once called him in one of his novels—will discover that medicine is part of a vast web of knowledge, in which sustained cognitive growth and technical prowess are going to make us, like our forebears, uncomfortable with the image we have of ourselves. The human condition is not something timeless; and we all live in a historical world shaped by what went before. Our particular danger seems to be weightlessness. For the sixteenth-century Tree of Life as depicted by the alchemist Robert Fludd, knowledge was just one aspect of the world, along with qualities like wisdom, mercy and beauty; now the entire world exists within knowledge. Failure to take that perspective into account condemns an author to saying nothing very meaningful about modern life.

My thanks are due to a number of people. Alec Logan, John and Mary Gillies, Christian and Barbara Schuetze, Ulrich and Franziska Spandau, Olivier Wong, Douglas and Alex Shenson, John Shreffler formerly of Basel, Desmond and Ann Avery and Peter and Maria McCarey in Geneva, Bruce Charlton, George Szirtes, Michael Schmidt, Isabel Coutinho, and others who have discussed the book with me, or helped me track down obscure authors. Special thanks in this connection are due to the staff of Strasbourg's Bibliothèque Nationale et Universitaire. Marjorie Farquharson generously put her time and talent into the translation of several Russian texts. The now out-of-print *Faber Book of Fevers and Frets* (1989), which was put together from hundreds of sources by the late D.J. Enright, is a model anthology, although this book differs from it in both approach and material. The writings on medicine of the late, lamented Roy Porter were a provocation in the best sense of the term. My former patient Jean Cowderoy introduced me, ever so astutely, to Robertson Davies's *A Cunning Man*. Acknowledgement is also due to the editors of the *British Journal of General Practice* and *Quadrant* in Australia, which first published some of my translations. My wife Cornelia deserves special mention for her support and encouragement through hard times, especially after I had proved to myself that I was incapable of running a medical practice as a grocer's shop. I would also like to express my gratitude for an award from The Authors' Foundation of the Society of Authors in 1999, which helped me to complete some of my research. Special thanks are also due to my desk and copy editors Tim Clark and Emma Smith for their painstaking work on the manuscript. All errors are of course my own.

Iain Bamforth
Strasbourg, September 2003

BIBLIOGRAPHY

Michael Balint, *The Doctor, His Patient and the Illness*, Edinburgh, 1957.

Jorge Luis Borges, "The Library of Babel," *Labyrinths*, Harmondsworth, 1987.

W. F. Bynum and Roy Porter, eds., *Medicine and the Five Senses*, Cambridge, 1993.

David Le Breton, *La Chair à Vif: Usages médicaux et mondains du corps humain*, Paris, 1993.

F. Gonzalez-Crussi, *The Notes of an Anatomist*, New York, 1985.

G. W. F. Hegel, *Philosophie des Rechts*, Frankfurt am Main, 1983.

Immanuel Kant, *Gesammelte Schriften*, Berlin and Leipzig, 1904.

Thomas Laqueur, "Even Immortality," *London Review of Books*, 29 July, 1999.

Marshall McLuhan, *The Gutenberg Galaxy*, Toronto, 1962.

Blaise Pascal, *Pensées*, Paris, 1976.

Lynn Payer, *Medicine and Culture*, New York, 1988.

Roy Porter, *Blood and Guts: A Short History of Medicine*, London, 2002.

Roy Porter, *The Greatest Benefit to Mankind: A Medical History of Humanity from Antiquity to the Present*, London, 1997.

Philip Rieff, *The Triumph of the Therapeutic: Uses of Faith after Freud*, Chicago, 1966.

Peter Sloterdijk, *Kränkungen durch Machinen, Nicht Gerettet: Versuche nach Heidegger*, Frankfurt am Main, 2000.

Bernard Williams, *Ethics and the Limits of Philosophy*, London, 1985.

Peter Worsley, *Knowledges: Culture, Counterculture, Subculture*, London, 1997.

Marguerite Yourcenar, *L'œuvre au Noir*, Paris, 1968.

CHARLES DICKENS

The Black Veil

This eerie Gothic story presents a young doctor who gets more than he bargains for (and Dickens can't resist a moralizing squeeze of sentiment at the close of his story) in a London undergoing radical technological and social change in the early years of the nineteenth century, even if it is not yet the gas-lit and police-patrolled metropolis of Empire. Burke, referred to in the story, is the famous Edinburgh grave-robber who was to fascinate Robert Louis Stevenson; the dead body as commodity is the unspoken premise underlying this doctor's start in his professional career. The Black Veil *appeared in Dickens's first, largely journalistic book,* Sketches by Boz, *in 1836.*

One winter's evening towards the close of the year 1800, or within a year or two of that time, a young medical practitioner, recently established in business, was seated by a cheerful fire in his little parlour, listening to the wind which was beating the rain in pattering drops against the window, and rumbling dismally in the chimney. The night was wet and cold: he had been walking through mud and water the whole day, and was now comfortably reposing in his dressing-gown and slippers, more than half asleep and less than half awake, revolving a thousand matters in his wandering imagination. First he thought how hard the wind was blowing, and how the cold, sharp rain would be at that moment beating in his face if he were not comfortably housed at home. Then his mind reverted to his annual Christmas visit to his native place and dearest friends; he thought how glad they would all be to see him, and how happy it would make Rose if he could only tell her that he had got a patient at last, and hoped to have more, and to come down again in a few months' time and marry her, and take her home to gladden his lonely fireside, and stimulate him to fresh exertions. Then he began to wonder when his first patient would appear or whether he was destined by a special dispensation of Providence never to have any patients at all; and then he thought about Rose again, and dropped to sleep and dreamed about her, till the very tones of her sweet merry voice sounded in his ears, and her soft tiny hand rested on his shoulder.

There *was* a hand upon his shoulder, but it was neither soft nor tiny; its owner being a corpulent round-headed boy, who, in consideration of the sum of one shilling per week and his food, was let out by the parish to carry medicine and messages. As there was no demand for the one, however, and no necessity for the other, he usually occupied his unemployed hours— averaging fourteen a day—in abstracting peppermint drops, taking animal nourishment, and going to sleep.

"A lady, sir—a lady!" whispered the boy, rousing his master with a shake.

"What lady?" cried our friend, starting up, not quite certain that his dream was an illusion, and half expecting that it might be Rose herself.— "What lady? Where?"

"*There*, sir," replied the boy, pointing to the glass-door leading into the surgery, with an expression of alarm which the very unusual apparition of a customer might have tended to excite.

The surgeon looked towards the door, and started himself, for an instant, on beholding the appearance of his unlooked-for visitor.

It was a singularly tall female, dressed in deep mourning, and standing so close to the door that her face almost touched the glass. The upper part of her person was carefully muffled in a black shawl, as if for the purpose of concealment, and her face was shrouded by a thick black veil. She stood perfectly erect; her figure was drawn up to its full height, and though the surgeon *felt* that the eyes beneath the veil were fixed on him, she stood perfectly motionless, and evinced, by no gesture whatever, the slightest consciousness of his having turned towards her.

"Do you wish to consult me?" he inquired, with some hesitation, holding open the door. It opened inwards, and therefore the action did not alter the position of the figure, which still remained motionless on the same spot.

The female slightly inclined her head, in token of acquiescence.

"Pray walk in," said the surgeon.

The figure moved a step forward; and then turning its head in the direction of the boy—to his infinite horror—appeared to hesitate.

"Leave the room, Tom," said the young man, addressing the boy, whose large round eyes had been extended to their utmost width during this brief interview.—"Draw the curtain, and shut the door."

The boy drew a green curtain across the glass part of the door, retired into the surgery, closed the door after him, and immediately applied one of his large eyes to the key-hole on the other side.

The surgeon drew a chair to the fire, and motioned the visitor to a seat. The mysterious figure slowly moved towards it, and as the blaze shone upon the black dress, the surgeon observed that the bottom of it was saturated with mud and rain.

"You are very wet," he said.

"I am," said the stranger, in a low deep voice.

"And you are ill?" added the surgeon, compassionately, for the tone was that of a person in severe pain.

"I am," was the reply— "very ill: not bodily, but mentally. It is not for myself, or on my own behalf," continued the stranger, "that I come to you. If I laboured under bodily disease, I should not be out alone at such an hour, or on such a night as this; and if I were afflicted with it twenty four hours hence, God knows how gladly I would lie down and pray to die. It is for another that I beseech your aid, sir. I may be mad to ask it for him—I think I am: but, night after night through the long dreary hours of watching and weeping, the thought has been ever present to my mind; and though even *I* see the hopelessness of human assistance availing him, the bare thought of laying him in his grave without it, makes my blood run cold!" And a shudder, such as the surgeon well knew art could not produce, trembled through the speaker's frame.

There was a desperate earnestness in this woman's manner that went to the young man's heart. He was young in his profession, and had not yet witnessed enough of the miseries which are daily presented before the eyes of its members, to have grown comparatively callous to human suffering.

"If," he said, rising hastily, "the person of whom you speak be in so hopeless a condition as you describe, not a moment is to be lost. I will go with you instantly. Why did you not obtain medical advice before?"

"Because it would have been useless before—because it is useless even now," replied the woman, clasping her hands passionately.

The surgeon gazed for a moment on the black veil, as if to ascertain the expression of the features beneath it; its thickness, however, rendered such a result impossible.

"You *are* ill," he said, gently, "although you do not know it. The fever which has enabled you to bear without feeling the fatigue you have evidently undergone, is burning within you now. Put that to your lips," he continued, pouring out a glass of water—"compose yourself for a few moments, and then tell me, as calmly as you can, what the disease of the patient is, and how long he has been ill. The moment I know what it is necessary I should know, to render my visit serviceable to him, I am ready to accompany you."

The stranger lifted the glass of water to her mouth without raising the veil, put it down again untasted, and burst into tears.

"I know," she said, sobbing aloud, "that what I say to you now, seems like the ravings of fever. I have been told so before, less kindly than by you. I am not a young woman, sir; and they do say, that as life steals on towards its final close, the last short remnant, worthless as it may seem to all beside, is dearer to its possessor than all the years that have gone before, connected though they be with the recollection of old friends long since dead, and young ones—children perhaps—who have fallen off from, and forgotten one as completely as if they had died too. My natural term of life cannot be many years longer, and should be dear on that account; but I would lay it down without a sigh—with cheerfulness—with joy if what I tell you now were only false, or imaginary. To-morrow morning he of whom I speak will be, I *know*, though I would fain think otherwise, beyond the reach of human aid; and yet, to-night, though he is in deadly peril, you must not see, and could not serve him."

"I am unwilling to increase your distress," said the surgeon, after a short pause, "by making any comment on what you have just said, or appearing desirous to investigate a subject you seem so anxious to conceal; but there is an inconsistency in your statement which I cannot reconcile with probability. This person is dying to-night, and I cannot see him when my assistance might possibly avail; you apprehend it will be useless to-morrow, and yet you would have me see him then. If he be indeed as dear to you, as your words and manner would imply, why not try to save his life before delay and the progress of his disease render it impracticable?"

"God help me!" exclaimed the woman, weeping bitterly, "how can I hope strangers will believe what appears incredible, even to myself? You will *not* see him then, sir?" she added, rising suddenly.

"I did not say that I declined to see him," replied the surgeon; "but I warn you, that if you persist in this extraordinary procrastination, and the individual dies, a fearful responsibility rests with you."

"The responsibility will rest heavily somewhere," replied the stranger bitterly. "Whatever responsibility rests with me, I am content to bear and ready to answer."

"As I incur none," continued the surgeon, "by acceding to your request, I will see him in the morning, if you leave me the address. At what hour can he be seen?"

"*Nine,*" replied the stranger.

"You must excuse my pressing these inquiries," said the surgeon. "But is he in your charge now?"

"He is not," was the rejoinder.

"Then if I gave you instructions for his treatment through the night, you could not assist him?"

The woman wept bitterly, as she replied, "I could not."

Finding that there was but little prospect of obtaining further information by prolonging the interview; and anxious to spare the woman's feelings, which, subdued at first by a violent effort, were now irrepressible and most painful to witness, the surgeon repeated his promise of calling in the morning at the appointed hour; and his visitor, after giving him a direction to an obscure part of Walworth, left the house in the same mysterious manner as she had entered it.

It will be readily believed that so extraordinary a visit produced a considerable impression on the mind of the young surgeon, and that he speculated a great deal and to very little purpose on the possible circumstances of the case. In common with the generality of people, he had often heard and read of singular instances, in which a presentiment of death at a particular day or even minute had been entertained and realized. At one moment he was inclined to think that the present might be such a case, but then it occurred to him that all the anecdotes of the kind he had ever heard, were of persons who had been troubled with a foreboding of their own death. This woman, however, spoke of another person—a man; and it was impossible to suppose that a mere dream or delusion of fancy would induce her to speak of his approaching dissolution with such terrible certainty as she had done. It could not be that the man was to be murdered in the morning, and that the woman, originally a consenting party and bound to secrecy by an oath, had relented, and, though unable to prevent the commission of some outrage on the victim, had determined to prevent his death if possible by the timely interposition of medical aid. The idea of such things happening within two miles of the metropolis appeared too wild and preposterous to be entertained beyond the instant. Then his original impression that the woman's intellects were disordered, recurred; and as it was the only mode of solving the difficulty with any degree of satisfaction, he obstinately made up his mind to believe she was mad. Certain misgivings upon this point, however, stole upon his thoughts at the time, and presented themselves again and again through the long dull course of a sleepless night, during which, in spite of all his efforts to the contrary, he was unable to banish the black veil from his disturbed imagination.

The back part of Walworth, at its greatest distance from town, is a straggling, miserable place enough, even in these days; but five-and-thirty years ago the greater portion of it was little better than a dreary waste, inhabited by a few scattered people of most questionable character, whose poverty prevented their living in any better neighbourhood, or whose pursuits and mode of life rendered its solitude peculiarly desirable. Very many of the houses which have since sprung up on all sides, were not built until some years afterwards; and the great majority even of those which were sprinkled about at irregular intervals, were of the rudest and most miserable description.

The appearance of the place through which he walked in the morning was not calculated to raise the spirits of the young surgeon, or to dispel any feeling of anxiety or depression which the singular kind of visit he was about to make might have awakened. Striking off from the high road, his way lay across a marshy common, through irregular lanes, with here and there a ruinous and dismantled cottage fast falling to pieces with decay and neglect. A stunted tree, or pool of stagnant water, roused into a creeping sluggish action by the heavy rain of the preceding night, skirted the path occasionally; and now and then a miserable patch of garden-ground, with a few old boards knocked together for a summer house, and old palings imperfectly mended with stakes pilfered from the neighbouring hedges, bore testimony at once to the poverty of the inhabitants, and the little scruple they entertained in appropriating the property of other people to their own use. Occasionally, a filthy-looking woman would make her appearance from the door of a dirty house, to empty the contents of some cooking utensil into the gutter in front, or to scream after a little slipshod girl, who had contrived to stagger a few yards from the door under the weight of a sallow infant almost as big as herself; but scarcely any thing was stirring around, and so much of the prospect as could be faintly traced through the cold damp mist which hung heavily over it, presented a lonely and dreary appearance perfectly in keeping with the objects we have described.

After plodding wearily through the mud and mire; making many inquiries for the place to which he had been directed; and receiving as many contradictory and unsatisfactory replies in return, the young man at length arrived before the house which had been pointed out to him as the object of his destination. It was a small low building, one storey above the ground, with a more desolate and unpromising exterior than any he had yet passed. An old yellow curtain was closely drawn across the window up stairs, and the parlour shutters were closed, but not fastened. The house was detached from any other, and, as it stood at an angle of a narrow lane, there was no other habitation in sight.

When we say that the surgeon hesitated, and walked a few paces beyond the house before he could prevail upon himself to lift the knocker, we say nothing that need raise a smile upon the face of the boldest reader. The police of London were a very different body in that day to what they are now: the isolated position of the suburbs, when the rage for building and the progress of improvement had not yet begun to connect them with the main body of the city and its environs, rendered many of them (and this in particular) a place of resort for the worst and most depraved characters. Even the streets in the gayest parts of London were imperfectly lighted at that time, and such places as these were left entirely to the mercy of the moon and stars. The chances of detecting desperate characters, or of tracing them to their haunts, were thus rendered very few, and their offences naturally increased in boldness, as the consciousness of comparative security became the more impressed upon them by daily experience. Added to these considerations, it must be remembered that the young man had spent some time in the public hospitals of the metropolis; and although neither Burke nor Bishop had then gained a horrible notoriety, still his own observation might have suggested to him how easily the atrocities to which the former has since given his name, might be committed. Be this as it may, whatever reflection made him hesitate, he *did* hesitate; but, being a young man of strong mind and great personal daring, it was only for an instant;—he stepped briskly back, and knocked gently at the door.

A low whispering was audible immediately afterwards, as if some person at the end of the passage were conversing stealthily with another on the landing above. It was succeeded by the noise of a pair of heavy boots upon the bare floor. The door-chain was softly unfastened; the door opened, and a tall, ill-favoured man, with black hair, and a face, as the surgeon often declared afterwards, as pale and haggard as the countenance of any dead man he ever saw, presented himself.

"Walk in, sir," he said in a low tone.

The surgeon did so, and the man having secured the door again by the chain, led the way to a small back parlour at the extremity of the passage.

"Am I in time?"

"Too soon," replied the man. The surgeon turned hastily round, with a gesture of astonishment not unmixed with alarm, which he found it impossible to repress, though he would gladly have recalled it.

"If you'll step in here, sir," said the man, who had evidently noticed the action—"if you'll step in here, sir, you won't be detained five minutes, I assure you!"

The surgeon at once walked into the room. The man closed the door, and left him alone.

It was a little cold room, with no other furniture than two deal chairs and a table of the same material. A handful of fire unguarded by any fender, was burning in the grate, which brought out the damp if it served no more comfortable purpose; for the unwholesome moisture was stealing down the walls in long, slug-like tracks. The window, which was broken and patched in many places, looked into a small enclosed piece of ground almost covered with water. Not a sound was to be heard, either within the house or without. The young surgeon sat down by the fireplace, to await the result of his first professional visit.

He had not remained in this position many minutes when the noise of some approaching vehicle struck his ear. It stopped; the street-door was opened: a low talking succeeded, accompanied with a shuffling noise of footsteps along the passage and on the stairs, as if two or three men were engaged in carrying some heavy body to the room above. The creaking of the stairs a few seconds afterwards, announced that the new comers having completed their task, whatever it was, were leaving the house. The door was again closed, and the former silence was restored.

Another five minutes elapsed, and the surgeon had just resolved to explore the house in search of some one to whom he might make his errand known, when the room-door opened, and his last night's visitor, dressed in exactly the same manner, with the veil lowered as before, motioned him to advance. The singular height of her form, coupled with the circumstance of her not speaking, caused the idea to pass across his brain for an instant that it might be a man disguised in woman's attire. The hysteric sobs which issued from beneath the veil, and the convulsive attitude of grief of the whole figure, however, at once exposed the absurdity of the suspicion, and he hastily followed.

The woman led the way up stairs to the front room, and paused at the door to let him enter first. It was scantily furnished with an old deal box, a few chairs, and a tent bedstead without hangings or cross-rails, which was covered with a patchwork counterpane. The dim light admitted through the curtain which he had noticed from the outside, rendered the objects in the room so indistinct, and communicated to all of them so uniform a hue, that he did not at first perceive the object on which his eye at once rested when the woman rushed frantically past him, and flung herself on her knees by the bedside.

Stretched upon the bed, closely enveloped in a linen wrapper, and covered with blankets, lay a human form, stiff and motionless. The head and face, which were those of a man, were uncovered, save by a bandage which passed over the head and under the chin. The eyes were closed. The left arm lay heavily across the bed, and the woman held the passive hand.

The surgeon gently pushed the woman aside, and took the hand in his.

"My God!" he exclaimed, letting it fall involuntarily—"the man is dead!"

The woman started to her feet and beat her hands together.—"Oh! don't say so, sir," she exclaimed with a burst of passion, amounting almost to frenzy—"Oh! don't say so, sir! I can't bear it—indeed I can't! Men have been brought to life before when unskilful people have given them up for lost; and men have died who might have been restored, if proper means had been resorted to. Don't let him lie here, sir, without one effort to save him. This very moment life may be passing away. Do try, sir,—do, for God's sake!" And while speaking, she hurriedly chafed, first the forehead and then the breast of the senseless form before her, and then wildly beat the cold hands, which, when she ceased to hold them, fell listlessly and heavily back on the coverlet.

"It is of no use, my good woman," said the surgeon, soothingly, as he withdrew his hand from the man's breast. "Stay—undo that curtain."

"Why?" said the woman, starting up.

"Undo that curtain," repeated the surgeon, in an agitated tone.

"*I* darkened the room on purpose," said the woman, throwing herself before him as he rose to undraw it.—"Oh! sir, have pity on me! if it can be of no use, and he is really dead, do not—do not expose that corpse to other eyes than mine!"

"This man died no natural or easy death," said the surgeon. "I must see the body!" and with a motion so sudden, that the woman hardly knew that he had slipped from beside her, he tore open the curtain, admitted the full light of day, and returned to the bedside.

"There has been violence here," he said, pointing towards the body, and gazing intently on the face, from which the black veil was now for the first time removed. In the excitement of a minute before, the female had dashed off the bonnet and veil, and now stood with her eyes fixed upon him. Her features were those of a woman of about fifty, who had once been handsome. Sorrow and weeping had left traces upon them which not time itself would ever have produced without their aid: her face was deadly pale, and there was a nervous contortion of the lip, and an unnatural fire in her eye, which showed too plainly that her bodily and mental powers had nearly sunk beneath an accumulation of misery.

"There has been violence here," said the surgeon, preserving his searching glance.

"There has!" replied the woman.

"This man has been murdered."

"That I call God to witness he has," said the woman, passionately; "pitilessly, inhumanly murdered!"

"By whom?" said the surgeon, seizing the woman by the arm.

"Look at the butchers' marks, and then ask me," she replied.

The surgeon turned his face towards the bed, and bent over the body which lay full in the light of the window. The throat was swollen, and a blue livid mark encircled it. The truth flashed suddenly upon him.

"This is one of the men who were hanged this morning!" he exclaimed, turning away with a shudder.

"It is," replied the woman, with a cold, unmeaning stare.

"Who was he?" inquired the surgeon.

"*My son*," rejoined the woman; and fell senseless at his feet.

It was true. A companion equally guilty with himself, had been acquitted for want of evidence; and this man had been left for death, and executed. To recount the circumstances of the case at this distant period, must be unnecessary, and might give pain to some persons still alive. The history was an every-day one. The mother was a widow without friends or money, and had denied herself necessaries to bestow them on her orphan boy. That boy, unmindful of her prayers, and forgetful of the sufferings she had endured for him—incessant anxiety of mind, and voluntary starvation of body—had plunged into a career of dissipation and crime. And this was the result: his own death by the hangman's hands, and his mother's shame, and incurable insanity.

For many years after this occurrence, and when profitable and arduous avocations would have led many men to forget that such a miserable being existed, the young surgeon was a daily visitor at the side of the harmless mad woman; not only soothing her by his presence and kindness, but alleviating the rigour of her condition by pecuniary donations for her comfort and support, bestowed with no sparing hand. In the transient gleam of recollection and consciousness which preceded her death, a prayer for his welfare and protection as fervent as mortal ever breathed, rose from the lip of this poor friendless creature. That prayer flew to Heaven, and was heard. The blessings he was instrumental in conferring have been repaid to him a thousand fold; but, amid all the honours of rank and station which have since been heaped upon him, and which he has so well earned, he can have no one reminiscence more gratifying to his feelings than that connected with—The Black Veil.

"The Black Veil," *Sketches by Boz*, 1836.

GEORG BÜCHNER

Woyzeck and the Doctor

It took German literature eighty years, and German history a few years longer, to discover Georg Büchner's writings. Before he died of typhus in Zurich, not yet twenty-four, Büchner (MD Strassburg) committed a fragmentary drama to paper. It lay unread and unperformed until the First World War, when it became one of the most important plays in the modern repertoire. In this scene the doctor, a proto-Nazi who has been feeding Woyzeck a diet of peas for three months, abrades his (paid) subject for answering the call of nature and spoiling his twenty-four-hour urine collection. His notion of transfigured individuality is choice in the context, for it is clearly the doctor, not Woyzeck, who is the machine.

DOCTOR: What's this then, Woyzeck? And you call yourself a man of your word, do you!

WOYZECK: Beg pardon, Doctor?

DOCTOR: I saw it, Woyzeck. You relieved yourself on the street, pissed against the wall like a dog!—Despite the fact that you're earning three groschen a day. Not good, Woyzeck, not good. The world's on the skids, the skids.

WOYZECK: But, doctor, it was a call of nature!

DOCTOR: A call of Nature, a call of Nature! Nature? Haven't I demonstrated that the bladder sphincter muscle is subordinate to the will? Nature! Woyzeck, human beings are free, humankind is individuality transfigured as freedom. Can't control his bladder! [*Shakes his head, puts his hands behind his back, strides up and down*] Eaten your peas, Woyzeck? Nothing but peas, mind, or God help you! Science is going to be revolutionized, and I'm the man to blast it sky high. Point one percent urea, ammonium hydrochlorate, peroxide—Woyzeck, surely you can spring a leak for me again? Go behind the screen and have a try.

WOYZECK: I can't, Doctor.

DOCTOR [*heatedly*]: But pissing against the wall! I've got it in writing, the agreement you signed, here in my hand!—I saw it, I saw it with my very own eyes. Just poking my nose out the window to see if sunlight triggers paroxysmal sneezing. [*Makes to throttle him*] No, Woyzeck, I'm not angry, anger is unhealthy and unscientific. I'm calm, quite calm: pulse its usual 60, and I'm telling you so without a flicker of emotion. Good God, who'd want to bother his head over a human, a human being? Had it been a salamander dying on me, that would have been different ... But damn it, Woyzeck, you shouldn't have pissed against the wall.

WOYZECK: You know, Doctor, it's just that some folk are made that way, that's their character.—But with Nature it's different, you know, when it comes to Nature [*He cracks his knuckles.*] it's like, how can I put it, for instance ...

DOCTOR: Philosophizing again, Woyzeck!

WOYZECK [*confidentially*]: Doctor, have you ever caught a glimpse of Nature hidden in full sight? Sometimes, when the sun's high overhead in the middle of the day and the world seems about to go up in flames, this terrible voice starts talking to me.

DOCTOR: Woyzeck, you've got an *aberratio*!

WOYZECK [*puts his finger against his nose*]: It's the mushrooms, Doctor, it's all lurking in the mushrooms. Have you noticed how they grow in patterns on the ground? If only we could riddle out what they say.

DOCTOR: Woyzeck, you're exhibiting the most splendid *aberratio partialis*, grade two, a most florid case. A bonus for you, Woyzeck. Grade two: obsessional traits, otherwise generally rational ideation.—No change to your routine? Shaving your officer?

WOYZECK: Yes, sir.

DOCTOR: Eating your peas?

WOYZECK: Regular as per orders, Doctor. The wife gets the money for the housekeeping.

DOCTOR: Doing your duties?

WOYZECK: Yes, sir.

DOCTOR: You're an interesting case, Woyzeck. So, bonus for subject Woyzeck, if he keeps at it. Show me your pulse. Good!

"Beim Doktor," *Woyzeck*, 1836–37;
first stage performance in Munich, 1913.

FANNY BURNEY

Letter of 1812

Married to a Frenchman and living in Paris in 1811, the novelist and playwright Fanny Burney discovered that she had a tumour of the breast. After considerable hesitation (to the very last, as we shall read) she agreed to have an operation. In this hair-raising journal letter sent to her sister Esther (it would have been beyond the bounds of good taste for her to have written this "up" into a memoir), she describes in exact detail what was a routine experience, for those whose wits were not fuddled with alcohol, until considerably later in the century. Fanny Burney lived on for another forty years after being rid of the "peccant attom."

The sight of an immense quantity of bandages, compresses, spunges, Lint—Made me a little sick:—I walked backwards and forwards till I quieted all emotion, and became by degrees, nearly stupid—torpid, without sentiment or consciousness;—and thus I remained till the Clock struck three. A sudden spirit of exertion then returned,—I defied my poor arm, no longer worth sparing, and took my long banished pen to write a few words to M. d'Arblay—and a few more for Alex, in case of a fatal result. These short billets I could only deposit safely, when the Cabriolets—one—two—three—four—succeeded rapidly to each other in stopping at the door. Dr. Moreau instantly entered my room, to see if I were alive. He gave me a wine cordial, and went to the Sallon. I rang for my Maid and Nurses,—but before I could speak to them, my room, without previous message, was entered by 7 Men in black, Dr. Larry, M. Dubois, Dr. Moreau, Dr. Aumont, Dr. Ribe, and a pupil of Dr. Larry, and another of M. Dubois. I was now awakened from my stupor—and by a sort of indignation—Why so many? and without leave?—But I could not utter a syllable. M. Dubois acted as Commander in Chief. Dr. Larry kept out of sight: M. Dubois ordered a Bed stead into middle of the room.

Astonished, I turned to Dr. Larry, who had promised that an Arm Chair would suffice; but he hung his head, and would not look at me. Two *old mattrasses* M. Dubois then demanded, and an old Sheet. I now began to tremble violently, more with distaste and horrour of preparations even than of the pain. These arranged to his liking, he desired me to mount the Bed stead. I stood suspended, for a moment, whether I should not abruptly escape—I looked at the door, the windows—I felt desperate— but it was only for a moment, my reason then took command, and my fears and feeling struggled vainly against it. I called to my maid—she was crying, and the two Nurses stood, transfixed, at the door. "Let those women all go!" cried M. Dubois. This order recovered me my Voice— "No," I cried, "let them stay! *qu'elles restent!*" This occasioned a little dispute, that re-animated me—The Maid, however, and one of the nurses ran off—I charged the other to approach, and she obeyed. M. Dubois now tried to issue his commands *en militaire*, but I resisted all that were resistable—I was compelled, however, to submit to taking off my long robe de Chambre, which I had meant to retain—Ah, then, how did I think of My Sisters!—not one, at so dreadful an instant, at hand, to protect—adjust—guard me—I regretted that I had refused Mme De Maisonneuve—Mme Chastel—no one upon whom I could rely—my departed Angel!—how did I think of her!—how did I long—long for my Esther—my Charlotte!—My distress was, I suppose, apparent, though not my Wishes, for M. Dubois himself now softened, and spoke soothingly. "Can *You*," I cried, "feel for an operation that, to *You*, must seem to trivial?"—"Trivial?" he repeated—taking up a bit of paper, which he tore, unconsciously, into a million pieces, "*oui—c'est peu de chose—mais—*" he stammered, and could not go on. No one else attempted to speak, but I was softened myself, when I saw even M. Dubois grow agitated, while Dr. Larry kept always aloof, yet a glance shewed me he was pale as ashes. I knew not, positively, then, the immediate danger, but every thing convinced me danger was hovering about me, and that this experiment could alone save me from its jaws. I mounted, therefore, unbidden, the Bed stead—and M. Dubois placed me upon the Mattrass, and spread a cambric handkerchief upon my face. It was transparent, however, and I saw, through it, that the Bed stead was instantly surrounded by the 7 men and my nurse. I refused to be held; but when, Bright through the cambric, I saw the glitter of polished Steel—I closed my Eyes. I would not trust to convulsive fear the sight of the terrible incision. A silence the most profound ensued, which lasted for some minutes, during which, I imagine, they took their orders by signs, and made their examination—Oh what a horrible suspension!—I did not breathe—and M. Dubois tried vainly to find any pulse. This pause, at length was broken by Dr. Larry, who in a voice of solemn melancholy, said "*Qui me tendra ce sein?*—"

No one answered; at least not verbally; but this aroused me from my passively submissive state, for I feared they imagined the whole breast infected—feared it too justly,—for, again through the Cambric, I saw the hand of M. Dubois held up, while his fore finger first described a straight line from top to bottom of the breast, secondly a Cross, and thirdly a circle; intimating that the Whole was to be taken off. Excited by this idea, I started up, threw off my veil, and, in answer to his demand "*Qui me tendra ce sein*" cried "*C'est moi, Monsieur!*" and I held My hand under it, and explained the nature of my sufferings, which all sprang from one point, though they darted into every part. I was heard attentively, but in utter silence, and M. Dubois then, re-placed me as before, and, as before, spread my veil over my face. How vain, alas, my representation! immediately again I saw the fatal finger describe the Cross—and the circle—Hopeless, then, desperate, and self-given up, I closed once more my Eyes, relinquishing all watching, all resistance, all interference, and sadly resolute to be wholly resigned.

My dearest Esther,—all my dears to whom she communicates this doleful ditty, will rejoice to hear that this resolution once taken, was firmly adhered to, in defiance of a terror that surpasses all description, and the most torturing pain. Yet—when the dreadful steel was plunged into the breast—cutting through veins—arteries—flesh—nerves—I needed no injunctions not to restrain my cries. I began a scream that lasted unintermittingly during the whole time of the incision—and I almost marvel that it rings not in my Ears still! so excruciating was the agony! When the wound was made, and the instrument was withdrawn, the pain seemed undiminished, for the air that suddenly rushed into those delicate parts felt like a mass of minute but sharp and forked poniards, that were tearing the edges of the wound—but when again I felt the instrument—describing a curve—cutting against the grain, if I may so say, while the flesh resisted in a manner so forcible as to oppose and tire the hand of the operator, who was forced to change from the right to the left—then, indeed, I thought I must have expired. I attempted no more to open my Eyes,—they felt as if hermetically shut, and so firmly closed, that the Eyelids seemed indented into the Cheeks. The Instrument this second time withdrawn, I concluded the operation over,—Oh no! presently the terrible cutting was renewed—and worse than ever, to separate the bottom, the foundation of this terrible gland from the parts to which it adhered—Again all description would be baffled—yet again all was not over,—Dr. Larry rested but his own hand, and—Oh Heaven!—I then felt the Knife rackling against the breast bone—scraping it!—This performed, while I yet remained in utterly speechless torture, I heard the Voice of M. Larry,—(all others guarded a dead silence) in a tone nearly tragic, desire every one present to pronounce if anything more remained to be done; or if he thought the operation complete. The general voice was Yes,—but the finger of M. Dubois—which I literally *felt* elevated over the wound, though I saw nothing, and though he touched nothing, so indescribably sensitive was the spot—pointed to some further requisition—and again began the scraping!—and, after this, Dr. Moreau thought he discerned a peccant attom—and still, and still, M. Dubois demanded attom after attom—My dearest Esther, not for days, not for Weeks, but for Months I could not speak of this terrible business without nearly going through it! I could not *think* of it with impunity! I was sick, I was disordered by a single question—even now, 9 months after it is over, I have a head ache from going on with the account! and this miserable account, which I began 3 Months ago, at least, I dare not revise, nor read, the recollection is still so painful.

To conclude, the evil was so profound, the case so delicate, and the precautions necessary for preventing a return so numerous, that the operation, including the treatment and the dressing, lasted 20 minutes! a time, for sufferings so acute, that was hardly supportable—However, I bore it with all the courage I could exert, and never moved, nor stopt them, nor resisted, nor remonstrated, nor spoke—except once or twice, during the dressings, to say *"Ah Messieurs! que je vous plains"*—for indeed I was sensible to the feeling concern with which they all saw what I endured, though my speech was principally—*very* principally meant for Dr. Larry. Except this, I uttered not a syllable, save, when they re-commenced, calling out *"Avertissez moi, Messieurs! avertissez moi!—"* Twice, I believe, I fainted; at least I have two total chasms in my memory of this transaction, that impede my tying together what passed. When all was done, and they lifted me up that I might be put to bed, my strength was so totally annihilated, that I was obliged to be carried, and could not even sustain my hands and arms, which hung as if I had been lifeless; while my face, as the Nurse has told me, was utterly colourless. This removal made me open my Eyes—and then I saw my good Dr. Larry, pale nearly as myself, his face streaked with blood, and its expression depicting grief, appre-hension, and almost horrour.

Excerpt from a letter to Esther Burney, March–June, 1812.

RENÉ THÉOPHILE HYACINTHE LAËNNEC

Illness as a Musical Problem

Although this is not a book of great discoveries in medicine, it would be foolish to overlook Laënnec's invention of the stethoscope, a simple technological device which was to revolutionize not just the diagnosis of disease but also the very posture, as Foucault has reminded us, adopted by doctors with respect to their patients. It was almost certainly Laënnec's avocation as flautist which suggested to him the possibilities of applying "mediate" auscultation to the percussive bodily sound-chamber of air and fluids (as opposed to "immediate" auscultation, which required listening with the ear directly applied to the patient's torso). Subsequently modified with sound-amplifying diaphragms and flexible tubing, his device is still the profession's icon.

In 1816 I was consulted by a young woman presenting general symptoms of heart disease. Owing to her stoutness little information could be gathered by application of the hand and percussion. The patient's age and sex did not permit me to resort to the kind of examination I have just described (direct application of the ear to the chest). I recalled a well-known acoustic phenomenon, namely, if you place your ear against one end of a wooden beam the scratch of a pin at the other extremity is most distinctly audible. It occurred to me that this physical property might serve a useful purpose in the case with which I was then dealing. Taking a sheaf of paper, I rolled it into a very tight roll, one end of which I place over the precordial region, while I put my ear to the other. I was both surprised and gratified at being able to hear the beating of the heart with much greater clearness and distinctness than I had ever done before by direct application of my ear.

I at once saw that this means might become a useful method for studying not only the beating of the heart but likewise all movements capable of producing sound in the thoracic cavity, and that consequently it might serve for the investigation of respiration, the voice, râles, and even possibly the movements of a liquid effused into the pleural cavity or pericardium.

With this conviction, I at once began, and have continued to the present time, a series of observations at the Hôpital Necker. As a result I have obtained many new and certain signs, most of which are striking, easy of recognition, and calculated perhaps to render the diagnosis of nearly all complaints of the lungs, pleurae, and heart both more certain and more circumstantial than the surgical diagnosis obtained by use of the sound or by introduction of the finger.

★

The first instrument employed by me consisted of a cylinder or roll of paper, sixteen lines in diameter and one foot long, made of three quires of paper rolled very tightly round, and held in position with gummed paper and filed smooth at both ends. However tight the roll may be, there will always remain a tube three or four lines in diameter running up the centre, because the sheets of paper composing it can never be rolled completely on themselves. This fortuitous circumstance gave rise, as will be seen, to an important observation upon my part: I found that for listening to the voice the tube is an indispensable factor. An entirely solid body is the best instrument that can be used for listening to the heart; such an instrument would indeed suffice also for hearing respiratory sounds and râles; yet these last two phenomena yield greater intensity of sound if a perforated cylinder is used, hollowed out at one end into a kind of funnel one and one half inches in depth.

The densest bodies are not, as analogy would lead us to suppose, the best materials for constructing these instruments. Glass and metals, apart from their weight and the sensation of cold that they impart in winter, are not such good carriers of the heartbeats and the sounds produced by breathing and râles, as are bodies of lesser density.

Substances of medium density, such as paper, wood, and cane, are those which have always appeared to me preferable to all others. This result may be in contradiction with an axiom of physics; nonetheless I consider it to be quite established.

I consequently employ at the present time a wooden cylinder with a tube three lines in diameter bored right down its axis; it is divisible into two parts by means of a screw and thus more portable. One of the parts is hollowed out at its ends into a wide funnel-shaped depression one and one half inches deep leading into the central tube. A cylinder made like this is the instrument most suitable for exploring breath sounds and râles. It is converted into a tube of uniform diameter with thick walls all the way, for exploring the voice and the heartbeats, by introducing into the funnel or bell a kind of stopper made of the same wood, fitting it quite closely; this is made fast by means of a small brass tube running through it, entering a certain distance into the tubular space running through the length of the cylinder. This instrument is sufficient for all cases, although, as I have already said, a perfectly solid body might perhaps be better for listening to the beating of the heart.

The dimensions indicated above are not altogether unimportant; if the diameter is larger it is not always possible to apply the stethoscope closely against all points of the chest; if the instrument is longer, it becomes difficult to hold it exactly in place; if it were shorter, the physician would often be obliged to adopt an uncomfortable position, which is to be avoided above all things if he desires to carry out accurate observations.

I shall be careful, when discussing each variety of exploration, to mention the positions which experience has taught me to be most favourable for observations and least tiring for both physician and patient.

Suffice it to say for the moment that in all cases the stethoscope should be held like a pen, and that the hand must be placed quite close to the patient's chest in order to make sure that the instrument is properly applied.

The end of the instrument intended to rest on the patient's chest, that is to say the end provided with the stopper, should be very slightly concave; it is then less liable to wobble, and as this concavity is easily filled by the skin it in no case leaves an empty space even when placed on the flattest part of the chest.

Excerpt from *On Mediate Auscultation*, 1819; translated by John Forbes, 1834.

JOHANN PETER HEBEL

The Cure

Johann Peter Hebel (1760–1826) is one of the best story-tellers in the German language. He was a pastor and teacher who published his tolerant, wise and humorous stories in an almanac for the education of a wide, unschooled but by no means unsophisticated public in his native Baden. Perhaps it was his caring paternalism (he called himself Your Family Friend) and unaffectedness which made him so appealing to Tolstoy and Kafka. This mildly politically incorrect story (in which a doctor uses deception to "bring" his patient to the cure) comes from the famous collection of his works The Treasure Chest. *A lindworm, just for the record, is a mythical wingless dragon or dybbuk.*

Despite having bags of money rich people sometimes still have to put up with all kinds of trials and illnesses which, thank God, are completely unknown to the poor man. There are illnesses which lurk, not in the air, but in filled plates and glasses, and in easy chairs and satin beds.

A particular rich man in Amsterdam could tell you a thing or two about that! He'd spend all morning in his armchair smoking tobacco, provided he wasn't too lazy to fill his pipe, or stand taking in the view from his window, but then at midday he'd eat like a peasant back from the fields, and sometimes the neighbours said: "Is that a wind coming up or is it the neighbour snoring?"

All afternoon he ate and drank too, a cold slice perhaps, and then something hot, not because he was hungry or had a craving for anything but just to while away the time till evening, so that you couldn't really tell when his midday meal finished and he sat down to supper. After supper, he slumped in his bed, weary as if he'd been shifting stones or chopping logs all day.

In the fullness of time his body became fat and as lumpy as a sack of corn. Eating and sleeping were tribulations, and for a long time, as often happens, he was neither very well nor very ill. If you'd spoken to him in person though, he would have told you he had 365 illnesses, a different one for every day of the year. All the doctors of Amsterdam were called upon to treat him. He swallowed whole firebuckets full of mixtures, powders by the shovelful and pills as big as quail's eggs, and he was known to all and sundry as the chemist's-shop-on-two-legs.

But nothing the doctors prescribed for him helped, since he didn't follow their prescriptions, but said: "Damn it all, what's the good of being a rich man if I have to live a dog's life, and all my money can't pay for a doctor who'll make me better?"

Eventually he heard about a doctor who lived in the countryside, a hundred hours away by foot: he was said to be so adept that his patients got well as soon as he looked them in the face, and even Death slunk out of his way whenever he turned up. And so this rich man pinned his hopes on this doctor and wrote to him describing his condition.

It wasn't long before this doctor saw what the problem was, not one of medicines but of moderation and exercise, and said to himself: "Patience, I'll soon have you cured." So he sent him a letter which read as follows: "My friend, you are indeed in bad shape, but you can still be helped if you do as I say. You have a nasty creature in your stomach, a lindworm with seven mouths. I must deal with this lindworm personally, for which you'll have to visit me. But first, don't come by coach or on horseback, but on leather soles, otherwise you'll disturb the lindworm and it'll bite through your innards and cut to shreds all seven parts of your intestines. Second, eat no more than a plate of vegetables twice a day, with a sausage at midday and an egg in the evening, and a bowl of broth sprinkled with chives in the morning. Anything more than that will only make the lindworm grow bigger so that it'll crush your liver, and then it won't be your tailor who takes your measurements, but the undertaker. That's my advice, and if you don't heed it you won't hear the cuckoo next spring! But it's your decision!"

The very next morning, as soon as he had read the letter, the patient had his boots waxed and set out on his way, as the doctor had recommended. On the first day he made such slow progress that even a snail could have been his advance runner, and he snubbed those who greeted him on the way and trod on every tiny creature that crawled in his path. But already on the second and third morning he had the impression that the birds were singing more sweetly than they had for many a day, and he thought the dew so fresh and the poppies in the fields so red, and everyone he met on his path seemed so friendly, and he was too. And each morning when he set out from his lodgings the world was lovelier, and he walked more easily and brightly.

On the eighteenth day he reached the doctor's town, and when he got up the next day he felt so well that he said: "I couldn't have got better at a worse time, just when I'm about to see the doctor! If only my ears were ringing a little or if I had a touch of dropsy!"

When he went in to see the doctor, the doctor took him by the hand, and said to him: "Now then, tell me again from the beginning what the matter is."

He replied: "Doctor, nothing is wrong with me, praise the Lord, and I only hope your health is as good as mine."

The doctor said: "I see a good spirit told you to follow my advice. The lindworm has gone. But its eggs are still inside you, and that's why you must go back home on foot, and when you're back you must saw lots of wood where nobody can see you, and eat only as much as satisfies your hunger so that the eggs don't hatch out; and you may well live to a ripe old age." And he smiled.

And the rich man from the city said: "Doctor, you're an odd chap, but I get your meaning." Thereupon he followed his advice and lived to be 87 years, 4 months and 10 days, as fit as a fiddle, and every New Year sent the doctor twenty doubloons and his best regards.

"Der geheilte Patient," *Erzählungen des Rheinländischen Hausfreundes*, 1810.

GEORGE ELIOT

Employing Lydgate

Virginia Woolf called George Eliot's Middlemarch *one of the few English novels "written for grown-up people." It certainly shows a rich and subtle social world, and one teeming with material bounty and new ideas—"involuntary, palpitating life." Lydgate, who has trained in Paris and uses stethoscopy, is a settler in the provinces, a new kind of doctor: the unease he arouses among the established physicians (Minchin and Sprague) and apothecaries (Toller and Wrench) is a kind of backhanded testimony to the fact that he represents change. The dynamic Lydgate is finally outdone by the massed forces of conservatism: this is provincial life in Victorian England, after all.*

That opposition to the New Fever Hospital which Lydgate had sketched to Dorothea was, like other oppositions, to be viewed in many different lights. He regarded it as a mixture of jealousy and dunder-headed prejudice. Mr Bulstrode saw in it not only medical jealousy but a determination to thwart himself, prompted mainly by a hatred of that vital religion of which he had striven to be an effectual lay representative—a hatred which certainly found pretexts apart from religion such as were only too easy to find in the entanglements of human action. These might be called the ministerial views. But oppositions have the illimitable range of objections at command, which need never stop short at the boundary of knowledge, but can draw for ever on the vasts of ignorance. What the opposition in Middlemarch said about the New Hospital and its administration had certainly a great deal of echo in it, for heaven has taken care that everybody shall not be an originator; but there were differences which represented every social shade between the polished moderation of Dr Minchin and the trenchant assertion of Mrs Dollop, the landlady of the Tankard in Slaughter Lane.

Mrs Dollop became more and more convinced by her own asseveration, that Doctor Lydgate meant to let the people die in the Hospital, if not to poison them, for the sake of cutting them up without saying by your leave or with your leave; for it was a known "fac" that he had wanted to cut up Mrs Goby, as respectable a woman as any in Parley Street, who had money in trust before her marriage—a poor tale for a doctor, who if he was good for anything should know what was the matter with you before you died, and not want to pry into your inside after you were gone. If that was not reason, Mrs Dollop wished to know what was; but there was a prevalent feeling in her audience that her opinion was a bulwark, and that if it were overthrown there would be no limits to the cutting-up of bodies, as had been well seen in Burke and Hare with their pitch-plaisters—such a hanging business as that was not wanted in Middlemarch!

And let it not be supposed that opinion at the Tankard in Slaughter Lane was unimportant to the medical profession: that old authentic public-house—the original Tankard known by the name of Dollop's—was the resort of a great Benefit Club, which had some months before put to the vote whether its long standing medical man, "Doctor Gambit", should not be cashiered in favour of "this Doctor Lydgate", who was capable of performing the most astonishing cures, and rescuing people altogether given up by other practitioners. But the balance had been turned against Lydgate by two members, who for some private reasons held that this power of resuscitating persons as good as dead was an equivocal recommendation, and might interfere with providential favours. In the course of the year, however, there had been a change in the public sentiment, of which the unanimity at Dollop's was an index.

A good deal more than a year ago, before anything was known of Lydgate's skill, the judgments on it had naturally been divided, depending on a sense of likelihood, situated perhaps in the pit of the stomach or in the pineal gland, and differing in its verdicts, but not the less valuable as a guide in the total deficit of evidence. Patients who had chronic diseases or whose lives had long been worn threadbare, like old Featherstone's, had been at once inclined to try him; also, many who did not like paying their doctor's bills, thought agreeably of opening an account with a new doctor and sending for him without stint if the children's temper wanted a dose, occasions when the old practitioners were often crusty; and all persons thus inclined to employ Lydgate held it likely that he was clever. Some considered that he might do more than others "where there was liver";— at least there would be no harm in getting a few bottles of "stuff" from him, since if these proved useless it would still be possible to return to the Purifying Pills, which kept you alive, if they did not remove the yellowness. But these were people of minor importance. Good Middlemarch families were of course not going to change their doctor without reason shown; and everybody who had employed Mr Peacock did not feel obliged to accept a new man merely in the character of his successor, objecting that he was "not likely to be equal to Peacock".

Lydgate had not been long in the town before there were particulars enough reported of him to breed much more specific expectations and to intensify differences into partisanship; some of the particulars being of that impressive order of which the significance is entirely hidden, like a statistical amount without a standard of comparison, but with a note of exclamation at the end. The cubic feet of oxygen yearly swallowed by a full-grown man—what a shudder they might have created in Middlemarch circles! "Oxygen! nobody knows what that may be—is it any wonder the cholera has got to Dantzic? And there are people who say quarantine is no good!"

One of the facts quickly rumoured was that Lydgate did not dispense drugs. This was offensive both to the physicians whose exclusive distinction seemed infringed on, and to the surgeon-apothecaries with whom he ranged himself; and only a little while before, they might have counted on having the law on their side against a man who without calling himself a London-made M.D. dared to ask for pay except as a charge on drugs. Lydgate had not been experienced enough to foresee that his new course would be even more offensive to the laity; and to Mr Mawmsey, an important grocer in the Top Market, who, though not one of his patients, questioned him in an affable manner on the subject, he was injudicious enough to give a hasty popular explanation of his reasons, pointing out to Mr Mawmsey that it must lower the character of practitioners and be a constant injury to the public, if their only mode of getting paid for their work was by their making out long bills for draughts, boluses, and mixtures.

"It is in that way that hard-working medical men may come to be almost as mischievous as quacks," said Lydgate, rather thoughtlessly. "To get their own bread they must overdose the king's lieges; and that's a bad sort of treason, Mr Mawmsey—undermines the constitution in a fatal way."

Mr Mawmsey was not only an overseer (it was about a question of outdoor pay that he was having an interview with Lydgate), he was also asthmatic and had an increasing family: thus, from a medical point of view, as well as from his own, he was an important man; indeed, an exceptional grocer, whose hair was arranged in a flame-like pyramid, and whose retail deference was of the cordial, encouraging kind—jocosely complimentary, and with a certain considerate abstinence from letting out the full force of his mind. It was Mr Mawmsey's friendly jocoseness in questioning him which had set the tone of Lydgate's reply. But let the wise be warned against too great readiness at explanation: it multiplies the sources of mistake, lengthening the sum for reckoners sure to go wrong.

Lydgate smiled as he ended his speech, putting his foot into the stirrup, and Mr Mawmsey laughed more than he would have done if he had known who the king's lieges were, giving his "Good morning, sir, good morning, sir" with the air of one who saw everything clearly enough. But in truth his views were perturbed. For years he had been paying bills with strictly-made items, so that for every half-crown and eighteenpence he was certain something measurable had been delivered. He had done this with satisfaction, including it among his responsibilities as a husband and father, and regarding a longer bill than usual as a dignity worth mentioning. Moreover, in addition to the massive benefit of the drugs to "self and family", he had enjoyed the pleasure of forming an acute judgment as to their immediate effects, so as to give an intelligent statement for the guidance of Mr Gambit—a practitioner just a little lower in status than Wrench or Toller, and especially esteemed as an accoucheur, of whose ability Mr Mawmsey had the poorest opinion on all other points, but in doctoring, he was wont to say in an undertone, he placed Gambit above any of them.

Here were deeper reasons than the superficial talk of a new man, which appeared still flimsier in the drawing-room over the shop when they were recited to Mrs Mawmsey, a woman accustomed to be made much of as a fertile mother,—generally under attendance more or less frequent from Mr Gambit, and occasionally having attacks which required Dr Minchin.

"Does this Mr Lydgate mean to say there is no use in taking medicine?" said Mrs Mawmsey, who was slightly given to drawling. "I should like him to tell me how I could bear up at Fair time, if I didn't take strengthening medicine for a month beforehand. Think of what I have to provide for calling customers, my dear!"—here Mrs Mawmsey turned to an intimate female friend who sat by—"a large veal pie—a stuffed fillet—a round of beef—ham, tongue, *et* cetera, *et* cetera! But what keeps me up best is the pink mixture, not the brown. I wonder, Mr Mawmsey, with *your* experience, you could have patience to listen. I should have told him at once that I knew a little better than that."

"No, no, no," said Mr Mawmsey; "I was not going to tell him my opinion. Hear everything and judge for yourself is my motto. But he didn't know who he was talking to. I was not to be turned on *his* finger. People often pretend to tell me things, when they might as well say, 'Mawmsey, you're a fool.' But I smile at it: I humour everybody's weak place. If physic had done harm to self and family, I should have found it out by this time."

The next day Mr Gambit was told that Lydgate went about saying physic was of no use.

"Indeed!" said he, lifting his eyebrows with cautious surprise. (He was a stout husky man with a large ring on his fourth finger.) "How will he cure his patients then?"

"That is what *I* say," returned Mrs Mawmsey, who habitually gave weight to her speech by loading her pronouns. "Does *he* suppose that people will pay him only to come and sit with them and go away again?"

Mrs Mawmsey had had a great deal of sitting from Mr Gambit, including very full accounts of his own habits of body and other affairs; but of course he knew there was no innuendo in her remark, since his spare time and personal narrative had never been charged for. So he replied, humorously—

"Well, Lydgate is a good-looking young fellow, you know."

"Not one that *I* would employ," said Mrs Mawmsey. "*Others* may do as they please."

Hence Mr Gambit could go away from the chief grocer's without fear of rivalry, but not without a sense that Lydgate was one of those hypocrites who try to discredit others by advertising their own honesty, and that it might be worth some people's while to show him up. Mr Gambit, however, had a satisfactory practice, much pervaded by the smells of retail trading which suggested the reduction of cash payments to a balance. And he did not think it worth his while to show Lydgate up until he knew how. He had not indeed great resources of education, and had had to work his own way against a good deal of professional contempt; but he made none the worse accoucheur for calling the breathing apparatus "longs".

Other medical men felt themselves more capable. Mr Toller shared the highest practice in the town and belonged to an old Middlemarch family: there were Tollers in the law and everything else above the line of retail trade. Unlike our irascible friend Wrench, he had the easiest way in the world of taking things which might be supposed to annoy him, being a well-bred, quietly facetious man, who kept a good house, was very fond of a little sporting when he could get it, very friendly with Mr Hawley, and hostile to Mr Bulstrode. It may seem odd that with such pleasant habits he should have been given to the heroic treatment, bleeding and blistering and starving his patients, with a dispassionate disregard to his personal example; but the incongruity favoured the opinion of his ability among his patients, who commonly observed that Mr Toller had lazy manners, but his treatment was as active as you could desire:—no man, said they, carried more seriousness into his profession: he was a little slow in coming, but when he came he *did* something. He was a great favourite in his own circle, and whatever he implied to any one's disadvantage told doubly from his careless ironical tone.

He naturally got tired of smiling and saying, "Ah!" when he was told that Mr Peacock's successor did not mean to dispense medicines; and Mr Hackbutt one day mentioning it over the wine at a dinner-party,

Mr Toller said, laughingly, "Dibbitts will get rid of his stale drugs, then. I'm fond of little Dibbitts—I'm glad he's in luck."

"I see your meaning, Toller," said Mr Hackbutt, "and I am entirely of your opinion. I shall take an opportunity of expressing myself to that effect. A medical man should be responsible for the quality of the drugs consumed by his patients. That is the *rationale* of the system of charging which has hitherto obtained; and nothing is more offensive than this ostentation of reform, where there is no real amelioration."

"Ostentation, Hackbutt?" said Mr Toller, ironically. "I don't see that. A man can't very well be ostentatious of what nobody believes in. There's no reform in the matter: the question is, whether the profit on the drugs is paid to the medical man by the druggist or by the patient, and whether there shall be extra pay under the name of attendance."

"Ah, to be sure; one of your damned new versions of old humbug," said Mr Hawley, passing the decanter to Mr Wrench.

Mr Wrench, generally abstemious, often drank wine rather freely at a party, getting the more irritable in consequence.

"As to humbug, Hawley," he said, "that's a word easy to fling about. But what I contend against is the way medical men are fouling their own nest, and setting up a cry about the country as if a general practitioner who dispenses drugs couldn't be a gentleman. I throw back the imputation with scorn. I say, the most ungentlemanly trick a man can be guilty of is to come among the members of his profession with innovations which are a libel on their time-honoured procedure. That is my opinion, and I am ready to maintain it against any one who contradicts me." Mr Wrench's voice had become exceedingly sharp.

"I can't oblige you there, Wrench," said Mr Hawley, thrusting his hands into his trouser-pockets.

"My dear fellow," said Mr Toller, striking in pacifically, and looking at Mr Wrench, "the physicians have their toes trodden on more than we have. If you come to dignity it is a question for Minchin and Sprague."

"Does medical jurisprudence provide nothing against these infringements?" said Mr Hackbutt, with a disinterested desire to offer his lights. "How does the law stand, eh, Hawley?"

"Nothing to be done there," said Mr Hawley. "I looked into it for Sprague. You'd only break your nose against a damned judge's decision."

"Pooh! no need of law," said Mr Toller. "So far as practice is concerned the attempt is an absurdity. No patient will like it—certainly not Peacock's, who have been used to depletion. Pass the wine."

Mr Toller's prediction was partly verified. If Mr and Mrs Mawmsey, who had no idea of employing Lydgate, were made uneasy by his supposed declaration against drugs, it was inevitable that those who called him in should watch a little anxiously to see whether he did "use all the means he might use" in the case. Even good Mr Powderell, who in his constant charity of interpretation was inclined to esteem Lydgate the more for what seemed a conscientious pursuit of a better plan, had his mind disturbed with doubts during his wife's attack of erysipelas, and could not abstain from mentioning to Lydgate that Mr Peacock on a similar occasion had administered a series of boluses which were not otherwise definable than by their remarkable effect in bringing Mrs Powderell round before Michaelmas from an illness which had begun in a remarkably hot August. At last, indeed, in the conflict between his desire not to hurt Lydgate and his anxiety that no "means" should be lacking, he induced his wife privately to take Widgeon's Purifying Pills, an esteemed Middlemarch medicine, which arrested every disease at the fountain by setting to work at once upon the blood. This co-operative measure was not to be mentioned to Lydgate, and Mr Powderell himself had no certain reliance on it, only hoping that it might be attended with a blessing.

But in this doubtful stage of Lydgate's introduction he was helped by what we mortals rashly call good fortune. I suppose no doctor ever came newly to a place without making cures that surprised somebody—cures which may be called fortune's testimonials, and deserve as much credit as the written or printed kind. Various patients got well while Lydgate was attending them, some even of dangerous illnesses; and it was remarked that the new doctor with his new ways had at least the merit of bringing people back from the brink of death. The trash talked on such occasions was the more vexatious to Lydgate, because it gave precisely the sort of prestige which an incompetent and unscrupulous man would desire, and was sure to be imputed to him by the simmering dislike of the other medical men as an encouragement on his own part of ignorant puffing. But even his proud outspokenness was checked by the discernment that it was as useless to fight against the interpretations of ignorance as to whip the fog; and "good fortune" insisted on using those interpretations.

Mrs Larcher having just become charitably concerned about alarming symptoms in her charwoman, when Dr Minchin called, asked him to see her then and there, and to give her a certificate for the Infirmary; whereupon after examination he wrote a statement of the case as one of tumour, and recommended the bearer Nancy Nash as an out-patient. Nancy, calling at home on her way to the Infirmary, allowed the staymaker and his wife, in whose attic she lodged, to read Dr Minchin's paper, and by this means became a subject of compassionate conversation in the neighbouring shops of Churchyard Lane as being afflicted with a tumour at first declared to be as large and hard as a duck's egg, but later in the day to be about the size of "your fist". Most hearers agreed that it would have to be cut out, but one had known of oil and another of "squitchineal" as adequate to soften and reduce any lump in the body when taken enough of into the inside—the oil by gradually "soopling", the squitchineal by eating away.

Meanwhile when Nancy presented herself at the Infirmary it happened to be one of Lydgate's days there. After questioning and examining her, Lydgate said to the house-surgeon in an undertone, "It's not tumour: it's cramp." He ordered her a blister and some steel mixture, and told her to go home and rest, giving her at the same time a note to Mrs Larcher, who, she said, was her best employer, to testify that she was in need of good food.

But by-and-by Nancy, in her attic, became portentously worse, the supposed tumour having indeed given way to the blister, but only wandered to another region with angrier pain. The staymaker's wife went to fetch Lydgate, and he continued for a fortnight to attend Nancy in her own home, until under his treatment she got quite well and went to work again. But the case continued to be described as one of tumour in Churchyard Lane and other streets—nay, by Mrs Larcher also; for when Lydgate's remarkable cure was mentioned to Dr Minchin he naturally did not like to say, "The case was not one of tumour, and I was mistaken in describing it as such," but answered, "Indeed! ah! I saw it was a surgical case, not of a fatal kind." He had been inwardly annoyed, however, when he had asked at the Infirmary about the woman he had recommended two days before, to hear from the house-surgeon, a youngster who was not sorry to vex Minchin with impunity, exactly what had occurred: he privately pronounced that it was indecent in a general practitioner to contradict a physician's diagnosis in that open manner, and afterwards agreed with Wrench that Lydgate was disagreeably inattentive to etiquette. Lydgate did not make the affair a ground for valuing himself or (very particularly) despising Minchin, such rectification of misjudgments often happening among men of equal qualifications. But report took up this amazing case of tumour, not clearly distinguished from cancer, and considered the more awful for being of the wandering sort; till much prejudice against Lydgate's method as to drugs was overcome by the proof of his marvellous skill in the speedy restoration of Nancy Nash after she had been rolling and rolling in agonies from the presence of a tumour both hard and obstinate, but nevertheless compelled to yield.

How could Lydgate help himself? It is offensive to tell a lady when she is expressing her amazement at your skill, that she is altogether mistaken and rather foolish in her amazement. And to have entered into the nature of diseases would only have added to his breaches of medical propriety. Thus he had to wince under a promise of success given by that ignorant praise which misses every valid quality.

In the case of a more conspicuous patient, Mr Borthrop Trumbull, Lydgate was conscious of having shown himself something better than an everyday doctor, though here too it was an equivocal advantage that he won. The eloquent auctioneer was seized with pneumonia, and having been a patient of Mr Peacock's, sent for Lydgate, whom he had expressed his intention to patronize. Mr Trumbull was a robust man, a good subject for trying the expectant theory upon—watching the course of an interesting disease when left as much as possible to itself, so that the stages might be noted for future guidance; and from the air with which he described his sensations Lydgate surmised that he would like to be taken into his medical man's confidence, and be represented as a partner in his own cure. The auctioneer heard, without much surprise, that his was a constitution which (always with due watching) might be left to itself, so as to offer a beautiful example of a disease with all its phases seen in clear delineation, and that he probably had the rare strength of mind voluntarily to become the test of a rational procedure, and thus make the disorder of his pulmonary functions a general benefit to society.

Mr Trumbull acquiesced at once, and entered strongly into the view that an illness of his was no ordinary occasion for medical science.

"Never fear, sir; you are not speaking to one who is altogether ignorant of the *vis medicatrix*," said he, with his usual superiority of expression, made rather pathetic by difficulty of breathing. And he went without shrinking through his abstinence from drugs, much sustained by application of the thermometer which implied the importance of his temperature, by the sense that he furnished objects for the microscope, and by learning many new words which seemed suited to the dignity of his secretions. For Lydgate was acute enough to indulge him with a little technical talk.

It may be imagined that Mr Trumbull rose from his couch with a disposition to speak of an illness in which he had manifested the strength of his mind as well as constitution; and he was not backward in awarding credit to the medical man who had discerned the quality of patient he had to deal with. The auctioneer was not an ungenerous man, and liked to give others their due, feeling that he could afford it. He had caught the words "expectant method", and rang chimes on this and other learned phrases to accompany the assurance that Lydgate "knew a thing or two more than the rest of the doctors—was far better versed in the secrets of his profession than the majority of his compeers."

This had happened before the affair of Fred Vincy's illness had given to Mr Wrench's enmity towards Lydgate more definite personal ground. The new-comer already threatened to be a nuisance in the shape of rivalry, and was certainly a nuisance in the shape of practical criticism or reflections on his hard-driven elders, who had had something else to do than to busy themselves with untried notions. His practice had spread in one or two quarters, and from the first the report of his high family had led to his being pretty generally invited, so that the other medical men had to meet him at dinner in the best houses; and having to meet a man whom you dislike is not observed always to end in mutual attachment. There was hardly ever so much unanimity among them as in the opinion that Lydgate was an arrogant young fellow, and yet ready for the sake of ultimately predominating to show a crawling subservience to Bulstrode. That Mr Farebrother, whose name was a chief flag of the anti-Bulstrode party, always defended Lydgate and made a friend of him, was referred to Farebrother's unaccountable way of fighting on both sides.

Here was plenty of preparation for the outburst of professional disgust at the announcement of the laws Mr Bulstrode was laying down for the direction of the New Hospital, which were the more exasperating because there was no present possibility of interfering with his will and pleasure, everybody except Lord Medlicote having refused help towards the building, on the ground that they preferred giving to the Old Infirmary. Mr Bulstrode met all the expenses, and had ceased to be sorry that he was purchasing the right to carry out his notions of improvement without hindrance from prejudiced coadjutors; but he had had to spend large sums and the building had lingered. Caleb Garth had undertaken it, had failed during its progress, and before the interior fittings were begun had retired from the management of the business; and when referring to the Hospital he often said that however Bulstrode might ring if you tried him, he liked good solid carpentry and masonry, and had a notion both of drains and chimneys. In fact, the Hospital had become an object of intense interest to Bulstrode, and he would willingly have continued to spare a large yearly sum that he might rule it dictatorially without any Board; but he had another favourite object which also required money for its accomplishment: he wished to buy some land in the neighbourhood of Middlemarch, and therefore he wished to get considerable contributions towards maintaining the Hospital. Meanwhile he framed his plan of management. The Hospital was to be reserved for fever in all its forms; Lydgate was to be chief medical superintendent that he might have free authority to pursue all comparative investigations which his studies, particularly in Paris, had shown him the importance of, the other medical visitors having a consultative influence, but no power to contravene Lydgate's ultimate decisions; and the general management was to be lodged exclusively in the hands of five directors associated with Mr Bulstrode, who were to have votes in the ratio of their contributions, the Board itself filling up any vacancy in its numbers, and no mob of small contributors being admitted to a share of government.

There was an immediate refusal on the part of every medical man in the town to become a visitor at the Fever Hospital.

"Very well," said Lydgate to Mr Bulstrode, "we have a capital house-surgeon and dispenser, a clear-headed, neat-handed fellow; we'll get Webb from Crabsley, as good a country practitioner as any of them, to come over twice a-week, and in case of any exceptional operation, Protheroe will come from Brassing. I must work the harder, that's all, and I have given up my post at the Infirmary. The plan will flourish in spite of them, and then they'll be glad to come in. Things can't last as they are: there must be all sorts of reform soon, and then young fellows may be glad to come and study here." Lydgate was in high spirits.

"I shall not flinch, you may depend upon it, Mr Lydgate," said Bulstrode. "While I see you carrying out high intentions with vigour, you shall have my unfailing support. And I have humble confidence that the blessing which has hitherto attended my efforts against the spirit of evil in this town will not be withdrawn. Suitable directors to assist me I have no doubt of securing. Mr Brooke of Tipton has already given me his concurrence, and a pledge to contribute yearly: he has not specified the sum—probably not a great one. But he will be a useful member of the Board."

A useful member was perhaps to be defined as one who would originate nothing, and always vote with Mr Bulstrode.

The medical aversion to Lydgate was hardly disguised now.

Chapter 45, "The Dead Hand," *Middlemarch*, 1871–72.

NIKOLAI GOGOL

Question of a Nose

This description of a doctor comes from Gogol's famous story of a disappearing nose, which itself came from Laurence Sterne's story of Tristram Shandy's nose fashioned by Dr Slop from "a piece of cotton and a thin piece of whalebone out of Susannah's stays." Its humour derives from a form of metonymy run wild.

This doctor was a fine figure of a man with striking pitch-black sideburns, and a pink-faced, healthy-looking wife. He used to eat an apple every morning, and was painstaking about his dental hygiene, spending nearly three-quarters of an hour every morning rinsing out his mouth and cleaning his teeth with five different kinds of toothbrush. He was there in the drop of a hat. After asking the Major when exactly the mishap had occurred, he lifted Kovalyov's face by the chin and prodded him with his thumb in the place where his nose used to be with such force that the Major pulled back his head and banged it against the wall. The doctor told him not to fret about it and made him stand a little bit farther from the wall and tilt his head first to the right. Palpating the place where the nose had been he said "Hmm!" Then he ordered him to incline his head to the left, and said "Hmm!" again. Finally he prodded Kovalyov again, and he jerked back his head like a horse having its teeth inspected.

After this examination the doctor shook his head and said: "No, it can't be done. Best to leave things as they are, or you might make it even worse. Of course, it can be stuck on, and I could perhaps do this for you right away. But I have to tell you it would look dire."

"Oh, that's marvellous! How am I to carry on without a nose?" asked Kovalyov. "Whatever you do, it couldn't look worse than it does now. It's just awful! How can I display myself in public looking like a freak? I mix with decent people. I'm expected at two soirées this evening. I know nearly all the best people: State Counsellor Chekhtaryev's wife, the wife of staff officer Podtochin … though after what she's done I won't be having any more to do with her except through the police. I appeal to you," pleaded Kovalyov, "is there nothing you can do? Stick it on somehow; even if it looks bad, even if it's in danger of falling off, I could always hold it on with my hand at tricky moments. And I don't dance, which is a godsend, so I'm not likely to dislodge it with some careless movement. And you can rest assured as regards recompense, you will be fulsomely rewarded for your troubles, within my means of course …"

"Well, you ought to know," said the doctor in a voice that was neither loud nor soft, but was extremely persuasive and compelling, "I never treat patients out of pecuniary self-interest. That runs contrary to my principles and to my calling. It is true I charge for private visits, but only because refusal to take money often offends. Of course, I could put your nose back on. But I give you my word of honour: it will look far worse if I do. Let nature take its course. Rinse the area as often as you can with cold water and, believe me, you'll feel just as good without a nose as you would with one. As for the nose, I suggest you put it in a jar with alcohol or, better still, soak it in two tablespoonsful of neat vodka and warmed-up vinegar, and you'll be able to get good money for it. I'll buy it myself if you don't want too much for it."

"No, I won't sell it for anything!" exclaimed the Major in despair. "I'd rather lose it again."

"Then I'm sorry," said the doctor, bowing as he went out, "I tried to be of some use … What more can I do! At least you saw my intentions were good."

With these words, the doctor made a dignified exit. Kovalyov was so stunned he didn't even catch a glimpse his face. All he saw was the pristine white of the doctor's cuffs, peeping out from the black sleeves of his tailcoat.

Excerpt from *The Nose*, 1836; translated from the Russian
by Marjorie Farquharson.

GUSTAVE FLAUBERT

The Operation

Charles Bovary is a medical officer, a species of doctor which no longer exists in France. In this chapter from Flaubert's masterpiece Bovary recklessly decides, in order to boost his local standing, to perform a corrective tenotomy on the local idiot Hippolyte. It is an operation for which he has no experience, though it would appear that it is his poor aseptic technique rather than his technical inexperience which gets the better of him. In the end, the shame of not being able to lean on a solid reputation drives his wife Emma into the arms of her feckless lover. Ambroise Paré is the father of French surgery.

Homais, the local chemist, had recently read an article in praise of a pioneering method for correcting club-foot. Since he was a man of progress, he got the patriotic notion that Yonville, to keep up with the times, should offer club-foot operations.

"After all," he said to Emma, "what's the risk? Look—" And he counted on his fingers the benefits of correction. "Success is almost certain. A patient helped and an eyesore less. Instant fame for the surgeon. Why on earth wouldn't your husband want to help out poor Hippolyte at the *Lion d'Or?* You can be sure he wouldn't fail to chatter about his cure to all and sundry, and then—" Homais lowered his voice and glanced around him. "What's to stop me sending the papers a little report about it? Well, good Lord! An article does the rounds ... people talk ... and a rolling stone gathers no moss. And then what? Who knows?"

In short, Bovary would be a success. Nothing alerted Emma to the fact that he wasn't up to the job. What satisfaction it would give her to have shown him the way to boost his reputation and his fortune. She did so want to lean on something more solid than love.

Prodded by her and the chemist, Charles allowed himself to be talked into it. He got Dr Duval's book from Rouen, and every evening, head in hands, buried himself in its pages.

While he was studying the equinovarus and equinovalgus deformities, that is to say *strephocatopodia, strephendopodia* and *strephexopodia* (or, better said, the different deviations of the foot, downwards, inwards or outwards), also *strephypopodia* and *strephanopodia* (in other terms, downwards eversion and upwards inversion), M. Homais was finding all sorts of reasons to convince the inn's odd-job-man to let himself be operated upon.

"You'll hardly feel a thing! Well, just a twinge perhaps, a little jab, like when you're bled a bit, but really, it's less trouble than cutting a thick corn."

Hippolyte considered the matter, rolling his daft eyes.

"Quite honestly," continued the chemist, "it's none of my business really. You're the one I'm thinking of. Out of pure humanity! It would please me to see you, my friend, freed of your hideous limp, not to mention the tilting of your lower spine, which—however much you pretend otherwise —must hurt awfully while going about your job."

Then Homais gave him to know how much brawnier and nimbler he would be afterwards, hinting that he would also be better equipped to please the ladies, at which the ostler gave a thick-witted smile. Then he attacked his vanity. "You're a man, aren't you, goddam? What would you do if you were called up, to fight for your country? Eh, Hippolyte?" And Homais left, declaring that he couldn't understand this pigheadedness, this blindness that refused to countenance the benefits of science.

The poor man gave in; it had all become a plot. Binet, who of course never stuck his nose into other people's business, Madame Lefrançois, Artémise, the neighbours, even the mayor himself M. Tuvache, absolutely everybody buttonholed him, preached to him, positively shamed him. But what settled the issue was that *it wouldn't cost him a penny*. Bovary would even pay for the instruments he needed. This act of generosity was Emma's idea, and Charles agreed to it, telling himself from the bottom of his heart that his wife was an angel.

On the advice of the chemist, and after a couple of dummy runs, he got the local joiner, with the locksmith's help, to construct an amateurish box weighing about eight pounds, not sparing the iron, the wood, steelplating, leather, nuts and bolts.

But to know which of Hippolyte's tendons to incise, he had first to diagnose what variety of club-foot he had.

The foot was almost in a straight line with the leg, but that didn't prevent it turning inwards. It was a club-foot with slight tendency to equinovarus, or perhaps a slight equinovarus with a severe club-foot. But upon this club-foot, as clumpy as a horse's hoof, with its rough skin, thick tendons, deformed toes, and nails as black as a horseshoe's, the strephopodic patient leapt about from morning to night like a faun. He was always to be seen out in the town square, hopping round the carts while thrusting his deformed limb ahead of him. It even seemed to have more life than the other one. By dint of being used, it had developed moral qualities: patience and energy. It seemed to have rather a penchant for being overworked.

But since it happened to be a case of club-foot the Achilles tendon would have to be incised, with surgery some time thereafter to the anterior tibialis muscle in order to release the varus. The doctor didn't dare risk two operations at one go. He was already trembling with the fear that he might stumble into some anatomically important region of which he knew nothing.

Ambroise Paré, about to ligate an artery directly for the first time, after an interval of fifteen centuries, since Celsus; Dupuytren, about to lance an abscess through a thick mantle of brain; Gensoul, about to perform the first excision of the maxilla—none of them had so palpitating a heart, so trembling a hand, so tense a mind, as Monsieur Bovary approaching Hippolyte with a tenotomy scalpel in his fingers.

It was just like in the hospitals. On a side-table stood a pile of lint, waxed threads and piles of bandages—a pyramid of bandages, every bandage in the chemist's shop. M. Homais had been organising it all since daybreak, to dazzle the townspeople and to impress himself.

Charles incised the skin. A dry snap was heard. The tendon was incised, the operation was over. Hippolyte was dumbfounded. He fell upon Bovary's hands and covered them with kisses.

"Steady now," said the chemist, "you can express your gratitude to your benefactor later on."

He went downstairs to announce the outcome to the five or six curious bystanders standing about in the courtyard, who imagined that Hippolyte was going to reappear walking normally. Having first strapped his patient into the joiner's mechanical boot, Charles then went home where Emma was waiting nervously at the door. She hugged him; they moved to the dinner-table; he ate heartily, and even requested a cup of coffee with the dessert, an indulgence he permitted himself only on Sundays when they had guests.

The evening was captivating, full of conversation and shared dreams. He spoke of their coming fortune, of home improvements to be made. He could see his reputation swelling, his standing increasing, his wife loving him everlastingly. And she was delighted to bathe in new feelings, feelings which were healthier and better, and to feel at last a little tenderness for the poor boy who was besotted with her. The idea of Rudolph, for a moment, flitted through her mind. But her eyes went back to Charles. She even noticed, to her surprise, that his teeth were not at all bad.

They were in bed the next morning when M. Homais, despite the protestations of the cook, burst into their bedroom holding a sheet of paper still damp with ink. It was the publicity which he was going to put in the *Fanal de Rouen*. He had brought it for them to read.

"You read it," said Bovary.

He read: "'Despite the prejudices which still cover part of the face of Europe like a veil, light has begun to break upon our country region. This all happened because, last Tuesday, our little town of Yonville became the stage of a surgical procedure which was also an act of great philanthropy. M. Bovary, one of out most distinguished practitioners—'"

"Stop! That's overdoing it! That's too much!" said Charles, choked with emotion.

"No, no, not at all! Not in the least! 'Operated on a club-foot ...' I haven't used the scientific term, because in a newspaper, you know, nobody would understand it. It's important that the masses—"

"How right you are," said Bovary. "Go on."

"Where was I—" said the chemist. "'M. Bovary, one of our most distinguished practitioners, operated on a patient with club-foot known as Hippolyte Tautain, ostler for the last twenty-five years at the hotel

Lion d'Or, which is kept by Madame Lefrançois, widow, in the Place d'Armes. The novelty of this attempt, and the interest occasioned by the subject, had drawn such a number of spectators that a large crowd blocked the access to the inn. The operation worked like a magic spell: the few drops of blood which appeared on the skin were sole witness to the fact that the rebellious tendon had at last yielded to surgical art. Curiously, the patient experienced very little pain, as your reporter was able to testify. His present condition is entirely satisfactory. Everything suggests that his convalescence will be short. And who knows?—it may even be, at the next village fête, that we shall even see our good Hippolyte joining the revels, at the centre of a cheery chorus; his gusto and capers a living proof for every onlooker of his complete cure. All honour to our learned improvers! Honour to those who put their intelligence to work through the night for the betterment, or the relief of their fellows! Honour! Three times honour! Is this not the moment to state that the blind *shall* see, the deaf hear and the lame walk? But what was once a fanatical promise to the chosen few, science now brings about for everyone! We will keep our readers fully informed of the progress of this remarkable cure.'"

Which did not prevent, five days later, mother Lefrançois appearing in a right state and crying: "Help! He's dying! I don't know what to do!"

Charles hurried across to the *Lion d'Or*. The chemist, observing him cross the square without his hat on, abandoned his shop. He was out of breath himself, flushed and worried, and asking everyone going upstairs: "So what's wrong with our interesting case of club-foot?"

The club-foot was writhing in terrible convulsions which were so violent that the mechanical boot in which his leg was encased thumped against the wall, threatening to knock a hole in it.

With great care, to avoid having to shift the position of the limb, the box was removed. What they saw was frightful. The contours of the foot were bloated into a huge swelling, the whole skin seemed on the point of bursting, and bruised all over because of the legendary machine. Hippolyte had been complaining of pain, but nobody took a blind bit of notice. It had to be admitted now that he hadn't been entirely wrong, so the foot was left exposed for a few hours. But the oedema was barely reduced before the two wise men judged it opportune to put the limb back in the apparatus, doing the screws up tighter to move things along. Three days later, Hippolyte had finally had enough. They again removed the contraption, and were greatly startled at what they saw. The leg was one livid swollen mass covered, in places, with blisters from which exuded a black fluid. Things were not looking good.

Hippolyte began to get bored with the business. Old mother Lefrançois put him in a little room by the kitchen, so that at least he had some distraction. But the tax inspector who dined every day in the kitchen complained bitterly about his neighbour. So they shifted Hippolyte to the billiard-room.

He lay there whimpering under the thick blankets, pale, unshaven, hollow-eyed, turning his sweaty head now and again on the dirty pillow on which the flies settled. Madame Bovary came to see him. She brought him muslin for his poultices; and consoled and encouraged him. Not that he was short of company, on market-days in particular, when the country people around him knocked away at the billiard-balls, fenced with the cues, smoked, drank, sang and bellowed.

"How are you doing?" they said, slapping him on the shoulder. "Ah! It's nothing to brag about, that's obvious. But it's not your fault, is it?" Then they would tell him what he should do.

They told him stories of people who had been cured, all of them, but by other methods. By way of consolation, they would add: "Aren't you molly-coddling yourself a bit? Why don't you get up? You're pampering yourself like a pasha! Oh, it doesn't really matter, you old wag. But you certainly smell rich."

The gangrene was rising higher and higher. It made Bovary feel ill himself. He was there every hour, every moment he could. Hippolyte gazed at him with terror in his eyes and sobbed his broken phrases: "When will I be made better? Save me! Oh, how miserable I am! How miserable I am!" And the doctor left, always with a word of advice about his diet.

"Don't listen to a word of it," old mother Lefrançois told him. "Haven't they crucified you already? You'll just get feebler and feebler. Come on, drink up!"

And she brought him delicious broths, legs of lamb, slices of bacon, and sometimes tiny glasses of spirits that he didn't have the courage to raise to his lips.

Father Bournisien, hearing that he was worse, asked to see him. He told Hippolyte how sorry he was to hear about his illness, while declaring that he should come to terms with it, because it was God's will, and seize the opportunity to make his peace with heaven.

"It must be said that you neglect your duties a bit," said the priest in a fatherly tone. "We never see you in church. How many years is it since you went up to the altar? I know you've things to do, that the hugger-mugger of the world might distract you from thinking about your eternal salvation. Now's the right time to think about it. But don't despair: I've known great sinners who, on the point of appearing before the judgement seat (I know, I know, you're not at that stage yet) have implored His heavenly mercy and most surely died with circumstances in their favour. Let's hope that, just like them, you'll practise what I'm preaching! However, just to be on the safe side, what's to stop you reciting morning and evening a Hail Mary and Our Father Who Art in Heaven? Yes, do that. Do it for me, as a favour. It won't cost you a penny? Promise?"

The poor devil promised. The curé came back every day after. He chatted to the innkeeper, and even told her anecdotes peppered with comic turns and word play which were quite beyond Hippolyte. When circumstances allowed he returned to religious matters, and took on a priestly gravamen.

His zeal seemed to pay off, because soon the club-foot was expressing a wish to make the pilgrimage to Bon-Secours if he got better. To which M. Bournisien replied that he couldn't see any objection, fending for his eternal soul twice was better than doing it just once. And he wasn't risking anything, was he?

The chemist was up in arms at what he called this priestly manoeuvring. He asserted that it interfered with Hippolyte's convalescence, and he repeated to Madame Lefrançois: "Leave him be! Leave him be! You're messing about with his state of mind with all your mysticism."

But the good woman didn't want to hear a word of it. The whole mess was the chemist's fault. Out of contrariness, she fixed a stoup full of holy water at the bedside together with a twig of box-wood.

But religion seemed no more effective than surgery, and the gangrene continued rising inexorably from his legs towards his belly. No matter how often they varied the medicines and changed the poultices the muscles became more and more deliquescent, and eventually Charles nodded his head when old mother Lefrançois asked him if it wouldn't be an idea, as a desperate last measure, to summon the famous surgeon M. Canivet from Neufchâtel.

Doctor of medicine, fifty years old, a man of high standing and self-confident, Bovary's fellow practitioner couldn't hold back a dismissive snort of contempt when he saw the leg gangrenous to the knee. Having stated peremptorily that he would amputate, he crossed over to the chemist's shop to rail at the fools who had managed to reduce the unfortunate man to such a state. Grabbing M. Homais by the button on his frock-coat, he shouted through the shop: "This was one of those new-fangled ideas from Paris! So much for the ideas of those gentlemen in the capital! It's the same as squints, chloroform and surgery for renal stones, a lot of monstrous ideas that the government ought to ban. But they want to look clever, and sell you a bill of goods without worrying about the consequences. The rest of us don't put on airs and graces. We're not a bunch of sages, dandies and paragons. We're doctors, healers, and we wouldn't dream of operating on anyone who was in splendid health. Correcting club-feet! Can you straighten club-feet? You might as well straighten out a hunchback."

Homais squirmed beneath this lecture, disguising his discomfiture with a diplomatic smile. He needed to keep in with M. Canivet, whose prescriptions sometimes reached Yonville. He therefore refrained from springing to Bovary's defence; and in fact, did not make a single comment. Jettisoning his principles, he sacrificed his intellectual dignity to the more serious matter of holding on to his business.

A mid-thigh amputation by the surgeon Canivet—that was a big event in the village! Everybody got up at the crack of dawn, and the Grande-Rue, crammed with people, took on a rather gloomy air, as if someone were about to be executed. The talk at the grocer's was all about Hippolyte's illness.

The shops sold nothing; and Madame Tuvache, the mayor's wife, didn't budge from her window, such was her keenness to see the surgeon arrive.

He appeared in his gig, holding the reins himself. The springs on the right-hand side had with long use yielded to his corpulence, so that the carriage inclined a little to the side as it went along, revealing on the cushion next to him a vast box, covered with a red sheepskin, on which the three brass locks glittered splendidly.

Entering the porch of the *Lion d'Or* like a whirlwind, the surgeon ordered in a brassy voice for his horse to be unharnessed. Then he went into the stables to make sure it was eating its oats. He was in the habit, when he arrived at his patients' houses, of busying himself first with his mare and his carriage. And people would say: "Ah! M. Canivet, he's a character!" And they thought all the more of him for his steady self-assurance. The whole universe might go to rack and ruin, but M. Canivet would still be there maintaining his usual habits.

Homais presented himself.

"I'm counting on you," said the surgeon. "Are we ready? Let's go to work!" But the chemist confessed, reddening in the face, that he was too sensitive to watch such an operation. "When you're just a spectator," he said, "your imagination, you know, gets to you. And my nervous system is so—"

"Nonsense," interrupted Canivet. "On the contrary, you strike me as a case of incipient apoplexy. Which doesn't surprise me at all: you pharmacists are always poking about in your laboratories, which ends up by ruining your health. Look at me! I get up at four every morning, I have a shave in cold water (since I don't feel the cold), I never wear flannel, I never catch a chill—a constitution like an ox! I live life however it comes, like a philosopher; and I eat what's put before me. That's why I'm not a lily like you, and it doesn't make the slightest difference to me if I cut up a Christian or the first chicken that comes along. It's a matter of habit, wouldn't you say? Habit is the thing."

Without taking the slightest notice of Hippolyte, who was sweating anxiously between the sheets, the pair started up a conversation in which the chemist compared a surgeon's icy calm to that of a general, a comparison flattering to Canivet, who launched into a long discourse on the demands of his art. He regarded it as a holy calling, though one brought into disrepute by the local medical officers. Coming at last to the patient, he examined the bandages brought by Homais, the same ones as had appeared during the club-foot operation, and asked if he could have someone to hold the leg. They sent for Lestiboudois, and M. Canivet, having rolled up his sleeves, went into the billiard-room, while the chemist stayed with Artémise and the innkeeper, both whiter than their aprons, ears cocked towards the door.

Bovary meanwhile had not dared to leave his house. He remained downstairs in the lounge, sitting next to the unlit chimney, chin on chest, hands together, staring into space. What a disaster! he thought. What a disappointment! He had taken every imaginable precaution. The hand of fate had intervened. There was nothing to do about it. If Hippolyte were to die later, it was he who had killed him. What reason could he give when people asked him about it on his rounds? Perhaps he'd slipped up somewhere? He thought hard, but he couldn't see how. But even the most famous surgeons had made mistakes. No, people wouldn't believe it. On the contrary, how they'd laugh and gossip. It would get around as far as Forges! Neufchâtel! Rouen! Everywhere! Who knows?—even his colleagues might write things against him. A row would blow up, he'd have to reply in the newspapers. Hippolyte could even take him to court! He saw himself dishonoured, ruined, lost. Swamped by all these conjectures, his imagination bobbed along like an empty barrel tossed into the sea and rolling on the waves.

Emma, sitting opposite, looked at him. She didn't share his humiliation. She was suffering one of her own: to have imagined such a man might be worth something even though she had already observed a score of times just how completely second-rate he was.

Charles paced up and down the room. His boots squeaked on the floorboards.

"Sit down," she said. "You're getting on my nerves." He sat.

How was it that she (who was so intelligent!) had erred again? What awful pulsion was driving her to ruin her existence by making sacrifice after sacrifice? She called back to mind all her feelings for luxury, the privations of her soul, the contemptibility of her marriage and four walls, her dreams falling into the mud like wounded swallows, everything she had wanted, everything she had refused herself, everything she might have had. Why? Why?

A piercing scream broke through the silence that shrouded the village. Bovary went pale as if about to faint. Emma nervously raised her eyebrows, and went on with her thoughts. That cry was meant for him, for this man who understood nothing and felt nothing! There he was, standing unperturbed and without the least inkling of the ridicule that was going to besmirch his name, and hers along with it. She had really tried to love him, and it had made her cry, repenting of having given herself to another man.

"But perhaps it *was* a valgus?" exclaimed Bovary suddenly. He had been thinking.

The unexpected shock of the phrase fell on her own reflections like a ball of lead on a silver platter. Emma gave a start, and cocked her head to work out what he had meant. They stared at each other silently, as though astounded to see each other, so distant were they in thought from one another. Charles held her in view with the glazed look of a drunk, listening, motionless, to the last cries of the amputee—long, drawn-out moans broken by jerky shrill screams, like the far-off howl of some beast getting its throat slit.

Emma bit her pale lips, and, rolling some bits of coral she had broken off between her fingers, fixed Charles sharply with her pupils, as if they were two torches ready to shoot. Everything about him irritated her now. His face, his clothes, the things he never said, his whole being, his very existence. She repented of her former virtue as if it had been a crime, and what was left of it crumbled beneath the pummellings of her pride. She relished all the base ironies of adultery triumphant. Memories of her lover returned with an allure that made her dizzy; she threw herself heart and soul upon them, drawn towards his image with a new enthusiasm. Charles himself seemed totally removed from her life, gone for ever; someone utterly out of the question, a mere nothing, as if he were about to die and undergo his death agonies before her eyes.

They heard the sound of people moving about on the pavement. Charles peered out. Through the lowered blind he saw, at the edge of the covered market, the surgeon Canivet mopping his brow with his silk scarf in the broad sunlight. Behind him was Homais with a large red box in his hands. The two of them crossed towards the chemist's shop.

Through a sudden pang of tenderness and despondency, Bovary turned towards his wife and said: "Kiss me, my darling."

"Leave me alone," she snapped back, red with rage.

"What's wrong? What's the matter with you?" he replied, dumbfounded. "Calm down, pull yourself together! You know that I love you … come to me …"

"Enough!" she shouted, with a dreadful look on her face.

Rushing from the room, Emma slammed the door so hard that the barometer sprang from the wall and fell to the floor.

Charles slumped back into his chair, bewildered, wondering what had got into her, surmising that it must be a nervous affliction, starting to weep and vaguely feeling something gathering around him like a doom he didn't understand.

When Rudolph came into the garden that evening, he found his mistress waiting for him, perched on the step at the bottom of the stairs. They embraced each other, and all their malice melted like snow in the brazier of their kisses.

Chapter XI, Part II, *Madame Bovary*, 1857.

SØREN KIERKEGAARD

Making a Diagnosis

The demon of medicine in an age of numbers, as the existentialist philosopher Kierkegaard suggests in opposition to the early public health thinking of Nietzsche, is the irksome fact that patients insist on being singular.

The demonical is seen from a therapeutic perspective. As a routine measure: "'*Mit Pulver und mit Pillen*' [powders and pills]—and don't forget the enemas!" Now the chemist and the doctor have put their heads together. The patient has been isolated so that the others won't be afraid. In our courageous age one does not say to a patient that he will die, one dare not call the cleric for fear the patient may die of fright, one dare not say to the patient that someone else died recently of the same illness. The patient has been isolated, compassion made inquiries about him, the doctor promised to issue as soon as possible a tabulated statistical report in order to calculate the mean. And when one has the mean, everything is explained. The therapeutic way of considering the case regards the phenomenon as purely physical and somatic, and it does as physicians often do, especially in one of Hoffman's novels—it takes its pinch of snuff and says, "This case is giving cause for concern."

Excerpt from "Anxiety about the Good,"
The Concept of Anxiety, 1844.

EMILY DICKINSON

Poems

*Emily Dickinson's 1862 poem articulates an ideal—a counterideal—as old as our
civilization: that the proper way to know ourselves is to maintain a prudent
ignorance of what Reason presumes to know, Reason being human and limited,
and to hold fast to the personal. Vision and incising are practically the same thing
here; but Dickinson ends the poem on a startling and ambiguous image: is the
heart a bomb or a balm? Shorn of her Christian humility, the same urge feeds a
powerful contemporary yearning not to cover what we think we are, but to recover
what we imagine we ought to be. The ideal, of course, comes from Socrates: genuine
knowledge, were we to achieve it, would be happiness.*

> To cover what we are
> From Science—and from Surgery—
> Too Telescopic Eyes
> To bear on us unshaded—
> For their sake—not for Ours—
> 'Twould startle them—
> We—could tremble—
> But since we got a Bomb—
> And held it in our Bosom—
> Nay—Hold it—it is calm—
>
> Therefore—we do life's labor—
> Through life's Reward—be done—
> With scrupulous exactness—
> To hold our Senses—on—

★

Is Heaven a physician?
They say that He can heal;
But medicine posthumous
Is unavailable.

Is Heaven an Exchequer?
They speak of what we owe;
But that negotiation
I'm not a party to.

★

Pain has an element of blank;
It cannot recollect
When it began, or if there were
A day when it were not.

It has no future but itself,
Its infinite realms contain
Its past, enlightened to perceive
New periods of pain.

Excerpts from poem 443; poem 47; poem 19.

SAMUEL BUTLER

A Trial in Erewhon

Butler's Erewhon *(1872) is a satire on the Victorians and what they really held close to their hearts. Putting a consumptive on trial might strike us as grossly unfair, since we regard disease as belonging to the world of physical causes and actions (reputedly the area of competence of the medical profession) and not a matter of morality—the blame-laying positive laws administered by our courts. To be consistent, courts can only arraign us for our freely chosen acts. In the world satirized by Butler doctors are criminals, and the judge must assume that the man in the dock has chosen, or culpably not avoided, his disease. We are not quite there yet, but it is possible to envisage our own world reaching a stage in which the scientific view of man posits such a wide understanding of causation that very little room is left for free will—already defence lawyers are not shy of resorting to what Alan Dershowitz has called the "abuse excuse." So why does blame become ever more strident?*

But I shall perhaps best convey to the reader an idea of the entire perversion of thought which exists among this extraordinary people, by describing the public trial of a man who was accused of pulmonary consumption— an offence which was punished with death until quite recently. It did not occur till I had been some months in the country, and I am deviating from chronological order in giving it here; but I had perhaps better do so in order that I may exhaust this subject before proceeding to others. Moreover, I should never come to an end were I to keep to a strictly narrative form, and detail the infinite absurdities with which I daily came in contact.

The prisoner was placed in the dock, and the jury were sworn much as in Europe; almost all our own modes of procedure were reproduced, even to the requiring the prisoner to plead guilty or not guilty. He pleaded not guilty, and the case proceeded. The evidence for the prosecution was very strong; but I must do the court the justice to observe that the trial was absolutely impartial. Counsel for the prisoner was allowed to urge everything that could be said in his defence: the line taken was that the prisoner was simulating consumption in order to defraud an insurance company, from which he was about to buy an annuity, and that he hoped thus to obtain it on more advantageous terms. If this could have been shown to be the case he would have escaped a criminal prosecution, and been sent to a hospital as for a moral ailment. The view, however, was one which could not be reasonably sustained, in spite of all the ingenuity and eloquence of one of the most celebrated advocates of the country. The case was only too clear, for the prisoner was almost at the point of death, and it was astonishing that he had not been tried and convicted long previously. His coughing was incessant during the whole trial, and it was all that the two jailors in charge of him could do to keep him on his legs until it was over.

The summing up of the judge was admirable. He dwelt upon every point that could be construed in favour of the prisoner, but as he proceeded it became clear that the evidence was too convincing to admit of doubt, and there was but one opinion in the court as to the impending verdict when the jury retired from the box. They were absent for about ten minutes, and on their return the foreman pronounced the prisoner guilty. There was a faint murmur of applause, but it was instantly repressed. The judge then proceeded to pronounce sentence in words which I can never forget, and which I copied out into a note-book next day from the report that was published in the leading newspaper. I must condense it somewhat, and nothing which I could say would give more than a faint idea of the solemn, not to say majestic, severity with which it was delivered. The sentence was as follows:—

"Prisoner at the bar, you have been accused of the great crime of labouring under pulmonary consumption, and after an impartial trial before a jury of your countrymen, you have been found guilty. Against the justice of the verdict I can say nothing: the evidence against you was conclusive, and it only remains for me to pass such a sentence upon you, as shall satisfy the ends of the law. That sentence must be a very severe one. It pains me much to see one who is yet so young, and whose prospects in life were otherwise so excellent, brought to this distressing condition by a constitution which I can only regard as radically vicious; but yours is no case for compassion: this is not your first offence: you have led a career of crime, and have only profited by the leniency shown you upon past occasions, to offend yet more seriously against the laws and institutions of your country. You were convicted of aggravated bronchitis last year: and I find that though you are now only twenty-three years old, you have been imprisoned on no less than fourteen occasions for illnesses of a more or less hateful character; in fact, it is not too much to say that you have spent the greater part of your life in a jail.

"It is all very well for you to say that you came of unhealthy parents, and had a severe accident in your childhood which permanently undermined your constitution; excuses such as these are the ordinary refuge of the criminal; but they cannot for one moment be listened to by the ear of justice. I am not here to enter upon curious metaphysical questions as to the origin of this or that—questions to which there would be no end were their introduction once tolerated, and which would result in throwing the only guilt on the tissues of the primordial cell, or on the elementary gases. There is no question of how you came to be wicked, but only this—namely, are you wicked or not? This has been decided in the affirmative, neither can I hesitate for a single moment to say that it has been decided justly. You are a bad and dangerous person, and stand branded in the eyes of your fellow-countrymen with one of the most heinous known offences.

"It is not my business to justify the law: the law may in some cases have its inevitable hardships, and I may feel regret at times that I have not the option of passing a less severe sentence than I am compelled to do. But yours is no such case; on the contrary, had not the capital punishment for consumption been abolished, I should certainly inflict it now.

"It is intolerable that an example of such terrible enormity should be allowed to go at large unpunished. Your presence in the society of respectable people would lead the less able-bodied to think more lightly of all forms of illness; neither can it be permitted that you should have the chance of corrupting unborn beings who might hereafter pester you. The unborn must not be allowed to come near you: and this not so much for their protection (for they are our natural enemies), as for our own; for since they will not be utterly gainsaid, it must be seen to that they shall be quartered upon those who are least likely to corrupt them.

"But independently of this consideration, and independently of the physical guilt which attaches itself to a crime so great as yours, there is yet another reason why we should be unable to show you mercy, even if we were inclined to do so. I refer to the existence of a class of men who lie hidden among us, and who are called physicians. Were the severity of the law or the current feeling of the country to be relaxed never so slightly, these abandoned persons, who are now compelled to practise secretly and who can be consulted only at the greatest risk, would become frequent visitors in every household; their organization and their intimate acquaintance with all family secrets would give them a power, both social and political, which nothing could resist. The head of the household would become subordinate to the family doctor, who would interfere between man and wife, between master and servant, until the doctors should be the only depositaries of power in the nation, and have all that we hold precious at their mercy. A time of universal dephysicalization would ensue; medicine-vendors of all kinds would abound in our streets and advertise in all our newspapers. There is one remedy for this, and one only. It is that which the laws of this country have long received and acted upon, and consists in the sternest repression of all diseases whatsoever, as soon as their existence is made manifest to the eye of the law. Would that that eye were far more piercing than it is.

"But I will enlarge no further upon things that are themselves so obvious. You may say that it is not your fault. The answer is ready enough at hand, and it amounts to this—that if you had been born of healthy and well-to-do parents, and been well taken care of when you were a child, you would never have offended against the laws of your country, nor found yourself in your present disgraceful position. If you tell me that you had no hand in your parentage and education, and that it is therefore unjust to lay these things to your charge, I answer that whether your being in a consumption is your fault or no, it is a fault in you, and it is my duty to see that against such faults as this the commonwealth shall be protected. You may say that it is your misfortune to be criminal; I answer that it is your crime to be unfortunate.

"Lastly, I should point out that even though the jury had acquitted you—a supposition that I cannot seriously entertain—I should have felt it my duty to inflict a sentence hardly less severe than that which I must pass at present; for the more you had been found guiltless of the crime imputed to you, the more you would have been found guilty of one hardly less heinous—I mean the crime of having been maligned unjustly.

"I do not hesitate therefore to sentence you to imprisonment, with hard labour, for the rest of your miserable existence. During that period I would earnestly entreat you to repent of the wrongs you have done already, and to entirely reform the constitution of your whole body. I entertain but little hope that you will pay attention to my advice; you are already far too abandoned. Did it rest with myself, I should add nothing in mitigation of the sentence which I have passed, but it is the merciful provision of the law that even the most hardened criminal shall be allowed some one of the three official remedies, which is to be prescribed at the time of his conviction. I shall therefore order that you receive two tablespoonfuls of castor oil daily, until the pleasure of the court be further known."

When the sentence was concluded the prisoner acknowledged in a few scarcely audible words that he was justly punished, and that he had had a fair trial. He was then removed to the prison from which he was never to return. There was a second attempt at applause when the judge had finished speaking, but as before it was at once repressed; and though the feeling of the court was strongly against the prisoner, there was no show of any violence against him, if one may except a little hooting from the bystanders when he was being removed in the prisoners' van. Indeed, nothing struck me more during my whole sojourn in the country, than the general respect for law and order.

Excerpt from "Some Erewhonian Trials," in *Erewhon*, 1872.

FRIEDRICH NIETZSCHE
The Future of the Doctor

Nietzsche's recipes for improving the health of society are well-known. In this list of instructions, written during his "positivist" phase, he is rather terrifying in his endorsement of the type of "benefactor to society at large" figure he would in other circumstances have hated on sight.

No profession today seems set to better its standing like the medical profession, especially since manipulators of the mind (so-called soul doctors) are no longer able to practise their magic art to public applause, and a cultured person avoids them. A doctor is no longer at his intellectual peak just because he knows the best new methods inside out, and is practised in them; or understands how to proceed swiftly from effects to causes in the famed manner of diagnosticians. He must also have a talent for conversation that can adapt to every individual and pluck his heart out; a bonhomie which is enough to dispel despondency (the canker in all ill people); a diplomat's unction in mediating between those who need happiness to get better and those who must (and can) foster happiness for their health's sake; the tact of a police agent or lawyer in divining the secrets of a soul without betraying them—in short, a good doctor today needs the skills and prerogatives of all other professional groups. Armed accordingly, he can then go out as a benefactor to society at large by increasing good works, mental happiness and productivity; by staving off bad thoughts, evil intentions and brutishness (the vile source of which is so often the belly); by producing an intellectual–physical aristocracy (as marriage broker and censor); and by benevolent pruning of all those conditions popularly known as torments of the soul and pangs of conscience. Thus, from being a "medicine man" he will become a redeemer, and yet need neither work miracles nor end up crucified for his pains.

243, Menschlich, all-zu-menschlich, 1878.

LYTTON STRACHEY

Florence Nightingale

A book on doctors would hardly be complete without a glance at the task of attending to the body's needs, a task so menial it is entrusted to nurses. It is a fair bet that nursing is going to be a scarce resource in a knowledge-saturated future (that it might be thought of as a "resource" is perhaps part of the problem). In fact, most of the curing done in the nineteenth century came about as a result of simple caring: by cleaning up the hospital at Scutari during the Crimean War, Florence Nightingale brought mortality down from 42 to 2 per cent, a dramatic reversal of "fate" that finds a parallel only in the similar hospital clean-ups of the American Civil War, or in Ignaz Semmelweis's signal discovery, in Vienna, of the association between autopsies and childbed fever. Lytton Strachey's patronizing account of Nightingale's "lurid and heroic adventure" comes from his famous demolition job on the high moral seriousness of the greatest era of achievement the world has witnessed.

Miss Nightingale had been a year in her nursing-home in Harley Street, when Fate knocked at the door. The Crimean War broke out; the battle of the Alma was fought; and the terrible condition of our military hospitals at Scutari began to be known in England. It sometimes happens that the plans of Providence are a little difficult to follow, but on this occasion all was plain; there was a perfect co-ordination of events. For years Miss Nightingale had been getting ready; at last she was prepared—experienced, free, mature, yet still young—she was thirty-four—desirous to serve, accustomed to command: at that precise moment the desperate need of a great nation came, and she was there to satisfy it. If the war had fallen a few years earlier, she would have lacked the knowledge, perhaps even the power, for such a work; a few years later and she would, no doubt, have been fixed in the routine of some absorbing task, and moreover, she would have been growing old. Nor was it only the coincidence of Time that was remarkable. It so fell out that Sidney Herbert was at the War Office and in the Cabinet; and Sidney Herbert was an intimate friend of Miss Nightingale's, convinced, from personal experience in charitable work, of her supreme capacity. After such premises, it seems hardly more than a matter of course that her letter, in which she offered her services for the East, and Sidney Herbert's letter, in which he asked for them, should actually have crossed in the post. Thus it all happened, without a hitch. The appointment was made, and even Mrs. Nightingale, overawed by the magnitude of the venture, could only approve. A pair of faithful friends offered themselves as personal attendants; thirty-eight nurses were collected; and within a week of the crossing of the letters Miss Nightingale, amid a great burst of popular enthusiasm, left for Constantinople.

Among the numerous letters which she received on her departure was one from Dr. Manning, who at that time was working in comparative obscurity as a Catholic priest in Bayswater. "God will keep you," he wrote, "and my prayer for you will be that your one object of Worship, Pattern of Imitation, and source of consolation and strength may be the Sacred Heart of our Divine Lord."

To what extent Dr. Manning's prayer was answered must remain a matter of doubt; but this much is certain, that, if ever a prayer was needed, it was needed then for Florence Nightingale. For dark as had been the picture of the state of affairs at Scutari, revealed to the English public in the despatches of the *Times* correspondent and in a multitude of private letters, yet the reality turned out to be darker still. What had occurred was, in brief, the complete break-down of our medical arrangements at the seat of war. The origins of this awful failure were complex and manifold; they stretched back through long years of peace and carelessness in England; they could be traced through endless ramifications of administrative incapacity—from the inherent faults of confused systems to the petty bunglings of minor officials, from the inevitable ignorance of Cabinet Ministers to the fatal exactitudes of narrow routine. In the inquiries which followed it was clearly shown that the evil was in reality that worst of all evils—one which has been caused by nothing in particular and for which no one in particular is to blame. The whole organisation of the war machine was incompetent and out of date. The old Duke had sat for a generation at the Horse Guards repressing innovations with an iron hand. There was an extraordinary overlapping of authorities, an almost incredible shifting of responsibilities to and fro. As for such a notion as the creation and the maintenance of a really adequate medical service for the army— in that atmosphere of aged chaos, how could it have entered anybody's head? Before the war, the easy-going officials at Westminster were naturally persuaded that all was well—or at least as well as could be expected; when someone, for instance, actually had the temerity to suggest the formation of a corps of army nurses, he was at once laughed out of court. When the war had begun, the gallant British officers in control of affairs had other things to think about than the petty details of medical organisation. Who had bothered with such trifles in the Peninsula? And surely, on that occasion, we had done pretty well. Thus the most obvious precautions were neglected, the most necessary preparations put off from day to day. The principal medical officer of the army, Dr. Hall, was summoned from India at a moment's notice, and was unable to visit England before taking up his duties at the front. And it was not until after the battle of the Alma, when we had been at war for many months, that we acquired hospital accommodation at Scutari for more than a thousand men. Errors, follies, and vices on the part of individuals there doubtless were; but, in the general reckoning, they were of small account—insignificant symptoms of the deep disease of the body politic—the enormous calamity of administrative collapse.

Miss Nightingale arrived at Scutari—a suburb of Constantinople, on the Asiatic side of the Bosphorus—on November 4th, 1854; it was ten days after the battle of Balaclava, and the day before the battle of Inkerman. The organisation of the hospitals, which had already given way under the stress of the battle of the Alma, was now to be subjected to the further pressure which these two desperate and bloody engagements implied. Great detachments of wounded were already beginning to pour in. The men, after receiving such summary treatment as could be given them at the smaller hospitals in the Crimea itself, were forthwith shipped in batches of two hundred across the Black Sea to Scutari. This voyage was in normal times one of four days and a half; but the times were no longer normal, and now the transit often lasted for a fortnight or three weeks. It received, not without reason, the name of "the middle passage." Between, and sometimes on the decks, the wounded, the sick, and the dying were crowded—men who had just undergone the amputation of limbs, men in the clutches of fever or of frostbite, men in the last stages of dysentery and cholera—without beds, sometimes without blankets, often hardly clothed. The one or two surgeons on board did what they could; but medical stores were lacking, and the only form of nursing available was that provided by a handful of invalid soldiers, who were usually themselves prostrate by the end of the voyage. There was no other food beside the ordinary salt rations of ship diet; and even the water was sometimes so stored that it was out of reach of the weak. For many months, the average of deaths during these voyages was 74 in the thousand; the corpses were shot out into the waters; and who shall say that they were the most unfortunate? At Scutari, the landing-stage, constructed with all the perverseness of Oriental ingenuity, could only be approached with great difficulty, and, in rough weather, not at all. When it was reached, what remained of the men in the ships had first to be disembarked, and then conveyed up a steep slope of a quarter of a mile to the nearest of the hospitals. The most serious cases might be put upon stretchers—for there were far too few for all; the rest were carried or dragged up the hill by such convalescent soldiers as could be got together, who were not too obviously infirm for the work. At last the journey was accomplished; slowly, one by one, living or dying, the wounded were carried up into the hospital. And in the hospital what did they find?

Lasciate ogni speranza, voi ch'entrate: the delusive doors bore no such inscription; and yet behind them Hell yawned. Want, neglect, confusion, misery—in every shape and in every degree of intensity—filled the endless corridors and the vast apartments of the gigantic barrack-house, which, without forethought or preparation, had been hurriedly set aside as the chief shelter for the victims of the war. The very building itself was radically defective. Huge sewers underlay it, and cess-pools loaded with filth wafted their poison into the upper rooms. The floors were in so rotten a condition that many of them could not be scrubbed; the walls were thick with dirt; incredible multitudes of vermin swarmed everywhere. And, enormous as the building was, it was yet too small. It contained four miles of beds, crushed together so close that there was but just room to pass between them. Under such conditions, the most elaborate system of ventilation might well have been at fault, but here there was no ventilation. The stench was indescribable. "I have been well acquainted," said Miss Nightingale, "with the dwellings of the worst parts of most of the great cities in Europe, but have never been in any atmosphere which I could compare with that of the Barrack Hospital at night." The structural defects were equalled by the deficiencies in the commonest objects of hospital use. There were not enough bedsteads; the sheets were of canvas, and so coarse that the wounded men recoiled from them, begging to be left in their blankets; there was no bedroom furniture of any kind, and empty beer-bottles were used for candlesticks. There were no basins, no towels, no soap, no brooms, no mops, no trays, no plates; there were neither slippers nor scissors, neither shoe brushes nor blacking; there were no knives or forks or spoons. The supply of fuel was constantly deficient. The cooking arrangements were preposterously inadequate, and the laundry was a farce. As for purely medical materials, the tale was no better. Stretchers, splints, bandages—all were lacking; and so were the most ordinary drugs.

To replace such wants, to struggle against such difficulties, there was a handful of men overburdened by the strain of ceaseless work, bound down by the traditions of official routine, and enfeebled either by old age or inexperience or sheer incompetence. They had proved utterly unequal to their task. The principal doctor was lost in the imbecilities of a senile optimism. The wretched official whose business it was to provide for the wants of the hospital was tied fast hand and foot by red tape. A few of the younger doctors struggled valiantly, but what could they do? Unprepared, disorganised, with such help only as they could find among the miserable band of convalescent soldiers drafted off to tend their sick comrades, they were faced with disease, mutilation, and death in all their most appalling forms, crowded multitudinously about them in an ever increasing mass. They were like men in a shipwreck, fighting, not for safety, but for the next moment's bare existence—to gain, by yet another frenzied effort, some brief respite from the waters of destruction.

In these surroundings, those who had been long inured to scenes of human suffering—surgeons with a world-wide knowledge of agonies, soldiers familiar with fields of carnage, missionaries with remembrances of famine and of plague—yet found a depth of horror which they had never known before. There were moments, there were places, in the Barrack Hospital at Scutari, where the strongest hand was struck with trembling, and the boldest eye would turn away its gaze.

Miss Nightingale came, and she, at any rate, in that Inferno, did not abandon hope. For one thing, she brought material succour. Before she left London she had consulted Dr. Andrew Smith, the head of the Army Medical Board, as to whether it would be useful to take out stores of any kind to Scutari; and Dr. Andrew Smith had told her that "nothing was needed." Even Sidney Herbert had given her similar assurances; possibly, owing to an oversight, there might have been some delay in the delivery of the medical stores, which, he said, had been sent out from England "in profusion," but "four days would have remedied this." She preferred to trust her own instincts, and at Marseilles purchased a large quantity of miscellaneous provisions, which were of the utmost use at Scutari. She came, too, amply provided with money—in all, during her stay in the East, about £7000 reached her from private sources; and, in addition, she was able to avail herself of another valuable means of help. At the same time as herself, Mr. Macdonald, of the *Times*, had arrived at Scutari, charged with the duty of administering the large sums of money collected through the agency of that newspaper in aid of the sick and wounded; and Mr. Macdonald had the sense to see that the best use he could make of the *Times* Fund was to put it at the disposal of Miss Nightingale. "I cannot conceive," wrote an eye-witness, "as I now calmly look back on the first three weeks after the arrival of the wounded from Inkerman, how it could have been possible to have avoided a state of things too disastrous to contemplate, had not Miss Nightingale been there, with the means placed at her disposal by Mr. Macdonald." But the official view was different. What! Was the public service to admit, by accepting outside charity, that it was unable to discharge its own duties without the assistance of private and irregular benevolence? Never! And accordingly when Lord Stratford de Redcliffe, our ambassador at Constantinople, was asked by Mr. Macdonald to indicate how the *Times* Fund could best be employed, he answered that there was indeed one object to which it might very well be devoted—the building of an English Protestant Church at Pera.

Mr. Macdonald did not waste further time with Lord Stratford, and immediately joined forces with Miss Nightingale. But, with such a frame of mind in the highest quarters, it is easy to imagine the kind of disgust and alarm with which the sudden intrusion of a band of amateurs and females must have filled the minds of the ordinary officer and the ordinary military surgeon. They could not understand it; what had women to do with war? Honest Colonels relieved their spleen by the cracking of heavy jokes about "the Bird"; while poor Dr. Hall, a rough terrier of a man, who had worried his way to the top of his profession, was struck speechless with astonishment, and at last observed that Miss Nightingale's appointment was extremely droll.

Her position was, indeed, an official one, but it was hardly the easier for that. In the hospitals it was her duty to provide the services of herself and her nurses when they were asked for by the doctors, and not until then. At first some of the surgeons would have nothing to say to her, and, though she was welcomed by others, the majority were hostile and suspicious. But gradually she gained ground. Her good will could not be denied, and her capacity could not be disregarded. With consummate tact, with all the gentleness of supreme strength, she managed at last to impose her personality upon the susceptible, overwrought, discouraged, and helpless group of men in authority who surrounded her. She stood firm; she was a rock in the angry ocean; with her alone was safety, comfort, life. And so it was that hope dawned at Scutari. The reign of chaos and old night began to dwindle; order came upon the scene, and common sense, and forethought, and decision, radiating out from the little room off the great gallery in the Barrack Hospital where, day and night, the Lady

Superintendent was at her task. Progress might be slow, but it was sure. The first sign of a great change came with the appearance of some of those necessary objects with which the hospitals had been unprovided for months. The sick men began to enjoy the use of towels and soap, knives and forks, combs and tooth-brushes. Dr. Hall might snort when he heard of it, asking, with a growl, what a soldier wanted with a tooth-brush; but the good work went on. Eventually the whole business of purveying to the hospitals was, in effect, carried out by Miss Nightingale. She alone, it seemed, whatever the contingency, knew where to lay her hands on what was wanted; she alone could dispense her stores with readiness; above all she alone possessed the art of circumventing the pernicious influences of official etiquette. This was her greatest enemy, and sometimes even she was baffled by it. On one occasion 27,000 shirts, sent out at her instance by the Home Government, arrived, were landed, and were only waiting to be unpacked. But the official "Purveyor" intervened; "he could not unpack them," he said, "without a Board." Miss Nightingale pleaded in vain; the sick and wounded lay half-naked shivering for want of clothing; and three weeks elapsed before the Board released the shirts. A little later, however, on a similar occasion, Miss Nightingale felt that she could assert her own authority. She ordered a Government consignment to be forcibly opened, while the miserable "Purveyor" stood by, wringing his hands in departmental agony.

Vast quantities of valuable stores sent from England lay, she found, engulfed in the bottomless abyss of the Turkish Customs House. Other ship-loads, buried beneath munitions of war destined for Balaclava, passed Scutari without a sign, and thus hospital materials were sometimes carried to and fro three times over the Black Sea, before they reached their destination. The whole system was clearly at fault, and Miss Nightingale suggested to the home authorities that a Government Store House should be instituted at Scutari for the reception and distribution of the consignments. Six months after her arrival this was done.

In the meantime she had reorganised the kitchens and the laundries in the hospitals. The ill-cooked hunks of meat, vilely served at irregular intervals, which had hitherto been the only diet for the sick men were replaced by punctual meals, well-prepared and appetising, while strengthening extra foods—soups and wines and jellies ("preposterous luxuries," snarled Dr. Hall)—were distributed to those who needed them. One thing, however, she could not effect. The separation of the bones from the meat was no part of official cookery: the rule was that the food must be divided into equal portions, and if some of the portions were all bone—well, every man must take his chance. The rule, perhaps, was not a very good one; but there it was. "It would require a new Regulation of the Service," she was told, "to bone the meat." As for the washing arrangements, they were revolutionised. Up to the time of Miss Nightingale's arrival the number of shirts the authorities had succeeded in washing was seven. The hospital bedding, she found, was "washed" in cold water. She took a Turkish house, had boilers installed, and employed soldiers' wives to do the laundry work. The expenses were defrayed from her own funds and that of the *Times*; and henceforward the sick and wounded had the comfort of clean linen.

Then she turned her attention to their clothing. Owing to military exigencies the greater number of the men had abandoned their kit; their knapsacks were lost for ever; they possessed nothing but what was on their persons, and that was usually only fit for speedy destruction. The "Purveyor," of course, pointed out that, according to the regulations, all soldiers should bring with them into hospital an adequate supply of clothing, and he declared that it was no business of his to make good their deficiencies. Apparently, it was the business of Miss Nightingale. She procured socks, boots, and shirts in enormous quantities; she had trousers made, she rigged up dressing-gowns. "The fact is," she told Sidney Herbert, "I am now clothing the British Army."

All at once, word came from the Crimea that a great new contingent of sick and wounded might shortly be expected. Where were they to go? Every available inch in the wards was occupied; the affair was serious and pressing, and the authorities stood aghast. There were some dilapidated rooms in the Barrack Hospital, unfit for human habitation, but Miss Nightingale believed that if measures were promptly taken they might be made capable of accommodating several hundred beds. One of the doctors agreed with her; the rest of the officials were irresolute: it would be a very expensive job, they said it would involve building; and who could take the responsibility? The proper course was that a representation should be made to the Director-General of the Army Medical Department in London; then the Director-General would apply to the Horse Guards, the Horse Guards would move the Ordnance, the Ordnance would lay the matter before the Treasury, and, if the Treasury gave its consent, the work might be correctly carried through several months after the necessity for it had disappeared. Miss Nightingale, however, had made up her mind, and she persuaded Lord Stratford—or thought she had persuaded him—to give his sanction to the required expenditure. A hundred and twenty-five workmen were immediately engaged, and the work was begun. The workmen struck; whereupon Lord Stratford washed his hands of the whole business. Miss Nightingale engaged two hundred other workmen on her own authority, and paid the bill out of her own resources. The wards were ready by the required date; five hundred sick men were received in them; and all the utensils, including knives, spoons, cans and towels, were supplied by Miss Nightingale.

This remarkable woman was in truth performing the function of an administrative chief. How had this come about? Was she not in reality merely a nurse? Was it not her duty simply to tend to the sick? And indeed, was it not as a ministering angel, a gentle "lady with a lamp" that she actually impressed the minds of her contemporaries? No doubt that was so; and yet it is no less certain that, as she herself said, the specific business of nursing was "the least important of the functions into which she had been forced." It was clear that in the state of disorganisation into which the hospitals at Scutari had fallen the most pressing, the really vital, need was for something more than nursing; it was for the necessary elements of civilised life—the commonest material objects, the most ordinary cleanliness, the rudimentary habits of order and authority. "Oh, dear Miss Nightingale," said one of her party as they were approaching Constantinople, "when we land, let there be no delays, let us get straight to nursing the poor fellows!" "The strongest will be wanted at the wash-tub," was Miss Nightingale's answer. And it was upon the wash-tub, and all that the wash-tub stood for, that she expended her greatest energies. Yet to say that is perhaps to say too much. For to those who watched her at work among the sick, moving day and night from bed to bed, with that unflinching courage, with that indefatigable vigilance, it seemed as if the concentrated force of an undivided and unparalleled devotion could hardly suffice for that portion of her task alone. Wherever, in those vast wards, suffering was at its worst and the need for help was greatest, there, as if by magic, was Miss Nightingale. Her superhuman equanimity would, at the moment of some ghastly operation, nerve the victim to endure and almost to hope. Her sympathy would assuage the pangs of dying and bring back to those still living something of the forgotten charm of life. Over and over again her untiring efforts rescued those whom the surgeons had abandoned as beyond the possibility of cure. Her mere presence brought with it a strange influence. A passionate idolatry spread among the men: they kissed her shadow as it passed. They did more. "Before she came," said a soldier, "there was cussin' and swearin', but after that it was as 'oly as a church." The most cherished privilege of the fighting man was abandoned for the sake of Miss Nightingale. In those "lowest sinks of human misery," as she herself put it, she never heard the use of one expression "which could distress a gentlewoman."

She was heroic; and these were the humble tributes paid by those of grosser mould to that high quality. Certainly, she was heroic. Yet her heroism was not of that simple sort so dear to the readers of novels and the compilers of hagiologies—the romantic sentimental heroism with which mankind loves to invest its chosen darlings: it was made of sterner stuff. To the wounded soldier on his couch of agony she might well appear in the guise of a gracious angel of mercy, but the military surgeons, and the orderlies, and her own nurses, and the "Purveyor," and Dr. Hall, and even Lord Stratford himself could tell a different story. It was not by gentle sweetness and womanly self-abnegation that she had brought order out of chaos in the Scutari hospitals, that, from her own resources, she had clothed the British Army, that she had spread her dominion over the serried and reluctant powers of the official world; it was by strict method, by stern discipline, by rigid attention to detail, by ceaseless labour, by the fixed determination of an indomitable will. Beneath her cool and calm demeanour lurked fierce and passionate fires. As she passed through the wards in her plain dress, so quiet, so unassuming, she struck the casual observer simply as the pattern of a perfect lady; but the keener eye perceived something more than that—the serenity of high deliberation in the scope of the capacious brow, the sign of power in the dominating curve of the thin nose, and the traces of a harsh and dangerous temper—something peevish, something mocking, and yet something precise—in the small and delicate mouth. There was humour in the face; but the curious watcher might wonder whether it was humour of a very pleasant kind; might ask himself, even as he heard the laughter and marked the jokes with which she cheered the spirits of her patients, what sort of sardonic merriment this same lady might not give vent to, in the privacy of her chamber. As for her voice, it was true of it, even more than of her countenance, that it "had that in it one must fain call master." Those clear tones were in no need of emphasis: "I never heard her raise her voice," said one of her company. Only, when she had spoken, it seemed as if nothing could follow but obedience. Once, when she had given some direction, a doctor ventured to remark that the thing could not be done. "But it must be done," said Miss Nightingale. A chance bystander, who heard the words, never forgot through all his life the irresistible authority of them. And they were spoken quietly—very quietly indeed.

Late at night, when the long miles of beds lay wrapped in darkness, Miss Nightingale would sit at work in her little room, over her correspondence. It was one of the most formidable of all her duties. There were hundreds of letters to be written to the friends and relations of soldiers; there was the enormous mass of official documents to be dealt with; there were her own private letters to be answered; and, most important of all, there was the composition of her long and confidential reports to Sidney Herbert. These were by no means official communications. Her soul, pent up all day in the restraint and reserve of a vast responsibility, now at last poured itself out in these letters with all its natural vehemence, like a swollen torrent through an open sluice. Here, at least she did not mince matters. Here she painted in her darkest colours the hideous scenes which surrounded her; here she tore away remorselessly the last veils still shrouding the abominable truth. Then she would fill pages with recommendations and suggestions, with criticisms of the minutest details of organisation, with elaborate calculations of contingencies, with exhaustive analyses and statistical statements piled up in breathless eagerness one on the top of the other. And then her pen, in the virulence of its volubility, would rush on to the discussion of individuals, to the denunciation of an incompetent surgeon or the ridicule of a self-sufficient nurse. Her sarcasm searched the ranks of the officials with the deadly and unsparing precision of a machine-gun. Her nicknames were terrible. She respected no one: Lord Stratford, Lord Raglan, Lady Stratford, Dr. Andrew Smith, Dr. Hall, the Commissary-General, the Purveyor—she fulminated against them all. The intolerable futility of mankind obsessed her like a nightmare, and she gnashed her teeth against it. "I do well to be angry," was the burden of her cry. How many just men were there at Scutari? How many who cared at all for the sick, or had done anything for their relief? Were there ten? Were there five? Was there even one? She could not be sure.

At one time, during several weeks, her vituperations descended upon the head of Sidney Herbert himself. He had misinterpreted her wishes, he had traversed her positive instructions, and it was not until he had admitted his error and apologised in abject terms that he was allowed again into favour. While this misunderstanding was at its height an aristocratic young gentleman arrived at Scutari with a recommendation from the Minister. He had come out from England filled with a romantic desire to render homage to the angelic heroine of his dreams. He had, he said, cast aside his life of ease and luxury; he would devote his days and nights to the service of that gentle lady; he would perform the most menial offices, he would "fag" for her, he would be her footman—and feel requited by a single smile. A single smile, indeed, he had, but it was of an unexpected kind. Miss Nightingale at first refused to see him, and then, when she consented, believing that he was an emissary sent by Sidney Herbert to put her in the wrong over their dispute, she took notes of her conversation with him, and insisted on his signing them at the end of it. The young gentleman returned to England by the next ship.

This quarrel with Sidney Herbert was, however, an exceptional incident. Alike by him, and by Lord Panmure, his successor at the War Office, she was firmly supported; and the fact that during the whole of her stay at Scutari she had the Home Government at her back, was her trump card in her dealings with the hospital authorities. Nor was it only the Government that was behind her: public opinion in England early recognised the high importance of her mission, and its enthusiastic appreciation of her work soon reached an extraordinary height. The Queen herself was deeply moved. She made repeated inquiries as to the welfare of Miss Nightingale; she asked to see her accounts of the wounded, and made her the intermediary between the throne and the troops. "Let Mrs. Herbert know," she wrote to the War Minister, "that I wish Miss Nightingale and the ladies would tell these poor noble, wounded, and sick men that *no one* takes a warmer interest or feels more for their sufferings or admires their courage and heroism *more* than their Queen. Day and night she thinks of her beloved troops. So does the Prince. Beg Mrs. Herbert to communicate these my words to those ladies, as I know that *our* sympathy is much valued by these noble fellows." The letter was read aloud in the wards by the Chaplain. "It is a very feeling letter," said the men.

And so the months passed, and that fell winter which had begun with Inkerman and had dragged itself out through the long agony of the investment of Sebastopol, at last was over. In May, 1855, after six months of labour, Miss Nightingale could look with something like satisfaction at the condition of the Scutari hospitals. Had they done nothing more than survive the terrible strain which had been put upon them, it would have been a matter for congratulation; but they had done much more than that; they had marvellously improved. The confusion and the pressure in the wards had come to an end; order reigned in them, and cleanliness; the supplies were bountiful and prompt; important sanitary works had been carried out. One simple comparison of figures was enough to reveal the extraordinary change: the rate of mortality among the cases treated had fallen from 42 per cent to 22 per thousand. But still the indefatigable lady was not satisfied. The main problem had been solved—the physical needs of the men had been provided for; their mental and spiritual needs remained. She set up and furnished reading-rooms and recreation-rooms. She started classes and lectures. Officers were amazed to see her treating their men as if they were human beings, and assured her that she would only end by "spoiling the brutes." But that was not Miss Nightingale's opinion, and she was justified. The private soldier began to drink less, and even—though that seemed impossible—to save his pay. Miss Nightingale became a banker for the army, receiving and sending home large sums of money every month. At last, reluctantly, the Government followed suit, and established machinery of its own for the remission of money. Lord Panmure, however, remained sceptical; "it will do no good," he pronounced; "the British soldier is not a remitting animal." But, in fact, during the next six months, £71,000 was sent home.

Amid all these activities, Miss Nightingale took up the further task of inspecting the hospitals in the Crimea itself. The labour was extreme, and the conditions of life were almost intolerable. She spent whole days in the saddle, or was driven over those bleak and rocky heights in a baggage cart. Sometimes she stood for hours in the heavily falling snow, and would only reach her hut at dead of night after walking for miles through perilous ravines. Her powers of resistance seemed incredible, but at last they were exhausted. She was attacked by fever, and for a moment came very near death. Yet she worked on; if she could not move, she could at least write; and write she did until her mind had left her; and after it had left her, in what seemed the delirious trance of death itself, she still wrote. When, after many weeks, she was strong enough to travel, she was implored to return to England, but she utterly refused. She would not go back, she said, before the last of the soldiers had left Scutari.

This happy moment had almost arrived, when suddenly the smouldering hostilities of the medical authorities burst out into a flame. Dr. Hall's labours had been rewarded by a K.C.B.—letters which, as Miss Nightingale told Sidney Herbert, she could only suppose to mean "Knight of the Crimean Burial-grounds"—and the honour had turned his head. He was Sir John, and he would be thwarted no longer. Disputes had lately arisen between Miss Nightingale and some of the nurses in the Crimean hospitals. The situation had been embittered by rumours of religious dissensions, for, while the Crimean nurses were Roman Catholics, many of those at Scutari were suspected of a regrettable propensity towards the tenets of Dr. Pusey. Miss Nightingale was by no means disturbed by these sectarian differences, but any suggestion that her supreme authority over all the nurses with the Army was in doubt was enough to rouse her to fury; and it appeared that Mrs. Bridgeman, the Reverend Mother in the Crimea, had ventured to call that authority in question. Sir John Hall thought that his opportunity had come, and strongly supported Mrs. Bridgeman—or, as Miss Nightingale preferred to call her, the "Reverend Brickbat." There was a violent struggle; Miss Nightingale's rage was terrible. Dr. Hall, she declared, was doing his best to "root her out of the Crimea." She would bear it no longer; the War Office was playing her false; there was only one thing to be done—Sidney Herbert must move for the production of papers in the House of Commons, so that the public might be able to judge between her and her enemies. Sidney Herbert with great difficulty calmed her down. Orders were immediately despatched putting her supremacy beyond doubt, and the Reverend Brickbat withdrew from the scene. Sir John, however, was more tenacious. A few weeks later, Miss Nightingale and her nurses visited the Crimea for the last time, and the brilliant idea occurred to him that he could crush her by a very simple expedient—he would starve her into submission; and he actually ordered that no rations of any kind should be supplied to her. He had already tried this plan with great effect upon an unfortunate medical man whose presence in the Crimea he had considered an intrusion; but he was now to learn that such tricks were thrown away upon Miss Nightingale. With extraordinary foresight, she had brought with her a great supply of food; she succeeded in obtaining more at her own expense and by her own exertions; and thus for ten days, in that inhospitable country, she was able to feed herself and twenty-four nurses. Eventually the military authorities intervened in her favour, and Sir John had to confess that he was beaten.

It was not until July, 1856—four months after the Declaration of Peace—that Miss Nightingale left Scutari for England. Her reputation was now enormous, and the enthusiasm of the public was unbounded. The royal approbation was expressed by the gift of a brooch, accompanied by a private letter. "You are, I know, well aware," wrote Her Majesty, "of the high sense I entertain of the Christian devotion which you have displayed during this great and bloody war, and I need hardly repeat to you how warm my admiration is for your services, which are fully equal to those of my dear and brave soldiers, whose sufferings you have had the *privilege* of alleviating in so merciful a manner. I am, however, anxious of marking my feelings in a manner which I trust will be agreeable to you, and therefore send you with this letter a brooch, the form and emblems of which commemorate your great and blessed work, and which I hope you will wear as a mark of the high approbation of your Sovereign!"

"It will be a very great satisfaction to me," Her Majesty added, "to make the acquaintance of one who has set so bright an example to our sex."

The brooch, which was designed by the Prince Consort, bore a St. George's cross in red enamel, and the Royal cypher surmounted by diamonds. The whole was encircled by the inscription "Blessed are the Merciful."

Part II of "Florence Nightingale," in *Eminent Victorians*, 1918.

LÉON DAUDET

Portrait of Charcot

One thing everybody remarked about Professor Charcot was his eagle-eyed gaze. He himself asserted on more than one occasion: "all that I am is a photographer, I describe what I see." In the 1880s and 90s, his fame was so great that Freud— more of a neurologist than an alienist, as psychiatrists were then called—came on a visit to the Hôpital Salpêtrière in Paris to meet the great man. Charcot's assistants included some of the most famous names in neurology, Babinski and Sollier; his secretary was Gilles de la Tourette. Daudet's father Alphonse was a great friend of Charcot, and this somewhat diabolical portrait is based on intimate knowledge of the great man. Freud wrote in his obit that Charcot "had the nature of an artist— he was, as he himself said, a visuel, *a man who sees," although his own analytical methods offered a new suspicion of sight, and what it might conceal. Daudet's portrait corroborates the equally compelling one by Axel Munthe in his famous memoir* The Story of San Michele *(1929).*

Charcot, though his forehead was not quite high enough, had the ramrod face of a stout Napoleon. I imagine that this resemblance, which he carefully cultivated, influenced his habits and the entire course of his life. I never knew a man as authoritarian as he was, or who dominated those around him more completely. This was apparent at table, where he threw a suspicious glance around his assembled students or cut them off in mid-sentence with a harsh remark. He was thick-set and clean-shaven. His mouth formed a hard, thoughtful bow, his cheeks were pendulous, and his hair was brushed backwards. Bull-necked and compact, he walked on short, stout legs. When sitting, he would fiddle with his glasses, displaying a handsome but rather limp and cold hand. He spoke in an imperious voice, low-toned and a bit rough, and often his words were ironic and insistent. His eyes held a remarkable fire.

As an observer, Charcot was an outright genius. He could see at a glance the connection between the minds and the bodies of his patients, detecting diseases while they were still latent, ailments and conditions which their victims would not admit. He summed up his observations in succinct sentences that were comparable to the drawings of Ingres, or the sketches of a Forain or a Goya. When he wanted the ladies to leave the room, Charcot would simply say, "The clinic is now open," and launch into a story. "He was one of my most famous colleagues—a German— and he had taken a long trip to explain his case to me. Not a very amusing case, either. Sudden and very complete sexual inversion brought on by having gazed too long at a little bronze Renaissance faun that stood on his desk." Then Charcot added, with a broad smile, "You see, gentlemen, masterpieces frequently secrete a poison of their own," and then, after a pause, "Very commonly indeed."

His learning was immense. He knew the works of the great poets through and through, especially Aeschylus, Dante, and Shakespeare, and that of several philosophers, especially the Greeks, as well as European painting. He admired Beethoven but detested Wagner, whom he considered, not without reason, as being bombastic and windy. Without the slightest indulgence for humans, he was very tender towards animals, spoiling his dogs and pooches as though they were children, and forbidding anyone to talk in his presence of hunters and hunting. When he talked about science, it lost its abstract, bookish character, and became something vital and dramatic, something with an immediate impact. Entirely absorbed by its formal beauty and the working out of its fundamental laws, he looked down on therapeutic intervention; he considered the various disorders that afflict the human body in the same detached manner in which an astronomer might regard the movements of the planets. He partook of Montaigne's scepticism. Not only was he without belief himself, he was frequently hostile toward Catholicism, considering it to be entirely reactionary. For some reason I never knew—and nor did he perhaps—he had a mystic affinity towards Buddha.

He had no head for politics, though it didn't stop him being peremptory in his judgements. A fanatical supporter of Gambetta, a republican by education and class, he believed the Revolution had liberated the masses. He declared that he had only ever met one titled person with an ounce of intelligence, Dr de Sinety, author of a remarkable work on the liver in breast-feeding mothers. An artisan's son, he had acquired his culture only through great effort and although he was a brilliant clinician, he retained the mind of a schoolboy in his analysis of the laws governing civic bodies and the state. He would have been furious to have observed the gathering progress of the Action Française! I laugh when I think of it.

Charcot was unable to bear even the slightest contradiction. I remember him once saying to a well-known doctor who was generally disgustingly servile but in this instance failed to share his mind: "Monsieur, leave your napkin and get out!" The miscreant's family had to intervene to secure his pardon. Unfortunately, Charcot was always ready to listen to other people's say-so and gossip, which his jealous eavesdroppers purveyed to him, especially at the time of the competitive examinations. He became petty and even downright vicious in his harrying of anyone who, in his opinion, had treated him without due respect or dared to contest any of his theories about the nervous system, hysteria, aphasia or the liver and kidneys. Then he left no stone unturned to ruin his opponent's career, and evinced no satisfaction until his enemy was completely crushed or compelled to renounce his heresy. This attitude earned him the hatred of many young doctors, who hailed his death as a stroke of good fortune. What pleasure can it give a man who is famous, rich, keenly intelligent and blessed with perspicuity to play the petty tyrant?

A tireless worker, Charcot would spend the best part of the night studying some histological problem, or making a diagram or illustrative figure, such as his "bell" showing the various forms of aphasia. That figure cost him three months of sleep. He was never satisfied with what he produced. Even after five years, he would take up a case again and re-examine it, always trying to elucidate, to clarify, to get to the bottom of Nature. When Charcot lived at 217, boulevard Saint-Germain, there was a man who shoed horses just behind his beautiful garden, looking out on the rue Saint Simon. The blacksmith hammered incessantly. Like Alphonse

Daudet, who lived nearby at 31, rue de Bellechasse, Charcot pretended that the rhythmic noise of the hammer soothed him and helped him to work. He and my father used to joke about it, asking, "Which of us will be the first not to hear our blacksmith any more?" Charcot was certain he would outlive his patient. Nevertheless, he was the first to go, and the author of *L'Immortel* murmured, sadly, as he filled his little pipe, "That lucky devil of a Charcot—he, at least, is at rest!"

Although stupidity put Charcot on edge, his constant desire to be the ruler of all he surveyed caused him to surround himself with mediocrities. Social contact with writers and artists was thus a relief and stimulant for him. He has been accused of "playing to the gallery," but the expression is too mean-mouthed to do justice to his spirit. Like those who never humble themselves in prayer, his intellectual stance denied him the unsurpassed luxury of realising his feebleness and smallness in the face of life's great problems. He lacked the touch of moral perfection, the greatness of a Pascal. What a curiously obstructive being he was and how diabolical a glitter shone sometimes in his eyes that had seen so many terrible sights!

He was generous, even lavish, and entertained in style. He adored his son and daughter, who returned his affection; and he was extremely tolerant of the laughter, noise, songs and games with which we made his house reverberate. If it was an inferno for patients with nervous illnesses, it was a paradise for young people. When he lived on the Quai Malaquais, in the Hotel de Chimay, and even in his house on the boulevard Saint-Germain, we would dash in and out of the rooms and pay no attention to the glum and anxious patients sitting, in the company of their doctors or nurses, in armchairs and on sofas. In those days there was a vogue for pseudo-medieval furniture, stained-glass windows, embossed leather, vamped-up tapestries—anything that dated back to Louis XI, Louis XII or the Gothic era. Patients with hypochondria and ataxia writhed about on strangely shaped 13th-century prayer-stools; patients with muscle atrophy stretched their emaciated limbs on chairs decorated with gargoyles, griffins or armorial bearings. Imagine the effect we must have had, breaking like party-rousers into a museum of pathological curiosities! It must have been nightmarish for the German, Russian, American, Turkish, English, and Polish millionaires who had come to pay court to the great king of neurology for their prescriptions of nux vomica, bromides, or Lamalou water.

Charcot, before whom the entire scientific world prostrated itself, had a fierce humour and intentionally used expressions that were Rabelaisian. Speaking of a neurasthenic patient who had been describing the intricacies of his own case, he said: "I told him: 'you're like a man perched on a midden with a sword suspended over his head: either you dive in or you lose your head.'" Any comfort to be had was clearly trifling. Or he would quote between his teeth a Spanish or English proverb: "As flies to wanton boys, are we to the gods—they kill us for their sport." On other occasions, holding in his hand his little rubber tendon hammer for testing reflexes, he would hum a tune as he stood in front of his astonished patient. His unerring gaze hypothesised a likely disease the moment the patient entered the room. He even anticipated what they were going to tell him: "You feel this and that ... Yes, when you stand with your feet together you feel a sort of dizziness ... Yes, and you see things double, especially toward evening ... I don't ask you to interpret your symptoms. Just sit down and take off your shoes and trousers."

Oddly enough he was shy, and his abruptness with women, whom he claimed to despise, was due largely to this shyness. I noticed it on many occasions, and would have given a lot to know more about the sentimental and sensual aspects of his life, aspects which the wisest always keep most carefully hidden. But Charcot would have sent packing any such amateur student of psychology as I then was who should have so much as hinted at the subject. At times, he seemed haunted by some kind of immense dream, from which he emerged irascibly and discontentedly, disorientated like a traveller who has lost his way and ready to arraign people and things with his learning. He came out with fashionable put-downs: "They see too many beautiful women naked. It goes to their heads." It must be remembered that for thirty years he acted as a priest of the body, a confessor who believed in nothing but the immediate satisfactions of the acting self and the appeasement of the same. It was one of his beliefs that dreams were far more important in the conscious life than is generally admitted, even when they are already recognised to be considerable. What role did the subconscious play in his own life?

One evening, lingering later than usual in order to consult a medical volume on the balcony of the huge library which ran around his consulting room, I was surprised by his unexpected return. Curiosity held me there, squatting on my haunches and peering down through the balustrade at this sad figure of a man. Under the light cast by his lamp, he appeared careworn and stooped; he sat motionless and stared in front of him with an expression on his face I had never seen before. It was a look both passionate and hopeless, the look of a man who has made a pact with the devil and now has to pay the reckoning. He remained in that stance for an hour or so. Then he left the room to give an order to his secretary, who in those days must have been Gilles de la Tourette. I felt chilled to the core. "So that's what it's like to be famous? It doesn't look much fun."

His library was filled with works on magic and demonology, and was a complete archive of documents on mental disorders. It had a rather unwholesome reputation, although it probably contained few rare items. Charcot read English, German, Spanish, and Italian fluently; he could also read human beings, and was all ears whenever anyone brought him an exact bit of information on any subject. His methods were, in short, those of a true professional.

In summer he went with his family to his damp but pleasant little house at Neuilly Saint-James. There you could find him, on a Sunday, sitting in his little strip of garden, reading and annotating. "That Zola of yours is a swine, an utter swine," he would call out when he saw my father, holding in his hand a volume of the *Rougon-Macquart* series. He spoke highly of Balzac, had little to say about Flaubert, and always went straight for the psychological or physiological truth of a work of literature, especially in what the author saw and recorded unconsciously. He said to Daudet, in connection with *L'Arlésienne*, "I liked your putting a dim-witted child in the family of a man who kills himself over a love affair; that was a brilliant touch." Charcot had certainly gone deeper than anyone else has done into the enigma of heredity, and it is unfortunate he did not leave a general treatise on the subject: only he could have written it.

Excerpt from *Souvenirs des Milieux Littéraires, Politiques, Artistiques et Médicaux*, 1913–22.

ANTON CHEKHOV

Letter from Siberia

Chekhov is well known for his plays and stories, the best of which he wrote after his monumental journey to the penal colony of Sakhalin, near Japan, in 1890. He spent three months on the island, where he conducted a census and detailed the appalling conditions in which prisoners were housed. Nobody has ever determined precisely what drove the tubercular Chekhov to make the hazardous trip to the region of Russia traditionally reserved for convicts and troublemakers, ethnic groups, religious enthusiasts and the mad. Phenomenologically, Sakhalin was to separate the mature artist from the scribbler who had supported his family in Moscow with journalistic hack work. In this long letter addressed to his devoted sister Maria he gives a vivid and amusing account of his journey across Siberia, including a "driver asleep at reins" incident in which world literature almost lost one of its greatest practitioners.

May 14, 1890, Krasni Yar, near Tomsk

My wonderful Mama, excellent Masha, sweet Misha and everybody at home,

… I left Tyumen on 3 May after a stop of two or three days in Ekaterinburg, which I applied to the repair of my coughing and haemorrhoidal personage. Both post and private drivers make the trans-Siberian trip. I elected to use the latter, as it was all the same to me. They put your humble servant into a vehicle resembling a little wicker basket and off we drove with a pair of horses. You sit in the basket, and look out upon God's earth like a bird in a cage, without a thought on your mind.

It looks to me as if the Siberian plain commences right at Ekaterinburg and ends the devil knows where; I would say it is very like our South

Russian steppe, were it not for the small birch groves encountered here and there and the cold wind stinging one's cheeks. Spring hasn't yet arrived here. There is absolutely no greenery, the forests are bare, the snow has not all melted and lustreless ice sheathes the lakes. On 9 May, St. Nicholas Day, there was a frost, and today, 14 May, we had a snowfall of about three inches. Only the ducks hint of spring. How many of them there are! I have never in my life seen such a superabundance of ducks. They fly over your head, take wing over the carriage, swim the lakes and pools, in short, I could have shot a thousand of them in one day with a poor gun. You can hear the wild geese honking; they are also numerous here. Often files of cranes and swans head our way ... In the birch groves flutter grouse and woodcock. Rabbits, which are not eaten or shot here, sit up on their hind paws in a relaxed way and prick up their ears as they stare inquisitively at all comers. They run across the road so often that here it is not considered bad luck.

Travelling is a cold business. I am wearing my sheepskin jacket. I don't mind my body, that's all right, but my feet are always freezing. I wrap them in my leather coat but it doesn't help. I am wearing two pairs of trousers. Well, you go on and on. Road signs flash by, ponds, little birch groves ... Now we drive past a group of new settlers, then a file of prisoners ... We've met tramps with pots on their backs; these gentlemen promenade all over the Siberian plain without hindrance. On occasion they will murder a poor old woman to obtain her skirt for leg puttees; or they will tear off the tin numbers from the road signs, on the chance they may find them useful; another time they will bash in the head of a passing beggar or knock out the eyes of one of their own banished brotherhood, but they won't touch people in vehicles. On the whole, as far as robbery is concerned, travelling hereabouts is absolutely safe. From Tyumen to Tomsk neither the drivers of the post coaches nor the independent drivers can recall anything ever having been stolen from a traveller; when you get to a station, you leave your things outside; when you ask whether they won't be stolen you get a smile in reply. It is not good form to mention burglaries and murders on the road. I really believe that were I to lose my money at a station or in a vehicle the driver would return it to me without fail if he found it and wouldn't boast of his honesty. On the whole, the people here are good, kind, and have splendid traditions. Their rooms are furnished simply, but cleanly, with some pretension to luxury; the beds are soft, with feather mattresses and big pillows, the floors are painted or covered with handmade linen rugs. All this is due, of course, to their prosperity, to the fact that a family gets an allotment of about 50 acres of good black earth, and that good wheat grows on it (wheat flour here is 30 kopeks for 36 pounds). But not everything can be explained by comfortable circumstances and plenty to eat, some reference must be made to their way of life as well. When you enter a room full of sleeping people at night your nose isn't assailed, especially not by that notorious Russian smell. I must say, one old lady wiped a teaspoon on her hindside before handing it to me, but still you do not sit down to tea without a tablecloth, people do not belch in your presence and don't search for things in their heads; when they hand you water or milk, they don't put their fingers inside the glass, the dishes are clean, the kvas is as transparent as beer—in fact, they practise cleanliness of a sort our Little Russians can only dream about, and certainly Little Russians are far and away cleaner than Great Russians! They bake the most delicious bread; the first few days I made a pig of myself. Delicious also are the pies and pancakes, the fritters and dinner rolls which remind one of Little Russian spongy ring rolls. The pancakes are thin … On the other hand, the rest of their cuisine is not for the European stomach. For instance, I have been treated everywhere to "duck soup." This is absolutely awful, consisting of a muddy liquid in which float bits of wild duck and uncooked onion; the duck stomachs haven't been entirely cleaned of their contents and so, when you bite into them, cause you to think your mouth and rectum have changed places. One time I asked for soup cooked with meat and some fried perch. The soup was served oversalted, dirty, with weatherbeaten bits of skin instead of meat, and the perch arrived complete with scales. They cook cabbage soup here with corned beef; they also roast corned beef. I've just been served some of the latter; it's vile stuff and after chewing a little of it I pushed it aside. Brick tea is their beverage. This is an infusion of sage and cockroaches—both in taste and colour—not tea but something like our horrible Taganrog wine. I might mention that I brought a quarter of a pound of tea with me from Ekaterinburg, five pounds of sugar and three lemons. I've run out of tea and now there's no place to buy any. In the dumpy little towns even the officials drink brick tea and the very best shops don't sell any more expensive than 1 rouble 50 a pound. So I've just had to drink sage.

The distance between stations is determined by the distance between the villages, usually 14 to 28 miles. The villages here are large, and there are no hamlets or farms. Churches and schools are everywhere. You see wooden cabins, some of them of two storeys.

Towards evening the pools and roads begin freezing, and at night there is a regular frost; an extra fur coat would not be amiss. Brrr! The vehicle jolts because the mud has turned into hillocks. It is heartbreaking. By dawn you are terribly tired with the cold, the jolting and the jingle of the bells on your horses; you passionately crave warmth and a bed. While the horses are being changed, you curl up in some corner and immediately fall asleep, but a moment later your driver is already tugging at your sleeve and saying, "Get up, friend, time to leave!" On the second night I began feeling a sharp toothache in my heels. It was intolerably painful and I wondered whether they hadn't got frost-bitten.

Tomsk, May 16

The guilty party turned out to be my jack boots, too narrow in the back. Sweet Misha, if you ever have children, which I don't doubt will happen, advise them not to look for cheapness. A cheap price on Russian merchandise is a guarantee of its worthlessness. In my opinion going barefoot is preferable to wearing cheap boots ... I had to buy felt boots in Ishim ... So I have been travelling in felt boots until they decompose on me from dampness and mud.

Tea drinking in the cabins goes on at five or six in the morning. Tea on the road is a true boon ... It warms you up, dispels sleep and with it you eat a lot of bread; in the absence of other food, bread should be eaten in large amounts and that is why the peasant eats such a quantity of bread and starchy things. You drink tea and talk with the peasant women, who here are sensible, home-loving, tenderhearted, hard-working and more free than they are in Europe; their husbands do not curse or beat them because they are just as tall, and strong, and clever as their lords; when their husbands are not at home it is they who do the driving. They are great punsters. They do not raise their children strictly but are inclined to indulge them. The children sleep in comfortable beds for as long as they like, drink tea, ride with the peasants and use swear words when the latter tease them playfully. There is no diphtheria. Smallpox is widespread but curiously enough it is not as contagious here as it is elsewhere; two or three will come down with it and die—and that's the end of the epidemic. There are no hospitals or doctors. The doctoring is done by medical assistants. They go in for bloodletting and cupping on a grandiose, brutal scale. On the road I examined a Jew with cancer of the liver. The Jew was emaciated and hardly breathing, but this did not deter the medical assistant from putting twelve cupping glasses on him. By the way, on the subject of Jews. Here they work the land, drive, run ferryboats, trade and call themselves peasants [i.e. Christians], because they actually are de jure and de facto peasants. They enjoy universal respect and according to the police officer are not infrequently elected village elders. I saw a tall, thin Jew scowling in revulsion and spitting when the police officer told obscene stories; he had a clean mind and his wife cooked excellent fish soup. The wife of the Jew with the cancer treated me to some pike roe and the most delicious white bread. Exploitation by Jews is unheard of.

By the way, about the Poles. You run across exiles sent here from Poland in 1864. They are kind, hospitable and most considerate. Some enjoy real wealth, others are poverty-stricken and work as clerks at the stations. After the amnesty the former returned to their homeland, but soon came back to Siberia, where life is more opulent; the latter dream of their native land, although they are already old and ailing. In Ishim a certain Pan Zalesski, who is rich and whose daughter resembles Sasha Kiseleva, served me an excellent dinner for a rouble and gave me a room where I slept very well; he keeps a tavern, has become a kulak to the marrow of his bones, swindles everybody, but nevertheless the gentleman makes itself felt in his manners, in the table he sets, in everything. He won't go back home out of greed, out of greed he puts up with snow on St. Nicholas Day; when he dies his daughter, born in Ishim, will remain here forever, and so black eyes and delicate features will keep on multiplying in Siberia! These random mixtures of blood are all to the good, since Siberians are not handsome. There are absolutely no brunettes. Perhaps you'd like to hear about the Tatars as well? Here goes. They are not numerous here. Good people. In Kazan Province even the priests speak well of them, and in Siberia they are "better than the Russians"—so stated the police officer in the presence of Russians, whose silence gave assent. My God, how rich Russia is in good people! If it were not for the cold which deprives Siberia of summer, and were it not for the officials who corrupt the peasants and exiles, Siberia would be the very richest and happiest of territories.

Dinners are nothing in particular ... During the entire trip I have only had a real dinner twice, if you don't count the Yiddish fish soup which I ate after having filled up on tea. I haven't been drinking any vodka; the Siberian brand is vile, and besides I had got out of the habit of drinking before reaching Ekaterinburg. One should drink vodka, though. It acts as a stimulant on the brain, which, flabby and inert with the continual movement, makes one stupid and weak ...

The first three days of the voyage, what with the shaking and jolting, my collarbones, shoulders and vertebrae started aching. I couldn't sit, walk or lie down. On the other hand, though, all my chest and head aches disappeared, my appetite took an unbelievable spurt and the haemorrhoids—keep your fingers crossed—have given up the ghost. The strain, the continual worry over trunks and such, and perhaps the farewell drinking bouts in Moscow, gave rise to some blood-spitting in the mornings, and this infected me with a kind of despondency and stirred up gloomy thoughts; but it ceased toward the end of the trip and now I don't even have a cough; it is a long time since I have coughed as little as now, after two weeks spent in the fresh air. After the first three days of the trip my body accustomed itself to the jolts and the time arrived when I began not to notice the way midday arrived after morning, followed by evening and night. The days flitted by quickly, as in a lingering illness.

Now let me tell you of an adventure for which I am indebted to Siberian driving. Except that I ask Mama not to groan or lament, for everything came out all right. On 6 May, before dawn, I was being driven by a very nice old man with a team of horses. I was in a little buggy. I was drowsing and to make time pass was observing the tongues of flame darting about the fields and birch groves; people here burn the previous year's grass this way. Suddenly I heard the broken thud of wheels. Coming toward us at full tilt, like a bird, dashed a three-horse carriage. My old man quickly turned to the right, the post carriage sailed past and then I discerned in the shadows an enormous, heavy three-horse post wagon with a driver making the return trip. Behind this wagon I could see another tearing along, also at full speed. We hurried to turn right ... To my great bewilderment and alarm the cart turned to the left, not the right. I scarcely had time to think to myself, "My God, we'll collide!" when there was a desperate crash, the horses mingled into one dark mass, the yokes fell, my buggy stood on end, I lay on the ground and my baggage on top of me. But that wasn't all ... A third cart dashed upon us ... Verily, this should have crushed me and my suitcases, but thank God, I was not sleeping, didn't fracture any bones and managed to jump up quickly enough to run to one side. "Stop!" I yelled at the third cart, "Stop!" It hurled itself upon the second one and came to a halt. Of course, if I had been able to sleep in my buggy, or if the third wagon had flung itself immediately upon the second, I would have returned home a cripple or a headless horseman. Results of the collision: broken shafts, torn harness, yokes and baggage on the ground, scared, exhausted horses and terror at the thought of having experienced a moment of peril. It seemed that the first driver had urged on his horses, while the drivers of the other two wagons were asleep; nobody was steering. After recovering from the tumult my old fellow and the drivers of all three vehicles began swearing furiously at one another. How they cursed! I thought it would wind up in a free-for-all. You cannot conceive how alone you feel in the midst of this wild, cursing horde, in the open country, at dawn, in sight of flames lapping up the grass in the distance and close at hand, but not throwing off a bit of heat into the frigid night air! How grief-stricken was

my soul! You listen to the swearing, look down at the broken shafts and
your own torn baggage and you seem to be thrust into another world,
about to be trampled down. After an hour long of cursing, my old man
began tying up the shafts and harness with cord; my straps were pressed
into service too. We dragged ourselves to the station somehow, with
plenty of stops in between, and barely made it.

After the fifth or sixth day the rains began, accompanied by a stiff
wind. It poured day and night. Out came the leather coat to save me from
the rain and wind. It is a marvellous coat. The mud became practically
impassable and the drivers were unwilling to drive by night. But the most
terrible business of all, which I won't ever forget, were the river crossings.
You reach a river at night. You and the driver both start shouting ... Rain,
wind, sheets of ice creep along the river, you hear a splash. To enliven
things appropriately, we hear a bittern screeching. These birds live on
Siberian rivers. That means they don't recognize climate, but geographical
position. Well, sir, in an hour a massive ferryboat in the form of a barge
looms in the shadows; it has immense oars resembling the pincers of a
crab. The ferrymen are a mischievous lot, for the most part exiles, deported
here by society to atone for their sins. They use foul language to an
intolerable degree, shout, demand money for vodka ... It is a long, long
trip across the river ... one long agony! ...

On 7 May, when I asked the driver for horses, he told me the Irtish
had overflown its banks and flooded the meadows, that yesterday Kuzma
had gone that way and had scarcely managed to return, and that it was
impossible to go on, that we would have to wait. I asked until when.
Reply: "The Lord only knows!" Here was an indefinite answer for me,
and besides, I had promised myself to get rid of two vices en route which
had caused me considerable expense, trouble and inconvenience: a
readiness to comply and let myself be talked into things. I would quickly
come to terms with a driver and find myself riding on the devil knows
what, sometimes paying twice the usual price, and waiting for hours on
end. I decided not to give in and not to believe what was told me and
I've had less aches and pains. For instance, they would get out a plain,
jolting wagon instead of a carriage. I'd refuse to ride in it, lay down the

law, and a carriage would inevitably appear, although previously I had been assured there wasn't a single one in the whole village, etc.

Well, sir, suspecting that the flood on the Irtish had been dreamed up expressly to avoid driving through the mud at night, I protested and gave orders to go on ... Off we went. Mud, rain, a furious wind, cold ... and felt boots on. Do you know what wet felt boots are like? They are footwear made of gelatin. We kept on and suddenly before my vision spread an immense lake, with mounds of earth and bushes jutting out in clumps— these were the inundated meadows. In the distance ranged the Irtish's steep bank and on it the patches of snow lay white. We started negotiating the lake. We should have turned back, but my obstinacy stood in the way, I was in a sort of defiant fervour, that same fervour that compelled me to bathe in the midst of the Black Sea from the yacht, and which has led me to perform all sorts of foolish acts. It's probably a psychotic condition. On we went, picking out little islets and strips of land. Big and little bridges are supposed to show the way, but they had been washed out. To get past them the horses had to be unharnessed and led one at a time. The driver did so, and I jumped into the water—in my felt boots—to hold the horses ... What sport! And with it the rain, the wind. Save us, Heavenly Mother! Finally we made our way to an islet with a roofless cabin. Wet horses were wandering about in wet manure. A mujik with a long stick came out of the cabin and volunteered to show us the way. He measured the depth of the water with his stick and tested the ground. God bless him, he steered us to a long strip of ground which he called a "ridge." He showed us how to get our bearings from this ridge and take the road to the right, or maybe the left, I don't remember exactly, and land on another ridge. This we did.

On we went ... Finally—O Joy—we reached the Irtish. The other bank was steep, on our side it sloped ... The Irtish does not murmur, or roar, but resigns itself to its fate, which, as it were, is to hammer as though coffins were reposing on its bottom. Cursed impression! The other bank was high, mat brown, desolate.

We came to the cabin where the ferrymen lived. One of them came out to announce it was impossible to allow a ferry across, as a storm was brewing. The river, they told us, was wide and the wind strong. What to do? We had to spend the night in the cabin. I recall that night, the snoring of the ferrymen, and of my driver, the howl of the wind, the patter of the rain, the growling of the Irtish.

In the morning they were reluctant to ferry us across because of the wind. So we had to row our way over. There I was sailing across the river, with the rain beating down, the wind blowing, the baggage getting drenched, the felt boots, which had been dried overnight in the stove, again turning into jelly …

… Seated on my suitcase I spent a full hour waiting for horses to be sent from the village. As I recall, climbing the bank was very slippery business. In the village I warmed up and had some tea. Some exiles approached me for alms. Every family makes about forty pounds of wheat flour into bread for them every day, as a sort of compulsory service.

The exiles sell the bread for liquor in the taverns. One such, a ragged, shaven old fellow, whose eyes his fellow prisoners had knocked out in the tavern, upon hearing there was a traveller in the room, and taking me for a merchant, began chanting and saying prayers. Prayers for health, requiescats, the Easter "God Has Risen," and "Peace With the Saints"—what didn't he sing! Then he began lying that he came of a Moscow merchant family. I noticed that this sot held in contempt the mujiks on whose necks he hung!

On 11 May I travelled on post horses. To pass the time I read the complaint book at the stations. I made a discovery that astounded me and which in the rain and dampness constitutes a pearl beyond price: and that is that there are toilets in the entrance halls of the post stations. You cannot put too high a value on them!

…. In Tomsk the mud is impassable. Of the city and way of life here I will write in a few days, but so long for now. I have worn myself out writing …

… I embrace you all, kiss and bless you.

Your

A. Chekhov

Misha's letter has arrived. Thanks.

Excuse the letter's resembling a hotchpotch. It rambles, but what can I do? One can't do better sitting in a hotel room. Excuse its length, but I am not to blame. My pen has run away with me, and besides, I wanted to be talking to you for as long as I could. It's three in the morning, and my hand has wearied. The wick has burned down on the candle and I can scarcely make things out. Write me at Sakhalin every four or five days. It seems the mails reach there not only by the sea route, but also across Siberia, which means I will be receiving them in good time and often …

"Letter of 1890," *Correspondence*; translated from the Russian
by Sidonie Lederer.

WILLIAM OSLER

Nationalism in Medicine

Adam Smith expected the world to go straight from feudalism to universalism; but it didn't happen. Nations happened instead, and nationalism told a more meaningful story to people than religion or class. Even medicine, which was rapidly universalizing itself by 1900, was nationally inflected, as a by-product of the rise of state-administered educational systems: the limits of a culture (and language) are also the limits of a world in which an educated person can meaningfully live. As the Canadian physician Osler, genial pontifex of medical education, might have known: the modern social order leans not on the guillotine but on the shoulders of professors.

Nationalism has been the great curse of humanity. In no other shape has the Demon of Ignorance assumed more hideous proportions; to no other obsession do we yield ourselves more readily. For whom do the hosannas ring higher than for the successful butcher of tens of thousands of poor fellows who have been made to pass through the fire to this Moloch of nationalism? A vice of the blood, of the plasm rather, it runs riot in the race, and rages today as of yore in spite of the precepts of religion and the practice of democracy. Nor is there any hope of change; the pulpit is dumb, the press fans the flames, literature panders to it and the people love to have it so. Not that all aspects of nationalism are bad. Breathes there a man with soul so dead that it does not glow at the thought of what the men of his blood have done and suffered to make his country what it is? There is room, plenty of room, for proper pride of land and birth. What I inveigh against is a cursed spirit of intolerance, conceived in distrust and bred in ignorance, that makes the mental attitude perennially antagonistic, even bitterly antagonistic to everything foreign, that subordinates everywhere the race to the nation, forgetting the higher claims of human brotherhood.

While medicine is everywhere tinctured with national characteristics, the wider aspects of the profession, to which I have alluded—our common lineage and the community of interests—should always save us from the more vicious aspects of this sin, if it cannot prevent it altogether. And yet I cannot say, as I wish I could, that we are wholly free from this form of Chauvinism. Can we say, as English, French, German or American physicians, that our culture is always cosmopolitan, not national, that our attitude of mind is always as frankly open and friendly to the French as to the English, to the American as to the German, and that we are free at all times and in all places from prejudice, at all times free from a self-satisfied feeling of superiority the one over the other? There has been of late years a closer union of the profession of the different countries through the International Congress and through the international meetings of the special societies; but this is not enough, and the hostile attitude has by no means disappeared. Ignorance is at the root. When a man talks slightingly of the position and work of his profession in any country, or when a teacher tells you that he fails to find inspiration in the work of his foreign colleagues, in the words of the Arabian proverb—he is a fool, shun him! Full knowledge, which alone disperses the mists of ignorance, can only be obtained by travel or by a thorough acquaintance with the literature of the different countries. Personal, first-hand intercourse with men of different lands, when the mind is young and plastic, is the best vaccination against the disease. The man who has sat at the feet of Virchow, or has listened to Traube, or Helmholtz, or Cohnheim, can never look with unfriendly eyes at German medicine or German methods. Who ever met with an English or American pupil of Louis or of Charcot, who did not love French medicine, if not for its own sake, at least for the reverence he bore his great master? Let our young men, particularly those who aspire to teaching positions, go abroad. They can find at home laboratories and hospitals as well equipped as any in the world, but they may find abroad more than they knew they sought—widened sympathies, heightened ideals and something perhaps of a *Weltkultur* which will remain through life as the best protection against the vice of nationalism.

Next to a personal knowledge of men, a knowledge of the literature of the profession of different countries will do much to counteract intolerance and Chauvinism. The great works in the department of medicine in which a man is interested, are not so many that he cannot know their contents, though they be in three or four languages. Think of the impetus French medicine gave to the profession in the first half of the last century, of the debt we all owe to German science in the latter half, and of the lesson of the practical application by the English of sanitation and asepsis! It is one of our chief glories and one of the unique features of the profession that, no matter where the work is done in the world, if of any value, it is quickly utilized! Nothing has contributed more to the denationalization of the profession of this continent than, on the one hand, the ready reception of the good men from the old countries who have cast in their lot with us, and, on the other, the influence of our young men who have returned from Europe with sympathies as wide as the profession itself. There is abroad among us a proper spirit of eclecticism, a willingness to take the good wherever found, that augurs well for the future. It helps a man immensely to be a bit of a hero-worshipper, and the stories of the lives of the masters of medicine do much to stimulate our ambition and rouse our sympathies. If the life and work of such men as Bichat and Laënnec will not stir the blood of a young man and make him feel proud of France and of Frenchmen, he must be a dull and muddy mettled rascal. In reading the life of Hunter, of Jenner, who thinks of the nationality which is merged and lost in our interest in the man and in his work? In the halcyon days of the Renaissance there was no nationalism in medicine, but a fine catholic spirit made great leaders like Vesalius, Eustachius, Stensen and others at home in every country in Europe. While this is impossible to-day, a great teacher of any country may have a world-wide audience in our journal literature, which has done so much to make medicine cosmopolitan.

Excerpt from "Nationalism in Medicine," *Aequanimitas*, 1904.

ARTHUR CONAN DOYLE

The Curse of Eve

No attempt at a social history of medicine as told through literature would be complete without an entry from Arthur Conan Doyle, whose famous detective, Sherlock Holmes, was based on a careful character study of one of the author's demonstrators at Edinburgh, Joseph Bell. Holmes, though not a physician like his amanuensis Watson, or even properly a scientist, is a kind of semiotician, reading the legible traces of crime in the physical world. Conan Doyle, who also practised medicine, wrote a number of other stories about medical life, often with an anthropological twist to them: some of his doctors do not fit the "mould," either because they are coloured or—a novelty in the high Victorian era—female. It will be noted, however, in this psychologically darker story in which the birth of a child is allowed to seem ominous, that Robert Johnson's "quiet little woman" doesn't make any noise at all.

Robert Johnson was an essentially commonplace man, with no feature to distinguish him from a million others. He was pale of face, ordinary in looks, neutral in opinions, thirty years of age, and a married man. By trade he was a gentleman's outfitter in the New North Road, and the competition of business squeezed out of him the little character that was left. In his hope of conciliating customers he had become cringing and pliable, until working ever in the same routine from day to day he seemed to have sunk into a soulless machine rather than a man. No great question had ever stirred him. At the end of this snug century, self-contained in his own narrow circle, it seemed impossible that any of the mighty, primitive passions of mankind could ever reach him. Yet birth, and lust, and illness, and death are changeless things, and when one of these harsh facts springs out upon a man at some sudden turn of the path of life, it dashes off for the moment his mask of civilisation and gives a glimpse of the stranger and stronger face below.

Johnson's wife was a quiet little woman, with brown hair and gentle ways. His affection for her was the one positive trait in his character. Together they would lay out the shop window every Monday morning, the spotless shirts in their green cardboard boxes below, the neckties above hung in rows over the brass rails, the cheap studs glistening from the white cards at either side, while in the background were the rows of cloth caps and the bank of boxes in which the more valuable hats were screened from the sunlight. She kept the books and sent out the bills. No one but she knew the joys and sorrows which crept into his small life. She had shared his exultations when the gentleman who was going to India had bought ten dozen shirts and an incredible number of collars, and she had been as stricken as he when, after the goods had gone, the bill was returned from the hotel address with the intimation that no such person had lodged there. For five years they had worked, building up the business, thrown together all the more closely because their marriage had been a childless one. Now, however, there were signs that a change was at hand, and that speedily. She was unable to come downstairs, and her mother, Mrs. Peyton, came over from Camberwell to nurse her and to welcome her grandchild.

Little qualms of anxiety came over Johnson as his wife's time approached. However, after all, it was a natural process. Other men's wives went through it unharmed, and why should not his? He was himself one of a family of fourteen, and yet his mother was alive and hearty. It was quite the exception for anything to go wrong. And yet in spite of his reasonings the remembrance of his wife's condition was always like a sombre background to all his other thoughts.

Dr. Miles of Bridport Place, the best man in the neighbourhood, was retained five months in advance, and, as time stole on, many little packets of absurdly small white garments with frill work and ribbons began to arrive among the big consignments of male necessities. And then one evening, as Johnson was ticketing the scarfs in the shop, he heard a bustle upstairs, and Mrs. Peyton came running down to say that Lucy was bad and that she thought the doctor ought to be there without delay.

It was not Robert Johnson's nature to hurry. He was prim and staid and liked to do things in an orderly fashion. It was a quarter of a mile from the corner of the New North Road where his shop stood to the doctor's house in Bridport Place. There were no cabs in sight so he set off upon foot, leaving the lad to mind the shop. At Bridport Place he was told that the doctor had just gone to Harman Street to attend a man in a fit. Johnson started off for Harman Street, losing a little of his primness as he became more anxious. Two full cabs but no empty ones passed him on the way. At Harman Street he learned that the doctor had gone on to a case of measles, fortunately he had left the address—69 Dunstan Road, at the other side of the Regent's Canal. Robert's primness had vanished now as he thought of the women waiting at home, and he began to run as hard as he could down the Kingsland Road. Some way along he sprang into a cab which stood by the curb and drove to Dunstan Road. The doctor had just left, and Robert Johnson felt inclined to sit down upon the steps in despair.

Fortunately he had not sent the cab away, and he was soon back at Bridport Place. Dr. Miles had not returned yet, but they were expecting him every instant. Johnson waited, drumming his fingers on his knees, in a high, dim lit room, the air of which was charged with a faint, sickly smell of ether. The furniture was massive, and the books in the shelves were sombre, and a squat black clock ticked mournfully on the mantel-piece. It told him that it was half-past seven, and that he had been gone an hour and a quarter. Whatever would the women think of him! Every time that a distant door slammed he sprang from his chair in a quiver of eagerness. His ears strained to catch the deep notes of the doctor's voice. And then, suddenly, with a gush of joy he heard a quick step outside, and the sharp click of the key in the lock. In an instant he was out in the hall, before the doctor's foot was over the threshold.

"If you please, doctor, I've come for you," he cried; "the wife was taken bad at six o'clock."

He hardly knew what he expected the doctor to do. Something very energetic, certainly—to seize some drugs, perhaps, and rush excitedly with him through the gaslit streets. Instead of that Dr. Miles threw his umbrella into the rack, jerked off his hat with a somewhat peevish gesture, and pushed Johnson back into the room.

"Let's see! You *did* engage me, didn't you?" he asked in no very cordial voice.

"Oh, yes, doctor, last November. Johnson the outfitter, you know, in the New North Road."

"Yes, yes. It's a bit overdue," said the doctor, glancing at a list of names in a note-book with a very shiny cover. "Well, how is she?"

"I don't—"

"Ah, of course, it's your first. You'll know more about it next time."

"Mrs. Peyton said it was time you were there, sir."

"My dear sir, there can be no very pressing hurry in a first case. We shall have an all-night affair, I fancy. You can't get an engine to go without coals, Mr. Johnson, and I have had nothing but a light lunch."

"We could have something cooked for you—something hot and a cup of tea."

"Thank you, but I fancy my dinner is actually on the table. I can do no good in the earlier stages. Go home and say that I am coming, and I will be round immediately afterwards."

A sort of horror filled Robert Johnson as he gazed at this man who could think about his dinner at such a moment. He had not imagination enough to realise that the experience which seemed so appallingly important to him, was the merest everyday matter of business to the medical man who could not have lived for a year had he not, amid the rush of work, remembered what was due to his own health. To Johnson he seemed little better than a monster. His thoughts were bitter as he sped back to his shop.

"You've taken your time," said his mother-in-law reproachfully, looking down the stairs as he entered.

"I couldn't help it!" he gasped. "Is it over?"

"Over! She's got to be worse, poor dear, before she can be better. Where's Dr. Miles!"

"He's coming after he's had dinner." The old woman was about to make some reply, when, from the half-opened door behind a high whinnying voice cried out for her. She ran back and closed the door, while Johnson, sick at heart, turned into the shop. There he sent the lad home and busied himself frantically in putting up shutters and turning out boxes. When all was closed and finished he seated himself in the parlour behind the shop. But he could not sit still. He rose incessantly to walk a few paces and then fell back into a chair once more. Suddenly the clatter of china fell upon his ear, and he saw the maid pass the door with a cup on a tray and a smoking teapot.

"Who is that for, Jane?" he asked.

"For the mistress, Mr. Johnson. She says she would fancy it."

There was immeasurable consolation to him in that homely cup of tea. It wasn't so very bad after all if his wife could think of such things. So light-hearted was he that he asked for a cup also. He had just finished it when the doctor arrived, with a small black leather bag in his hand.

"Well, how is she?" he asked genially.

"Oh, she's very much better," said Johnson, with enthusiasm.

"Dear me, that's bad!" said the doctor. "Perhaps it will do if I look in on my morning round?"

"No, no," cried Johnson, clutching at his thick frieze overcoat. "We are so glad that you have come. And, doctor, please come down soon and let me know what you think about it."

The doctor passed upstairs, his firm, heavy steps resounding through the house. Johnson could hear his boots creaking as he walked about the floor above him, and the sound was a consolation to him. It was crisp and decided, the tread of a man who had plenty of self-confidence. Presently, still straining his ears to catch what was going on, he heard the scraping of a chair as it was drawn along the floor, and a moment later he heard the door fly open and someone come rushing downstairs. Johnson sprang up with his hair bristling, thinking that some dreadful thing had occurred, but it was only his mother-in-law, incoherent with excitement and searching for scissors and some tape. She vanished again and Jane passed up the stairs with a pile of newly aired linen. Then, after an interval of silence, Johnson heard the heavy, creaking tread and the doctor came down into the parlour.

"That's better," said he, pausing with his hand upon the door. "You look pale, Mr. Johnson."

"Oh no, sir, not at all," he answered deprecatingly, mopping his brow with his handkerchief.

"There is no immediate cause for alarm," said Dr. Miles. "The case is not all that we could wish it. Still we will hope for the best."

"Is there danger, sir?" gasped Johnson.

"Well, there is always danger, of course. It is not altogether a favourable case, but still it might be much worse. I have given her a draught. I saw as I passed that they have been doing up a little building opposite to you. It's an improving quarter. The rents go higher and higher. You have a lease of your own little place, eh?"

"Yes, sir, yes!" cried Johnson, whose ears were straining for every sound from above, and who felt none the less that it was very soothing that the doctor should be able to chat so easily at such a time. "That's to say no, sir, I am a yearly tenant."

"Ah, I should get a lease if I were you. There's Marshall, the watchmaker, down the street. I attended his wife twice and saw him through the typhoid when they took up the drains in Prince Street. I assure you his landlord sprung his rent nearly forty a year and he had to pay or clear out."

"Did his wife get through it, doctor?"

"Oh yes, she did very well. Hullo! hullo!"

He slanted his ear to the ceiling with a questioning face, and then darted swiftly from the room.

It was March and the evenings were chill, so Jane had lit the fire, but the wind drove the smoke downwards and the air was full of its acrid taint. Johnson felt chilled to the bone, though rather by his apprehensions than by the weather. He crouched over the fire with his thin white hands held out to the blaze. At ten o'clock Jane brought in the joint of cold meat and laid his place for supper, but he could not bring himself to touch it. He drank a glass of the beer, however, and felt the better for it. The tension of his nerves seemed to have reacted upon his hearing, and he was able to follow the most trivial things in the room above. Once, when the beer was still heartening him, he nerved himself to creep on tiptoe up the stair and to listen to what was going on. The bedroom door was half an inch open, and through the slit he could catch a glimpse of the clean-shaven face of the doctor, looking wearier and more anxious than before. Then he rushed downstairs like a lunatic, and running to the door he tried to distract his thoughts by watching what was going on in the street. The shops were all shut, and some rollicking boon companions came shouting along from the public-house. He stayed at the door until the stragglers had thinned down, and then came back to his seat by the fire. In his dim brain he was asking himself questions which had never intruded themselves before. Where was the justice of it? What had his sweet, innocent little wife done that she should be used so? Why was nature so cruel? He was frightened at his own thoughts, and yet wondered that they had never occurred to him before.

As the early morning drew in, Johnson, sick at heart and shivering in every limb, sat with his great coat huddled round him, staring at the grey ashes and waiting hopelessly for some relief. His face was white and clammy, and his nerves had been numbed into a half conscious state by the long monotony of misery. But suddenly all his feelings leapt into keen life again as he heard the bedroom door open and the doctor's steps upon the stair. Robert Johnson was precise and unemotional in everyday life, but he almost shrieked now as he rushed forward to know if it were over.

One glance at the stern, drawn face which met him showed that it was no pleasant news which had sent the doctor downstairs. His appearance had altered as much as Johnson's during the last few hours. His hair was on end, his face flushed, his forehead dotted with beads of perspiration. There was a peculiar fierceness in his eye, and about the lines of his mouth, a fighting look as befitted a man who for hours on end had been striving with the hungriest of foes for the most precious of prizes. But there was a sadness too, as though his grim opponent had been over-mastering him. He sat down and leaned his head upon his hand like a man who is fagged out.

"I thought it my duty to see you, Mr. Johnson, and to tell you that it is a very nasty case. Your wife's heart is not strong, and she has some symptoms which I do not like. What I wanted to say is that if you would like to have a second opinion I shall be very glad to meet anyone whom you might suggest."

Johnson was so dazed by his want of sleep and the evil news that he could hardly grasp the doctor's meaning. The other, seeing him hesitate, thought that he was considering the expense.

"Smith or Hawley would come for two guineas," said he. "But I think Pritchard of the City Road is the best man."

"Oh, yes, bring the best man," cried Johnson.

"Pritchard would want three guineas. He is a senior man, you see."

"I'd give him all I have if he would pull her through. Shall I run for him?"

"Yes. Go to my house first and ask for the green baize bag. The assistant will give it to you. Tell him I want the A. C. E. mixture. Her heart is too weak for chloroform. Then go for Pritchard and bring him back with you."

It was heavenly for Johnson to have something to do and to feel that he was of some use to his wife. He ran swiftly to Bridport Place, his footfalls clattering through the silent streets and the big dark policemen turning their yellow funnels of light on him as he passed. Two tugs at the night-bell brought down a sleepy, half-clad assistant, who handed him a stoppered glass bottle and a cloth bag which contained something which clinked when you moved it. Johnson thrust the bottle into his pocket, seized the green bag, and pressing his hat firmly down ran as hard as he could set foot to ground until he was in the City Road and saw the name of Pritchard engraved in white upon a red ground. He bounded in triumph up the three steps which led to the door, and as he did so there was a crash behind him. His precious bottle was in fragments upon the pavement.

For a moment he felt as if it were his wife's body that was lying there. But the run had freshened his wits and he saw that the mischief might be repaired. He pulled vigorously at the night-bell.

"Well, what's the matter?" asked a gruff voice at his elbow. He started back and looked up at the windows, but there was no sign of life. He was approaching the bell again with the intention of pulling it, when a perfect roar burst from the wall.

"I can't stand shivering here all night," cried the voice. "Say who you are and what you want or I shut the tube."

Then for the first time Johnson saw that the end of a speaking-tube hung out of the wall just above the bell. He shouted up it,—

"I want you to come with me to meet Dr. Miles at a confinement at once."

"How far?" shrieked the irascible voice.

"The New North Road, Hoxton."

"My consultation fee is three guineas, payable at the time."

"All right," shouted Johnson. "You are to bring a bottle of A. C. E. mixture with you."

"All right! Wait a bit!"

Five minutes later an elderly, hard-faced man, with grizzled hair, flung open the door. As he emerged a voice from somewhere in the shadows cried,—

"Mind you take your cravat, John," and he impatiently growled something over his shoulder in reply.

The consultant was a man who had been hardened by a life of ceaseless labour, and who had been driven, as so many others have been, by the needs of his own increasing family to set the commercial before the philanthropic side of his profession. Yet beneath his rough crust he was a man with a kindly heart.

"We don't want to break a record," said he, pulling up and panting after attempting to keep up with Johnson for five minutes. "I would go quicker if I could, my dear sir, and I quite sympathise with your anxiety, but really I can't manage it."

So Johnson, on fire with impatience, had to slow down until they reached the New North Road, when he ran ahead and had the door open for the doctor when he came. He heard the two meet outside the bedroom, and caught scraps of their conversation. "Sorry to knock you up—nasty case—decent people." Then it sank into a mumble and the door closed behind them.

Johnson sat up in his chair now, listening keenly, for he knew that a crisis must be at hand. He heard the two doctors moving about, and was able to distinguish the step of Pritchard, which had a drag in it, from the clean, crisp sound of the other's footfall. There was silence for a few minutes and then a curious drunken, mumbling sing-song voice came quavering up, very unlike anything which be had heard hitherto. At the same time a sweetish, insidious scent, imperceptible perhaps to any nerves less strained than his, crept down the stairs and penetrated into the room. The voice dwindled into a mere drone and finally sank away into silence, and Johnson gave a long sigh of relief, for he knew that the drug had done its work and that, come what might, there should be no more pain for the sufferer.

But soon the silence became even more trying to him than the cries had been. He had no clue now as to what was going on, and his mind swarmed with horrible possibilities. He rose and went to the bottom of the stairs again. He heard the clink of metal against metal, and the subdued murmur of the doctors' voices. Then he heard Mrs. Peyton say something, in a tone as of fear or expostulation, and again the doctors murmured together. For twenty minutes he stood there leaning against the wall, listening to the occasional rumbles of talk without being able to catch a word of it. And then of a sudden there rose out of the silence the strangest little piping cry, and Mrs. Peyton screamed out in her delight and the man ran into the parlour and flung himself down upon the horse-hair sofa, drumming his heels on it in his ecstasy.

But often the great cat Fate lets us go only to clutch us again in a fiercer grip. As minute after minute passed and still no sound came from above save those thin, glutinous cries, Johnson cooled from his frenzy of joy, and lay breathless with his ears straining. They were moving slowly about. They were talking in subdued tones. Still minute after minute passing, and no word from the voice for which he listened. His nerves were dulled by his night of trouble, and he waited in limp wretchedness upon his sofa. There he still sat when the doctors came down to him—a bedraggled, miserable figure with his face grimy and his hair unkempt from his long vigil. He rose as they entered, bracing himself against the mantelpiece.

"Is she dead?" he asked.

"Doing well," answered the doctor.

And at the words that little conventional spirit which had never known until that night the capacity for fierce agony which lay within it, learned for the second time that there were springs of joy also which it had never tapped before. His impulse was to fall upon his knees, but he was shy before the doctors.

"Can I go up?"

"In a few minutes."

"I'm sure, doctor, I'm very—I'm very—" he grew inarticulate. "Here are your three guineas, Dr. Pritchard. I wish they were three hundred."

"So do I," said the senior man, and they laughed as they shook hands.

Johnson opened the shop door for them and heard their talk as they stood for an instant outside.

"Looked nasty at one time."

"Very glad to have your help."

"Delighted, I'm sure. Won't you step round and have a cup of coffee?"

"No, thanks. I'm expecting another case."

The firm step and the dragging one passed away to the right and the left. Johnson turned from the door still with that turmoil of joy in his heart. He seemed to be making a new start in life. He felt that he was a stronger and a deeper man. Perhaps all this suffering had an object then. It might prove to be a blessing both to his wife and to him. The very thought was one which he would have been incapable of conceiving twelve hours before. He was full of new emotions. If there had been a harrowing there had been a planting too.

"Can I come up?" he cried, and then, without waiting for an answer, he took the steps three at a time.

Mrs. Peyton was standing by a soapy bath with a bundle in her hands. From under the curve of a brown shawl there looked out at him the strangest little red face with crumpled features, moist, loose lips, and eyelids which quivered like a rabbit's nostrils. The weak neck had let the head topple over, and it rested upon the shoulder.

"Kiss it, Robert!" cried the grandmother. "Kiss your son!"

But he felt a resentment to the little, red, blinking creature. He could not forgive it yet for that long night of misery. He caught sight of a white face in the bed and he ran towards it with such love and pity as his speech could find no words for.

"Thank God it is over! Lucy, dear, it was dreadful!"

"But I'm so happy now. I never was so happy in my life."

Her eyes were fixed upon the brown bundle.

"You mustn't talk," said Mrs. Peyton.

"But don't leave me," whispered his wife.

So he sat in silence with his hand in hers. The lamp was burning dim and the first cold light of dawn was breaking through the window. The night had been long and dark but the day was the sweeter and the purer in consequence. London was waking up. The roar began to rise from the street. Lives had come and lives had gone, but the great machine was still working out its dim and tragic destiny.

"The Curse of Eve," *Round the Red Lamp*, 1897.

HJALMAR SÖDERBERG

Doctor Glas

Söderberg's 1905 masterpiece is a tightly ironic novel that allows the reader to observe Dr Tyko Gabriel Glas, a doctor in his thirties, as he keeps up his diary. This soured and fastidious man seems to have made the worst possible choice of career: the physicality and occasional sordidness of medicine dismays him. Throughout much of the novel he steels himself to take judgement and power into his own hands, and dispense with the life of a pastor called Gregorius, who has been forcing himself on his younger wife Helga, also one of Glas's patients. Cyanide pills hidden in a hollow watchcase ultimately do the trick. But Dr Glas is not just a knight errant; this entry proves him to be something of a Social Darwinist too. It is a frank passage that is remarkable for its anticipation of what was to become government policy in Sweden between 1936 and 1976 when 63,000 women were sterilized in the interests of "positive eugenicism."

No, sometimes life shows a face altogether too vile. Only a moment ago I came home from a night call. I was woken by the telephone ringing, took a name and address—it was quite close by—and a hint of what the trouble was: a child had suddenly fallen seriously ill, probably with the croup, at the home of so-and-so, a wholesaler. A cloud of drunken night-birds and whores swarming about my coat-tails, I hurried through the streets. It was the fourth floor of a house in a side-street. The name I'd just heard on the telephone, and which I now saw on the front door, seemed familiar; although I could not place it. The wife received me in dressing-gown and petticoat,—it was the lady from Djurgårdsbrunn, the same I remembered from that time years ago. So, I thought, it's the pretty little boy! I was shown through a narrow dining-room and an idiotic hall-way, illuminated, just then, by a greasy kitchen lamp placed in the corner of a whatnot; and so into a bedroom. Evidently the master wasn't at home. "It's our eldest boy who is ill," the wife explained. She led me over to a little bed. In it lay, not the pretty little lad, but another, a monster. Enormous ape-like cheek-bones, a flattened cranium, little evil stupid eyes. It was obvious at first glance: an idiot.

So—this was her first-born! It was him she was carrying under her heart, that time. This was the seed she begged me on her knees to free her from; and I answered with duty. Life, I don't understand you!

And now death at last wished to take pity on him and on them, take him away from the life he should never have entered. But it's not to be. There is nothing they long for so much as to be quit of him. Yet their cowardly hearts impel them, even so, to send for me, the doctor, to drive away kind merciful death and keep this monster alive. And I, no less a coward, do "my duty"—do it now, as I did then.

All these thoughts, of course, did not immediately pass through my head as I stood there, wide awake in that strange room, beside a sickbed. I merely followed my calling, thought nothing—stayed as long as was necessary, did what had to be done; and left. In the hall I met the husband and father, who had just come home, somewhat under the influence.

And the ape-boy is going to live—perhaps for many years yet. The loathsome brutish face with its evil stupid eyes pursues me, even into my room. I sit reading in them the whole story.

He has been given those very eyes the world looked at his mother with, when she was big with him. And with those same eyes the world fooled her into looking at what she had done.

And now, here's the fruit—a lovely fruit!

The brutal father who hit her, the mother whose head was full of what friends and relatives would say, the servants who looked askance at her, giggling and rejoicing in their hearts at this confirmation that their "betters" are no better than their inferiors, aunts and uncles who became stiff with idiotic indignation and half-witted morality, the clergyman who made short work of his sermon at the humiliating wedding, a little embarrassed, perhaps rightly, at having to exhort the contracting parties on our Lord's behalf to do what so blatantly was already done—all, all contributed their mite, all had their little part in what ensued. Not even the doctor was missing—the doctor, that was me.

Couldn't I have helped her that time when, in her hour of utmost need and despair, she went down on her bended knees in this room? Instead, I replied with duty, in which I did not believe.

But neither could I know, or guess ...

Her case, at least, was one of those where I was sure of myself. Even if I did not believe in "duty"—did not believe it to be the supremely binding law it gives itself out as being—yet it was perfectly clear to me that in this case the right, the prudent thing to do was what others call their duty. And I did not hesitate to do it.

Life, I don't understand you.

★

"When a child is born deformed, it is drowned."

(Seneca)

★

Every idiot at the Eugenia House costs more in annual upkeep than a healthy young labourer earns in annual income.

"July 17," *Doctor Glas*, 1905; translated from the Swedish by Paul Britten Austin.

JEROME K. JEROME

Victim to One Hundred and Seven Fatal Maladies

Jerome K. Jerome's parents fell on hard times and he grew up in cramped conditions in the East End of London which left him with "a haunting terror" of the poverty and hopeless faces he saw as a child; like many furtively melancholy people, his mode of expression was humour. His most popular novel Three Men in a Boat *captures the sunny disposition of Europe before it "fled from peace" in 1914. His winsome narrator convinces himself, like many after him, that an entire medical textbook was written expressly with him in mind. We might call his problem "sympathetic contagion." Now that so many people believe in—and don't even have to visit the British Museum for—Information the problem has hardly disappeared, and in fact is rarely treated with anything like humour. Humour about oneself might be too close to cure.*

There were four of us—George, and William Samuel Harris, and myself, and Montmorency. We were sitting in my room, smoking, and talking about how bad we were—bad from a medical point of view I mean, of course.

We were all feeling seedy, and we were getting quite nervous about it. Harris said he felt such extraordinary fits of giddiness come over him at times, that he hardly knew what he was doing; and then George said that *he* had fits of giddiness too, and hardly knew what *he* was doing. With me, it was my liver that was out of order. I knew it was my liver that was out of order, because I had just been reading a patent liver-pill circular, in which were detailed the various symptoms by which a man could tell when his liver was out of order. I had them all.

It is a most extraordinary thing, but I never read a patent medicine advertisement without being impelled to the conclusion that I am suffering from the particular disease therein dealt with in its most virulent form. The diagnosis seems in every case to correspond exactly with all the sensations that I have ever felt.

I remember going to the British Museum one day to read up the treatment for some slight ailment of which I had a touch—hay fever, I fancy it was. I got down the book, and read all I came to read; and then, in an unthinking moment, I idly turned the leaves, and began to indolently study diseases, generally. I forget which was the first distemper I plunged into—some fearful, devastating scourge, I know—and, before I had glanced half down the list of "premonitory symptoms", it was borne in upon me that I had fairly got it.

I sat for a while, frozen with horror; and then, in the listlessness of despair, I again turned over the pages. I came to typhoid fever—read the symptoms—discovered that I had typhoid fever, must have had it for months without knowing it—wondered what else I had got; turned up St. Vitus's Dance—found, as I expected, that I had that too,—began to get interested in my case, and determined to sift it to the bottom, and so started alphabetically—read up ague, and learnt that I was sickening for it, and that the acute stage would commence in about another fortnight. Bright's disease, I was relieved to find, I had only in a modified form, and, so far as that was concerned, I might live for years. Cholera I had, with severe complications; and diphtheria I seemed to have been born with. I plodded conscientiously through the twenty-six letters, and the only malady I could conclude I had not got was housemaid's knee.

I felt rather hurt about this at first; it seemed somehow to be a sort of slight. Why hadn't I got housemaid's knee? Why this invidious reservation? After a while, however, less grasping feelings prevailed. I reflected that I had every other known malady in the pharmacology, and I grew less selfish, and determined to do without housemaid's knee. Gout, in its most malignant stage, it would appear, had seized me without my being aware of it; and zymosis I had evidently been suffering with from boyhood. There were no more diseases after zymosis, so I concluded there was nothing else the matter with me.

I sat and pondered. I thought what an interesting case I must be from a medical point of view, what an acquisition I should be to a class! Students would have no need to "walk the hospitals," if they had me. I was a hospital in myself. All they need do would be to walk round me, and, after that, take their diploma.

Then I wondered how long I had to live. I tried to examine myself. I felt my pulse. I could not at first feel any pulse at all. Then, all of a sudden, it seemed to start off. I pulled out my watch and timed it. I made it a hundred and forty-seven to the minute. I tried to feel my heart. I could not feel my heart. It had stopped beating. I have since been induced to come to the opinion that it must have been there all the time, and must have been beating, but I cannot account for it. I patted myself all over my front, from what I call my waist up to my head, and I went a bit round each side, and a little way up the back. But I could not feel or hear anything. I tried to look at my tongue. I stuck it out as far as ever it would go, and I shut one eye, and tried to examine it with the other. I could only see the tip, and the only thing that I could gain from that was to feel more certain than before that I had scarlet fever.

I had walked into that reading-room a happy, healthy man. I crawled out a decrepit wreck.

I went to my medical man. He is an old chum of mine, and feels my pulse, and looks at my tongue, and talks about the weather, all for nothing, when I fancy I'm ill; so I thought I would do him a good turn by going to him now. "What a doctor wants," I said, "is practice. He shall have me. He will get more practice out of me than out of seventeen hundred of your ordinary, commonplace patients, with only one or two diseases each." So I went straight up and saw him, and he said:

"Well, what's the matter with you?"

I said:

"I will not take up your time, dear boy, with telling you what is the matter with me. Life is brief, and you might pass away before I had finished. But I will tell you what is *not* the matter with me. I have not got housemaid's knee. Why I have not got housemaid's knee, I cannot tell you; but the fact remains that I have not got it. Everything else, however, I *have* got."

And I told him how I came to discover it all.

Then he opened me and looked down me, and clutched hold of my wrist, and then he hit me over the chest when I wasn't expecting it—a cowardly thing to do, I call it—and immediately afterwards butted me with the side of his head. After that, he sat down and wrote out a prescription, and folded it up and gave it me, and I put it in my pocket and went out.

I did not open it. I took it to the nearest chemist's, and handed it in. The man read it, and then handed it back.

He said he didn't keep it.

I said:

"You are a chemist?"

He said:

"I am a chemist. If I was a co-operative stores and family hotel combined, I might be able to oblige you. Being only a chemist hampers me."

I read the prescription. It ran:

"1 lb. beefsteak, with
1 pt. bitter beer
                every 6 hours.
1 ten-mile walk every morning.
1 bed at 11 sharp every night.
And don't stuff up your head with things you don't understand."

I followed the directions, with the happy result—speaking for myself—that my life was preserved, and is still going on.

In the present instance, going back to the liver-pill circular, I had the symptoms, beyond all mistake, the chief among them being "a general disinclination to work of any kind."

What I suffer in that way no tongue can tell. From my earliest infancy I have been a martyr to it. As a boy, the disease hardly ever left me for a day. They did not know, then, that it was my liver. Medical science was in a far less advanced state than now, and they used to put it down to laziness.

"Why, you skulking little devil, you," they would say, "get up and do something for your living, can't you?"—not knowing, of course, that I was ill.

And they didn't give me pills; they gave me clumps on the side of the head. And, strange as it may appear, those clumps on the head often cured me—for the time being. I have known one clump on the head have more effect upon my liver, and make me feel more anxious to go straight away then and there, and do what was wanted to be done, without further loss of time, than a whole box of pills does now.

You know, it often is so—those simple, old-fashioned remedies are sometimes more efficacious than all the dispensary stuff.

We sat there for half-an-hour, describing to each other our maladies. I explained to George and William Harris how I felt when I got up in the morning, and William Harris told us how he felt when he went to bed; and George stood on the hearth-rug, and gave us a clever and powerful piece of acting, illustrative of how he felt in the night.

George *fancies* he is ill; but there's never anything really the matter with him, you know.

At this point, Mrs. Poppets knocked at the door to know if we were ready for supper. We smiled sadly at one another, and said we supposed we had better try to swallow a bit. Harris said a little something in one's stomach often kept the disease in check; and Mrs. Poppets brought the tray in, and we drew up to the table, and toyed with a little steak and onions, and some rhubarb tart.

I must have been very weak at the time; because I know, after the first half-hour or so, I seemed to take no interest whatever in my food—an unusual thing for me—and I didn't want any cheese.

This duty done, we refilled our glasses, lit our pipes, and resumed the discussion upon our state of health. What it was that was actually the matter with us, we none of us could be sure of; but the unanimous opinion was that it—whatever it was—had been brought on by overwork.

"What we want is rest," said Harris.

"Rest and a complete change," said George. "The overstrain upon our brains has produced a general depression throughout the system. Change of scene, and absence of the necessity for thought, will restore the mental equilibrium."

George has a cousin, who is usually described in the charge-sheet as a medical student, so that he naturally has a somewhat family-physicianary way of putting things.

I agreed with George, and suggested that we should seek out some retired and old-world spot, far from the madding crowd, and dream away a sunny week among its drowsy lanes—some half-forgotten nook, hidden away by the fairies, out of reach of the noisy world—some quaint-perched eyrie on the cliffs of Time, from whence the surging waves of the nineteenth century would sound far-off and faint.

Harris said he thought it would be humpy. He said he knew the sort of place I meant; where everybody went to bed at eight o'clock, and you couldn't get a *Referee* for love or money, and had to walk ten miles to get your baccy.

"No," said Harris, "if you want rest and change, you can't beat a sea trip."

I objected to the sea trip strongly. A sea trip does you good when you are going to have a couple of months of it, but, for a week, it is wicked.

You start on Monday with the idea implanted in your bosom that you are going to enjoy yourself. You wave an airy adieu to the boys on shore, light your biggest pipe, and swagger about the deck as if you were Captain Cook, Sir Francis Drake, and Christopher Columbus all rolled into one. On Tuesday, you wish you hadn't come. On Wednesday, Thursday, and Friday, you wish you were dead. On Saturday, you are able to swallow a little beef tea, and to sit up on deck, and answer with a wan, sweet smile when kind-hearted people ask you how you feel now. On Sunday, you begin to walk about again, and take solid food. And on Monday morning, as, with your bag and umbrella in your hand, you stand by the gunwale, waiting to step ashore, you begin to thoroughly like it.

I remember my brother-in-law going for a short sea trip once, for the benefit of his health. He took a return berth from London to Liverpool; and when he got to Liverpool, the only thing he was anxious about was to sell that return ticket.

It was offered round the town at a tremendous reduction, so I am told; and was eventually sold for eighteenpence to a bilious-looking youth who had just been advised by his medical men to go to the sea-side, and take exercise.

"Sea-side!" said my brother-in-law, pressing the ticket affectionately into his hand; "why, you'll have enough to last you a lifetime; and as for exercise! why, you'll get more exercise, sitting down on that ship, than you would turning somersaults on dry land."

He himself—my brother-in-law—came back by train. He said the North-Western Railway was healthy enough for him.

Another fellow I knew went for a week's voyage round the coast, and, before they started, the steward came to him to ask whether he would pay for each meal as he had it, or arrange beforehand for the whole series.

The steward recommended the latter course, as it would come so much cheaper. He said they would do him for the whole week at two pounds five. He said for breakfast there would be fish, followed by a grill. Lunch was at one, and consisted of four courses. Dinner at six—soup, fish, entree, joint, poultry, salad, sweets, cheese, and dessert. And a light meat supper at ten.

My friend thought he would close on the two-pound-five job (he is a hearty eater), and did so.

Lunch came just as they were off Sheerness. He didn't feel so hungry as he thought he should, and so contented himself with a bit of boiled beef, and some strawberries and cream. He pondered a good deal during the afternoon, and at one time it seemed to him that he had been eating nothing but boiled beef for weeks, and at other times it seemed that he must have been living on strawberries and cream for years.

Neither the beef nor the strawberries and cream seemed happy, either—seemed discontented like.

At six, they came and told him dinner was ready. The announcement aroused no enthusiasm within him, but he felt that there was some of that two-pound-five to be worked off, and he held on to ropes and things and went down. A pleasant odour of onions and hot ham, mingled with fried fish and greens, greeted him at the bottom of the ladder; and then the steward came up with an oily smile, and said:

"What can I get you, sir?"

"Get me out of this," was the feeble reply.

And they ran him up quick, and propped him up, over to leeward, and left him.

For the next four days he lived a simple and blameless life on thin captain's biscuits (I mean that the biscuits were thin, not the captain) and soda-water; but, towards Saturday, he got uppish, and went in for weak tea and dry toast, and on Monday he was gorging himself on chicken broth. He left the ship on Tuesday, and as it steamed away from the landing-stage he gazed after it regretfully.

"There she goes," he said, "there she goes, with two pounds' worth of food on board that belongs to me, and that I haven't had."

He said that if they had given him another day he thought he could have put it straight.

So I set my face against the sea trip. Not, as I explained, upon my own account. I was never queer. But I was afraid for George. George said he should be all right, and would rather like it, but he would advise Harris and me not to think of it, as he felt sure we should both be ill. Harris said that, to himself, it was always a mystery how people managed to get sick at sea—said he thought people must do it on purpose, from affectation—said he had often wished to be, but had never been able.

Then he told us anecdotes of how he had gone across the Channel when it was so rough that the passengers had to be tied into their berths, and he and the captain were the only two living souls on board who were not ill. Sometimes it was he and the second mate who were not ill; but it was generally he and one other man. If not he and another man, then it was he by himself.

It is a curious fact, but nobody ever is sea-sick on land. At sea, you come across plenty of people very bad indeed, whole boat-loads of them; but I never met a man yet, on land, who had ever known at all what it was to be sea-sick. Where the thousands upon thousands of bad sailors that swarm in every ship hide themselves when they are on land is a mystery.

If most men were like a fellow I saw on the Yarmouth boat one day, I could account for the seeming enigma easily enough. It was just off Southend Pier, I recollect, and he was leaning out through one of the port-holes in a very dangerous position. I went up to him to try and save him.

"Hi! come further in," I said, shaking him by the shoulder. "You'll be overboard."

"Oh my! I wish I was," was the only answer I could get; and there I had to leave him.

Three weeks afterwards, I met him in the coffee-room of a Bath hotel, talking about his voyages, and explaining, with enthusiasm, how he loved the sea.

"Good sailor!" he replied in answer to a mild young man's envious query; "well, I did feel a little queer *once*, I confess. It was off Cape Horn. The vessel was wrecked the next morning."

I said:

"Weren't you a little shaky by Southend Pier one day, and wanted to be thrown overboard?"

"Southend Pier!" he replied, with a puzzled expression.

"Yes; going down to Yarmouth, last Friday three weeks."

"Oh, ah—yes," he answered, brightening up; "I remember now. I did have a headache that afternoon. It was the pickles, you know. They were the most disgraceful pickles I ever tasted in a respectable boat. Did you have any?"

For myself, I have discovered an excellent preventive against sea-sickness, in balancing myself. You stand in the centre of the deck, and, as the ship heaves and pitches, you move your body about, so as to keep it always straight. When the front of the ship rises, you lean forward, till the deck almost touches your nose; and when its back end gets up, you lean backwards. This is all very well for an hour or two; but you can't balance yourself for a week.

George said:

"Let's go up the river."

He said we should have fresh air, exercise and quiet; the constant change of scene would occupy our minds (including what there was of Harris's); and the hard work would give us a good appetite, and make us sleep well.

Harris said he didn't think George ought to do anything that would have a tendency to make him sleepier than he always was, as it might be dangerous.

He said he didn't very well understand how George was going to sleep any more than he did now, seeing that there were only twenty-four hours in each day, summer and winter alike; but thought that if he DID sleep any more, he might just as well be dead, and so save his board and lodging.

Harris said, however, that the river would suit him to a "T". I don't know what a "T" is (except a sixpenny one, which includes bread-and-butter and cake *ad lib.*, and is cheap at the price, if you haven't had any dinner). It seems to suit everybody, however, which is greatly to its credit.

It suited me to a "T" too, and Harris and I both said it was a good idea of George's; and we said it in a tone that seemed to somehow imply that we were surprised that George should have come out so sensible.

The only one who was not struck with the suggestion was Montmorency. He never did care for the river, did Montmorency.

"It's all very well for you fellows," he says; "you like it, but I don't. There's nothing for me to do. Scenery is not in my line, and I don't smoke. If I see a rat, you won't stop; and if I go to sleep, you get fooling about with the boat, and slop me overboard. If you ask me, I call the whole thing bally foolishness."

We were three to one, however, and the motion was carried.

Chapter I, *Three Men in a Boat*, 1889.

Various Aphorisms

I too believe that humanity will triumph in the long run; I'm only afraid that at the same time the world will have been transformed into one huge hospital where everyone is everybody else's humane nurse.

—WOLFGANG VON GOETHE (1749–1832)

DOCTOR: Always preceded by "the good". Is a marvel while he enjoys your confidence, a fool as soon as you've fallen out. Are all materialists: "You can't find the soul with a scalpel."

—GUSTAVE FLAUBERT (1821–1880)

Physician, help yourself: thus you help your patient too. Let his best help be to see with his own eyes the man who makes himself well.

—FRIEDRICH NIETZSCHE (1844–1900)

I myself should always regret not being a doctor.

—VINCENT VAN GOGH (1853–1890)

One should not be taken in by disguises such as empathy, social obligation or the glittering saviour's mask that doctors sport.

—ROBERT MUSIL (1880–1942)

The ill person is the tactical, the illness the strategic object of medicine.

—ERNST JÜNGER (1895–1998)

The aim of medicine is surely not to make men virtuous; it is to safeguard and rescue them from the consequences of their vices. The true physician does not preach repentance; he offers absolution.

—H.L. MENCKEN (1880–1956)

All professions are conspiracies against the laity.

—GEORGE BERNARD SHAW (1856–1950)

You—a doctor! It would have taken a single patient to spell your downfall. Woe to you if you hadn't saved him!

—ELIAS CANETTI (1905–1994)

No cry of torment can be greater than the cry of one human being, and no torment can be greater than that which a single human being can suffer.

—LUDWIG WITTGENSTEIN (1889–1951)

I also expect a doctor to be an evolutionist, and, as such, regard all habits as acquired habits, a man being nothing but an amoeba with acquirements.

—GEORGE BERNARD SHAW (1856–1950)

And how comfortless is the thought that the sickness of the normal does not necessarily imply as its opposite the health of the sick, but that the latter usually only present, in a different way, the same disastrous pattern.

—THEODOR ADORNO (1903–1969)

The Doctor and the Public Hangman require the same qualifications.

—W.H. AUDEN (1907–1973)

MARCEL PROUST

People with Neuroses

Marcel Proust grew up in a medical family; his father Adrien was an expert on neurasthenia, and his brother Robert a famous Paris doctor. Marcel's asthma attacks began at the age of nine after a walk in the Bois de Boulogne with his parents, and he profited from the persistance of his asthma in adult life to withdraw from society in order to begin work on his great novel whose rhythm, it has been claimed, resembles that of the "asthmatic's shortness of breath." What is not in doubt is that hypochondria, in Proust's work, receives its apotheosis as a disgressive literary technique.

People with neuroses are perhaps, despite the phrase earmarked for them, those who are least accustomed to "listening to their insides": they hear so many things inside them crying wolf and later learn they were wrong to get worried that they end up paying no attention to any of them. So often have their nervous systems cried out for help as if it were a serious disease, just when it was about to start snowing or they were going to a new apartment, that they've acquired the habit of paying no more heed to these alerts than a soldier who, in the heat of battle, so little perceives them that he is capable, though mortally wounded, of carrying on for a few days more as if he were a man in the pink of health. One morning, bearing neatly ranged within me all my usual ailments, from whose constant circulation in my viscera I kept my mind turned as resolutely away as from that of my blood, I skipped lightheartedly into the dining-room where my parents were already at table, and—telling myself, in my usual way, that to feel cold meant not that I ought to warm myself but instead, for instance, that I'd just been reprimanded, and that not to feel hungry meant that it was going to rain and not that I ought to desist from eating—sat beside them when, in the very act of swallowing the first mouthful of a appetizing chop, a feeling of nausea and vertigo stopped me, the feverish reaction of a beginning illness, the symptoms of which had been veiled and impeded by my cold indifference, but which stubbornly declined the nourishment I was hardly in a state to absorb. Then, at the same moment, the consideration that I would not be allowed to go out if I were seen to be unwell gave me, like the instinct of self-preservation in a wounded man, enough strength to drag myself off to my room, where I discovered that my temperature was 40, and then to get ready to go out to the Champs-Elysées. Through the languid and heightened senses of the body enveloping them, my thoughts were eagerly anticipating, even clamouring for the coddling delight of a game of prisoner's base with Gilberte, and an hour later, barely able to stay upright, but happy to be with her, I still had the energy to savour it.

Françoise, on our return, declared that I was "feeling poorly", that I must have come down with a "chill", while the doctor, who was called in at once, wished rather to talk about the "severity", the "virulence" of the acute temperature rise which accompanied my congestion of the lungs, and would be no more than "a flash in the pan" in relation to other more "insidious" and "covert" forms. For some time now I had been prone to shortness of breath, and our doctor, braving the disapproval of my grand-mother, who could already see me dying a alcoholic's death, had suggested that I take, along with the caffeine which had been prescribed to aid my breathing, beer, champagne or brandy as soon as I felt an attack coming on. These attacks would be nipped in the bud, he said, in the "euphoria" produced by the alcohol. In order that my grandmother should allow it to be given me, I was often obliged not to disguise, but almost to make a display of my breathlessness. I must add that, whenever I felt it coming on, and never quite sure what proportions it would assume, I would get upset at the thought of my grandmother's anxiety, of which I was afraid far more than my own symptoms. But at the same time my body, either because it was too weak to keep those symptoms to itself, or because it was frightened that, unawares of the imminent crisis, people might demand of me some strenuous task it would have found impossible or dangerous, gave me the urge to warn my grandmother of my symptoms with a punctiliousness which I ultimately reinforced as a kind of physiological scruple. Should I observe in myself a troublesome symptom I had not previously encountered my body remained in distress so long as I had not described the symptom to my grandmother. If she pretended to take no notice, it became insistent. Sometimes I went too far; and that beloved face, which was no longer able always to hide its emotion as in the past, would betray a look of pity, a pained grimace. Then my heart was pierced by the sight of her grief; thinking that my kisses had the power to expel that grief and that my affection could offer my grandmother as much joy as my own content, I flung myself into her arms. And since the scruples were moreover appeased by the certainty that she was now aware of this current malaise, my body offered no opposition to my reassuring her. I protested that this ailment was not in the least distressing, that I was not at all deserving of pity, that she could be quite sure that I was content; my body had wished to obtain exactly its just measure of pity and, provided that someone knew that it had a pain in its right side, it could see no disadvantage to my declaring that this pain was trifling and not a hindrance to happiness; for my body did not pride itself on its philosophy: that was outside its purview. Almost every day during my convalescence I suffered from these attacks of breathlessness. One evening, after my grandmother had left me in a fairly stable condition, she returned to my room very late and, seeing me gasping for breath, exclaimed, her face distraught, "Oh dear God, you must be suffering awfully." She left me at once; I heard the latch on the street door, and in a little while she came back with some brandy she had gone out to buy since there was none in the house. Soon I began to feel better. My grandmother, who was a little bit flushed in the face, seemed harassed, and her expression was tired and dejected.

"I'll leave you alone now, and let you benefit a little from your improvement," she said, rising abruptly to go. I held her back though, for a kiss, and could feel on her cold cheeks something moist, but I couldn't tell whether it was the dampness of the night air through which she had just gone. The following day, she did not come to my room until the evening, having had, she told me, to go out. I thought this an act of blatant indifference to my welfare, and had to bite my tongue in order not to reproach her with it.

Since my breathlessness persisted long after any congestion which might have accounted for it, my parents called on the services of Professor Cottard. It is not enough that a physician who is requested to treat cases of this nature should be learned. Faced with symptoms which may be common to three or four different diseases, it is ultimately his flair and intuition that determine which disease he is likely to be dealing with, over and above the great similarities between them. This mysterious gift does not entail any superiority in the other subdivisions of the intellect, and a very vulgar person, someone who admires the worst kind of painting and music, someone without the slightest curiosity of mind, may perfectly well possess it. In my own case, the physical signs of my illness might just as well have been caused by nervous spasms, by early tuberculosis, by asthma, by a toxic alimentary dyspnoea accompanied by renal failure, by chronic bronchitis, or even by a complex state in which several of these factors were implicated. However, nervous spasms required to be treated with a firm hand, tuberculosis with a great deal of care and fuss and the kind of "fattening-up" which would have been bad for an arthritic condition such as asthma and might indeed have been dangerous in a case of toxic alimentary dyspnoea, which calls for a strict diet that, in turn, might be detrimental for a tubercular patient. But Cottard barely hesitated and his orders were imperious: "Laxatives, violent and drastic purges; milk for a few days, but only milk. No meat. No alcohol." My mother murmured that I needed, all the same, to be "built up", that I was already very highly-strung, and that this positively horselike washout and diet would make me worse. I could see in Cottard's eyes, as anxious as those of a man afraid of missing a train, that he was wondering if he had perhaps erred too much on the side of his natural gentleness. He was trying to remember whether he had told himself to put on his mask of coldness, much as men look for a mirror to make sure they haven't forgotten to knot their tie. In his moment of doubt, and at the same time riding slipshod over it, he barked out gruffly: "I'm not in the habit of repeating my orders. Give me a pen. Mark my word, milk! Later on, when we've dealt with the acute attacks and the insomnia, I'm prepared to let you take a little clear broth, and then some blended food, but always with milk—*au lait!* You'll enjoy that, since

Spain is all the rage just now—*olé, olé!*" (His pupils could see this joke coming, since he made it at the hospital every time he put a heart or liver patient on his milk diet.) "After that, you'll gradually return to your normal life. But whenever you have any coughing fits or breathlessness—laxatives, intestinal washouts, bed, milk!" He listened to my mother's final objections with an icy calm, but made no reply; and since he had gone without so much as having condescended to explain why this diet was necessary, my parents concluded that it had no bearing on my case and would weaken me for no good reason, and therefore did not subject me to it. Naturally they sought to conceal their non-compliance from the professor, and to make sure of it avoided all the households in which they might have bumped into him. Then, when my condition got worse, they decided to make me follow Cottard's order to the the letter; in three days my wheezing and cough had gone, and I was breathing freely. We then realised that Cottard, while finding me, as he told us later on, somewhat asthmatic, and above all "bonkers," had perceived that what was really wrong with me at that moment was a kind of toxaemia, and that by lightening my liver and purging my kidneys he would be able to relieve the congestion in my bronchial tubes and thus give me back my breath, my sleep and my vital forces. And we realised that this imbecile was a great clinician.

Excerpt from "Autour de Mme Swann,"
A la Recherche du Temps Perdu, 1913.

G.K. CHESTERTON

The Medical Mistake

Chesterton is known today for his novels and Father Brown mysteries, but he was also a mercurial journalist and brilliant polemicist. In this chapter from a tract written when fascist Italy was recommending corporatism as a political philosophy, he lays bare what is known as the "organic fallacy," the belief that societies work like bodies (or minds like genes). Hobbes's Leviathan is merely the most famous of such mythical beasts. Yet Chesterton's assertion that medicine seeks only to restore the normal human body has clearly been superseded by events: public health, with its abstract notions of personhood and justice, is becoming ever more influential in a trend that parallels what Wittgenstein once referred to as "the contemptuous attitude towards the individual case." Suffice it to say that a perfect society of that kind, a health utopia, in which medical problems have been addressed by altering the social order, is incompatible with one in which people have moral relationships.

A book of modern social inquiry has a shape that is somewhat sharply defined. It begins as a rule with an analysis, with statistics, tables of population, decrease of crime among Congregationalists, growth of hysteria among policemen, and similar ascertained facts; it ends with a chapter that is generally called "The Remedy." It is almost wholly due to this careful, solid, and scientific method that "The Remedy" is never found. For this scheme of medical question and answer is a blunder; the first great blunder of sociology. It is always called stating the disease before we find the cure. But it is the whole definition and dignity of man that in social matters we must actually find the cure before we find the disease.

The fallacy is one of the fifty fallacies that come from the modern madness for biological or bodily metaphors. It is convenient to speak of the Social Organism, just as it is convenient to speak of the British Lion. But Britain is no more an organism than Britain is a lion. The moment we begin to give a nation the unity and simplicity of an animal, we begin to think wildly. Because every man is a biped, fifty men are not a centipede. This has produced, for instance, the gaping absurdity of perpetually talking about "young nations" and "dying nations," as if a nation had a fixed and physical span of life. Thus people will say that Spain has entered a final senility; they might as well say that Spain is losing all her teeth. Or people will say that Canada should soon produce a literature; which is like saying that Canada must soon grow a new moustache. Nations consist of people; the first generation may be decrepit, or the ten thousandth may be vigorous. Similar applications of the fallacy are made by those who see in the increasing size of national possessions, a simple increase in wisdom and stature, and in favour with God and man. These people, indeed, even fall short in subtlety of the parallel of a human body. They do not even ask whether an empire is growing taller in its youth, or only growing fatter in its old age. But of all the instances of error arising from this physical fancy, the worst is that we have before us: the habit of exhaustively describing a social sickness, and then propounding a social drug.

Now we do talk first about the disease in cases of bodily breakdown; and that for an excellent reason. Because, though there may be doubt about the way in which the body broke down, there is no doubt at all about the shape in which it should be built up again. No doctor proposes to produce a new kind of man, with a new arrangement of eyes or limbs. The hospital, by necessity, may send a man home with one leg less: but it will not (in a creative rapture) send him home with one leg extra. Medical science is content with the normal human body, and only seeks to restore it.

But social science is by no means always content with the normal human soul; it has all sorts of fancy souls for sale. Man as a social idealist will say "I am tired of being a Puritan; I want to be a Pagan," or "Beyond this dark probation of Individualism I see the shining paradise of Collectivism." Now in bodily ills there is none of this difference about the ultimate ideal. The patient may or may not want quinine; but he certainly wants health. No one says "I am tired of this headache; I want some toothache," or "The only thing for this Russian influenza is a few German measles," or "Through this dark probation of catarrh I see the shining paradise of rheumatism." But exactly the whole difficulty in our public problems is that some men are aiming at cures which other men would regard as worse maladies; are offering ultimate conditions as states of health which others would uncompromisingly call states of disease. Mr. Belloc once said that he would no more part with the idea of property than with his teeth; yet to Mr. Bernard Shaw property is not a tooth, but a toothache. Lord Milner has sincerely attempted to introduce German efficiency; and many of us would as soon welcome German measles. Dr. Saleeby would honestly like to have Eugenics; but I would rather have rheumatics.

This is the arresting and dominant fact about modern social discussion; that the quarrel is not merely about the difficulties, but about the aim. We agree about the evil; it is about the good that we should tear each other's eyes out. We all admit that a lazy aristocracy is a bad thing. We should not by any means all admit that an active aristocracy would be a good thing. We all feel angry with an irreligious priesthood; but some of us would go mad with disgust at a really religious one. Everyone is indignant if our army is weak, including the people who would be even more indignant if it were strong. The social case is exactly the opposite of the medical case. We do not disagree, like doctors, about the precise nature of the illness, while agreeing about the nature of health. On the contrary, we all agree that England is unhealthy, but half of us would not look at her in what the other half would call blooming health. Public abuses are so prominent and pestilent that they sweep all generous people into a sort of fictitious unanimity. We forget that, while we agree about the abuses of things, we should differ very much about the uses of them. Mr. Cadbury and I would agree about the bad public house. It would be precisely in front of the good public house that our painful personal fracas would occur.

I maintain, therefore, that the common sociological method is quite useless: that of first dissecting abject poverty or cataloguing prostitution. We all dislike abject poverty; but it might be another business if we began to discuss independent and dignified poverty. We all disapprove of prostitution; but we do not all approve of purity. The only way to discuss the social evil is to get at once to the social ideal. We can all see the national madness; but what is national sanity? I have called this book "What Is Wrong with the World?" and the upshot of the title can be easily and clearly stated. What is wrong is that we do not ask what is right.

"The Medical Mistake," *What's Wrong with the World?*, 1910.

MIKHAIL BULGAKOV

The Killer

*Mikhail Bulgakov studied at Kiev University and after qualifying in 1916 spent
18 hard months as a solo general practitioner in the Smolensk province. The sometimes lurid experiences of this period are recounted in his book* A Country
Doctor's Notebook. *With one or two concessions to cliché, Bulgakov's stories
convey a strong sense of the doctor as a beacon of enlightenment in a vast and
threatening sea of ignorance. In this story, a doctor's sense of justice overrides what
we could call medicine's Kantian principle: thou shalt not kill—in any circumstances.
"The Killer" was first published in* Meditsinsky Rabotnik, *and was retrieved
from a Moscow archive long after Bulgakov's death in 1940.*

Doctor Yashvin cleared his throat and with a wry smile on his face asked:

"May I tear a page off the calendar? It's exactly 12 o'clock, so today
must be the second."

"Be my guest," I said.

Yashvin grasped a corner of the top sheet with his slender white fingers
and carefully detached it. Beneath was a page of cheap paper stamped
with the number "2" and the caption "Tuesday." Something about the
greyish paper held him spellbound. He narrowed his eyes to peer at it,
then looked up and gazed into the distance. It was evidently something
only he could see: an inscrutable scene somewhere beyond the wall of my
room and perhaps far beyond Moscow looming in the gloom of that
freezing February night.

"What's bitten him?" I wondered, looking up at my colleague. He had
always intrigued me, because his looks were at odds with his profession.
People who didn't know him always took him for an actor. He had dark
hair and very pale skin, which made him both very attractive and eye-
catching. He was always smoothly shaven, he dressed fastidiously, he was

fond of going to the theatre and whenever he talked about acting did so with genuine taste and insight. But what really made him stand out from the other house officers were his shoes. Of the five of us standing in the room four had cheap tawed leather boots with clunky rounded toecaps but Dr Yashvin was wearing pointed patent leather shoes and yellow gaiters. It must be said, however, that his dandified appearance rarely raised hackles, and he was, to give him his due, a very good doctor. He was intrepid, got across well to patients and, most importantly, was able to keep up with the literature in spite of his regular outings to *The Valkyrie* and *The Barber of Seville*.

His footwear was not what interested me most, however; there was something else about him. I was intrigued by a remarkable side of his character: the talent, which he would reveal from time to time, of being a wonderful storyteller—even though at all other times he was a quiet and even taciturn man. He could speak authoritatively and compellingly about the most fascinating things, and what he said was utterly lacking in mannerisms or rhetorical padding. This reserved and elegant doctor would come to life. With his right hand he made the occasional sparing gesture in the air, as though punctuating his story. He never smiled when recounting something funny, and his similes were sometimes so apt and telling that as I listened to them I would think: "You're no mean doctor, but you've missed your calling. You should have been a writer."

Now, once again, I was struck by the same thought although Yashvin was silent, looking into the distance beyond the number "2," his eyes narrowed.

"What could he be looking at—a picture perhaps?" I looked over my shoulder and saw a quite ordinary and uninspiring picture of a workhorse with an improbably broad chest standing next to an engine. Underneath it read: "comparative power: horse (1)—engine (500)."

"This is all rubbish," I said, continuing the conversation, "all nonsense and prejudice. Those so-and-sos have got it in for doctors and for us surgeons especially. Think about it: someone does a hundred appendectomies and the hundred-and-first patient dies on the operating table. So—does that mean the doctor killed him?"

"That's what they will say. Definitely," one doctor said.

"And if the patient was somebody's wife, her husband will come round to the clinic and throw a chair at you," Doctor Plonsky added firmly, even managing a wan smile. We all smiled with him, although there's nothing very much to laugh at when people hurl chairs around a clinic.

"I can't stand these phoney confessions," I went on: "I've killed him! That makes me a murderer! No doctor sets out to kill anyone and if a patient dies on you, it's sheer bad luck. It's quite ridiculous! Murder is alien to the very nature of our profession. Good God! I call it murder when you kill someone quite deliberately or, if you insist, have a burning desire to see them dead. A surgeon with a gun in his hand—that, I concede, might be murder. But I've never met a surgeon like that in my life and I'm not likely to."

Doctor Yashvin suddenly turned his head towards me, his expression darkening, and said:

"The honour is all mine."

As he spoke, he adjusted his tie with one finger and the corner of his mouth twisted in another wry smile, though not his eyes.

We looked at him in astonishment.

"Meaning what?" I asked.

"Meaning that I murdered someone," Yashvin explained.

"When?" I asked thickly.

Yashvin pointed at the number "2" and said:

"Imagine the coincidence. As soon as you began talking about hospital deaths I looked at the calendar and saw it was the 2nd. It is a date I remember every year, by the way. Because exactly seven years ago tonight, or perhaps even …"Yashvin pulled out his black watch and glanced at it. "… yes, almost to the hour in fact, on the night of 1st and 2nd February I murdered someone."

"A patient?" Gins asked.

"Yes."

"But not intentionally?" I asked.

"Yes, quite deliberately," Yashvin said.

"Well, I can imagine," conceded Plonsky, ever the doubting Thomas, "that he had cancer and was probably dying an agonising death and you slipped him ten times the normal dose of morphine."

"No. Morphine had absolutely nothing to do with it," Yashvin said. "Nor did he have cancer. It was freezing cold, I remember clearly: the temperature was about fifteen degrees below zero and the stars were out. Oh what stars we have in Ukraine! I've lived nearly seven years in Moscow but I still long for home. I pine so badly that sometimes I'd love to jump on the first train for Ukraine, to see its ravines filled with snow, the Dnieper. There's no city on earth more beautiful than Kiev."

Yashvin put the leaf of calendar paper into his wallet, sat down in the armchair and continued:

"It was a frightening city, in frightening times ... and I'd seen terrible things that you here in Moscow haven't. It was 1919: the first of February as I said, at about six o'clock in the evening when it was already growing dark. In the gloaming I found myself doing something very strange. A lamp was burning on the table in my chambers, the room was cosy and warm, and there I was, crouching on the floor over a small suitcase, forcing something into it and mumbling one word: 'Run. Run.'

"I stuffed a shirt in the case and pulled it out again—the damned thing wouldn't fit. The suitcase was for hand-luggage and quite small, and my underwear took up so much space, not to mention the hundreds of cigarettes and my stethoscope, which were all poking out of it. I tossed the shirt away, then listened hard. The window frames were sealed for the winter and muffled every sound but you could still hear it. Far far away, the low roar of heavy guns—boo-oom, boo-oom. The echo died away, then it was silent. I looked out of the window. I lived on the heights above Kiev, at the top of Alekseyev Rise, and could see the whole of Podol, the lower city. Night was coming in from the Dnieper and swallowing up the houses. Windows would be lit, one by one, in little chains of light. Then another salvo. Soon it would be dawn again. Every time I heard an explosion across the Dnieper I would whisper:

"'Go on, go on, keep at it.'

"You see: by this time the whole city knew that Petlyura, the nationalist commander fighting the Communists, was on the point of clearing out—if not that night then the following one. On the other side of the Dnieper, the Bolsheviks were rumoured to be advancing in great numbers, and the whole city was awaiting their arrival, not just impatiently, I'd say, but enthusiastically. Because what Petlyura and his men had done in the last month in Kiev beggared belief. Pogroms would flare up at the drop of a hat. Every day people would be murdered—Jews first of course. Something or other would be requisitioned, and suddenly cars would be careening around the town filled with people with red ribbons fluttering on their sheepskin hats. In the last few days, the sound of heavy field ordnance in the outskirts had been relentless. Day and night. People were exhausted, and everybody had a wary, frightened look on his face. Only the day before, two dead bodies had lain the whole afternoon in the snow under my window. One was in a grey greatcoat, the other in a black shirt and both were barefoot. Passers-by either sidestepped them, or huddled round to stare. Some old women ran out of an alley, not stopping to pin up their hair, and shook their fists at the sky, shouting: 'Just you wait. They're coming. The Bolsheviks are coming.' My blood ran cold at the pitiful sight of these two men, murdered for no reason.

"I, too, started looking forward to the arrival of the Bolsheviks. They were coming closer and closer. The horizon lit up and a deep rumbling came as if from the very bowels of the earth. So with my lamp giving off a cosy, unsteady glow, there I was, entirely alone in my flat, my books strewn around me (for in all this chaos I still had the wild idea of studying for my thesis), crouching over my suitcase.

"Then, believe it or not, events flew straight into the flat, grabbed me by the hair and dragged me away, as though in some hellish nightmare. I'd come back that evening from a workers' clinic in the outskirts of the city where I was registrar in the women's surgery unit, and found a disconcertingly official-looking envelope wedged in the crack of the door. I opened it there and then on the landing, read what was on the page and sat down on the stairs. The note, typed in dark-blue ink, read in Ukrainian:

"'You are hereby summoned to report to the Army Medical Service within two hours to await further instructions.'

"Here was this brilliant army strewing corpses behind it all over the streets, Papa Petlyura and the pogroms—and I was to be a part of them, with a red cross on my sleeve.

"Crouched there on the landing I gave it no more than a moment's thought. I sprang up, went into my flat; and this is where my suitcase materialised. I quickly worked out a plan. I'd quit the flat with just a change of underwear and go to a medical assistant I knew in the outskirts, a gloomy looking man who was a Bolshevik sympathiser. I'd stay with him until Petlyura was driven out of the city.

"But what if he was never forced to leave? What if these long-awaited Bolsheviks were a myth? Where was the artillery? Silence. No, there was the booming sound—again.

"I angrily pulled out the shirt, and snapped shut the lock of the suitcase. I put my Browning and a spare cartridge clip in my pocket, threw on my coat with the red cross armband, cast a last desperate look round me, dimmed the lamp and felt my way out into the hall through the evening shadows. I switched on the light, picked up a balaclava and opened the door onto the landing.

"That very moment two figures with snub cavalry rifles on their shoulders stepped, coughing, into the hallway. One was wearing spurs, and both had tall sheepskin hats with jaunty blue ribbons dangling down to their cheeks.

"My heart pounded.

"'Are you Doc Yashvin?' the first cavalryman asked.

"'Yes, that's me,' I answered dully.

"'You're coming with us,' the first man said.

"'What's the meaning of this?' I asked, recovering some presence of mind.

"'Refusal to obey orders, that's what,' the first one said, rattling his spurs and giving me a knowing leer. 'Medics who don't want to be mobilised will have to answer to the law.'

"The hall light went out, the door creaked open, we went down the stairs and out onto the street.

"'Where are you taking me?' I asked, fingering the cool butt of the revolver in my trouser pocket.

"'To the First Cavalry Regiment,' answered the one with spurs.

"'Why?'

"'What do you mean why?' the other one asked. 'You're going to be our doctor.'

"'Who's the commander?'

"'Colonel Leshchenko,' the first one answered with a note of pride, his spurs jangling rhythmically at my left side.

"You stupid bastard,' I thought to myself, 'agonising over a suitcase—all because of your underwear. Why didn't you get out five minutes earlier?'

"By the time we reached the villa where the regiment was billeted the city was decked with a black frosty sky and the stars were coming out. Electric lights blazed through the ice patterns on the windowpanes. Spurs rattling, the men led me into a bare dusty room lit by a single bulb, dazzlingly bright under its cracked opal-glass shade. A rifle barrel stood in the corner and my gaze was drawn to the brown and red stains next to it, where an expensive tapestry hung in tatters. 'Blood,' I thought, and flinched inwardly.

"'Colonel,' the man with the spurs said quietly, 'we've brought the doctor.'

"'Is he a Yid?' barked a dry, hoarse voice from somewhere.

"From behind the needlework shepherds of the tapestry a door swung silently open and a man burst in. He was dressed in a magnificent greatcoat and boots with spurs. A Caucasian belt encrusted with silver decorations was drawn tight at his waist, and a Caucasian sabre that glinted in the electric light sat at his hip. He was wearing a red hat lined with fleece and braided with gold. His slanting eyes had a cruel and oddly feverish look to them, darting in their sockets like little black beads, and the clipped black moustache on his pockmarked face quivered with tension.

"'No, he's not,' the cavalryman said.

"Then the colonel leapt up towards me and looked me straight in the eye.

"'You're not a Yid,' he began in a heavy accent, speaking broken Ukrainian and Russian, 'but you're no better than one, and as soon as the fighting's over I'll have you court-martialled. You'll be shot for refusing to obey orders. Don't let him out of your sight!' he instructed the cavalryman, 'and bring him a horse.'

"I stood there and didn't say a word. The blood had no doubt drained from my face. Then the bad dream started up again. Somebody in the corner said in a wheedling voice: 'Have mercy, Colonel, sir.'

"I half-glimpsed a quivering beard and a soldier's torn greatcoat. Cavalrymen's faces pressed around it. 'On a deserter?' the now familiar hoarse voice rasped. 'Some chance, you scum. You scab.'

"I saw the colonel's mouth twitch as he drew an elegant black pistol from his holster and smashed its butt in the scruffy man's face. The man staggered sideways, choking up blood as he fell to his knees. He was weeping.

"And then the frost-white city was behind us, and a tree-lined road stretched along the bank of the frozen black waters of the mysterious Dnieper, and along this road in a long crocodile wended the First Cavalry Regiment. At the rear of the column the supply wagons creaked and groaned. Black bayonets nodded up and down and the peaks of frozen balaclavas made a forest in the air. I was astride a cold saddle, wriggling my toes in my boots from time to time when they started to throb, and breathing through the icy hole of my balaclava. I could feel the weight of my suitcase strapped to the pommel of the saddle pressing against my left thigh. My escort shadowed me silently. Inwardly, I was as frozen as my feet. Now and then I'd tilt my head and look up at the huge stars, and that deserter's howl would echo in my ears as though it had congealed there and would fade only with time. Colonel Leshchenko had ordered his soldiers to flog him with their rifle gun rods and they'd done it in that room.

"Far off in the dark it was silent now and to my utter dismay it seemed that the Bolsheviks had been driven back. My situation was desperate. We were heading for the Sloboda, the shanty town where we would take up position guarding the bridge over the Dnieper. If things were quiet and I was not immediately needed, Colonel Leshchenko would court-martial me. The thought of this petrified me and I gazed up at the stars, in an agony of worry. It was not hard to guess the outcome for someone who had failed to report for duty in times like these. A bizarre fate for a medical man.

"Two hours later everything had shifted again like a kaleidoscope. Now the dark road had disappeared. I was in a room with white plastered walls and a wooden table on which there was a lantern, a hunk of bread and an open medical bag. I had lost all feeling in my feet and I was warming them by the heat of the little purple flame flickering in a black iron stove. Cavalrymen came to see me every so often and I would treat them. Most had frostbite. They took off their boots, unwound the cloths wrapped around their feet and huddled down in front of the fire. The room stank of sour sweat, cheap tobacco and iodine.

"At other times my escort left me and I was alone. My first instinct was to make a break for it, and by the light of a guttering tallow candle I would open the door from time to time and peek out at the faces and bayonets on the stairway. The whole place was bristling with people: it would be hard to run away. I was in the centre of Petlyura's headquarters. I retreated from the door to the table, slumped down exhausted, put my head in my hands and listened. I'd noticed for some time a howl coming up from the room below mine every five minutes. I knew by then what it was: someone was being flogged with ramrods. The howl sometimes turned into a wild lion's roar and sometimes crept through the floorboards like gentle pleading or reproaches, as though someone was deep in intimate conversation with a friend. Sometimes it stopped abruptly as though severed by a knife.

"'What's all that about?' I asked one of Petlyura's men, who was stretching out his hand to the fire, shivering. His bare foot was propped on the stool and I was daubing white ointment onto the abscess on his blackened big toe.

"'The opposition has infiltrated the shanty town. Communists and Yids. The Colonel's interrogating them.'

"I said nothing. When he left I wrapped a balaclava round my head to block out the sound and spent a quarter of an hour like that, haunted by the vision of a pock-marked face under a gold-braided fur hat, until I was startled from my dozing by my escort's voice: 'The Colonel wants to see you.'

"I got up, unwound the balaclava while my escort looked on uncomprehendingly and followed him out. We went down to the floor below and I stepped into a white room. Here lit by a lantern I saw Colonel Leshchenko stripped to the waist and crouched over a stool, pressing a piece of bloodstained gauze to his chest. A young-faced soldier stood next to him not knowing what to do, and shifted his feet with a clank of his spurs.

"'The bastard,' the Colonel said, then turned to me. 'Well, doctor, bandage me up.' 'Get out,' he instructed the young soldier, who made his way to the door. The whole building was silent, then suddenly the window frame shuddered. The Colonel squinted over to the black window and so did I. 'Heavy guns,' I thought, and sighed convulsively as I asked:

"'What did this?'

"'A penknife,' retorted the Colonel angrily.

"'Who did it?'

"'None of your business,' he said contemptuously, and added: 'Oh doctor, things don't look good for you.'

"It suddenly dawned on me that someone who had been unable to take the torture had flown at him with the knife. That could be the only explanation.

"'Take away the gauze,' I said, and bent down to his hairy black chest. But before he was able to lift the blood-stained wad we heard footsteps outside the door, a scuffle, and then a coarse voice shouted:

"'Stop! Stop! Where the hell do you think ...'

"The door was flung open and a dishevelled woman burst in. Her face was tensed in such a way I thought she was jubilant: it was only much later I learned what strange forms extreme distress can take. A grey cuff tried to grab her by the headscarf but merely succeeded in pulling it off.

"'Back off, boy, back off,' the Colonel ordered his soldier, and the cuff drew back.

"The woman gazed at the half-naked Colonel and asked in a dry emotionless voice:

"'Why did you shoot my husband?'

"'Why? Because he had to be shot. That's why,' the Colonel answered and grimaced with pain. Under his fingers the pad of gauze was getting redder and redder. She gave such a scream of laughter that without stopping what I was doing I looked up at her eyes. I'd never seen such an expression.

"Suddenly she turned on me and said: 'And you, a doctor!' She poked the red cross on my sleeve, shook her head and continued: 'You bastard. Good God, you go to university, and then you side with swine like him. You even bandage them up. This man beats people in the face until they lose their minds. And you're bandaging him up!'

"Everything blurred before my eyes and I felt I was going to be sick. I felt as if the most terrible episode in my miserable doctor's life was just about to start. 'Are you talking to me?' I asked, and must have been trembling. 'Me? I ...'

"But she wasn't listening. She turned back to the Colonel and spat straight in his face. He jumped up and shouted for his men. When they ran in, he told them, furious, to flog her twenty-five times with a ramrod. She said nothing as they dragged her out of the room by the arms. The Colonel closed the door, slipped the lock, sat down on the stool and tossed away the gauze pad. Blood was seeping out of a small cut. He wiped the gob of spit from the right side of his moustache.

"'Twenty five for a woman?' I asked, in a voice I hardly recognised as my own.

"Anger flared in his eyes.

"'What?' he snapped. He gave me an ominous look. 'Now I see what a wimp they've given me for a doctor.'

"I must have fired one bullet into his mouth because I remember him swaying with blood running out of it; then in no time blood pouring down his chest and stomach, and his black eyes turning dim and clouding over as he slumped from the stool to the floor. As I pulled the trigger I remember being afraid that I might lose count and spend my last bullet, the seventh. 'That one will be for me,' I thought, relishing the smell of sulphur from the Browning.

"They'd barely tried the door before I flew to the window, smashed the glass and jumped. Fate was kind to me: I landed in a back yard and ran out past stacks of cut firewood into a dark street. They would almost certainly have caught me if I hadn't darted into a narrow gap between two walls and spent several hours holed up in a brick funnel that was like a cave. I could hear horsemen galloping past. The street led down to the Dnieper and for a long time they trotted up and down the riverbank, looking for me. Through the crack I could see one star, which for some reason I was convinced was Mars. I thought it had exploded. When the first shell fell, the star went out.

"That night was filled with explosions and rumblings. I stood silently in my brick burrow, thinking about my degree and wondering whether the woman had died under the onslaught of her flogging. At first light everything fell silent. I could endure the discomfort no longer and crept out of my funnel—both my feet were frostbitten. The shanty town was dead. Not a sound could be heard. The stars were growing dim. When I reached the bridge it was as though there had never been a Colonel Leshchenko or a First Cavalry Regiment. Only horse dung on a trampled track.

"I walked all the way back to Kiev alone, reaching the city in daylight. An unfamiliar-looking patrol wearing odd headgear with earflaps stopped me and asked for my papers. I said:

"'I'm Dr Yashvin. I'm on the run from Petlyura's men. Where are they?'

"'They retreated in the night. There's a Revolutionary Committee in Kiev now.'

"I could see one of the patrol looking at my face, and then he said with a rather sympathetic wave of his hand:

"'Off you go home, doctor.'

"So I did."

After a silence I asked Yashvin:

"Did he die? Did you kill him, or just wound him?"

Yashvin answered with his wry little smile:

"Oh, don't worry. I killed him. You can rely on my experience as a surgeon."

Meditsinsky Rabotnik, 1925; translated from the Russian by
Marjorie Farquharson and Iain Bamforth.

GOTTFRIED BENN
Three Expressionist Poems

Gottfried Benn, a dermatologist-venereologist in Berlin for much of his life, was notorious in his younger years for his volume of poems Morgue, *a chronicle of extremely "unpoetic" material: last insults to the bodies of autopsy cases. An air of technical radicalism marks Benn's work, partly in response to the First World War's equally radical annihilation of European values. Benn's vision of life is not unlike that of his French contemporary Céline (q.v.): his bedside manner is a kind of bierside sarcasm. The first two poems are clearly out to shock, offering a piece of reality "sectioned" from the body on the slab. "Night Café" parodies a doctor's use of objectification, eliding a personality in favour of a condition ("she's the appendicitis") or even a bed number ("Have you examined No. 24 yet?").*

CIRCULATION

The only molar of a whore
who'd died without next of kin
sported a gold filling.
(As if by tacit agreement her other teeth
had all decamped.)
It was swiped by the mortician's assistant
and pawned, so he could go dancing,
for, as he put it,
"only dust should go back to dust".

LOVELY CHILDHOOD

The mouth of a girl who'd been a long time
lying in the reeds had been gnawed at.
When her breastcage was opened, the gullet was full of holes.
Finally, in a canopy under the diaphragm
a nest of baby rats was discovered.
One little dam was dead.

The others fed on liver and kidneys,
nourished themselves on clotted blood and thereby spent
an altogether lovely childhood in the nest.
And death came quick and sweet for them too:
they were all tossed in the bucket.
Oh how their little muzzles squeaked!

NIGHT CAFÉ

824: The Love and Life of Women.
The cello knocks one back. The flute trills over
a three-beat belch: steak and chips.
The drum trips on to the thriller's last page.

Verdigris teeth, face pocked with acne
waves to Blepharitis.

Seborrhoea chats
to Mouth-agape-with-Tonsils,
"Faith Hope & Charity" around his neck.

Young Goitre has the hots for Saddlenose.
He stands her three half-pints.

Shaver's-rash buys carnations
to soften up Double-chin.

B-flat minor: sonata opus 35.
Eyes on stalks bark out:
Don't spray Chopin's blood around this joint
for these no-goods to ponce about in!
Hey, Gigi, cut it out!—

The door melts on the floor: a woman.
Desert dried-out. Caananite brown.
Pure as the driven. Hollowed-out. A scent comes too. Hardly a scent.
It's only a sweet tumescence of the air
curving past my brain.

A larded corpulence waddles in behind her.

"Kreislauf," "Schöne Jugend," "Nachtcafé," from *Morgue*, 1912.

ALAIN

On Medicine

Alain is the pseudonym of the philosopher Emile-Auguste Chartier; though not particularly well-known outside France, he had a major influence as a teacher on several generations of French thinkers and writers, including Simone Weil. The lion's share of his philosophical writings is occupied by his "propos," short comments which subject even the most apparently insignificant events and operations to comment and judgement. Written almost daily from 1906, Alain left more than 5000 of these articles: "On Medicine" appears in the best known collection of them, On Happiness, *published in 1922.*

"I know," says the scientist, "quite a few truths, and I've a fairly good idea of those I don't know. I know what a machine is and how it comes about that everything grinds to a halt when a screw works itself loose, all for want of a little maintenance, a few minutes' attention, and always because the expert wasn't consulted at the right time. That's why I set some of my time aside for looking after this elaborate machine I call my body. That's why at the least sign of chafing or creaking I put myself in the hands of an expert so that he can examine the part that is ill, or that appears to be ill. And thanks to his care, in accordance with the advice given by the celebrated Descartes, I am assured of extending my life, barring some act of fate, to the full life span of the instrument received from my ancestors. That is what I call wisdom." Those were his words, but he lived a drab life.

"I know," says the attentive reader, "quite a few false ideas that complicated human lives back in the age of credulity. These errors have taught me some important truths which our scientists are barely aware of. Imagination, according to the books I've read, is the sovereign of the human world. The great Descartes in his *Treatise on the Passions* admirably set out, for me, the reasons why. It is in the nature of things for a worry, even if I succeed in overcoming it, to upset my stomach; or a sudden shock to affect my heartbeat. And the mere idea of coming across a worm in my salad makes me feel quite genuinely sick. All these weird ideas, even though I may not credit them, grip me viscerally, in my very depths, and all of a sudden modify the flow of blood and body fluids: that is something my will could never do. Well, whatever invisible enemies I might swallow with every mouthful of food, they can't affect my heart or my stomach any more than the swings of my mood or the reveries of my imagination. First of all, I have to be as happy as I can be. Secondly, I must avoid the kind of thinking that broods over my own body: there is no more certain way of disturbing the vital functions. For aren't there stories to be found in the histories of all peoples of men who died because they believed themselves to be cursed? Isn't it the case that spells worked very well provided the person in question had been informed of the hexing? What can the best doctor do except put a spell on me? What good can be expected of his pills if just one from him is enough to change my heart rate? I really don't know what I can hope for from medicine, but I know very well what there is to fear in it. And indeed, whatever dysfunction I feel in this machine I call myself, it is my greater consolation to know that it is precisely my concern and worry that cause almost all the disorder, and that the best and surest remedy is therefore to have no more fear of a pain in the stomach or a sore back than I would of a corn on my foot. But what a splendid lesson in patience—the fact that a spot of calloused skin can cause just as much suffering!"

"Médecine," *Propos sur le bonheur*, 1922.

FRANZ KAFKA

A Country Doctor

Kafka's negative fairy tale is every doctor's nightmare: a night visit that goes wrong; though it's not a malpractice claim that threatens this country doctor. Just as in several of Bulgakov's stories, Kafka's doctor is pitted against elemental forces. He goes out into a traditional world of trust which has been infected by the language of suspicion: one false gesture when the diagnosis is out of the bag and he is stripped naked, briefly thrown into bed with his patient, and then chased out of the village to wander the universe. Thus do darlings become scapegoats.

I was at wits' end: an urgent journey lay ahead of me; a seriously ill patient was expecting me in a village ten miles off; a dense snowstorm filled the wide space between him and me; I had a trap, a light trap with big wheels, just right for our country roads; muffled in furs, instrument bag in my hand, I stood ready and waiting in the courtyard; but not a horse was to be had, not a horse. My own horse had died in the night, worn out by the grind of this icy winter; my servant girl was now running round the village to get the loan of a horse; but it was hopeless, I knew it, and there I stood aimlessly, more and more snowed under, more and more rooted to the spot. The girl appeared in the gateway, alone, and swung the lantern; but who lends his horse at a time like this for a journey like that? I strode across the courtyard again; I could find no alternative; upset, I absentmindedly gave a kick to the ramshackle door of the ancient unused pig-sty. It flew open and flapped back and forth on its hinges. Warmth and the stench of horses hit me in the face. Inside, a dim stable lantern was swinging on a rope. A man, squatting down in that low shed, showed his face, frank and blue-eyed. "Shall I harness up?" he asked, crawling out on all fours. I didn't know what to say and merely bent down to see what else was in the shed. The servant-girl was standing beside me. "You just don't know what you're going to stumble across in your own house," she said, and we both laughed. "Hey Brother, hey Sister!" the stable boy called, and one after the other two horses, huge beasts with strong flanks, legs flush against the torso, shapely heads bent like camels, only by the sheer force of their buttocking squeezed out through the keyhole which they completely filled. At once they were standing upright, high-legged, their bodies thick clouds of steam. "Give him a hand," I said, and the girl promptly hurried over to help the stable boy with the harnessing. Hardly was she beside him when he grabbed hold of her and pressed his face against hers. She screamed and fled back to me; the imprint of two rows of teeth stood out red on her cheek. "You beast, " I yelled in fury, "do you want a whipping?", but at the same time realised he was a stranger; that I didn't know where he'd come from, and that he was volunteering to help me out when everyone else had turned a deaf ear. As if he'd read my mind, he took no offence at my threat, and instead simply turned towards me once more while he worked with the horses. "Get in," he said, and sure enough: everything was ready. I'd never ridden, I thought, with such a splendid pair of horses, and I climbed in cheerfully. "But I'll take the reins," I said, "You don't know the way." "Sure," he said, "I'm not coming with you anyway, I'm staying with Rose." "No," shrieked Rose and rushed into the house, knowing in her bones that her fate was not to be run from; I heard the door-chain clatter as she put it up; I heard the key scrape in the lock; I also saw how she put the lights out, first in the corridor and then from room to room, to prevent herself from being found. "You're coming with me," I said to the stable boy, "or I'm not going at all, urgent though the journey is. I wouldn't even think of paying for it by handing you the girl." "Gee up!", he said; clapped his hands; the trap sprang off like a log in a rapid; I could just hear the door of my house split and burst under the stable boy's assault, and then I was blinded and deafened by a roaring noise that buffeted all my senses. But that too for only a moment, since already I was there as if my patient's yard had opened out just in front of my own front gate; the horses were standing quietly; it had stopped snowing; moonlight all around; my patient's parents hurrying out of the house; his sister behind them; they almost lifted me out of the carriage; I couldn't catch anything of their confused talking all at once; in the sick-room the air was hardly fit to breathe; the stove was unattended and smoking away; I thought to heave open the window; but first I wanted to see my patient. Gaunt, no fever, not cold, not warm, his eyes vacant, the young man hauled himself up shirtless from under his eiderdown, clasped my neck, and whispered in my ear: "Doctor, let me die." I glanced around; nobody had heard it; the parents stood stooped and silent, awaiting my verdict; the sister had set a chair for my doctor's bag. I opened the bag and rummaged through my instruments; the young man kept leaning out of bed to grasp me, and remind me of his plea; I picked up a pair of forceps, examined them in the candle light and put them down again. "Yes," I thought blasphemously, "in cases like this the gods help out, send the missing horse, couple it with another because of the urgency, and then to crown it all donate a stable boy—" And only then did I think of Rose again; what was I to do, how could I rescue her, how could I pull her out from under that stable boy, ten miles away from her, my carriage drawn by horses with a will of their own? These horses, they'd somehow slipped loose of the reins; pushed open the windows, I don't know how, from outside; each stuck a head in through a window and undeterred by the family's commotion, ogled the patient. "I'll go back straightaway," I thought, as if the horses were summoning me for the trip, but I allowed the sister, who thought me dazed by the heat, to relieve me of my fur coat. A glass of rum was laid out for me, the old man clapped me on the shoulder, his familiarity justified by the offer of his prized rum. I shook my head; in the immediate confines of the old man's thinking I felt ill; only for that reason did I decline the drink. The mother stood by the bed and enticed me towards it; I yielded and while one of the horses brayed loudly at the ceiling laid my head on the young man's chest which shuddered at the touch of my wet beard. It confirmed what I already knew: the young man was healthy, a few circulatory problems, saturated with coffee by the solicitous mother, but healthy and best bundled out of bed with a good shove. I'm no world reformer, so I let him lie. I'm the district doctor and do my duty as far as possible, to the brink of overdoing it. Badly paid, but I give what I have, ready to help the poor. I still have to look after Rose, and then the young man might be right and I too about to die. What was I doing here in this endless winter! My horse was dead, and nobody in the village would lend me another. I'd had to get my team out of the pig-sty; if they hadn't happened to be horses, I would have been travelling with pigs. That's how it was. And I nodded to the family. They knew nothing about it, and had they known, wouldn't have believed it. Writing prescriptions is easy, but coming to an understanding with people is hard. So, that should have been that, my visit ended, called out unnecessarily once again: I was used to it, the whole district tormented me with my night-bell; but that I'd had to surrender Rose this time too, the lovely girl who'd lived in my house for years without my hardly noticing—this sacrifice was too much, and I somehow had to make sense of it in my head by splitting hairs, so as not to fly straight for this family which, with the best will in the world, couldn't give Rose back to me. But when I shut my bag and beckoned for my fur coat, the family standing together, the father sniffing at the glass of rum in his hand, the mother in all likelihood disappointed by me—but what do people expect?—biting her lips, tears in her eyes, the sister brandishing a blood-drenched handkerchief, I was somehow ready to concede the young man might possibly be ill after all. I approached him, he greeted me with a smile as if I were bringing him the most nutritious broth—ah, now both the horses were neighing; the noise must surely have been ordered from above to facilitate my examination—and this time I discovered the young man was indeed ill. In his right side, near the hip, a wound had opened, as big as my palm. Rose-red, in variegated hues, dark at its base and lighter at the margins, slightly granulated, with irregular pockets of blood, open like a mine to the day above. So it looked from the distance. On closer inspection, there was an added complication. Who could look at that without whistling under his breath? Worms, as long and broad as my little finger, themselves rose-red and blood-spattered besides, squirmed up from their fastness within the wound towards the light, with small white heads and lots of tiny legs. Poor young man, there's no helping you. I've discovered your great wound; this blossom in your flank is dragging you down. The family was pleased, watched me busying myself; sister told mother, mother father, father a few guests who were coming in on tiptoe through the moonlight from the open door, arms outstretched to hold their balance. "Will you save me?" sobbed the young man in a whisper, quite blinded by the life in his wound. That's what people are like in this region, always expecting the impossible from the doctor. They've lost their old beliefs; the cleric sits at home and unpicks his vestments, one after another; but the doctor is expected to be able to do everything with his gentle surgeon's hand. Well, as they wish it: I didn't thrust my services on them; should they misuse me for sacred purposes, I wouldn't stand in their way with that either; how could I expect anything better, old country doctor that I am, robbed of my servant girl! And so they came, the family and the village elders, and stripped me of my clothes; a school choir with the teacher at its head stood in front of the house and sang these words to a tune that couldn't have been simpler:

> *Strip him naked, then he'll heal us*
> *And should he fail to, kill him quick!*
> *Only a mediciner, only a mediciner.*

Then my clothes were off and I looked at the people quietly, fingers in my beard and my head to one side. I was calm and collected and a match for the situation, and I stayed calm and collected, although it wouldn't help me, for now they took me by the head and feet and carried me to the bed. They laid me beside the wall, on the side of the wound. Then they all left the room; the door was shut; the singing ceased; clouds covered the moon; the bedding was warm around me; the horses' heads flickered like shadows in the window-frames. "Do you know," said a voice in my ear, "I don't have much confidence in you. After all, you were only blown in here, you didn't come on your own two feet. Instead of helping, you're cramping my death bed. I'd like best to scratch your eyes out." "You're right," I said, "it's a disgrace. But then I'm just a doctor. What was I to do? Believe me, it's none too easy for me either." "Am I supposed to accept your apology? Oh, I have to: I always have to put up with things. I came into the world with a fine wound; that's all I have to my name."

"Young friend," I said, "your error is this: you lack perspective. I've been in all the sick-rooms, far and wide, and I tell you: your wound isn't so bad. Done in a tight jam with two blows of the axe. Many a person offers up his side and hardly hears the axe in the forest, much less that it's nearing him." "Is that really so, or are you deluding me in my fever?" "That's the truth, take the word of honour of a medical officer." And he took it and lay quiet. But now it was time for me to think of saving myself. The horses were still standing faithfully in their place. Clothes, fur coat and bag were quickly grabbed; I didn't want to waste time dressing; if the horses raced home the way they'd come, I'd only be leaping in a manner of speaking from this bed into my own. Obediently a horse backed away from the window; I threw my bundle into the carriage; the fur coat flew too far and snagged on a hook only by the sleeve. Good enough. I swung myself on the horse. The reins loosely dragging, one horse barely coupled to the other, the carriage lurching behind, the fur coat straggling in the snow. "Gee up!" I said, but the going was not brisk; like old men we crept slowly through the snowy wastes; a long time resounding behind us the children's latest, if mistaken song:

> *Now be cheerful, all you patients,*
> *Doctor's laid in bed beside you!*

At this rate I'll never reach home; my flourishing practice has gone to the wall; my successor is robbing me, but in vain, since he can't replace me; the loathsome stable boy is running riot in my house; Rose is his victim; I can't bear to think about it. Naked, exposed to the frost of this most unfortunate of times, with an earthly carriage, unearthly horses, old vagrant that I am. My fur coat's hanging at the back of the carriage, but I can't reach it, and not one of my agile pack of patients lifts a finger. Betrayed! Betrayed! Respond to a false alarm on the night-bell—and it can't be made good, ever again.

"Ein Landarzt," *Ein Landarzt: Kleine Erzählungen*, 1919.

GEORGES DUHAMEL

The Machine Inside Us

With the First World War began a new era in history: not just the age of the machine but the age of machine rhythm. Time-and-motion studies, F.W. Taylor's theories of "scientific management," and the bun-on-the-run concept that would eventually become McDonald's all come from the early years of the twentieth-century. In this impassioned essay, the surgeon Georges Duhamel, conscripted to an ambulant unit of the French 1st Army Corps for much of the war, deplores the deadening effects of mechanization on what he calls the "animal passion" of sympathy, medicine's oldest ally. It was to take more than 80 years before the advent of the personal computer made it possible to extend Taylorization into the heart of medical practice itself.

At the beginning of 1917, I was posted as head of a surgical team to one of those units that are barbarously referred to as *autochirs*, which, in good French, stands for "ambulances chirurgicales automobiles" (motorized surgical ambulances).

For two years, in other words until the end of the war, I shared the life of this ambulant unit and, day in day out, noted the curious effects of the industrialization of the war. This "autochir" was under the command of a remarkable surgeon, a good-hearted man who is one of my dearest friends. Most of my companions were excellent practitioners, open-minded and generous. Several of them still enjoy a special place in my affections. The historical evolution that we followed wasn't our own doing, it was the doing of an entire epoch—the perfect expression of the method and triumph of technique. I'd like to give you an impressionistic account of it, giving due recognition to its great benefits but also teasing out its deep meaning for the world's future.

The autochirs were not particularly nimble units. They have been compared, not without reason, to heavy artillery. Indeed, they were the heavy ambulances of the mobile health service units. Originally set up to bring the equipment needed for immaculate surgery close to the battlefields, they became stationary in the trench war, when their facilities underwent constant expansion. Towards the end of the conflict, they possessed an excellent and fully equipped surgical arsenal. They could transport not only this arsenal but even the equipment required for sterilizing the instruments and dressings, electricity generators, laboratories, a radiographic service, tents and barracks, an entire world to itself. Motorized ambulances? They were motorized, it is true: when we moved position, it was in a convoy of twenty-two or twenty-three lorries, without counting the vans and buses for the staff. On the road, that made us look for all the world like an enormous itinerant enterprise, a travelling circus. It was unusual for us, then, to shift position. Barely arrived at the next worksite, the circus unpacked its luggage. It retained its itinerant appearance, while taking on its true nature—its industrial nature. The circus became a factory. Think of the big modern fairgrounds: they are nothing but a concatenation of humming dynamos, stamping motors, electric fulgurations, hissing vapour, howling sirens, grinding gears, gliding belts, spatterings of grease. Pleasure and pain are mechanized in almost the same way. This comparison between ambulance and village fair returns in all my war books. And how could I rid myself of it?

Technical improvement and material enrichment go together. The autochir had four regular teams and, on heavy days, could call on back-up teams. We decided fairly quickly that getting all the teams to work simultaneously until they were completely exhausted was the wrong method, out of step with an industrial economy. We adopted the principle of shift-work, which is applied in the mines and in some branches of the metallurgical industry where work has to continue without interruption. The surgical manpower of the autochir was divided into two sections. And to circumvent the drawbacks of working constantly in the day or at night, the 24-hour cycle itself was divided into three periods of eight hours. One team would therefore work from midday to eight in the evening, then pause from eight until four in the morning before returning to duty from four until midday, and would finally be off-duty from midday until eight in the evening. I wouldn't really say that this roster gave us the chance to work in broad daylight as well as under artificial light since, in this extraordinary factory, electric lighting almost always came to heaven's help.

A strict division of work was imposed, little by little. To produce his best work, the surgeon was unable to carry out the triage and preparation of the wounded himself. Two teams, specialized in this task, worked in eight-hourly relays in a barrack adjoining the operating block; they categorized the wounded, eliminating those who were beyond help, shaving, washing and disinfecting the others and sending them, equipped with a record and a provisional diagnosis, to the radiology department. The radiologists themselves formed two teams and worked, like the others, in eight-hour shifts. They examined the wounded, outlined the X-rays or even took the prints and drafted a report. Kitted out with this dossier, the wounded soldier was brought to the operating room. I've already given an account in my war books of how this room looked, what was done there and what we saw, and I won't repeat myself. I simply wish to mention some technical rules that were applied. Often the surgeon worked at two tables. While he operated at one table with his assistant and the male surgical nurses, a second wounded patient was attached to the other table and given the first lungful of anaesthetic. Moving from one table to the other, the surgeon would change gloves, scrub his hands, have a look at the X-rays and dossier. When things were hectic, he hardly had any time to question the wounded soldier just brought in. Sometimes he relied on the examination conducted by the preparatory teams. It sometimes happened that, when the shifts changed, a man with multiple critical wounds requiring five or six separate operations had only undergone one or two of them. In exceptional cases, the patient was handed over to the relief team, especially when the planned operations might require an hour or more of surgery and upset the normal working rhythm.

Once his shift had ended, the surgeon had eight hours, sometimes during the day, sometimes at night, sometimes in between. Given the extreme division of work, the surgeon was not able to put dressings on those who had to remain in the recovery room because of their injuries. Dressing teams made up of doctors and nurses worked all day long in the barracks and reported any unusual findings to the surgeon. In his eight-hour rest period, the surgeon first took the time to make a careful visit.

He examined the wounded men he had operated upon, studied their temperature chart, checked their drains and equipment, and discussed all kinds of matters with the physicians in the dressing teams. If an additional or repeat operation was necessary, it had to take place during his off-duty period. He would then have the patient wheeled into an empty operating room and send for his assisting personnel. Once all these tasks had been completed, all that was left for the surgeon to do, while waiting to start work again, was to get something to eat, catch some rest and spruce himself up. Twenty minutes before the hour, he would be wakened and prepare to assume his place again in the round, like an athlete in a relay race. During his eight hours on the job, the surgeon would sometimes ask for his mask to be taken off and drink copious amounts of water, the temperature in the room being similar to that of a bakehouse or boiler room.

Regulated and mechanized in this way, work could be continued for weeks and months. Set up in the battle sectors, the autochir was like a high-output machine. It *was* a factory, and to borrow the language used by modern economists, a factory for rationalized work. I repeat: in this organization we followed the general rhythm of an industrial war. But I should immediately say that we did a lot of very fine work. In 1915, had an inspector learned that teams could eat and sleep in the middle of an offensive he would have cried blue murder, called for sanctions, put everyone on the spot. In 1918, the health service allowed each surgical unit to establish its own working pattern and measured not just throughput but staying power too. After four years, we knew that war was both a trial of force and a test of character. So we did a lot of excellent work. Our instrumentation left almost nothing to be desired. Every day our methods gained in daring and certainty. We operated on more wounded men, and we operated better than before.

And nevertheless, whenever I turn back to this phase of the war I understand immediately how I acquired such clarity about the excesses of the future world.

The climate of mechanization is not the climate of sympathy. I'll quote a few lines from a diary in which I wrote down my impressions. "Naked beneath my whites, at the moment of entering that dazzling stove, I sometimes felt a bit like those athletes who give their all in endurance sports. But this image is still too human, and it is tending to vanish. A machine, a machine without soul, heated to the right temperature, calibrated to run for ages and do lots of work. Brotherly love, fond help, communion in suffering ... Ah! how far we were from all that. I operated, ever more efficiently, ever more effectively, on men who remained unknown to me, men whose nationality I didn't always know."

We will say nothing about tiredness and callousness. This rigid mechanical order just had to relent for a minute, and I felt myself becoming, once again, a man of flesh among men of flesh. Sympathy regained its dominion. But soon I heard steam whistling, dynamos vibrating, electricity sparking and crackling, and, right away, the automaton expelled the humanist.

It was my lot to live this terrible, deceiving experience at a time when I enjoyed so much friendship, when most of my companions—top surgeons, decent men—inspired me, through their character and conduct, with admiration and gratitude. To see so many magnificent human virtues dispensed so unstintingly could only make me anticipate the future triumph of automatism with even more horror and foreboding.

At the beginning of our talk, I mentioned, paraphrasing J. R. Bloch, "the machine which is inside us". Granted, the machine is within us, automatism is within us, inside our soul and inside our body. We have made the automaton not in our image, but in the image of a part of ourselves. And this is the nature of the game: the creature remakes us, moulds us again, remodels us in its turn and, this time, in its image. The contagion of the machine is the greatest peril awaiting the future. That is what I understood in the last years of the war, years during which I provided, on a daily basis, intelligent, exact, effective care to the wounded, though the lack of opportunity prevented me from always giving them the indefinably priceless: a scrap of myself, a spark of my own life.

Man has handed in his notice; now human impoverishment and reduction are what we ought to fear and forestall.

Excerpt from "L'humaniste et l'automate," 1933.

BERTOLT BRECHT

A Worker's Speech to a Doctor

Bert Brecht from Augsburg thought of studying medicine before he went on to become Germany's most famous—and famously committed—poet, balladeer and dramatist. Some of his poems in communist party support mode are so stripped of aesthetic effect as to make them about as interesting as real propaganda: doctors are targeted in several as class enemies. Cultures can still be found on apartment walls, though these days a carpet would surely cost less than 5000 consultations and workers are better paid all round. But the force of Brecht's charge remains: why have doctors not proved to be, as the German pathologist Virchow put it, "the natural allies of the poor"?

We know what makes us ill.
When we're ill word says
You're the one to make us well.

For ten years, so we hear
You learned how to heal in elegant schools
Built at the people's expense
And to get your knowledge
Dispensed a fortune.
That means you can make us well.

Can you make us well?

When we visit you
Our clothes are ripped and torn
And you listen all over our naked body.
As to the cause of our illness
A glance at our rags would be more
Revealing. One and the same cause wears out
Our bodies and our clothes.

The pain in our shoulder comes
You say, from the damp; and this is also the cause
Of the patch on the apartment wall.
So tell us then:
Where does the damp come from?

Too much work and too little food
Make us weak and scrawny.
Your prescription says:
Put on more weight.
You might as well tell a fish
Go climb a tree.

How much time can you give us?
We see: one carpet in your flat costs
The fees you take from
Five thousand consultations.

You'll no doubt protest
Your innocence. The damp patch
On the wall of our apartments
Tells the same story.

"Rede eines Arbeiters an einen Arzt,"
Spätere Gedichte und Satiren aus Svendborg, 1936–38.

WILLIAM CARLOS WILLIAMS
Jean Beicke

William Carlos Williams is better known as a poet, but he wrote thirteen laconic "doctor stories," all of which comment, sometimes with great insight, on the nature of medical practice. This harsh story set during the Depression relates a sequence of events in which a doctor fails to diagnose meningitis—a "clear miss"—and a patient dies. The heartlessness of the narrator's stance masks his sentiment. It also raises a subtle challenge: the reader is being asked to retain faith in the narrator's authority even though he admits to incompetence, in fact precisely because he does—for this story reveals how much medical authority, in the mid-twentieth century, could rely not just on rhetoric and status, but also on honesty. I doubt this is true now.

During a time like this, they kid a lot among the doctors and nurses on the obstetrical floor because of the rushing business in new babies that's pretty nearly always going on up there. It's the Depression, they say, nobody has any money so they stay home nights. But one bad result of this is that in the children's ward, another floor up, you see a lot of unwanted children.

The parents get them into the place under all sorts of pretexts. For instance, we have two premature brats, Navarro and Cryschka, one a boy and one a girl; the mother died when Cryschka was born, I think we got them within a few days of each other, one weighing four pounds and one a few ounces more. They dropped down below four pounds before we got them going but there they are; we had a lot of fun betting on their daily gains in weight but we still have them. They're in pretty good shape though now. Most of the kids that are left that way get along swell. The nurses grow attached to them and get a real thrill when they begin to pick up. It's great to see. And the parents sometimes don't even come to visit them, afraid we'll grab them and make them take the kids out, I suppose.

A funny one is a little Hungarian Gypsy girl that's been up there for the past month. She was about eight weeks old maybe when they brought her in with something on her lower lip that looked like a chancre. Everyone was interested but the Wasserman was negative. It turned out finally to be nothing but a peculiarly situated birthmark. But that kid is still there too. Nobody can find the parents. Maybe they'll turn up some day.

Even when we do get rid of them, they often come back in a week or so—sometimes in terrible condition, full of impetigo, down in weight—everything we'd done for them to do over again. I think it's deliberate neglect in most cases. That's what happened to this little Gypsy. The nurse was funny after the mother had left the second time. I couldn't speak to her, she said. I just couldn't say a word I was so mad. I wanted to slap her.

We had a couple of Irish girls a while back named Cowley. One was a red head with beautiful wavy hair and the other a straight haired blonde. They really were good looking and not infants at all. I should say they must have been two and three years old approximately. I can't imagine how the parents could have abandoned them. But they did. I think they were habitual drunkards and may have had to beat it besides on short notice. No fault of theirs maybe.

But all these are, after all, not the kind of kids I have in mind. The ones I mean are those they bring in stinking dirty, and I mean stinking. The poor brats are almost dead sometimes, just living skeletons, almost, wrapped in rags, their heads caked with dirt, their eyes stuck together with pus and their legs all excoriated from the dirty diapers no one has had the interest to take off them regularly. One poor little pot we have now with a thin purplish skin and big veins standing out all over its head had a big sore place in the fold of its neck under the chin. The nurse told me that when she started to undress it it had on a shirt with a neckband that rubbed right into that place. Just dirt. The mother gave a story of having had it in some sort of home in Paterson. We couldn't get it straight. We never try. What the hell? We take 'em and try to make something out of them.

Sometimes, you'd be surprised, some doctor has given the parents a ride before they bring the child to the clinic. You wouldn't believe it.

They clean 'em out, maybe for twenty-five dollars—they maybe had to borrow—and then tell 'em to move on. It happens. Men we all know too. Pretty bad. But what can you do?

And sometimes the kids are not only dirty and neglected but sick, ready to die. You ought to see those nurses work. You'd think it was the brat of their best friend. They handle those kids as if they were worth a million dollars. Not that some nurses aren't better than others but in general they break their hearts over those kids, many times, when I, for one, wish they'd never get well.

I often kid the girls. Why not? I look at some miserable specimens they've dolled up for me when I make the rounds in the morning and I tell them: Give it an enema, maybe it will get well and grow up into a cheap prostitute or something. The country needs you, brat. I once proposed that we have a mock wedding between a born garbage hustler we'd saved and a little female with a fresh mug on her that would make anybody smile.

Poor kids! You really wonder sometimes if medicine isn't all wrong to try to do anything for them at all. You actually want to see them pass out, especially when they're deformed or—they're awful sometimes. Every one has rickets in an advanced form, scurvy too, flat chests, spindly arms and legs. They come in with pneumonia, a temperature of a hundred and six, maybe, and before you can do a thing, they're dead.

This little Jean Beicke was like that. She was about the worst you'd expect to find anywhere. Eleven months old. Lying on the examining table with a blanket half way up her body, stripped, lying there, you'd think it a five months baby, just about that long. But when the nurse took the blanket away, her legs kept on going for a good eight inches longer. I couldn't get used to it. I covered her up and asked two of the men to guess how long she was. Both guessed at least half a foot too short. One thing that helped the illusion besides her small face was her arms. They came about to her hips. I don't know what made that. They should come down to her thighs, you know.

She was just skin and bones but her eyes were good and she looked straight at you. Only if you touched her anywhere, she started to whine and then cry with a shrieking, distressing sort of cry that no one wanted to hear. We handled her as gently as we knew how but she had to cry just the same.

She was one of the damnedest looking kids I've ever seen. Her head was all up in front and flat behind, I suppose from lying on the back of her head so long the weight of it and the softness of the bones from the rickets had just flattened it out and pushed it up forward. And her legs and arms seemed loose on her like the arms and legs of some cheap dolls. You could bend her feet up on her shins absolutely flat—but there was no real deformity, just all loosened up. Nobody was with her when I saw her though her mother had brought her in.

It was about ten in the evening, the interne had asked me to see her because she had a stiff neck, and how! and there was some thought of meningitis—perhaps infantile paralysis. Anyhow, they didn't want her to go through the night without at least a lumbar puncture if she needed it. She had a fierce cough and a fairly high fever. I made it out to be a case of broncho-pneumonia with meningismus but no true involvement of the central nervous system. Besides she had inflamed ear drums.

I wanted to incise the drums, especially the left, and would have done it only the night superintendent came along just then and made me call the ear man on service. You know. She also looked to see if we had an operative release from the parents. There was. So I went home, the ear man came in a while later and opened the ears—a little bloody serum from both sides and that was that.

Next day we did a lumbar puncture, tapped the spine that is, and found clear fluid with a few lymphocytes in it, nothing diagnostic. The X-ray of the chest clinched the diagnosis of broncho-pneumonia, there was an extensive involvement. She was pretty sick. We all expected her to die from exhaustion before she'd gone very far.

I had to laugh every time I looked at the brat after that, she was such a funny looking one but one thing that kept her from being a total loss was that she did eat. Boy! how that kid could eat! As sick as she was she took her grub right on time every three hours, a big eight ounce bottle of whole milk and digested it perfectly. In this depression you got to be such a hungry baby, I heard the nurse say to her once. It's a sign of intelligence, I told her. But anyway, we all got to be crazy about Jean. She'd just lie there and eat and sleep. Or she'd lie and look straight in front of her by the hour. Her eyes were blue, a pale sort of blue. But if you went to touch her, she'd begin to scream. We just didn't, that's all, unless we absolutely had to. And she began to gain in weight. Can you imagine that? I suppose she had been so terribly run down that food, real food, was an entirely new experience to her. Anyway she took her food and gained on it though her temperature continued to run steadily around between a hundred and three and a hundred and four for the first eight or ten days. We were surprised.

When we were expecting her to begin to show improvement, however, she didn't. We did another lumbar puncture and found fewer cells. That was fine and the second X-ray of the chest showed it somewhat improved also. That wasn't so good though, because the temperature still kept up and we had no way to account for it. I looked at the ears again and thought they ought to be opened once more. The ear man disagreed but I kept after him and next day he did it to please me. He didn't get anything but a drop of serum on either side.

Well, Jean didn't get well. We did everything we knew how to do except the right thing. She carried on for another two—no I think it was three—weeks longer. A couple of times her temperature shot up to a hundred and eight. Of course we knew then it was the end. We went over her six or eight times, three or four of us, one after the other, and nobody thought to take an X-ray of the mastoid regions. It was dumb if you want to say it, but there wasn't a sign of anything but the history of the case to point to it. The ears had been opened early, they had been watched carefully, there was no discharge to speak of at any time and from the external examination, the mastoid processes showed no change from the normal. But that's what she died of, acute purulent mastoiditis of the left side, going on to involvement of the left lateral sinus and finally the meninges. We might, however, have taken a culture of the pus when the ear was first opened and I shall always, after this, in suspicious cases. I have been told since that if you get a virulent bug like the streptococcus mucosus capsulatus it's wise at least to go in behind the ear for drainage if the temperature keeps up. Anyhow she died.

I went in when she was just lying there gasping. Somehow or other, I hated to see that kid go. Everybody felt rotten. She was such a scrawny, misshapen, worthless piece of humanity that I had said many times that somebody ought to chuck her in the garbage chute—but after a month watching her suck up her milk and thrive on it—and to see those alert blue eyes in that face—well, it wasn't pleasant. Her mother was sitting by the bed crying quietly when I came in, the morning of the last day. She was a young woman, didn't look more than a girl, she just sat there looking at the child and crying without a sound.

I expected her to begin to ask me questions with that look on her face all doctors hate—but she didn't. I put my hand on her shoulder and told her we had done everything we knew how to do for Jean but that we really didn't know what, finally, was killing her. The woman didn't make any sign of hearing me. Just sat there looking in between the bars of the crib. So after a moment watching the poor kid beside her, I turned to the infant in the next crib to go on with my rounds. There was an older woman there looking in at that baby also—no better off than Jean, surely. I spoke to her, thinking she was the mother of this one, but she wasn't.

Before I could say anything, she told me she was the older sister of Jean's mother and that she knew that Jean was dying and that it was a good thing. That gave me an idea—I hated to talk to Jean's mother herself—so I beckoned the woman to come out into the hall with me.

I'm glad she's going to die, she said. She's got two others home, older, and her husband has run off with another woman. It's better off dead—never was any good anyway. You know her husband came down from Canada about a year and a half ago. She seen him and asked him to come back and live with her and the children. He come back just long enough to get her pregnant with this one then he left her again and went back to the other woman. And I suppose knowing she was pregnant, and suffering, and having no money and nowhere to get it, she was worrying and this one never was formed right. I seen it as soon as it was born. I guess the condition she was in was the cause. She's got enough to worry about now without this one. The husband's gone to Canada again and we can't get a thing out of him. I been keeping them, but we can't do much more. She'd work if she could find anything but what can you do with three kids in times like this? She's got a boy nine years old but her mother-in-law sneaked it away from her and now he's with his father in Canada. She worries about him too, but that don't do no good.

Listen, I said, I want to ask you something. Do you think she'd let us do an autopsy on Jean if she dies? I hate to speak to her of such a thing now but to tell you the truth, we've worked hard on that poor child and we don't exactly know what is the trouble. We know that she's had pneumonia but that's been getting well. Would you take it up with her for me, if—of course—she dies.

Oh, she's gonna die all right, said the woman. Sure, I will. If you can learn anything, it's only right. I'll see that you get the chance. She won't make any kick, I'll tell her.

Thanks, I said.

The infant died about five in the afternoon. The pathologist was dog-tired from a lot of extra work he'd had to do due to the absence of his assistant on her vacation so he put off the autopsy till next morning. They packed the body in ice in one of the service hoppers. It worked perfectly.

Next morning they did the postmortem. I couldn't get the nurse to go down to it. I may be a sap, she said, but I can't do it, that's all. I can't. Not when I've taken care of them. I feel as if they're my own.

I was amazed to see how completely the lungs had cleared up. They were almost normal except for a very small patch of residual pneumonia here and there which really amounted to nothing. Chest and abdomen were in excellent shape, otherwise, throughout—not a thing aside from the negligible pneumonia. Then he opened the head.

It seemed to me the poor kid's convolutions were unusually well developed. I kept thinking it's incredible that that complicated mechanism of the brain has come into being just for this. I never can quite get used to an autopsy.

The first evidence of the real trouble—for there had been no gross evidence of meningitis—was when the pathologist took the brain in his hand and made the long steady cut which opened up the left lateral ventricle. There was just a faint color of pus on the bulb of the choroid plexus there. Then the diagnosis all cleared up quickly. The left lateral sinus was completely thrombosed and on going into the left temporal bone from the inside the mastoid process was all broken down.

I called up the ear man and he came down at once. A clear miss, he said. I think if we'd gone in there earlier, we'd have saved her.

For what? said I. Vote the straight Communist ticket.

Would it make us any dumber? said the ear man.

"Jean Beicke," from *The Doctor Stories*, 1938.

ALFRED DÖBLIN

My Double

Alfred Döblin is perhaps the most distinguished doctor-writer of the twentieth-century. This amusing reflexive portrait, in which the writer fawns on the doctor, and the doctor ignores the writer, was written in the period before Döblin's great montage novel Berlin Alexanderplatz *(1929), a brilliantly sympathetic portrait of an ex-convict's attempt, in a world of brute process, to lead a decent life. His first novels were, as the neurologist points out (at the time Döblin was working in the poor eastern suburbs of Berlin), historical epics and dystopian fantasies: one of them,* Mountains, Seas and Giants *(1924), in which industrial scientists and researchers have arrogated the right to rule society, has been claimed as a forerunner of Ridley Scott's influential film* Bladerunner.

THE NEUROLOGIST DÖBLIN TALKS ABOUT
THE WRITER DÖBLIN

Speaking as a doctor, I have to confess to only the sketchiest knowledge of the writer who bears my name. To be perfectly honest, I really don't know him at all. I work in a medium-sized (not very big at all), insurance-scheme practice in the east of Berlin; I'm a neurologist and that keeps me pretty busy for most of the day. My literary leanings are not well developed; books bore me stiff and that goes particularly for books by the man who, as you say, bears my name. Once or twice at friends' houses his books have come into my hands, but what I've glimpsed in them is completely alien to me and leaves me absolutely cold. This gentleman appears to have a wild imagination; there I draw a blank. My income doesn't allow me to travel to either India or China. I therefore have no way of verifying what he writes. Besides, I prefer to read that kind of thing in the original, I mean as straight travel literature: that's something I happen to enjoy reading very much. I can't get anywhere at all either with the style adopted by the gentleman, I mean the author who has the same name as I do. It's just too complicated for me; you can't expect people who are tired out by their job to struggle through something like that out of their own free will. Allow me in passing to make a general comment which sounds somewhat political or ethical. I actually know this author's occasional statements better than his books: I see them in the newspaper which I do of course read. I have to say though, that the man doesn't shed much light, politically or generally. If I ever had any urge to meet him it isn't stronger after these statements. Sometimes I get the impression that he is decidedly leftwing, even far left, left to the power of two perhaps, and then he comes out with phrases which are either ill-considered, which for a man of his age is quite inadmissible, or he's pretending to be above politics, having a little poetic snigger. So: you were the person, dear editor, who asked for my opinion about the author, the man with the red rose: the coincidence of us having the same name gave you the idea, for I personally would never have had dealings with him, as few as with other young authors, and I'll repeat myself briefly: the gentleman is almost entirely unknown to me; he doesn't interest me; I'm neither a relation nor an in-law, and I'm ready to accept his judgement regarding myself since, as you've told me, you intend to ask him about me. His ostensibly facetious reproaches will leave me unmoved.

THE WRITER DÖBLIN TALKS ABOUT
THE NEUROLOGIST DÖBLIN

I'm very grateful to you, dear editor, although at Easter, as you can imagine, I have rather a lot to put up with, questionnaires and the like, for having sent this remarkable query my way and in many respects added to my store of knowledge. At the moment I'm busy with a Berlin novel, an epic work in everyday language which deals with the east of Berlin, the area around the Alexanderplatz and the Rosenthaler Gate. So your asking me to give my opinion on the neurologist with my name was a nod in the right direction. Perhaps I can get some extra material out of it, I thought, not just the stuff with the Salvation Army, at the slaughterhouse, from the criminal records. I drove there and want to tell you what I saw. The gentleman makes a lively and not too bad impression. I attended his consultation and sat in the waiting room. A waiting room like that is the strangest place you can imagine. And when I introduced myself to the gentleman and we exchanged pleasantries—God knows, we come from areas that could hardly be less alike—he told me lots which I duly, with his permission, entered in my notebook. These insurance-scheme doctors are not to be envied. I saw the oddly compelling work with which he is occupied, and some of his patients have very odd diseases. I'm sure he's by no means a unique specimen in his line of business, but I was very taken with the way he worked away, quite anonymously. He is my exact opposite, it struck me in passing, the objective way he handles, speaks, attends to things; while I'm a solo dancer, a prima donna, as my publisher once said, a grey soldier in a silent army. I'm sure I failed to make any great impression on my namesake. A few times I got quite hot under the collar when he gave me one of those psychotherapeutic stares. I have all kinds of quirks, probably complexes, and the expert probably got a whiff of them. Please don't be angry with me when I admit that for this reason I failed to extend my knowledge or broaden our acquaintance very much with the man who bears my name. To be quite honest I didn't feel entirely well on the chair across from him; far too many unpleasant things come to mind. Nevertheless I retain a very clear memory of the thin, not very tall man with the doctor's glasses and would be really delighted to hear, if you wouldn't mind telling me, what this anon, for whom I was certainly not an author but merely a man, told you about me.

Döblin über Döblin, 1927.

JULES ROMAINS

The Triumph of Medicine

Knock, a great theatrical success in Paris before the war, was always thought to be a parable on the rise of the great dictators. Medicine simply wasn't therapeutically effective enough in the 1930s to explain the anxiety-generating power of Knock, personified for an entire generation by the debonair actor Louis Jouvet. In the climactic scene from Act III, Knock explains to his predecessor, the pleasant old bumbler Dr Parpalaid, how, in the space of three months, he has gone about stunning the people of the imaginary borough of Saint-Maurice with the evidence of scientific things unseen. Céline (see Doctor in the Zone*) is known to have participated in public health measures in Brittany at this time, singing the refrain "va t'en, microbe!" to groups of presumably startled schoolchildren.*

DR PARPALAID: I hope you won't be accusing me now of having "fleeced" you?

KNOCK: It was certainly the intention, my dear colleague.

DR PARPALAID: You can't deny I almost gifted it to you, and the practice was worth a bit after all.

KNOCK: Oh, you could have stayed. We wouldn't have cramped each other's style. Did Monsieur Mousquet tell you about our initial figures?

DR PARPALAID: He mentioned them in passing.

KNOCK [*rummaging in his case*]: On a confidential basis, I can show you some of my charts. Bear in mind our conversation of three months ago when you look at them. First of all: consultations. This curve displays the weekly figures. As a starting point it takes your own figure which I don't recall, but which I set at approximately 5.

DR PARPALAID: Five consultations a week! Let's say at least twice that, my dear colleague.

KNOCK: As you wish. Here are my figures. Naturally I haven't included the free Monday consultations. Mid-October: 37. End of October: 90. End of November: 128. End of December: I haven't yet made the count, but we're in excess of 150. Now lack of time is going to oblige me to sacrifice the consultation curve to the treatment curve. In itself the consultation is only of partial interest: it's a rather primitive art, like weeding. But treatment: that's a fine art, horticulture ...

DR PARPALAID: Forgive me, dear colleague, but are your figures absolutely watertight?

KNOCK: Absolutely.

DR PARPALAID: You mean to tell me that in one week, in the circumscription of Saint-Maurice, one hundred and fifty people took the trouble to leave their sitting rooms to come and queue up at the doctor's surgery and then paid for this pleasure? That they left home without being forced to or under duress of any kind?

KNOCK: Neither the gendarmes nor the army.

DR PARPALAID: It defies understanding.

KNOCK: To move on now to the treatment curve. This was the situation you left me at the beginning of October: patients undergoing regular domiciliary treatment: 0. That's right isn't it? [*Parpalaid protests feebly*] End of October: 32. End of November: 121. End of December ... the figure will be somewhere between 245 and 250.

DR PARPALAID: I get the impression you're taking me for a ride.

KNOCK: I don't see anything excessive in these figures. Don't forget that there are 2853 households in the district, of which 1502 have an annual income of over 12 000 francs.

DR PARPALAID: What is all this about incomes?

KNOCK [*moving over to the washbasin*]: In all good conscience you can't lumber a family making less than 12,000 francs with the costs of a chronic illness. That would be exploitation. A uniform treatment for the other patients is unrealistic too. I have four treatment scales. The basic, for families earning beween 12,000 and 20,000 francs, comprises only one visit a week, and about 50 francs of pharmaceutical expenses a month. At the top end of the scale, the deluxe treatment, for incomes in excess of 50,000 francs, includes a minimum of four visits a week, and expenses of 300 hundred francs every month for various items: X-rays, radium, electric massage, blood tests, routine medication, et cetera …

DR PARPALAID: But how do you know your patients' incomes?

KNOCK [*he starts scrubbing his hands meticulously*]: Not through the inland revenue, that's for sure! And just as well for me. I have 1,502 households with incomes above 12,000; the tax inspector has 17. The highest income on his list is 20,000. The highest on mine is 120,000. Not one of our figures coincides. But then he's working for the state.

DR PARPALAID: And where do you get your information?

KNOCK [*smiling*]: I have my sources. It's a colossal task. I spent almost the whole month of October on it. And I'm constantly revising my figure. Look at this: it's pretty isn't it?

DR PARPALAID: It looks like a map of the district. But what do these red dots signify?

KNOCK: It is a map of medical penetration of the district. Each red dot shows where I have a regular patient. A month ago you would have seen an enormous grey patch here: the Chabrières bulge.

DR PARPALAID: The what?

KNOCK: Yes, that's the name of the hamlet in the middle. For the last few weeks I've concentrated most of my efforts in this area. The patch hasn't quite disappeared, but it has been dispersed. You hardly notice it, do you?

[*Silence*]

DR PARPALAID: Even if I wanted to hide my stupefaction from you, dear colleague, I couldn't. I don't doubt your results for a moment: I've seen confirming evidence from several sides. You're an amazing chap. Others might hesitate telling you so to your face, but they'd think it. Otherwise they wouldn't be doctors. But would you allow me to ask you something on a matter of principle?

KNOCK: Go ahead.

DR PARPALAID: If I had your method ... if I had it properly mastered like you ... if all I had to do was apply it ...

KNOCK: Yes.

DR PARPALAID: Wouldn't I feel a pang of conscience? [*Silence*] Tell me that.

KNOCK: That's for you to answer, I believe.

DR PARPALAID: I'm not making judgements, as you'll observe. But I'm raising an extremely delicate matter.

[*Silence*]

KNOCK: It would help if I could follow you more closely.

DR PARPALAID: You'll say that I'm being puritanical, that I'm splitting hairs. But wouldn't you say that in your method the patient's interest has been more than a little subordinated to the doctor's interest?

KNOCK: Doctor Parpalaid, you're forgetting that there is another interest, higher than either.

DR PARPALAID: Which?

KNOCK: That of medicine. It's the only one of concern to me.

[*Silence. Dr Parpalaid ponders*]

DR PARPALAID: Yes, yes, yes.

[*From this moment and until the end of the play, the stage lighting gradually becomes more and more like the light of medicine which, as is commonly known, is richer in green and violet rays than the simple terrestrial sort ...*]

KNOCK: You gave me a district peopled by a few thousand individuals, non-committal and dithering. My role is to prompt decision in their lives, to bring them to medicine. I put them to bed, and wait to see what emerges: a diabetic, a hypertensive, an asthmatic, whatever you like, but something, dear God, something! Nothing irritates me as much as this entity—neither fish nor fowl—you call a healthy person.

DR PARPALAID: But all the same you can't confine the whole district to bed!

KNOCK [*while drying his hands*]: That is a matter for discussion. I've known five persons in the same family, all ill at the same time, all in bed at the same time, who got by rather nicely. Your objection reminds me of those notorious economists who said that a major modern war couldn't last more than six weeks. The truth is that we all lack the courage of our convictions, that nobody—not even myself—would dare to go all the way and put an entire populace to bed, just to find out, just to find out! So be it. I concede that we need healthy people, if only to look after the others, or create a kind of reserve behind the patients in the front-line. What I don't like is to see healthy people getting cocky. I think you'll agree that's just too much. We have to close our eyes to a certain number of cases: some we allow to indulge their mask of well-being. But if they try to strut about in front of us, or take the mickey, I lose my patience. That's what happened to Monsieur Raffalens.

DR PARPALAID: Oh, the giant? The one who boasted he could carry his mother-in-law on one arm?

KNOCK: That's the one. He defied me for almost the three months ... But it's over.

DR PARPALAID: What?

KNOCK: He's in bed. His bragging was starting to weaken the town's medical resolve.

DR PARPALAID: There's still a serious quandary.

KNOCK: What would that be?

DR PARPALAID: You claim to think only of medicine … But the rest? Aren't you concerned that the widescale application of your methods is leading to a certain falling off in other social activities, some of which are not, after all, unpleasurable?

KNOCK: That's of no concern to me. I practise medicine, and medicine only.

DR PARPALAID: True enough: when an engineer's building a railway he doesn't ask the country doctor what he thinks about it.

KNOCK: Good Lord, no! [*He goes to the back of the stage and approaches a window*] Look here for a moment, Doctor Parpalaid. You know the view from this window. You must have taken it in between many a frame of billiards in the old days. It's all set out: Mount Aligre marking the boundary of the district. You can make out the villages of Mesclat and Trébures to the left; and if the houses of Saint-Maurice on this side didn't obstruct the view, you'd be able to see all the villages in a line down the valley. But you probably only ever had an eye, as is your wont, for the beauties of nature. You were contemplating a wild landscape, barely cultivated by human hand. Now I offer it to you impregnated by medicine, fired by the spirit of our subterranean art. When I stood here the first time, the day after my arrival, I wasn't too proud: I realised that my presence didn't count for much. This vast expanse of France had the temerity to spurn me and my coevals. But now, I'm as much at ease here as an organist sitting down to play his instrument. In two hundred and fifty of these houses—not all of which are apparent because of the distance and the greenery—there are two hundred and fifty bedrooms where someone's confessing the power of medicine, two hundred and fifty beds where a recumbent body attests that life has a purpose, and—thanks to me—a medical purpose. At night the view is even more beautiful, for then their lights shine out. And almost all these lights are mine. Non-patients sleep in the outer dark. They cease to exist. But patients leave on their night-lights or their lamps. For me, night banishes everything that remains outside medicine, wipes away its irritation and provocation. Instead of the district we know there is a kind of firmament of which I am the continual creator. And I haven't mentioned the bells. Their first office for all these people is call them to my prescriptions; the bells intone my orders. Think of it: in a few moments, ten o'clock is going to sound, and for all my patients ten o'clock is when they read their rectal temperature for the second time: just think, in a few moments, two hundred and fifty thermometers will be inserted at the same time …

DR PARPALAID [*seizes Knock's arm in some emotion*]: Dear colleague, I have a proposal to offer you.

KNOCK: What?

DR PARPALAID: A man like you is wasted in a small county town like this. You need a city.

KNOCK: I shall have one, sooner or later.

DR PARPALAID: Caution, caution! At the moment you're at the height of your powers. In a few years, they'll begin to decline. Take my word for it.

KNOCK: So?

DR PARPALAID: So, you shouldn't put it off.

KNOCK: Do you know of a suitable opening?

DR PARPALAID: My practice. I'll give it to you. I can't give you any better proof of my admiration.

KNOCK: Yes … And what would become of you?

DR PARPALAID: Me? I'd be happy enough to return to Saint-Maurice.

KNOCK: Yes.

DR PARPALAID: And I'd go further. For the few thousand francs you owe me, we're quits.

KNOCK: Yes … You know, you're not as daft as people think.

DR PARPALAID: What do you mean?

KNOCK: You don't produce much, but you know how to buy and sell. Those are the attributes of the small businessman.

DR PARPALAID: I can assure you …

KNOCK: And in your way, you're even a fairly good psychologist. You guessed that I don't care much about money as soon as I'm making a lot; and that the prospect of medically penetrating one of the districts of Lyons made me quickly forget my charts for Saint-Maurice. No, I don't intend to grow old here. But that doesn't mean I'd throw myself on the first opportunity to present itself!

Scene VI, Act III, *Knock ou Le Triomphe de la Médecine*, 1923.

ROBERT MUSIL

Oedipus in Danger

As Robert Musil sarcastically wrote in the epigraph to this short piece (one of the feuilletons he wrote when relaxing from his great novel The Man Without Qualities*), "though malicious and biased, this critique does not claim to be scientifically objective." With his solid background in the sciences, Musil is justifiably suspicious of Freud's reenchantment technique and its claims to be able to "adjust" the uncomfortably duplicated self that emerges from the way we understand and manipulate the world: an agent with a minimal kind of freedom who is constrained to know him or herself as an aspect of nature.*

In ancient times humankind had its Scylla and Charybdis; in modern times humankind has its Wasserman and Oedipus—for if it has succeeded in evading the former and getting an offspring up on his feet, then it can be even surer that said offspring will succumb to the latter. It may even be said that without Oedipus almost nothing is possible these days, family life as little as architecture.

Since I myself grew up without Oedipus, I must speak my mind on the subject only with the greatest circumspection, though I go in wonder at the methods of psychoanalysis. I recall the following from my youth: when one of us boys was fed up with insults from another and wanted to retort with a slur as insulting as the first, but couldn't think one up no matter how he tried, he simply took the little phrase "yours with knobs on" and plugged it into the space where the other paused for breath: this short-circuited all the insults and sent them back to source. And in my study of psychoanalytical literature I was delighted to come across the fact that all those who fail to believe in the infallibility of psychoanalysis are immediately shown to have reasons for their disbelief; these are of course demonstrably psychoanalytical in nature. There can be no more splendid proof of the fact that even scientific methods are acquired before puberty.

If therapeutics, however, in its use of the "return to sender" harks back to the good old days of the mail coach, it does so unconsciously but not without deep psychological coherence. For one of its greatest achievements, now that time is scarce, is to educate us in its more leisurely use, indeed in mild squandering of this fleeting natural product. Once you've put yourself in the hands of the soul improver, all you know is that one day treatment will come to an end, but that for the time being you're most satisfied with the progress made. Impatient patients ditch their neurosis and start on a fresh one straightaway, but the patient who has acquired a proper appreciation of psychoanalysis won't be so hasty. He steps into his friend's office from the quotidian bustle, and though the outside world might be exploding with its mechanical energy—there he finds it, good old time. A sympathetic question about how he's been sleeping, and what he's dreaming. Family feeling, otherwise so sadly neglected nowadays, is restored to its natural standing, and it becomes apparent that what Auntie Sadie said when the serving girl broke the plate is not at all ridiculous but in fact, if looked at correctly, more telling than one of Goethe's maxims. And we can entirely overlook the fact that it is apparently not embarrassing to talk about cuckoos either, the ones in the nest, especially if the nest happens to be a stork's. More importantly than any details in such a treatment—indeed of crowning importance— is that the person, gently and mesmerically caressed, should learn once again to feel himself to be the measure of all things. Down through the centuries he has been told that the way he behaves is entirely the fault of his culture, which was far more important than he was anyway; and now that we've all but finally rid ourselves of this culture in the latest generation, it has given way to the era of innovation and discovery running riot, beside which the individual looks like a nothing: now psychoanalysis takes this atrophied individual by the hand and shows him all he needs is courage and gonads. May psychoanalysis never come to grief! That is the wish of a layman; but I believe my wish concurs with what the experts say on the matter.

I am therefore put out by a suspicion, which may well stem from my lay ignorance but is perhaps well-founded after all. As far as I know, the aforementioned Oedipus complex is now, more than ever, at the core of the theory; almost all phenomena are traced back to it, and I fear that in one or two generations there won't be any more Oedipuses! Oedipus, it is revealed, arises from the nature of the wee man who finds his pleasure in his mother's lap, and is reputedly jealous of his father who ousts him from the same lap. What then if the mother no longer has a lap?! Now, we know where this is leading: "lap" isn't just the body part to which the word in its strictest sense applies; psychologically it also signifies the whole incubating motherliness of the woman, the bosom, the warm adiposity, the tender caring softness; it even signifies the skirt whose broad pleats form a mysterious nest. Accordingly, the fundamental experiences of psychoanalysis are indubitably derived from the dress modes of the 1870s and 1880s, not from the ski outfit. Not to mention the modern bathing suit: where are today's laps? If, with psychoanalytical longing, I attempt to return embryonically to the lap imagined as the running and swimming girls' and women's bodies that are all the rage today, then— all my respect for their peculiar beauty notwithstanding—I can see no reason why the next generation shouldn't be just as eager to go back to the father's lap.

And what then?

Will we instead of Oedipus have an Orestes? Or will psychoanalysis have to renounce its beneficial effect?

"Der bedrohte Oedipus," from *Nachlass zu Lebzeiten*, 1929.

VIRGINIA WOOLF

Illness

In this lyrical exploration, a condensed version of her essay On Being Ill, *Virginia Woolf fingers a contentious issue: the fact that illness in general and pain in particular have precious few referents. Whether undiscovered countries alive with a "primitive, subtle, sensual, obscene" language are really to be found on the other side of the flatlands of ordinary experience is questionable: it would seem that pain, especially severe and protracted pain, actually destroys our ability to express it and, a fortiori, the imagination's attempt to shift it into the realm of fiction or myth. Nobody can be indifferent to illness, should it arrive, but it is likely to resist representation; and free-floating sympathy, as Woolf herself recognizes, would bring all human activities to a halt.*

Considering how common illness is, how tremendous the spiritual change that it brings, how astonishing, when the lights of health go down, the undiscovered countries that are then disclosed, what wastes and deserts of the soul a slight attack of influenza brings to light, what precipices and lawns sprinkled with bright flowers a little rise of temperature reveals, what ancient and obdurate oaks are uprooted in us in the act of sickness, how we go down into the pit of death and feel the waters of annihilation close above our heads and wake thinking to find ourselves in the presence of the angels and the harpers when we have a tooth out and come to the surface in the dentist's arm-chair and confuse his "Rinse the mouth—rinse the mouth" with the greeting of the Deity stooping on the floor of Heaven to welcome us,—when we think of this and infinitely more as we are so frequently forced to think of it, it becomes strange indeed that illness has not taken its place with love, battle, and jealousy among the prime themes of literature. Novels, one would have thought, would have been devoted to Influenza; epic poems to Typhoid; odes to Pneumonia,

Appendicitis, and Cancer; lyrics to Toothache. But no; with a few exceptions,—De Quincey attempted something of the sort in *The Opium Eater*; there must be a volume or two about disease scattered through the pages of Proust,—literature does its best to maintain that its concern is with the mind; that the body is a sheet of plain glass through which the soul looks straight and clear, and, save for one or two passions such as desire and greed, is null and negligible and non-existent.

On the contrary, the very opposite is true. All day, all night the body intervenes; blunts or sharpens, colours or discolours; turns us to wax in the warmth of June, hardens us to tallow in the murk of February. The creature within can only gaze through the pane—smudged or rosy; it cannot separate off from the body like the sheath of a knife or the pod of a pea for a single instant; it must go through the whole unending procession of changes, heat and cold, comfort and discomfort, hunger and satisfaction, health and illness, until there comes the inevitable catastrophe: the body smashes itself to smithereens, and the soul (it is said) escapes.

But of all this daily drama of the body there is no record. People write always about the doings of the mind, the thoughts that come to it; its noble plans; how it has civilised the universe. They show it ignoring the body in the philosopher's turret; or kicking the body, like an old leather football, across leagues of snow and desert in the pursuit of conquest or discovery. Those great wars which it wages by itself, with the mind a slave to it in the solitude of the bedroom against the assault of fever or the oncome of melancholia, are neglected. Nor is the reason far to seek. To look these things squarely in the face would need the courage of a lion tamer, of ten thousand lion tamers,—for these lions are within us not without; and a robust philosophy; and a reason rooted in the bowels of the earth. Short of these, this monster, this miracle, of the body and pain, will soon make us taper into mysticism, or rise with rapid beats of the wings into the raptures of transcendentalism.

More practically speaking, the public would say that a novel devoted to influenza lacked plot; they would complain that there was no love in it, wrongly however, for illness often takes on the disguise of love, and plays the same odd tricks, investing certain faces with divinity, setting us to wait hour after hour with pricked ears for the creaking of a stair, and wreathing the faces of the absent (plain enough in health, Heaven knows) with a new significance, while the mind sports with them, and concocts legends and romances about them for which it has not time nor liberty in health.

Finally, among the drawbacks of illness as matter for literature there is the poverty of the language. English which can express the thoughts of Hamlet and the tragedy of Lear has no words for the shiver and the headache. It has all grown one way. The merest schoolgirl, when she falls in love, has Shakespeare, Donne, Keats to speak her mind for her; but let a sufferer try to describe a pain in his head to a doctor, and language at once runs dry. There is nothing ready-made for him. He is forced to coin words himself, and, taking his pain in one hand and a lump of pure sound in the other (as perhaps the inhabitants of Babel did in the beginning), crush them together that a brand new word in the end will emerge, and it will be something laughable. For who of English birth can take liberties with the language? It is a sacred thing to us and therefore doomed to die, unless the Americans, whose genius is so much happier in the making of new words than in the artful disposition of the old, will come to our help, and set the springs aflow again.

But it is not only a new language that we need,—primitive, subtle, sensual, obscene,—but a new hierarchy of the passions; love must be deposed in favour of a temperature of 104 degrees; jealousy give place to the pangs of sciatica; sleeplessness play the part of villain, and the hero become a white liquid with a sweet taste, that mighty prince with the moth's eyes and the feathered feet, one of whose names is Chloral.

But to return to the invalid. "I am in bed with influenza," he says, and actually complains that he gets no sympathy at all. "I am in bed with influenza," but what does that convey of the great experience: how the world has changed its shape; the tools of business have grown remote; the sounds of festival romantic become like a merry-go-round across the fields; and friends have changed, some putting on a strange beauty, others deformed to the squatness of toads while the whole landscape of life lies remote, fair, silent, like the shore seen from a ship out at sea; and he is now exalted on a peak and needs no help from man or God, and now grovels supine on the floor glad of a kick from a housemaid. The experience cannot be imparted and, as is always the way with these dumb things, his own suffering serves but to wake memories in his friends' minds of their influenzas, their aches and pains which went unwept last February, and now cry out, desperately, clamorously, for the divine relief of sympathy.

But sympathy we cannot have. Wisest Fate says no. If her children, whose lot is hard enough already, were to take on them that burden too, adding in imagination others' pains to their own, buildings would cease to rise, roads would peter out into grassy tracks, there would be an end of music and of painting; one great sigh alone would rise to Heaven, and the only attitudes for men and women would be those of horror and despair. As it is, there is always some little distraction—an organ grinder at the corner of the Hospital, a shop with a book or a picture to decoy one past the prison or the workhouse, some absurdity of cat or dog to prevent one from turning the old beggar's hieroglyphic of misery into volumes of sordid suffering—and the vast effort of sympathy which those barracks of pain and discipline, those dried symbols of sorrow, ask us to exert on their behalf is uneasily shuffled off for another time.

Sympathy nowadays is dispensed chiefly by the laggards and failures, women for the most part (in whom the obsolete exists so strangely side by side with anarchy and newness) who, having dropped out of the race, have time to spend upon fantastic and unprofitable excursions; C. L. for example who, sitting by the stale sickroom fire, builds up with touches at once sober and imaginative the nursery fender, the loaf, the lamp, barrel organs in the West, and all the simple old wives' tales of pinafores and escapades; A. R. the rash, the magnanimous, who if you fancied a giant tortoise to solace you, and a theorbo to cheer you, would ransack the markets of London and procure them somehow, wrapped in paper, before the end of the day; the frivolous K. T. who, dressed in silks and feathers, painted and powdered (which takes time too) as if for a banquet of Kings and Queens, spends her whole brightness in the gloom of the sick room, and makes the medicine bottles ring and the flames shoot up with her gossip and her mimicry.

But such follies have had their day; civilisation points to a different goal; if the cities of the Middle West are to blaze with electric light, Mr Insull "must keep twenty or thirty engagements every day of his working months,"—and then what place is there for the tortoise and the theorbo?

There is, let us confess it (and illness is the great confessional), a childish outspokenness in illness; things are said, truths blurted out, which the cautious respectability of health conceals. About sympathy for example; we can do without it. That illusion of a world so shaped that it echoes every laugh, every tear, of human beings so tied together by common needs and fears that a twitch of one wrist jerks another, where however far you penetrate into your own mind someone has been there before you—is all an illusion. We do not know our own souls, let alone the souls of others. Human beings do not go hand in hand the whole stretch of the way. There is a virgin forest, tangled, pathless, in each; a snow field where even the print of a bird's feet is unknown. Here we go alone, and like it better so. Always to have sympathy, always to be accompanied, always to be understood would be intolerable. But in health the genial pretence must be kept up and the effort renewed—to communicate, to civilise, to share, to cultivate the desert, educate the native, to work by day together and by night to sport.

In illness this make-believe ceases. Directly the bed is called for, or sunk deep among pillows in one chair we raise our feet even an inch above the ground on another, we cease to be soldiers in the army of the upright; we become deserters. They march to battle. We float with the sticks on the stream; helter-skelter with the dead leaves on the lawn, irresponsible and disinterested, and able perhaps for the first time for years, to look round, to look up—to look at the sky, for example.

The first impression of that extraordinary spectacle is strangely overcoming. Ordinarily to look at the sky for any length of time is impossible. Pedestrians would be impeded and disconcerted by a public sky gazer. What snatches we get of it are mutilated by chimneys and churches, serve as a background for man, signify wet or fine weather, daub windows gold, and, filling in the branches, complete the pathos of dishevelled autumnal plane trees in London squares. Now, become as the leaf or the daisy, lying recumbent, staring straight up, the sky is discovered to be something so different from this that really it is a little shocking. This then has been going on all the time without our knowing it! This incessant making up of shapes and casting them down, this buffeting of clouds together, and drawing vast trains of ships and wagons across the sky, this incessant ringing up and down of curtains of light and shade, this interminable experiment with gold shafts and blue shadows, with veiling the sun and unveiling it, with making rock ramparts and wafting them away, this endless activity with the waste of Heaven-knows-how-many million horse power of energy has been left to work its will year in year out, and we have not known it. The fact seems to call for comment and indeed for censure. Use should be made of it. One could not let this gigantic cinema play perpetually to an empty house.

But watch a little longer, and another emotion drowns the stirrings of civic ardour. Divinely beautiful it is also divinely heartless. Immeasurable resources are used for some purpose which has nothing to do with human pleasure or human profit. If we were all laid prone, frozen, stiff, still the sky would be experimenting with its blues and golds. Perhaps, then, looking down at something very small and close and familiar we shall find sympathy. Let us examine the rose. We have seen it so often flowering in bowls, connected it so often with beauty in its prime, or June, or youth, that we have forgotten how it stands still and steady throughout an entire afternoon in the earth. It preserves a demeanour of perfect dignity and self-possession. The suffusion of its petals is of inimitable rightness. Now perhaps one deliberately falls; now all the flower, the voluptuous purple, the creamy, in whose waxen flesh a spoon has left a swirl of cherry juice, gladioli, dahlias, lilies, sacerdotal, ecclesiastical, flowers with prim cardboard collars tinged apricot and amber, all gently incline their heads to the breeze—all, with the exception of the heavy sunflower, who proudly acknowledges the sun at midday, and perhaps at midnight rebuffs the moon. There they stand; and it is of these, the stillest, the most self-sufficient of all things that human beings have made companions; these that symbolise their passions, decorate their festivals, and lie (as if they knew sorrow) upon the pillows of the dead. Wonderful to relate, poets have found religion in nature; people live in the country to learn virtue from plants. It is in their indifference that they are comforting. That snowfield of the mind, where man has not been, rejoices in the cloud itself perhaps, in the upright rose, as, in another sphere, it is the great artists, the Miltons, the Popes, who console, not by thinking of us, but by forgetting us entirely.

Meanwhile, with the heroism of the ant or the bee, however indifferent the sky may be or disdainful the flowers, the army of the upright marches to battle. Mrs Jones catches her train, Mr Smith mends his motor. The cows are driven home to be milked. Men thatch the roof. The dogs bark. The rooks rising in a net fall in a net upon the elm trees. The wave of life flings itself out indefatigably. It is only the recumbent who know what, after all, Nature is at no pains to conceal—that she in the end will conquer; the heat will leave the world; stiff with frost we shall cease to drag our feet about the fields; ice will lie thick upon factory and engine; the sun will go out. Even so, when the whole earth is sheeted with ice, some undulation, some irregularity of surface will mark the boundary of an ancient garden, and there, thrusting its head up undaunted in the starlight the rose will flower, the crocus will burn.

But with the hook of life within us still we must wriggle. We cannot stiffen peaceably into glassy mounds. Even the recumbent spring up at the mere imagination of frost about the toes and stretch out to avail themselves of the universal hope—Heaven, immortality. Surely, since men have been wishing all these ages they will have wished something into existence; there will be some green isle for the mind to rest on even if the foot cannot plant itself there. The co-operative imagination of mankind will have drawn some firm outline. But no such thing. One opens the Morning Post and reads the Bishop of Lichfield on Heaven—a vague discourse, weak, watery, inconclusive. One watches the churchgoers file to church, those gallant temples where, on the bleakest day in the wettest fields, lamps will be burning, bells punctually ringing, and however the autumn leaves may shuffle and the winds sigh, hopes and desires will be changed to beliefs and certainties. Do they look serene? Are their eyes filled with the light of their sublime conviction? Would one of them dare leap straight into Heaven off Beachy Head?

None but a simpleton would ask such questions; they lag and drag and pry and gossip; the mother is worn, the children fidget, the father is tired. The Bishops are tired too. Frequently we read in the same paper how the Diocese has presented its Bishop with a motor car, how at the presentation some leading citizen has remarked, with obvious truth, that the Bishop has more need of motor cars than any of his flock. But this making Heaven available needs time and concentration. It needs the imagination of a poet. Left to ourselves we can but trifle with it— imagine Pepys in Heaven, adumbrate little interviews with celebrated people on tufts of thyme, soon fall into gossip about such of our friends as have stayed in Hell, or, worse still, revert again to earth and choose, since there is no harm in choosing, to live over and over, now as man, now as woman, as sea captain, court lady, Emperor, farmer's wife, in splendid cities and remote moors, in Teheran and Tunbridge Wells, at the time of Pericles or Arthur, Charlemagne or George the Fourth—to live and live till we have lived out those embryo lives which attend about us in early youth and fade in the shadow of that tyrannical "I" who has conquered so far as this world is concerned but shall not, if wishing can alter it, usurp Heaven too, and condemn us who have played our parts here as Mr Jones or Mrs Smith to remain Mr Jones and Mrs Smith for ever. Left to ourselves we speculate thus carnally. We need the poets to imagine for us. The duty of Heaven-making should be attached to the office of Poet Laureate.

Indeed, it is to the poets that we turn. Illness makes us disinclined for the long campaigns that prose exacts. We cannot command all our faculties and keep our reason and our judgement and our memory at attention while chapter swings on top of chapter, and, as one settles into place, we must be on the watch for the coming of the next, until the whole structure—arches, towers, battlements—stands firm on its foundations. *The Decline and Fall of the Roman Empire* is not the book for influenza, nor *The Golden Bowl*, nor *Madame Bovary*. On the other hand, with responsibility shelved and reason in abeyance—for who is going to exact criticism from an invalid or sound sense from the bedridden?—other tastes assert themselves; sudden, fitful, intense. We rifle the poets of their flowers. We break off a line or two and let them open in the depths of the mind, spread their bright wings, swim like coloured fish in green waters:

> ... and oft at eve
> Visits the herds along the twilight meadows
> Wandering in thick flocks along the mountains
> Shepherded by the slow, unwilling wind—

Or there is a whole three-volume novel to be mused over and spread out in a verse of Hardy's, or a sentence of La Bruyère's. We dip in Lamb's Letters (some prose writers are to be read as poets) and find, "I am a sanguinary murderer of time, and would kill him inch-meal just now. But the snake is vital", and who shall explain the delight of that? or open Rimbaud and read

> O saisons, o châteaux
> Quelle âme est sans défauts?

and who shall rationalise the charm? In illness words seem to possess a mystic quality. We grasp what is beyond their surface meaning, gather instinctively this, that, and the other—a sound, a colour, a stress, a pause which the poet, knowing words to be meagre in comparison with ideas, has strewn about his page to evoke, when collected, a state of mind which is not in one word or in one sentence, nor can the reason explain it. Incomprehensibility has an enormous power over us, more legitimately perhaps than the upright will allow. In health, meaning has encroached upon sound. Our intelligence domineers over our senses. But in illness, with the police off duty, we creep beneath some obscure poem by Mallarmé or Donne, some phrase in Latin or Greek, and the words give out their scent, and ripple like leaves, and chequer us with light and shadow, and then if at last we grasp the meaning it is all the richer for having travelled slowly up with all the bloom upon its wings. Foreigners to whom the tongue is strange have us at a disadvantage. The Chinese must know better what *Antony and Cleopatra* sounds like than we do.

"Illness—An Unexploited Mine," *Forum*, 1926.

GOTTFRIED BENN

Irrationalism and Modern Medicine

Can an essayist leap from warts to apocalpyse in the same paragraph? Benn does. His arguifying is not beyond reproach, but it gives an emotional timbre to what the sociologist Max Weber was calling, at roughly the same time, "the disenchantment of the world." Benn's—or rather his alter-ego Rönne's—realization that he, the modern doctor, is still a shaman, but a shaman whose superstition is numbers, force and mass, propels him into a kind of existential vertigo. Warts (viral tumours) can indeed disappear under the effects of suggestion, an occurrence which makes no sense in terms of conventional theories of disease causation. Once again, a charismatic connection between medicine and politics emerges, in things "decreed by the right man in the right way."

Imagine a doctor in practice in today's Germany able to find time, despite the daily grind, to read the scientific literature on biology: he might come across the book by Erwin Liek entitled "Miracles in medicine" (Lehmann Verlag, Munich). Excited by this book, pondering some remarks from no lesser academic authorities than Professors Kraus, Krehl and Goldscheider, even inspired to carry out certain tests on his own patients, this doctor could find himself being led by the train of thought set out below, the starting point for which is something as trite as the treatment of warts, towards a crisis which could pose a serious threat to his nature as a person.

This doctor—let's call him Dr. Rönne and allow him to experience it directly—strolls one day down the street and meets a colleague. "Well, have you used the new wart paint yet?" asks the colleague. "No", replies Rönne. They discuss it, weigh it up, Rönne shakes his head, smiles, goes to the office to begin his consultations. Rönne is a dermatologist; he has many patients with warts among his clientele—warts, these inoffensive little growths, mostly flat, horny proliferations which grow fairly deep down into the subdermal layer and may sometimes be found, especially on the back of the hand in young people, in their unwelcome hundreds. Usually they have to be destroyed one by one with caustic; but Rönne has heard it said many times that only one hand apparently needs to be treated, since the other gets better too. He has never witnessed this phenomenon himself, but he has heard about it; now, after what has been reported about the new wart procedure, it appears in a completely new light.

Rönne begins his examinations. The first patient comes in, a young wart carrier. "I'll treat just the one big wart", says Rönne, and says it in a particularly melodic tone of voice: "I'll burn it away with the nitric acid, then the others will vanish along with it; the substance spreads under the skin and nibbles away at the roots; return in a week and we'll have another look." The patient turns up in a week again, and both hands are smooth and unblemished. Naturally nitric acid is not something that spreads about under the skin or anywhere else; it stays where it is deposited and evaporates immediately. But the whole point of this manner of speaking will become clear.

Rönne works on. He deals with his new wart patients as follows: he gets them to put their hands on a piece of paper, outlines the hands with a pen and inserts the warts in the drawing, lifesize. Then he blindfolds his patients, rubs the warts lightly with a little rod while intoning: "from today on you will no longer be able to feel the warts, they will vanish, you're not to touch them any more." With rebellious cases, particularly where the warts are large, he repeats the session several times; in the most extreme case he requests the patient to bring a photograph of his hands—in other words, just like a customs inspection over which a threatening question hangs: why is the wart still there? And the warts vanish in every case. The author of the method, whom he follows in its application, proudly asserts that in thirty years' practice he has never had a single failure.

Rönne changes his approach. Now he has the patients led from the consulting room, eyes bound, to an adjoining room where they place their wart-covered hands on an electrical apparatus. The apparatus is switched on without the electric field touching the patient's body even in the slightest; only the noise is apparent, a hissing noise. The now familiar assertions take effect: the warts will heal, and then the affected person is led back into the consulting room and the bind removed. Outcome: a 90 percent cure rate and, unlike the conventional treatment, no scars. In some people this is a matter of thousands of warts over the entire body.

Finally Rönne tries out the method suggested to him by the colleague he had met on the street. He injects some purified water through a needle under the skin, wherever he likes but usually in the upper arm, casually remarking: "during the injection you'll feel a mild burning in the warts; it'll soon go, but expect it to return a couple of times until the warts fall off." And in due course, the mild burning settles, and the warts fall off.

Appeal to them, and warts fall off, thinks Rönne; in other words, warts, pathologically well demarcated structures, examined hundreds of times under the microscope, vanish by persuasion. Small tumours caused by viruses dry up through the force of the word. Quite obviously human beings are something completely different, quite incomprehensibly different, from what my science taught me; nothing so reducible, nothing so viscous, nothing whose cadaver has to be worked on with gas pipes and rubber drains in order to cure it and spy on its being.

Now other medical fields attract his interest; he hunts for observations similar to his own. He discovers that an eminent surgeon attributes gastroptosis to an inadequate abdominal cover and performs an operation to extend it, after which patients' symptoms disappear. A second, perhaps even more eminent surgeon finds, on the contrary, that the abdominal cover is too extensive and carries out an operation to trim it; and after this procedure, too, patients are relieved of their pain. Healing a specific chronic infectious disease through a salt-free diet, which is all the rage just now, was preceded just a short time ago in another country by a method in which the same patients were most sternly instructed by their doctors to salt their food as much as possible; and patients who had been given up on as incurable were saved by both methods. And a book could be written just about spas, all of which really do bring about rejuvenation. They used to take fluids from ancient elephants which had eaten the berries of eternal youth in the jungle; then they adopted the indirect approach using rabbits which, after being fed on the appropriate magic-mix (photomatonically proven), simply cannnot be held back from exhibiting their lust for life and springing over tables and benches out of sheer youthfulness; sometimes terribly complicated chemical extracts are used, purified brain perhaps, or ground testicles; even Egyptian papyri, emulsified with the abdominal fat of the long-lived crocodile, turn up as rejuvenation creams: and everything helps, the juices rise, the hairs sprout, the mood is youth from top to toe, provided it gets decreed by the right man in the right way.

Modern medicine, Rönne realises, certainly not in the business of allowing itself to be swindled, but a hugely serious and responsible public work, puts no emphasis on particular organs and highly specific treatments—it applies itself to something quite general, to the organism as a whole, to its totality. If my warts vanish through being stroked with quite indifferent materials to the accompaniment of a phrase; if people paint the sign of the dove on warts in Japan because the word "mame" means pea as well as wart and doves eat peas: and the warts vanish, then here the word becomes flesh, blood becomes water, and we are only a step away from going over to the contents of the coffin, and saying: Arise and go forth—then there are possibilities and transitions, and no end in sight.

The body is obviously something fugitive, not the chemical-physic morass of the 19th century with positivism pressed in its face: it is nothing but an inner principle, and when it is touched, everything moves. Provided the right man touches it with the right word: this is the basic requirement. This right man can be the Tlinkit shaman, who dances around sick people, on his head a crown of twigs to resemble the horns of the mountain-goat which rub against each other festively. He can be the conjurer with his metal pendulum, the shepherd, the mud priest, the masseur with the mystic equipment; he can be found in Lourdes and in Christian Science. He must act only on this inner principle, on this heart made of soul, from which you can die just as surely as from a rock that falls on you. From which you can die like Penthesilea: she gave the dagger to Prothoe and said: "Do you want the arrows too?" She dug an annihilating feeling underneath herself and died there without the bloody roses or crown of wounds around her head.

Human beings are clearly something far, far more primitive than the West's intellectual elite asserts, something quite general behind a schematic ego. Even life and death are evidently nothing like the catastrophes individualism has made of them. Stevenson reports from the South Sea: young people who have offended the taboo prescriptions in some way, or who simply imagine they have, withdraw to a hut and die in a few days of no apparent cause. Clearly they die on account of this inner principle, the internal creator, the metaphysical blueprint that passes through the entire animal kingdom. Yes, a blueprint: how else are we to understand the foresight of adaptation which is unexplainable when we look at the individual? The larva of the stag beetle, for instance, scrapes a smooth hole inside a clump of hard clay where it can undergo further metamorphosis. The male larva makes its hole much bigger. How does it know that a bigger hole is required because of the greater jaw size of the future fully-formed insect? It is hardly conceivable that the future insect is somehow already modelled in the pupa. The interior of the pupa collapses into an amorphous pap. Only a few cells remain, out of which the complete insect then goes on to develop. It is the inner principle, you begin to notice, that moves even what is called the inanimate: geologists are just beginning to recognise that certain crystals always occur together in geological deposits, while others always seem to avoid each other: the inner principle is present even in the stones, in mute sympathy and antipathy, arousal, forces, bonds.

The wart theme runs through all of nature, Rönne realises: feeling and the rousing word. It begins to be recognised, and not only that: it is put to use. The entire medical literature is full of the word as actual stimulus, its manifest therapeutic possibilities. The intoxicating word, the killer word, thinks Rönne. The right man with the right word—he thinks the situation through again, but far more exactitude. Not the pure man with the pure word, not the great man with the great word, not the word on behalf of some ideal or belief, not as a part of some great former community, not as a sound from some inner memory. No. The right word: integrated into modern therapy, pressed into the general cultural context ... how did it look then, what would it mean?

Whom would the West heal with this new method? More urgently, blemish-free and classically than ever before? What kind of person? Why *this* person? The biology of the inductive age, which Rönne learned around 1900, this kind of objective safeguarding of the automatism of the individual life, a kind of pacificism of the juices or better said: the individual glandular idyll as the last idol of the white race—that was the age of power and matter, the Darwinian era, that was what was taught and it was swallowed whole. But if biology took in the other stuff too, the irrational, the vague, but in the same hands, under the same social conditions—but again only as a new trick, a new fashion, a new trend, a new palaver, in short an incantation with balance due, creation as big business—is there anything else to be gained from it? Did it ever have any deeper meaning for the human condition that rationalized individual life acquire perhaps an extra three days' or three weeks' or even three months' life-expectancy if there is no epochal sense to it, if no more is made of this rationalized individual life than horse-power, utilities, work-related calories, autonomic reflexes, glandular discharge? Does it still have any kind of historical meaning to get western man back into physical shape with hypodermics, ointments, trusses and now methods of suggestion too, when he sits on the same old rotten ideology of utilitarian positivism, the same washed-up, helpless, running-on-empty hymnology that was always progress's favourite, nursed back to health with nose baths and colonic irrigations, from the cradle to the bier?

Health as an economic good—the American formulation, stems from I. Dublin, head of the statistical office of the Metropolitan Life Insurance Company, New York. This formulation has been adopted by all the capitalist conglomerates east and west of the Atlantic. That is where the modern Napoleons reside—the hygienists, radiologists, statisticians—and survey their armies: hearts worn out early: wars, crises, fall in the share prices; general hypertension, arterial tone of the irritable, the masses under tension ... Six new institutes with a two million dollar budget for circulatory and blood vessel research yields 4 percent interest on the original investment by deferring disablement payments by an average ten days. On then to the vagus, nerve of lability, voiding frequency and intestinal syndromes ... Canteens with calcium-supplemented food, stabilization therapy, written off as reinvestment, industrially accounted for, that means an increased horse-power rating of 3.27 percent. In the boom times Prosperity keeps the individual fit for the galley-ships of the slave economy with calcium and bromide and afterwards dumps it as fertilizing waste product in the prairies ... That is the health of the age, hardly the health of mosquitoes, less than that of a pampered dog.

This age! Chancellor Bacon comes to mind, wrote Goethe to Jacobi, as a Hercules who purged a stable of dialectical muck only to fill it with empirical muck. Modern science, the inductive age—empirical muck! Instructive, thinks Rönne. Yes, it can surely be illuminating seen like that, this great big bubble greased in formulas; it can surely be pricked, this skin puffed up with pension gases from the state and public purse, this amorphous, eyeless, appetite-driven mass, prostrate before things like a mirror with a hundred eyes. Yes, it can surely be walked the length of, this front bonded by very special cement: the data validate the proportions, and the proportions validate the laws, and the laws validate the data again, and the mathematics validates the physics, and the physics validates the chemistry, and the chemistry validates the mathematics again ... In picture-postcard terms, it's like a bunch of peasants in the time of the Thirty Years War playing cards to avoid getting conscripted: the problem is they're all cheating according to the rules and can't expose the dupe since they're all holding marked cards.

And biology at the heart of it. Now they're all in it together and bumping up the percentage. Where you go, there I shall go, too; and where you make money, there I want to make money too. In 1870, a newborn had the chance of becoming forty years old, today sixty—that's the starting point. Twenty years for the masses on the galley-oars, and twenty years for the upper class sipping soda water from Gastein and Carlsbad. And now the spirit pipes up too and speaks in business jargon: arise and go forth, walk your soles out another two decades, great son of the intellectual era, you'll find the cheapest spare parts at my cousin next door and the cheapest rejuvenation glands at my auntie round the corner, and now go forth and multiply, and your warts will fade away, and fatten your carcass and monitor your blood pressure, and if, despite all that, the camphor injections and the cardiac massage and the oxygen apparatus and even my inspiring phrases fail, and you're done for, and enter accounts only as a groundwater impurity, then please only in a churchyard the model of which was shown to general acclaim at the international hygiene fair in Atananarivo, since it brought the emotional and sanitary aspects of funeral service together so impeccably—one of those really super-duper churchyards with installations to reduce urban noise disturbance and provide simultaneous air sterilisation using the ozone- and uplift-spray system for surviving relatives!

That was man, and his idea of life and death. For that too he still has to pay, paste, stamp, fight, famish, and even his dreams torment him. The image that was godlike. Time was. Great, cruel, unhuman thoughts surfaced in Rönne. In twilight he saw the Creation, its veils and lights silvery and diffuse as after a cloudburst. And in the Creation a species, a particular species between the animals that came before and the animals that survived it. Within this species he saw a race—a white, domineering, godless, positivistic race: decomposition hubris and creative apathy. This race felt its hour approaching. With all the cruelty of their brains the groups fought it out among themselves, each wanted to overcome, each wanted to survive; victory and long life, everything for it, always for it, its hunger, its bones, its life, even measured against the animals its greed was great. But its hour had come—it began in the coal-mining forests, and it will end between the ice floes, not a moment longer, as it was in the beginning. Rönne saw it for a moment, then walked back and looked into his rooms: the instruments, glasses, hypodermics, the test-tubes, all the aspects of a highly developed biological industry. And as great as this industry was, it seemed to him too small for his perspective. The conviction suddenly arose within him: the productive power of his race resided solely in the fact of always being able to greet a new age with a new pathos, a kind of vertigo induced by world change, a kind of tapeworm of glad tidings …

if it now decided to change sides and turn the irrational, the vague, the creative ground too, into no more than a new business based on a senseless and purposeless reconstruction therapy—then out of this place, away from this kind of thinking: pure pension neurosis developed in a degenerative lag that has lasted centuries. Let it come: chaos, fall, doom and mortal panic.

Those could be final thoughts for a doctor, and what was alluded to at the outset might emerge: a serious threat to his person, indeed to his very existence, lies ahead of him. It would take this form: he would disappear from society and not enter his practice again, because it had become physically impossible for him to show charity for the type of human around him, impossible to turn his thoughts, his work towards restoring the individual glandular idyll of the white race. He would disappear; but his gaze remain fixed on an eternal mythical remainder of our race from which he believed he had learned, something we owe to it alone, of times when we were great and may still be for an hour or two.

"Irrationalismus und moderne Medizin," *Essays*, 1931.

KURT TUCHOLSKY
Apprehension

Kurt Tucholsky, a brilliant humorist who wrote for a number of German newspapers between the wars, penned this little squib under one of his several disguises, Kaspar Hauser. He doesn't seem to be familiar with Montaigne's reassurance in his essay On physiognomy: *"If you don't know how to die, never mind. Nature will instruct you how to do it there and then, plainly and adequately."*

Shall I know how to die? Sometimes I'm afraid I shan't.

What I'm wondering is this: how will you bear up when the time comes? Oh I don't mean the stiff upper lip—not that business against the wall, the shout "Long live ..." something or other while you get it in the neck; not the minute before the gas attack, your breeks full of courage and your heroically distorted face grimacing at the foe ... not that. No, merely the senseless business in bed: weariness, pain, and now The Dread Thing. Will you know how to do it?

Take an example: for years I could never manage to sneeze properly. I sneezed like a small dog with hiccups. And, if you'll pardon the expression, until I was twenty-eight I didn't know how to eructate; then I met Charlie, an old university friend, and he taught me. But who's going to show me how to die?

Oh yes, I've seen it happen. I've been to an execution, and I've seen sick people die—it seemed as if they made very heavy weather of it. But what'll happen if I ham it up so much it amounts to nothing? After all, it's not inconceivable.

"Don't worry, old chap, it'll sink down on you, this hard thing. You have a false idea of death. It'll ..." Is someone speaking from experience here? It's the truest of all democracies, this democracy of death. Which must account for the haughty superiority of clergymen, who all act as if they'd died a hundred times already, as if they got their information from the other side—and now they play the messengers of death among the living.

Perhaps it won't be so hard after all. A doctor will help me to die. And if my pain isn't too excruciating, I shall put on an embarrassed, modest little smile and say: "Please excuse me—it's my first time ..."

"Befürchtung," 1929.

GEORGE ORWELL

How the Poor Die

George Orwell (Eric Blair) died of pulmonary tuberculosis just months before a successful treatment was developed for it in the form of streptomycin and PAS. Twenty years before, during his period of rough living in Paris, a bout of pneumonia compelled him to visit the Hôpital St Jacques: it produced this sharp-eyed and compassionate essay which recalls dismal folk memories of the hospital as well as anticipating the National Health Service, launched in Britain the year after he published his essay. No hospital today would be quite so brazen in revealing the cynical allegiance of doctors to disease-processes rather than the people who suffer them, though Orwell would no doubt be perplexed to learn that cupping is making something of a revival. His technique of reflexive ethnography lies at the heart of this book: the "bronchial rattle" becomes moral observer of the French medical tradition.

In the year 1929 I spent several weeks in the Hôpital X, in the fifteenth arrondissement of Paris. The clerks put me through the usual third-degree at the reception desk, and indeed I was kept answering questions for some twenty minutes before they would let me in. If you have ever had to fill up forms in a Latin country you will know the kind of questions I mean. For some days past I had been unequal to translating Réaumur into Fahrenheit, but I know that my temperature was round about 103, and by the end of the interview I had some difficulty in standing on my feet. At my back a resigned little knot of patients, carrying bundles done up in coloured handkerchiefs, waited their turn to be questioned.

After the questioning came the bath—a compulsory routine for all newcomers, apparently, just as in prison or the workhouse. My clothes were taken away from me, and after I had sat shivering for some minutes in five inches of water I was given a linen nightshirt and a short blue flannel dressing-gown—no slippers, they had none big enough for me, they said—and led out into the open air. This was a night in February and I was suffering from pneumonia. The ward we were going to was 200 yards away and it seemed that to get to it you had to cross the hospital grounds. Someone stumbled in front of me with a lantern. The gravel path was frosty underfoot, and the wind whipped the nightshirt round my bare calves. When we got into the ward I was aware of a strange feeling of familiarity whose origin I did not succeed in pinning down till later in the night. It was a long, rather low, ill-lit room, full of murmuring voices and with three rows of beds surprisingly close together. There was a foul smell, faecal and yet sweetish. As I lay down I saw on a bed nearly opposite me a small, round-shouldered, sandy-haired man sitting half naked while a doctor and a student performed some strange operation on him. First the doctor produced from his black bag a dozen small glasses like wine glasses, then the student burned a match inside each glass to exhaust the air, then the glass was popped on to the man's back or chest and the vacuum drew up a huge yellow blister. Only after some moments did I realize what they were doing to him. It was something called cupping, a treatment which you can read about in old medical text-books but which till then I had vaguely thought of as one of those things they do to horses.

The cold air outside had probably lowered my temperature, and I watched this barbarous remedy with detachment and even a certain amount of amusement. The next moment, however, the doctor and the student came across to my bed, hoisted me upright and without a word began applying the same set of glasses, which had not been sterilized in any way. A few feeble protests that I uttered got no more response than if I had been an animal. I was very much impressed by the impersonal way in which the two men started on me. I had never been in the public ward of a hospital before, and it was my first experience of doctors who handle you without speaking to you or, in a human sense, taking any notice of you. They only put on six glasses in my case, but after doing so they scarified the blisters and applied the glasses again. Each glass now drew about a dessert-spoonful of dark-coloured blood. As I lay down again, humiliated, disgusted and frightened by the thing that had been done to me, I reflected that now at least they would leave me alone. But no, not a bit of it. There was another treatment coming, the mustard poultice, seemingly a matter of routine like the hot bath. Two slatternly nurses had already got the poultice ready, and they lashed it round my chest as tight as a strait-jacket while some men who were wandering about the ward in shirt and trousers began to collect round my bed with half-sympathetic grins. I learned later that watching a patient have a mustard poultice was a favourite pastime in the ward. These things are normally applied for a quarter of an hour and certainly they are funny enough if you don't happen to be the person inside. For the first five minutes the pain is severe, but you believe you can bear it. During the second five minutes this belief evaporates, but the poultice is buckled at the back and you can't get it off. This is the period the onlookers enjoy most. During the last five minutes, I noted, a sort of numbness supervenes. After the poultice had been removed a waterproof pillow packed with ice was thrust beneath my head and I was left alone. I did not sleep, and to the best of my knowledge this was the only night of my life—I mean the only night spent in bed—in which I have not slept at all, not even a minute.

During my first hour in the Hôpital X I had had a whole series of different and contradictory treatments, but this was misleading, for in general you got very little treatment at all, either good or bad, unless you were ill in some interesting and instructive way. At five in the morning the nurses came round, woke the patients and took their temperatures, but did not wash them. If you were well enough you washed yourself, otherwise you depended on the kindness of some walking patient. It was generally patients, too, who carried the bedbottles and the grim bedpan, nicknamed *la casserole*. At eight breakfast arrived, called army-fashion *la soupe*. It was soup, too, a thin vegetable soup with slimy hunks of bread floating about in it. Later in the day the tall, solemn, black-bearded doctor made his rounds, with an interne and a troop of students following at his heels, but there were about sixty of us in the ward and it was evident that he had other wards to attend to as well. There were many beds past which he walked day after day, sometimes followed by imploring cries. On the other hand if you had some disease with which the students were warned to familiarize themselves you got plenty of attention of a kind. I myself, with an exceptionally fine specimen of a bronchial rattle, sometimes had as many as a dozen students queuing up to listen to my chest. It was a very queer feeling—queer, I mean, because of their intense interest in learning their job, together with a seeming lack of any perception that the patients were human beings. It is strange to relate, but sometimes as some young student stepped forward to take his turn at manipulating you he would be actually tremulous with excitement, like a boy who has at last got his hands on some expensive piece of machinery. And then ear after ear—ears of young men, of girls, of negroes—pressed against your back, relays of fingers solemnly but clumsily tapping, and not from any one of them did you get a word of conversation or a look direct in your face. As a non-paying patient, in the uniform nightshirt, you were primarily *a specimen*, a thing I did not resent but could never quite get used to.

After some days I grew well enough to sit up and study the surrounding patients. The stuffy room, with its narrow beds so close together that you could easily touch your neighbour's hand, had every sort of disease in it except, I suppose, acutely infectious cases. My right-hand neighbour was a little red-haired cobbler with one leg shorter than the other, who used to announce the death of any other patient (this happened a number of times, and my neighbour was always the first to hear of it) by whistling to me, exclaiming "Numéro 43!" (or whatever it was) and flinging his arms above his head. This man had not much wrong with him, but in most of the other beds within my angle of vision some squalid tragedy or some plain horror was being enacted. In the bed that was foot to foot with mine there lay, until he died (I didn't see him die—they moved him to another bed), a little weazened man who was suffering from I do not know what disease, but something that made his whole body so intensely sensitive that any movement from side to side, sometimes even the weight of the bedclothes, would make him shout out with pain. His worst suffering was when he urinated, which he did with the greatest difficulty. A nurse would bring him the bedbottle and then for a long time stand beside his bed, whistling, as grooms are said to do with horses, until at last with an agonized shriek of "*Je pisse!*" he would get started. In the bed next to him the sandy-haired man whom I had seen being cupped used to cough up blood-streaked mucus at all hours. My left-hand neighbour was a tall, flaccid-looking young man who used periodically to have a tube inserted into his back and astonishing quantities of frothy liquid drawn off from some part of his body. In the bed beyond that a veteran of the war of 1870 was dying, a handsome old man with a white imperial, round whose bed, at all hours when visiting was allowed, four elderly female relatives dressed all in black sat exactly like crows, obviously scheming for some pitiful legacy. In the bed opposite me in the farther row was an old bald-headed man with drooping moustaches and greatly swollen face and body, who was suffering from some disease that made him urinate almost incessantly. A huge glass receptacle stood always beside his bed. One day his wife and daughter came to visit him. At sight of them the old man's bloated face lit up with a smile of surprising sweetness, and as his daughter, a pretty girl of about twenty, approached the bed I saw that his hand was slowly working its way from under the bedclothes. I seemed to see in advance the gesture that was coming—the girl kneeling beside the bed, the old man's hand laid on her head in his dying blessing. But no, he merely handed her the bedbottle, which she promptly took from him and emptied into the receptacle.

About a dozen beds away from me was Numéro 57—I think that was his number—a cirrhosis-of-the-liver case. Everyone in the ward knew him by sight because he was sometimes the subject of a medical lecture. On two afternoons a week the tall, grave doctor would lecture in the ward to a party of students, and on more than one occasion old Numéro 57 was wheeled in on a sort of trolley into the middle of the ward, where the doctor would roll back his nightshirt, dilate with his fingers a huge flabby protruberance on the man's belly—the diseased liver, I suppose— and explain solemnly that this was a disease attributable to alcoholism, commoner in the wine-drinking countries. As usual he neither spoke to his patient nor gave him a smile, a nod or any kind of recognition. While he talked, very grave and upright, he would hold the wasted body beneath his two hands, sometimes giving it a gentle roll to and fro, in just the attitude of a woman handling a rolling-pin. Not that Numéro 57 minded this kind of thing. Obviously he was an old hospital inmate, a regular exhibit at lectures, his liver long since marked down for a bottle in some pathological museum. Utterly uninterested in what was said about him, he would lie with his colourless eyes gazing at nothing, while the doctor showed him off like a piece of antique china. He was a man of about sixty, astonishingly shrunken. His face, pale as vellum, had shrunken away till it seemed no bigger than a doll's.

One morning my cobbler neighbour woke me up plucking at my pillow before the nurses arrived. "Numéro 57!"—he flung his arms above his head. There was a light in the ward, enough to see by. I could see old Numéro 57 lying crumpled up on his side, his face sticking out over the side of the bed, and towards me. He had died some time during the night, nobody knew when. When the nurses came they received the news of his death indifferently and went about their work. After a long time, an hour or more, two other nurses marched in abreast like soldiers, with a great clumping of sabots, and knotted the corpse up in the sheets, but it was not removed till some time later. Meanwhile, in the better light, I had had time for a good look at Numéro 57. Indeed I lay on my side to look at him. Curiously enough he was the first dead European I had seen. I had seen dead men before, but always Asiatics and usually people who had died violent deaths. Numéro 57's eyes were still open, his mouth also open, his small face contorted into an expression of agony. What most impressed me, however, was the whiteness of his face. It had been pale before, but now it was little darker than the sheets. As I gazed at the tiny, screwed-up face it struck me that this disgusting piece of refuse, waiting to be carted away and dumped on a slab in the dissecting room, was an example of "natural" death, one of the things you pray for in the Litany. There you are, then, I thought, that's what is waiting for you, twenty, thirty, forty years hence: that is how the lucky ones die, the ones who live to be old. One wants to live, of course, indeed one only stays alive by virtue of the fear of death, but I think now, as I thought then, that it's better to die violently and not too old. People talk about the horrors of war, but what weapon has man invented that even approaches in cruelty some of the commoner diseases? A death, almost by definition, means something slow, smelly and painful. Even at that, it makes a difference if you can achieve it in your own home and not in a public institution. This poor old wretch who had just flickered out like a candle-end was not even important enough to have anyone watching by his deathbed. He was merely a number, then a "subject" for the students' scalpels. And the sordid publicity of dying in such a place! In the Hôpital X the beds were very close together and there were no screens. Fancy, for instance, dying like the little man whose bed was for a while foot to foot with mine, the one who cried out when the bedclothes touched him! I dare say "*Je pisse!*" were his last recorded words. Perhaps the dying don't bother about such things— that at least would be the standard answer: nevertheless dying people are often more or less normal in their minds till within a day or so of the end.

In the public wards of a hospital you see horrors that you don't seem to meet with among people who manage to die in their own homes, as though certain diseases only attacked people at the lower income levels. But it is a fact that you would not in any English hospitals see some of the things I saw in the Hôpital X. This business of people just dying like animals, for instance, with nobody standing by, nobody interested, the death not even noticed till the morning—this happened more than once. You certainly would not see that in England, and still less would you see a corpse left exposed to the view of the other patients. I remember that once in a cottage hospital in England a man died while we were at tea, and though there were only six of us in the ward the nurses managed things so adroitly that the man was dead and his body removed without our even hearing about it till tea was over. A thing we perhaps underrate in England is the advantage we enjoy in having large numbers of well-trained and rigidly-disciplined nurses. No doubt English nurses are dumb enough, they may tell fortunes with tea-leaves, wear Union Jack badges and keep photographs of the Queen on their mantelpieces, but at least they don't let you lie unwashed and constipated on an unmade bed, out of sheer laziness. The nurses at the Hôpital X still had a tinge of Mrs Gamp about them, and later, in the military hospitals of Republican Spain, I was to see nurses almost too ignorant to take a temperature. You wouldn't, either, see in England such dirt as existed in the Hôpital X.

Later on, when I was well enough to wash myself in the bathroom, I found that there was kept there a huge packing case into which the scraps of food and dirty dressings from the ward were flung, and the wainscotings were infested by crickets. When I had got back my clothes and grown strong on my legs I fled from the Hôpital X, before my time was up and without waiting for a medical discharge. It was not the only hospital I have fled from, but its gloom and bareness, its sickly smell and, above all, something in its mental atmosphere stand out in my memory as exceptional. I had been taken there because it was the hospital belonging to my arrondissement, and I did not learn till after I was in it that it bore a bad reputation. A year or two later the celebrated swindler, Madame Hanaud, who was ill while on remand, was taken to the Hôpital X, and after a few days of it she managed to elude her guards, took a taxi and drove back to the prison, explaining that she was more comfortable there. I have no doubt that the Hôpital X was quite untypical of French hospitals even at that date. But the patients, nearly all of them working men, were surprisingly resigned. Some of them seemed to find the conditions almost comfortable, for at least two were destitute malingerers who found this a good way of getting through the winter. The nurses connived because the malingerers made themselves useful by doing odd jobs. But the attitude of the majority was: of course this is a lousy place, but what else do you expect? It did not seem strange to them that you should be woken at five and then wait three hours before starting the day on watery soup, or that people should die with no one at their bedside, or even that your chance of getting medical attention should depend on catching the doctor's eye as he went past. According to their traditions that was what hospitals were like. If you are seriously ill and if you are too poor to be treated in your own home, then you must go into hospital, and once there you must put up with harshness and discomfort, just as you would in the army. But on top of this I was interested to find a lingering belief in the old stories that have now almost faded from memory in England—stories, for instance, about doctors cutting you open out of sheer curiosity or thinking it funny to start operating before you were properly "under". There were dark tales about a little operating-room said to be situated just beyond the bathroom. Dreadful screams were said to issue from this room. I saw nothing to confirm these stories and no doubt they were all nonsense, though I did see two students kill a sixteen-year-old boy, or nearly kill him (he appeared to be dying when I left the hospital, but he may have recovered later) by a mischievous experiment which they probably could not have tried on a paying patient. Well within living memory it used to be believed in London that in some of the big hospitals patients were killed off to get dissection subjects. I didn't hear this tale repeated at the Hôpital X, but I should think some of the men there would have found it credible. For it was a hospital in which not the methods, perhaps, but something of the atmosphere of the nineteenth century had managed to survive, and therein lay its peculiar interest.

During the past fifty years or so there has been a great change in the relationship between doctor and patient. If you look at almost any literature before the later part of the nineteenth century, you find that a hospital is popularly regarded as much the same thing as a prison, and an old-fashioned, dungeon-like prison at that. A hospital is a place of filth, torture and death, a sort of antechamber to the tomb. No one who was not more or less destitute would have thought of going into such a place for treatment. And especially in the early part of the last century, when medical science had grown bolder than before without being any more successful, the whole business of doctoring was looked on with horror and dread by ordinary people. Surgery, in particular, was believed to be no more than a peculiarly gruesome form of sadism, and dissection, possible only with the aid of bodysnatchers, was even confused with necromancy. From the nineteenth century you could collect a large horror-literature connected with doctors and hospitals. Think of poor old George III, in his dotage, shrieking for mercy as he sees his surgeons approaching to "bleed him till he faints"! Think of the conversations of Bob Sawyer and Benjamin Allen, which no doubt are hardly parodies, or the field hospitals in *La Débâcle* and *War and Peace*, or that shocking description of an amputation in Melville's *Whitejacket*! Even the names given to doctors in nineteenth-century English fiction, Slasher, Carver, Sawyer, Fillgrave and so on, and the generic nickname "sawbones", are about as grim as they are comic. The anti-surgery tradition is perhaps best expressed in Tennyson's poem, *The Children's Hospital*, which is essentially a pre-chloroform document though it seems to have been written as late as 1880. Moreover, the outlook which Tennyson records in this poem had a lot to be said for it. When you consider what an operation without anaesthetics must have been like, what it notoriously was like, it is difficult not to suspect the motives of people who would undertake such things. For these bloody horrors which the students so eagerly looked forward to ("A magnificent sight if Slasher does it!") were admittedly more or less useless: the patient who did not die of shock usually died of gangrene, a result which was taken for granted. Even now doctors can be found whose motives are questionable. Anyone who has had much illness, or who has listened to medical students talking, will know what I mean. But anaesthetics were a turning point, and disinfectants were another. Nowhere in the world probably would you now see the kind of scene described by Axel Munthe in *The Story of San Michele*, when the sinister surgeon in top hat and frock coat, his starched shirtfront spattered with blood and pus, carves up patient after patient with the same knife and flings the severed limbs into a pile beside the table. Moreover, the national health insurance has partly done away with the idea that a working-class patient is a pauper who deserves little consideration. Well into this century it was usual for "free" patients at the big hospitals to have their teeth extracted with no anaesthetic. They didn't pay, so why should they have an anaesthetic—that was the attitude. That too has changed.

And yet every institution will always bear upon it some lingering memory of its past. A barrack-room is still haunted by the ghost of Kipling, and it is difficult to enter a workhouse without being reminded of *Oliver Twist*. Hospitals began as a kind of casual ward for lepers and the like to die in, and they continued as places where medical students learned their art on the bodies of the poor. You can still catch a faint suggestion of their history in their characteristically gloomy architecture. I would be far from complaining about the treatment I have received in any English hospital, but I do know that it is sound instinct that warns people to keep out of hospitals if possible, and especially out of the public wards. Whatever the legal position may be, it is unquestionable that you have far less control over your own treatment, far less certainty that frivolous experiments will not be tried on you, when it is a case of "accept the discipline or get out". And it is a great thing to die in your own bed, though it is better still to die in your boots. However great the kindness and the efficiency, in every hospital death there will be some cruel, squalid detail, something perhaps too small to be told but leaving terribly painful memories behind, arising out of the haste, the crowding, the impersonality of a place where every day people are dying among strangers.

The dread of hospitals probably still survives among the very poor, and in all of us it has only recently disappeared. It is a dark patch not far beneath the surface of our minds. I have said earlier that when I entered the ward at the Hôpital X I was conscious of a strange feeling of familiarity. What the scene reminded me of, of course, was the reeking, pain-filled hospitals of the nineteenth century, which I had never seen but of which I had a traditional knowledge. And something, perhaps the black-clad doctor with his frowsy black bag, or perhaps only the sickly smell, played the queer trick of unearthing from my memory that poem of Tennyson's, *The Children's Hospital*, which I had not thought of for twenty years. It happened that as a child I had had it read aloud to me by a sick-nurse whose own working life might have stretched back to the time when Tennyson wrote the poem. The horrors and sufferings of the old-style hospitals were a vivid memory to her. We had shuddered over the poem together, and then seemingly I had forgotten it. Even its name would probably have recalled nothing to me. But the first glimpse of the ill-lit murmurous room, with the beds so close together, suddenly roused the train of thought to which it belonged, and in the night that followed I found myself remembering the whole story and atmosphere of the poem, with many of its lines complete.

"How the Poor Die," *Now*, 1946.

KARL KRAUS

Aphorisms

Karl Kraus (1874–1936) was a great Viennese satirist and columnist who had an ear for condemning people out of their own mouths. Living in Vienna he of course had the privilege of witnessing the spectacle of Psychoanalysis emerging, fully-armoured, from Sigmund Freud's head: Kraus promptly declared it stillborn. His quip about diagnosis being a disease is properly understandable only in the light of the therapeutic nihilism which had taken root in Viennese medicine in the late nineteenth century: out of fear of distorting symptoms the only drug used by doctors in the General Hospital was cherry brandy.

Medicine: "your money *and your* life".

Anaesthesia: wounds without suffering. Neurasthenia: suffering without wounds.

One of the most widespread diseases at present is diagnosis.

He died, bitten by Asclepius's snake.

Psychoanalysis is the mental disease for which it purports to be the treatment.

Today's literature: prescriptions written by patients.

"Aphorismen," *Die Fackel*, 1899–1936.

LOUIS-FERDINAND CÉLINE

Doctor in the Zone

Céline's first novel, Voyage to the End of the Night, *which appeared in 1933, is one of the most striking novels written by a doctor. It is also one of the hardest boiled books written by anybody. Published after the debacle of the First World War, in a period in which frankness had become a literary convention, Céline's disgust with the moral code brings his characters to assume a kind of reductive nec plus ultra: morality is a con-trick, man an egoist, and life a mirage. Much of* Voyage *is based on Céline's medical experiences in the Paris suburbs, the Zone being the strip of land around the outskirts of the old city. Candour makes the fire-sale philosophy of the novel seem like an explanation of existence: it was a political trap Céline was to walk straight into himself at the end of the 1930s.*

It was about then I was put in charge of a small neighbourhood tuberculosis clinic. I won't make any bones about it: it brought in eight hundred francs a month. My patients were mostly people from the Zone, that weird village that never quite manages to extricate itself from the sludge and litter, with its lanes where wee lassies, snotty-nosed and way too sassy, skip school under the fences in order to get a few bob, a handful of chips and a dose of clap from some sex monster. A setting for avant-garde films: trees rank with dirty laundry and lettuces sopping with urine on Saturday night. No miracles were performed in those few months of specialized practice, though a miracle or two was what was needed. Not that my patients wanted me to perform miracles, quite the opposite—tuberculosis was the vouchsafe that might raise them from the state of absolute misery they'd been festering in for as long as they could remember to the state of relative misery afforded by a piddly government pension. Their sputum, as good as positive whenever it was tested, had got them out of military service since the war. Fever made them thinner and thinner;

and they stayed in a fever through eating little, vomiting a lot, drinking prodigious quantities of wine, and working through it all, if only one day in three.

Hope of a pension possessed them body and soul. It would descend on them one day like grace, but only if they had the strength to bide their time a bit longer before they finally kicked the bucket. Nobody really knows what it is to recover and wait for something if you haven't seen all the recovering and waiting poor people do for the sake of a pension.

With the rain coming down outside, they'd spend whole afternoons and even weeks hoping in the entrance and doorway of my dilapidated health centre, conjuring up their dreams of percentages, their longings for frankly positive sputum, genuine sputum, absolutely proven and confirmed TB sputum. The hope of remission came a long way behind their hope of a pension. Sure, they thought too about getting cured, but not much: they were so enthralled by their dream of getting an income, no matter how piddling, no matter how. This desire, peremptory and absolute as it was, left them with no proclivity for anything else but small and insignificant wishes: even their death became by comparison a subordinate issue, at the very most a sporting risk. Death after all was only a business of a few hours, perhaps minutes, but a pension was like poverty: it lasted a lifetime. Rich people are under the influence in a different way; they can't understand this craze for security. Being rich is another kind of inebriation, it's the drunkenness of forgetting it all. But that's the very reason for getting rich: to forget.

Little by little I'd rid myself of my bad habit of promising them good health, my patients. The prospect of getting well could hardly have thrilled them. Good health was only ever a stopgap. Being healthy means you can work—and then what? While a government pension, even the littlest, is manna from heaven, pure and simple.

If you've no money to offer the poor, better keep your trap shut. If you talk to them about anything but money, you're either tricking them or pulling a fast one. Almost always. It's easy to amuse the rich. All you need, for one thing, is mirrors. Mirrors for them to catch themselves in, because there's nothing better in the world to look at than the rich. Want to keep the rich cheerful? Just notch them up a rack in the Legion of Honour every ten years, like a pair of saggy boobs, that'll keep them busy for another ten years. That's all. My patients were poor and wrapped up with themselves. They were materialists who could think of nothing more than their sordid hope: positive blood-streaked sputum equals pension. They couldn't give a fig for anything else. Not even the seasons. All they knew and cared to know about the seasons was that they affected their cough and their general condition: in the winter, for instance, they got lots more colds than in the summer, but then they were more likely to spit blood in the springtime, and if it was really hot they might lose as much as six pounds in a week … Sometimes I heard them chatting together when they were waiting their turn, and thought I was somewhere else. Story after story, endless horror stories about me. Lies that would take the top of your head off. Taking me down a rung like that must have given them a fillip, given them some kind of strange courage they needed to be harder and tougher, to be vicious old buggers, able to survive and stick it out. Having someone they could run down, despise and threaten made them feel better. No doubt about it. And yet I did all I could to humour them. I took their side; I tried to help them; I gave them plenty of iodine to help them spit up their disgusting bacilli—I did all that, but I never managed to disarm their nastiness.

When I asked them questions, they stood in front of me, smiling like servants; but they never warmed to me, mainly because I was helping them but also because I wasn't rich. Having me for a doctor meant they were being treated free of charge, which is never flattering for a sick person, even if he is hoping for a pension. There was no malicious rumour they wouldn't have spread behind my back. Most of the doctors in the neighbourhood had cars but I didn't, and to them it was a further confir-mation that I wasn't up to it. Given the slightest encouragement, something my colleagues were never slow to do, they'd get back at me, or so it seemed, for all my helpfulness, for my cooperativeness and concern. That's the way of the world. Time passed anyway.

One evening when my waiting room had almost emptied, a priest came in to see me. I didn't know him, and almost showed him the door.

I didn't much care for priests. I had my reasons, especially since the time they'd press-ganged me at San Tapeta. But hard as I tried to place this one, to bawl him out with a mouthful just for him, the fact was that I'd never seen him before. Still, he must have done a lot of night calls like me in Rancy; he lived nearby. Was he trying to avoid me then, when he did his rounds? I considered the odds. Maybe somebody had told him I didn't like priests. You could tell it by the way he got his words in edgeways. One thing was sure—we had never bumped ito each other around the same sickbeds. He had been doing the duties at a nearby church for the last twenty years, he said. Plenty of parishioners, but not that many who paid. A kind of beggar, in fact. That much we had in common. The cassock he was wearing struck me as a most impractical bit of clothing for trudging through the muck of the Zone. I thought so, and I said so. I went so far as to stress the extravagant discomfort of such a garment.

"You get used to it," he said.

The impertinence of my remark didn't put him off, and he became even more affable. Obviously he had something to ask of me. His voice rarely rose above a kind of off-the-record monotone which, or so I imagined, came from his calling. While he was getting around to the gist of what he had to say, I tried to form a mental picture of what he did every day to earn his calories, all those facial contortions and promises, pretty much like my own ... And then, to amuse myself, I imagined him stark naked at the altar ... That's what you have to do when people come to see you for the first time: strip them naked in your mind, and you'll see through them in a flash, whoever it is; you'll see straightaway the maggot-reality inside everybody, giant and devouring. It's a wee trick of imagination. Lousy prestige fades away, evaporates. And once the person's naked, you've got nothing more in front of you than a puffed-up, pretentious beggar, who's bursting his guts to splutter out something or other. Nothing withstands this test. In a moment you know what's what. All that's left are ideas, and ideas never scared anybody. Nothing gets lost with ideas, everything can be straightened out. Whereas it's sometimes hard to stand up to the prestige of a fully clothed man. Nasty smells and inscrutabilities cling to his clothes.

This Abbé had dreadful teeth, decayed and stained, with deposits of greenish tartar at their necks, in short a fine case of alveolar pyorrhoea. I was going to talk to him about his pyorrhoea, but he was too busy telling me things. The things he was telling me kept squirting against the stumps of his teeth under the lashings of his tongue, no movement of which escaped me. Spots on the margin of his tongue were peeled and bleeding.

This kind of punctilious personal observation was a habit of mine. A predilection you might say. If you stop to look at how words are formed and uttered, our phrases have a hard time surviving the disaster of their slobbery surroundings. The mechanical effort of conversation is harder and more intricate than defaecation. That corolla of bloated flesh, the mouth, which stiffens itself to whistle, which sucks in breath and contorts itself wildly, propels all kinds of viscous sound across the fetid blockade of decaying teeth—what a punishment! Yet that is what we're called upon to sublimate into an ideal. No easy task. Being nothing but bundles of lukewarm, half-rotten viscera, we'll always have trouble with feelings. Falling in love is a cakewalk, it's staying together that's difficult. Ordure doesn't try to last or grow. On that score we're worse off than excrement; our mad frenzy to hang on to what we are—that's the unbearable torture.

No doubt about it: we worship nothing more divine than our smell. All our misery comes from wanting to go on being Tom, Dick or Harry, year in year out. No matter what it costs. This body of ours, this veil put on by a cloud of agitated molecules, is in perpetual rebellion against the awful farce of having to endure. Our dear little molecules just want to disperse across the universe as fast they can! They're really up against it being nothing but "us", infinity's has-beens! If we had the courage we'd burst apart, and there are days we come close to it. Our cherished torture is locked up inside us, atoms in our very skin, along with our pride.

Since I was silent, stunned by the biological abominations I'd conjured up, the Abbé, thinking he had it wrapped up and that I was entirely in his pocket, took on a benevolent and almost familiar manner. Obviously he had got the low-down on me beforehand. With the greatest care and delicacy he broached the subject of my medical reputation in the area. My reputation might have been better, he gave me to understand, even within a few months of having started, had I done otherwise when setting up practice in Rancy. "We mustn't forget, my dear doctor, that the sick are deeply conservative ... They live in fear, as you doubtless know, that heaven and earth will fail them ..."

In other words, I should have come to terms with the Church from the start. That was his spiritual and eminently practical conclusion as well. The idea was sound enough. I held myself back from interrupting him and waited and waited for him to come to the point of his visit.

Excerpt from *Voyage au Bout de la Nuit*, 1933.

DEZSÖ KOSZTOLÁNYI

The Stranger

Dezsö Kosztolányi (1885–1936) was one of the brilliant generation of Hungarian writers who congregated around the literary journal Nyugat *(West), founded in 1908 and heavily influenced by the "Budapest correspondent" of the burgeoning psycho-analytic movement, Sandor Ferenczi, who thought the idea of professional neutrality was a fiction. His pupil, Michael Balint, founder of the method that bears his name, went on to have a major impact on general practice in the British NHS in the 1950s. The stranger in this simple little story guards the secret of his personal identity to the end, while infecting those around him with something like common humanity.*

In those days, the world wasn't yet a little fleck of earth scored with telephone lines and electricity grids you could fly around in a couple of days: each country, each individual was able to keep secrets. People didn't move about like they do today: travelling took longer and cost more. On the other hand, you didn't have to hand over your passport at the end of every field or enter your civil status in all kinds of registers. In those days there were still vagabonds and strangers.

The stranger I'm going to tell you about came from a distant Nordic country. But he wasn't Norwegian or Swedish or Danish, and not only could he speak just the one language, his mother-tongue, but nobody could understand it.

In the little hotel in which he had landed, he communicated by signs. In the restaurant where he took his meals, morning and evening, he beckoned the waiter over, "scrutinised" the menu and pointed to a dish, at random, with his finger. When it was brought to him, he nodded his head in approval. He was always satisfied with what he got.

"Who could he be?" wondered the other guests who saw him day in day out.

But nobody could answer their question.

There was nothing strange about the stranger, nothing noteworthy, other than the fact that nobody knew who he was.

He was a placid and unassuming fifty-year-old man. Not in the least a shrinking violet, he looked in fact a bit crumpled and disillusioned.

After the meal, he stayed behind at the table, lit a cigarette and casually glanced around at the other guests.

"But who is this man?" the waiters and chambermaids asked each other, but in vain. Not knowing what to say, they just shrugged their shoulders and smiled.

Every morning, the stranger went into town. He walked with a measured step, not hurried, but not dawdling either. Always back first at mealtimes, he ate his way through some dish selected at random, nodded with his head, paid, and then went out, not without having once again nodded his head. He never asked for anything else. He seemed to be a man without a past.

He lived in this manner at the hotel for a month.

One morning, he rang the bell unexpectedly. He was in bed and wanted to explain something at all costs to the waiter who had run in. He pointed to his heart. Since his face was unusually pale, the waiter called a doctor.

The doctor tried to ask him a few questions, firstly in the local language, and then, one after the other, in German, French and English, but the stranger could understand none of these languages. To all these questions he replied with a single strange-sounding word the doctor didn't understand.

The doctor felt the patient's heart, then grasped both his wrists at once, trying to find a pulse, the beats of which had become imperceptible.

The stranger was lying in the bed as calmly as before.

As for the feverish doctor, he opened his bag in a hurry, took out his syringe and gave him an injection. He knew what was happening. He had often been present at this kind of event before. In any corner of the globe, the scene is always the same. He waited a little before pushing the syringe back into the patient's flesh.

Eyes half-closed, face blanched, the stranger lay prone on his white pillow.

A few moments later, his eyes opened and his chin sagged.

The doctor rang the bell.

The floor waiter was the first to come in, followed by the hotel director and two or three chambermaids, who had heard the news in the corridor.

Dumbfounded, they circled round the bed in silence.

The youngest thought of their grandparents, the less young of their father, of their mother, or another member of the family, since they had all seen a similar sight before.

Henceforth, the stranger was familiar. They knew who he was.

A man, who, like them, had lived on this earth and who had left as they would leave one day.

He wasn't a stranger any more. He was a brother.

"Az idegen," *Hét Köver Esztendö*, 1930.

PAUL VALÉRY

Socrates and his Physician

The elevated tone of this dialogue might seem to keep odd company, but Valéry's observations on the nature of knowledge in the encounter between Hippocratic doctor and patient are insightful and not lacking in humour. Flight, says Socrates of the departing Eryximachus, whose ministrations are themselves a drug, is in the physician's nature. In his pregnant concept of the ill which "is itself a thinking force," Valéry anticipates the dynamic of the therapeutic culture that would emerge in full bloom only after the war.

SOCRATES

Are you leaving me?

ERYXIMACHUS

I have to dash to the bedside of a woman patient ...

SOCRATES

But I'm still suffering, by the Gods ... My head is throbbing but vacant; my limbs are in pieces; my mouth is dry and bitter; my entire body is weighed down and leaden and prone to pins and needles, as though I carried within me a fatal principle governing all contradictions ...

ERYXIMACHUS

You'll feel better this evening; and well tomorrow.

SOCRATES

Please stay. I know that as soon as you're out of reach, my pains will worsen, and I'll have to send someone to fetch you ... Leave your coat and stick where they are, your lantern too ...

ERYXIMACHUS

Someone else is ill, another call. Someone is writhing with pain on another couch, begging the Gods to bring the sound of my footsteps. I beseech you Socrates, you the man I admire above all mortals—summon to your help the sublime calm of your great intelligence: let it dispel your fears, which I know to be quite groundless. Continue to sip lukewarm water. Think, but in moderation. Remain on your couch. Watch how the day dissipates on your wall, and how the balance between light and shadow shifts imperceptibly into night. Time itself is a great remedy. I tell you the fight is over; you are the conqueror, and your body's cause has won. You will feel refreshed and full of life when dawn comes. Now I must go ...

SOCRATES

Go ... But don't go until you've answered a question ... Just one. You mustn't leave until you've satisfied my mind about an issue which troubles it. I'm anxious to know ...

ERYXIMACHUS

Look how much better you are already ... Our philosopher is already feeling better, reinvigorated by a thought more universal than the idea of fever and glum ruminations induced by nausea.

SOCRATES

Oh! no ... I'm not feeling so well! ... But the ill in me is itself a thinking force. Listen! If you leave without giving me an answer, the question will haunt me, the fever return, sleep overwhelm me or escape me—your ministrations thwarted by yourself ... Listen, Eryximachus.

ERYXIMACHUS

Alright ... I'm listening. But I swear to you that three-quarters of my soul is elsewhere.

SOCRATES

Tell me: you assert that I'm regaining the fullness of good health, and that my existence will reappropriate all its virtues, much as a branch, bent by a child's hand or a dove's weight, and then restored to itself, returns to its place in the tree after a few wavering movements ...

ERYXIMACHUS

I assure you it will.

SOCRATES

You also say that you're running off to help another mortal who's summoning your help; and from this one you will no doubt go off on your winged feet to bring succour to a third, and so on ... But how can you so acutely foretell, in the face of such dissimilar adversities, what will become of the various ills, whether the visceral problems of all these bodies which have nothing in common but disease and suffering will get better or worse?

ERYXIMACHUS

Aren't you yourself flitting from idea to idea? Don't you switch interlocutor and therefore tactics? Don't you know (as if you didn't!) that Zeno is seduced differently from Phaedrus? Do you try to enter, treat and cure every soul with just one method, using the same approach every time?

SOCRATES

Wait ... You shouldn't be questioning me. Your time may be precious, but my thoughts are fleeting. If I want to know something, the very instant of my will also happens to be the very instant in which my mind is most happily poised to be imbued by the enlightenment offered it. A mind is all the more receptive the closer it is to producing itself what it desires ... Isn't this true, by the way, of all nourishment, and isn't it said too about fertilization?

ERYXIMACHUS

I've heard it said ...

SOCRATES

Allow me then to tell you, while the thought is fresh, what arouses my curiosity. It's you yourself. You're the one who does or who seeks to do me good: now I want to consider solely the person who possesses the power to do this good, to me and to many others. It's your art itself which intrigues me. I ask myself: how do you know what you know, and what kind of mind do you have to be able to speak to me as you did just now, without falsehood or presumption, when you told me—foretold me— that I shall be cured tomorrow, and at ease with my body when I waken in the morning? I marvel at what you must be, you and your medicine, in order to elicit from my nature this happy oracle and to anticipate its turning for the better. This body of mine confides in you, not in me; all it addresses me are hurt, fatigue and pains—as if they were the insults and blasphemies extended by its displeasure. It speaks to my mind as to a beast, a beast led not by explanation, but with blows and curses; whereas it tells you clearly what it wishes and doesn't wish, and why it is the way it is. It's strange that you should know a thousand times more than I do about myself, and that I should be, as it were, transparent to the light of your knowledge, while to myself I appear obscure and opaque. What am I saying! … You even see what I've yet to become, and assign a certain good to my body to which it must respond, as though on your express orders and at an appointed time … Wait. You're staring at me as though my astonishment astonished you, as if I were making you listen to some childish question.

ERYXIMACHUS

I'm waiting, O greatest among wise men, I'm waiting; it is true that I stand astonished. But please don't forget: each word uttered *here* adds a tiny grain of unbearable duration *there* to someone else's anxious waiting.

SOCRATES

Listen then. You often come to take part in the conversations between myself and my friends: you know that once business and practical affairs are concluded I spend my time questioning myself, either alone or by following the dialectical twists of well-constructed conversations, seeking by every possible means to form an idea of myself as right and sincere as possible, and believing no other object worthier of being fathomed. I haven't found any other object worth living for, for the purpose of a life seems to me to be to use its time and strength to make, or to create, or to perceive something which makes the idea of recommencing existence quite pointless, and even inconceivable and absurd. *Living should therefore, in my view, be directed against reliving.* In other words, the essential aim of a life's course is a self-knowledge so accomplished that nothing thereafter, when it reaches its highest point, is able to alter the structure, forms or ways of expression of that life. It is just like the growth of a child: all of its blunderings and risky experiments after birth gradually coalesce to give it possession of its body and of the sensate world, and once this possession is definitively acquired it can no longer be increased or changed, or even imagined other than it is.

To be able to experience this extreme knowledge would also be the last thought possible, and like the last drop of liquid that trembles on the brim of a vase. The measure being full, the duration of my life would seem to me in that exact moment exhausted.

I've done my best, friend Eryximachus, to follow the way of this ending. While I could certainly never claim to have an intimate knowledge of my mortal body or to imagine all the hazards which might befall it, I flattered myself that my soul would always dominate and be master, if not of the entire force of my body (for overweening sufferings and unbearable ordeals do exist) then, at least, of all that which, stemming from this body, tends to lead it astray and into error regarding the good and true and beautiful. Now you're causing me to entertain great fears about the very substance of my principle and my hope. If you can·show me that you know me better than I myself, and can even predict how I'll be feeling next, seeing me already cheerful and full of life when I actually feel quite low and down in the mouth, there is surely only one conclusion—that my whole effort is puerile, that my intimate tactics fade away in the face of your entirely exterior art, which envelops both my body and my mind within a finely woven web of exact knowledge, thereby seizing the universe of my person in one fell motion.

ERYXIMACHUS

Don't make me sound so impressive, great Socrates ... I'm not the monster of knowledge and power which your words are conjuring up. My limitations are all too certain.

I'm interested solely in phenomena; I try to find my bearings inside their complexity and confusion so as to bring as much relief as possible to the beings who consult me, and in the act of relief to cause them the least harm (for the physician ought to fear his art and not make unlimited use of its weapons).

It is true that I know you better than you know yourself in that you are ignorant of yourself; but infinitely less well in that you do know yourself. I know much better than you what's in your belly and between the bones of even your wonderfully gifted head; I can say with some, though not absolute assurance how you'll be, and your mood, when the night is over. But what you make of that mood, and of all the fine surprises which it'll bring to your mind and delight us with in the evenings—all this escapes me, and necessarily so, for if not your fame would be mine, and in the eyes of men and the gods I should be a more-than-Socrates ... You are ignorant of yourself, Socrates, in so far as you are mortal, for in its purity your mind is engaged here and now in separating its essence from everything perishable: if you knew what I know, you couldn't know what you do know ... Goodbye. I leave you with your daemon, and your body to the clement hands of Asclepius.

SOCRATES

But ... He's already far away! ... Flight, I can see now, is in the nature of physicians. True enough—I don't know what would become of medicine and mortals if a physician were attached to each and every one of them, a physician who never left them night or day and who kept them under perpetual observation. This one here turns his back on me. He leaves me divided between what he knows and what I don't know on the one hand, and what he doesn't know and what I do on the other ... A strange, ambiguous sentence keeps repeating itself in my mind, still rather dulled and clouded, like an oracle: EVERYTHING DEPENDS ON ME AND I'M HANGING BY A THREAD ...

"Socrate et son médecin," *Mélange*, 1941.

ERNST WEISS

Heart Suture

Ernst Weiss (1882–1940) was an ophthalmologist, close friend of Franz Kafka and productive novelist. It is interesting to compare this melodrama in which surgery is an extreme expedient (a quasi-military procedure conducted by "the General" with, as we would say, "surgical precision") with the lurid description given by Léon Daudet of the famous surgeon Péan: "After two hours of this activity, he was drenched in blood and sweat, with his hands—or rather, his clubs—as red as a murderer's, his feet dyed crimson, and he was always very cheerful … This scientific massacre was at once butchershop, scaffold, and bullfight … Never have I seen such a mincemeat of human flesh, such a mountain of torsos, trunks, and stumps." It will be noted, in the impersonal if more humane theatre of surgery depicted by Weiss, that the would-be suicide instrument is a pen.

Medical student Friedrich von B., tall, blond and young, passionately fond of "major surgery," but certainly not averse to other kinds of passions, among which a certain Hildegard Anneliese had played a considerable if, in recent times, not entirely happy role, was taken on at the beginning of December as an unpaid assistant in the surgical clinic of privy councillor O., known to his students because of his military appearance and his imposing bearing as the General. This appointment was not unrelated to an old duelling club friendship between the professor and the student's father. Friedrich von B did all sorts of jobs in the clinic, initially without attracting the notice of his father's friend; they were odd jobs, but essential and responsible tasks: anaesthesics, dressings, minor operations. Sometimes he found himself just mooning about, waiting to be asked to do something, or he portered patients to the lectures that took place on week-days between a quarter to ten and eleven.

On one of these occasions, on January 17, the Professor gave a lecture on malignant tumours. With pride, he wheeled forward his permanent successes, patients he had operated on three or five years before, even one person he had treated seven and a half years before when he had just taken up his surgical teaching post in the city, and who, like the others, had stayed healthy and not relapsed. The operations had been difficult; and the fact that the patients were in remission for so long was a triumph of surgery, the benefit of early and radical intervention. So the university clinic sent letters to the old patients summoning them back, reassuring them that if they came from the outlying areas their travelling expenses would be met.

Now they were parked on a bench in the wide corridor which led from the wards to the lecture hall. Five men, three women; four from the town, and four from the country. Although the registrar had told them not to talk about their illness (a general prohibition for all patients in the clinic), they had now been talking with each other for an hour about nothing else; a couple of them rucked up their shirts in order to display their operation scars, others merely making a sign over their clothes to show where and how long the incision had been, although they tended to exaggerate just how long. Then they proudly followed the students into the lecture room, smoothing their clothes, and one of the women broke out in a sweat having, in her haste, been unable to put her gloves on quickly enough.

The General revelled in surgical optimism. He compared the fate of the patients in remission with the fate of others with the same illness who had long since been pushing up the daisies, during which he put his giant arms on the shoulders of his frail patient, who was getting on a bit, and rotated the woman like a puppet to the right and left, then promptly turned his back to her so that he could draw a schema of the operation procedure on the blackboard for his students, and while doing so held the chalk in his right hand, and the patient's notes in his left containing in detail all the exact facts of the case, the very same dossier which his registrar had just handed over to him. Then in a formally perfect recital he explained the operating technique, gave a critical evaluation of the pros and cons of each method, estimated the corresponding prognoses with the help of carefully applied statistics and completely forgot, while doing so, that the eight people all this was about were standing in the lecture room, which also happened to be an operating theatre.

He was still completely absorbed in his surgical considerations when his old registrar, Professor E., suddenly burst into the lecture room and flustered something in his ear. The excitement transmitted itself immediately to the surgeon, flushing his face red as if he had drunk a good claret: only the old duelling club scar shone out in its bright cherry red. A deep crease appeared in the General's forehead indicating that he was deep in thought, while the registrar shooed the eight healed patients out of the hall like a gaggle of geese. The Professor immediately let the water run in a washing stand set aside for his exclusive use. Then he reversed the hourglass that was standing on a glass shelf. Ten minutes' worth of brown sand started running out: the exact length of time for hand rinsing and surgical antisepsis. The student helped the General with his "toilet," and while the General alternately spoke and scrubbed his hands he tied a large yellow waterproof gown with a brass chain around his bullish neck which was now as claret-red as his face. Without looking, the General put his feet into black galoshes that went over his ankles.

In a moment he was transformed from the academic lecturer into another kind of human being; his voice, his bearing, his glance were all different. With his stiff brush he scrubbed at his fingers, hands, front and back, and forearms up to the elbows. With a press of his foot he squeezed soap from an automatic dispenser, and soon his arm was covered with white soapsuds. Once again everything would be rinsed, the blotchy skin, redder and redder because of the scrubbing, would re-emerge, only to disappear again in lather.

Standing beside him, his assistant was his spitting image.

Now the General turned to the lecture room: "A stroke of luck, regrettably increasingly rare. A suicide attempt in the vicinity of the clinic. A young woman, mere slip of a girl. Stabbed herself in the heart. Probably requires suturing. Timely operation. Most untimely suicide instrument, an old-fashioned pen with a nasty steel nib. Office girl. Relatively advantageous circumstances, gentlemen, given that the fell object has lodged in the wound and thereby hindered exsanguination. Fortune in her misfortune.

"By the way, an achievement too, to hit the heart with such a crude weapon. The method, which hopefully all of you now, even the gentlemen in the top row (please don't stand up gentlemen whatever you do, the dust is frightful and terribly dangerous)—now, the method which I hope to demonstrate to you is new and is one of the many, quite sterling contributions to science of the late Professor Rehn in Frankfurt. First assistant, as usual, will be yourself, Herr Oberarzt, the second Herr Glikker, and the third Herr Schillerling; anaesthesia will be in the hands of our model student here, one of your own number, gentlemen, who is already quite a little anaesthetist. In cases like this we need anaesthesia by the book, not just any kind but excess pressure anaesthesia; after all we'll be guddling about inside the chest cage. Once medicine could do nothing for injuries to the heart, but that was ages ago; since Rehn we have been able to deal with stab, and even—though, of course, only in the rarest cases— bullet wounds to the heart; we can tackle all these situations, provided, gentlemen, that the patient is brought to us alive on the table! No less than three of every five cases survive provided they can be operated upon in time. There can be no doubt that if the Austrian archduke, heir to the throne, had, after his heart wound in Sarajevo … Well, let us move on from that painful chapter!—Warm the saline apparatus. Sister, prepare the adrenalin, one in a thousand solution, yes, I merely wanted to say, there are methods against every kind of injury, the only thing we can't prevent is murder. You can suture the wound, but you can't cure the heart. Our anaesthetist will monitor the pulse. Don't forget the rib dilator, in fact have all bone instruments ready. Indications for operation in such cases are straightforward: you start the operation as soon as the patient is in front of you. First aid is decisive. So not a second to lose, where have you put the patient, wheel her in straightaway! Formalities and extensive paperwork are superfluous; I operate even without the consent of the patient who, in such cases, is often not quite compus mentis, and without the consent of the relatives, who don't have a blind shimmer—No matter: let's go get 'em, but only in strictest adherence to the rules of bacterial antisepsis. No excuses here; we must and most certainly will follow the rules of asepsis, for we're on the point of opening one of the most susceptible cavities of the body, and one prone moreover to suppuration, in a word the chest cage and the pericardium. Ah, there she is. Forwards! Be careful! Gently does it!"

Tall, blond, somewhat thoughtless medical student Friedrich von B. saw Hildegard Anneliese again, the person who had played such a considerable, even if not always happy role in his recent past.

The instruments were being boiled in their very own electrically heated sterilisers. Thick clouds of steam rose from the instrument drums and thinned out in the amphitheatrical space. Even though it was almost midday, the lecture room was gloomy. "Light!" said the General. The lamps, which were positioned immediately under the ceiling like stage lights, hissed on, and an almost pure white shadowless light poured out over the operation table, the professor and his assistant and over the lowest row of the audience. The face of a clock, which had been indistinct until that moment, now showed not quite two minutes past eleven. The General was silent. All that could be heard was the bubbling of the water, the metallic clatter of the instruments shifting here and there in the seething water, and the whispering of the spectators.

Now the girl who had tried to kill herself gave a dull groan. She didn't cry out; she seemed to be holding her breath in, for every movement of her ribcage caused her pain. The students looked down into the depths and saw the girl's face under the glare of the ceiling lights, sickly yellow, the upper lip drawn down over the lower, moist, and around her face a tangle of damp, light-brown hair. She screwed her pale green eyes tight shut, then opened them again wide, the eyelids trembling, and the reflection of the lights kept flitting from one side of her eye to the other. The clothing on the upper part of her body had already been cut with scissors, and a fine gauze dressing spread over her chest; in one place it stuck up jaggedly, and this place moved rhythmically. There was calm. The General and the assistants had stopped scouring their arms and hands with their brushes, and eyed the patient.

It seemed as if it were deepest night. Stillness. Only the seething of the water, the bubbling of the instrument holder, the hissing of the light and the groaning that came every time the patient breathed out. The General had motioned to the Chief Sister. With sterile forceps she removed the gauze dressing very gently from the patient, a woman like herself, as if she were afraid of hurting her. Beneath the left breast of the patient the shaft of the pen was visible; it bobbed up and down with the heart beat, as if it were being pulled down by a hidden power until it was no more than a mere dot, and then it forced itself up again as if drawing a fine line.

"The very first thing to notice," said the General while scrubbing his now lobster-red arms with renewed intensity, "is that consciousness is entirely intact. Apart from the understandable degree of shock associated with such cases. And no haemorrhage. External bleeding has ceased. It can only have been minimal anyway."

He beckoned the student Friedrich von B. to come closer to the victim. His muscular male arms shone in the blazing light like glossy metal.

"Onwards! Let's get started! Anaesthesia!"

The student heaved his shoulders. His entire body trembled in horror and he was able to control himself only by summoning all his strength.

For excess pressure anaesthesia he needed a special apparatus which should have been at hand. But being in need of minor repair it had been taken into another room, and now, where every second counted, it was missing, and nobody dared tell the boss. The nurses were rapidly opening large nickel-plated drums with protective coats, drapes, hoods, rubber gloves and dressing material; in tandem they pulled out white square-shaped sheets, opened them out, spread them under the patient while the Chief Sister lifted the girl's upper body with extreme delicacy. The lower body was then draped, only the upper body and the face that was becoming paler with every second remained free. The hands were strapped down, and a broad strap tightened across the thighs.

In the hourglass nine minutes had elapsed. The great clacking sieves containing the instruments were lifted out of the seething water. Huge clouds of steam rose up. With practised movements the Chief Sister separated the metal instruments out in systematically ordered rows on small, mobile tables; similar types of instrument next to each other, the larger ones on the right, the smaller on the left. Scissors, straight and curved, four-finger crochets, bone extractors, vessel clamps, forceps, needle holders, boxes with sickle-shaped needles and boxes with straight needles, silk and cat-gut thread wound on glass bobbins ordered according to tensile strength.

The hourglass had almost run out, the student looked around the hall, but the anaesthetic apparatus was still not there. The sound of running water stopped abruptly. "Iodine!" said the surgeon.

Only now, in the last minute, was the anaesthetic device trundled in, a complicated apparatus. The rust–coloured bomb with the red valve was the oxygen cylinder, the blue bomb with the blue valve was liquid air, and the green valve supplied the anaesthetic agent. Flashing manometer, gleaming, with fluid-filled gauges for controlling every breath.

While the professor was being gowned in a white operating costume and someone else was putting a white bonnet on his head, the student held the close-fitting reddish rubber mask over the girl's nose and mouth. Mixed with air the anaesthetic agent trickled through a transparent glass tube in large beads. "Breathe deeply! Breathe deeply!" said the student in a flat voice to the girl. Without a word the girl stubbornly shook her head. With feeble movements she pushed the mask away as best she could. The mask slipped back in place, but her pale face turned and tried to evade it. She opened her mouth, she wanted to scream, she wanted to defend herself. She tried to whisper a request and pursed her mouth. But not a word, only the same long-drawn-out dull groaning emerged from completely bloodless lips that had taken on the pallor of her skin.

"Iodine!" repeated the General as he pulled on rubber gloves. Both breasts, the skin up to the throat and down to the navel were now covered with a metallic blue-brown sheet, and a broad piece of dressing material had been applied to the operating field.

In the middle of the brown expanse the steel-nibbed pen moved up and down, but less energetically now, faster and weaker, thrilling, driven by the helpless trembling heart. Her respiratory movements which until now had been visible became flatter. The eyes were now wide open, they darted desperately, but lucidly, around the large room.

Difficult to believe that a human being with such a wound was still lucid, that she knew what she was doing, what she was suffering.

Already the General's face bore that peculiar, almost serene, quite disengaged expression indicating that he had thought the operation down to the last detail with all possible complications so that its technical execution was a mere formality—but why was the patient still conscious? Yes, she almost showed more signs of life than before, and her eyes sought and finally found the eyes of her former lover.

Not a second to lose, thought the student, it has to be. But what should he say to her, how could he make her understand everything, bring her to reason, what should he remind her of? Who was guilty? Who would make it good again? Two minutes before death? Twelve past eleven.

"And the pulse?" asked the General.

The young medical student fumbled on the beautiful soft neck of the girl, the contours of which were known to him from what seemed ages ago. With the tips of his index and middle fingers he softly touched the moist, smooth, lukewarm skin.

"Carotid impalpable. I can feel nothing on the carotid." But the girl had felt his hand. Did she still love him? Did she still want to live? Did she regret it? Was she still the same girl she had been a couple of minutes before?

The eyelids closed then, the long eyelashes came together and formed a thick, light-brown line that almost looked brazen in the glare of the lights. The lips opened delicately. The milk-white teeth stood out amid the pale coral red of the gums. She breathed out in his face, she drew the ether-air mixture in with shallow, rapid breaths. Thirteen minutes past eleven. "We must get started now. Is she under? No, not yet? Doesn't matter. Life is the main thing, anaesthesia is secondary. War is war. Up and at 'em. Tilt the head as deep as you can. Avoid cerebral anaemia, preserve the spinal breathing centres and so on above all else. The blood leaking from the wound is pressing on the heart externally and filling the pericardial sac. The brilliant Ernst Bergmann has termed this cardiac tamponade. There we are, a little lower yet, fine, enough." The table had noiselessly lowered itself by means of a hydraulic device. The student felt the girl's head, with its matted silken hair, sink in his lap. Was she still alive? Was she suffering? She wasn't groaning any more. Was she sleeping? Was she awake? Was she dead?

"Instruments, please!"

From a dazzlingly bright alcohol-filled dish the Oberarzt lifted a thin curved nickel scalpel with a steely blue gleaming blade; it was as fine as the fin of a fish. The General took it at the upper end, almost in the same way as a painter takes a brush, and with the cutting edge, as if he was trying to outline an arabesque, drew an arcuate line which started in the middle of the upper torso and circled round the bottom edge of the left breast. Pale streaks of red appeared at the margins of the line, but without any obvious blood loss. The assistants hooked their dilators to the margins of the wound on the right and left and pulled it apart. The patient groaned. Then she was silent. The student gave ether. The knife vanished from the surgeon's hand, although nobody saw how, and now a series of instruments appeared in his right hand, large and small, sharp and blunt, ablating and extirpating, invasive and dilating. The surgeon's hands and those of his assistants were sheathed in close-fitting, red-coloured gloves made of the thinnest rubber which clung so intimately to the fingers that the contours of the nails were apparent. All that was apparent in the operating field was the General's long-fingered hand making gestures that seemed casual and fortuitous, but in fact were absolutely precise and methodical. Other hands were busy holding the wound margins open, handing over instruments or little bundles of gauze, and doing all the various ancillary tasks which the General directed mostly with his gaze; his voice was reserved only for the most important commands. What he said was more for the students in the gallery, to make the particular step of his operation clear to them. "You see, unfortunately hardly any blood to be seen. Blood pressure is minimal. Careful with the anaesthesia. Let her groan if you must, only the bare minimum so that she doesn't come to on us. She's in shock, will hardly be sensitive to pain. Here, in the subcutaneous tissue is a crepitus, air's coming out under pressure from the wounded rib cage. What to do? First we'll remove a section of sternum, and then we'll open the ribs. We're making an access to the heart, a kind of door. There we have to cut through two, three, in fact four ribs while sparing the periosteum because everything has to knit together again. The whole thing is very straightforward. Air again. With every breathing motion the wound sucks in air from the exterior. Heads not too close to the wound! We don't want any infection. Give more pressure with the anaesthesia! Just a trace of ether and lots of oxygen. Now we can have a go at the enemy. Grip the suicide instrument externally with a pair of forceps, hold it firm. And now we're forcing it back the way it came, that is the trajectory the pen took: you can see the track still marked with ink. Now we're going to remove it, turn it externally a little, good! Careful traction now, a bit more force, more, splendid! It's out now. Good, into the collection with it. Silly woman, in her despair she grabs for the nearest thing to hand. And now for the ribs, be careful, rib cutters, yes, oppose them carefully, first the finger underneath and now I'm pressing through and here's the next. Finger under and then lift skin, bone and membrane in a single flap upwards, without exerting force. One, two, and another one, one, two, back, back and let it go, but don't slip, hold the skin flap steady, damn it, easy does it, gently, gently, good!"

Friedrich von B. held his hand over the girl's mouth; the flow of her breathing was hardly perceptible. "Don't let air in the mask! Continue excess pressure. Don't worry, she's still breathing, the situation is easier to assess at our end, we can see the lung inflating; check your anaesthesia, do the best you can. Watch out! There is the pericardium! Onwards!

"Toothed clamp. Clamp. Larger! Smaller! Medium-sized, be careful and turn the thing a little towards the exterior! Another one, another one, keep going just like that! Here's the wound in the pericardium, jagged, zigzag, it must have gone in that way, not a simple incision obviously, because at the moment it was wounded the pericardium was under tension, torquing, as with every heart beat. Goitre-probe, we want to go in, deeper, deeper!"

The probe, an elongated finger-like instrument made of nickel-plated steel slipped smoothly through the wound into its depths, blood-filled and dark.

"Right. Please hold the probe underneath. And now the scissors above it, please, a straight line would be best, yes, and support it from beneath, hold the probe exactly under the scissors. Cut! Good. And now for the first time a clear view! Everything full of clotted blood. This has to go! Now we're removing the clot. Gently wipe it away, don't rub the pericardium, it doesn't like that. Now we have a clear sighting, it won't be long now, we must be at the wound. Don't dilly-dally! It is probably straight ahead of us though it doesn't have to be. Where's the bleeding point? Where's it bleeding from? Look at this sweat! Swab that. Head away, I need to have a look, get out of my way! Swab, don't put your hand in, swab just with the forceps, more gently, energetically, gently I said, gently and energetically at the same time and don't rub, don't chafe! Be careful! Again! Soon we'll have daylight! How's the pulse? Something to feel? Nothing? Give her some saline then, as much as you can get in. Blood would be better, blood transfusion, would take too long, we need to know her blood group first, takes too long, saline into the cubital vein, as much as will go—life ersatz, trick blood! And can one of you gentlemen get the laboratory to work out her blood group fast, do we have any blood donors? You once gave us blood, Herr B. Which blood group are you? Watch out, only another hundred seconds! Quiet! Let go! Fixation of the heart! With the heart flouncing about like this we'll never do a decent job. It has to be held. It needs to come out of its hiding hole! Out, you coward! I say. We really have to get a hold of it and make it accessible if we want to suture it. Sutures for fixation! Yes, that's the right thread. Thin silk, curved needle, this size must be right, give here, what's all this shilly-shally, don't thread it too short and give me the needleholder at the same time: you hold the pericardium up, and take the end of the thread so that it doesn't trail. Now watch: I'm going to insert it in the serosa of the heart, left ventricle, apex, in, and out again here; now we have a loop; colleague here will hold it for us, and the same again somewhat higher up and somewhat to the right and another loop on the side; now watch, I bring the needle up the heart muscle, needle in, follow through, needle out, remove the needle and tie the ends, and we've done it. Cut the threads and carefully now bring the heart out of the cavity. Is it bleeding? Let it bleed. Of course it's bleeding. Lift it up! Faster, more gently, higher! A little higher perhaps. Nothing to report this side. Nothing on this wall of the heart. Nothing there either. So the other way round! Lift a little please, and around the right side! Firmly and swab again, very finely, without pressing. Stop! Stop! Here it is! Here's the wound! Finger in the wound, you, finger on the wound, I said. Bring the wound margins very gently together, give with your hand when the heart beats! That's good. But we want to see something too! Don't press. That's enough. That's good, fine. Ahead now to the heart suture! The same silk as before. First suture, obliquely inserted. Left wound margin, right wound margin, thread out, knot gathered, thread clamped and held. Correct. Take the upper layers. Registrar, take over the suturing and hold the heart wall up to me, no, turn it somewhat to the right, and continue to give with each pulsation of the heart. Good. Second suture. Go somewhat deeper to be on the safe side. In, out, gather the knot, pull together slowly and equally from both sides, and knot again. Less bleeding now, but we're still not quite there! Any pulse to feel? Still nothing? And how is the breathing? Awful? Calmly now. Hand away. Third suture. Good. Bleeding stopped. The heart wound is closed. Scissors, cut the threads of the three sutures! Not too short! But no tail either! No. Good. A fourth? No, that'll do. Leave it. The suture is solid enough, it'll hold when the blood pressure returns and the vessels fill normally. Pulse? None? Come then! If the heart's still beating, the man's still living. Look, the heart muscle is recovering visibly, the beats are more prominent, we can see proper systole and diastole now, not the hysterical twitching and fluttering we had earlier. This was a patient in extremis, no doubt about it. So, give a good dose of saline into the cubital, but don't disturb us up here and don't come too close to us with that dirty stuff. Let the mediastinum slip back in, draw the threads out, everything in the right order. Do you see already how the heart muscle is jerking on the three reins like an untrained colt, it is growing stronger under our hands. Good, and the pulse? Hardly palpable. But we can correct that! Give the adrenalin now, we can simply inject the adrenalin solution directly into heart. Good. That was that. And now?"

"The pulse is—there, I think."

"We think so too. And the breathing?"

The student watched the silvery beads of inspired air climb more and more animatedly in the gauge of the anaesthetic device. "Doing well," he said.

"Now the pericardial suture. We'll use catgut for that. We couldn't use it for the heart. Silk is safer. But the pericardium doesn't have to withstand the powerful stroke of the heart. That's it, that'll do. Now the ribs back in their old position, we can suture the periosteum with a couple of quick tacks.

"A glass drain under the skin. Here, down in the deepest site. Muscle-fascia-wound closure, that is: skin suture, fine silk, only a couple of needle points. Anaesthesia?"

"Off ages ago."

"Good. Continue the pure oxygen, three-and-a-half litres, four litres, for ever and amen. And camphor to be on the safe side. Head down once she's up in the recovery room too. Blood transfusion only if necessary. Give it if you're in doubt. What blood group is she? A? And you, Herr B.?"

"A, too."

"We can't have it better than that. Herr Oberarzt and Herr B.: remain with the patient. When did we start?"

"Thirteen minutes past eleven."

"Operating time: seven and a half minutes. A hundred years ago Napoleon's personal physician could take a leg off at the hip in the same time, with stump and pedicle, haemostasis included. They were craftsmen too, but in a different way from us. So, take a hold of the patient very carefully and lift her into the bed; better still, let me do that. There ... there ... Are the bed warmers handy? Cover her! Cover her! Cover her! Splendid. Everything in order. The rest we leave in the hands of fortune. Good morning, gentlemen, good morning."

"Die Herznaht," *Gesammelte Werke: Die Erzählungen*, 1982.

MICHEL LEIRIS

Two Memoirs

Michel Leiris was an extraordinarily self-conscious anthropologist and writer on the fringes of the Surrealist movement who produced an extraordinarily poised and self-conscious autobiography called Manhood: A Journey from Childhood into the Fierce Order of Virility. *Both extracts below involve deception: the first advertises the advantages of adopting the sick-role, the second suggests how a well-meaning lie, in this case one reinforced by all the adults involved, can itself become a trauma which never heals: according to his other autobiographical works, Leiris had a lifelong fear of losing his voice. Consent before surgery, even minor and involving minors, is now obligatory in most countries.*

THE GENIUS OF THE HEARTH

In the middle of the night, I was abruptly awakened by a violent cough which racked my throat and trachea and seemed to cut deeper and deeper into me, like a chock or a hatchet. It hurt, but it also gave me a certain pleasure to wait for the spasms which, with each paroxysm of coughing, became more violent and made my whole body shudder. I also knew what would follow—the worry and compassion my mother would display, the care she would lavish on me—and I was vaguely pleased that something had made me a focus of *interest*. Since that time I've often enjoyed being sick, provided the illness is not too painful, revelling in the sense of irresponsibility—and consequently of total freedom—that sickness confers, the unstinting attentions it gets me, and also the fever itself, with the resultant heightened sensitivity of the skin it gives rise to, a state of tension and skin-deep awareness that are distinctly euphoric.

I was brought into the dining room and my mother took me on her lap beside the salamander stove which we called La Radieuse, after its trademark. With its hot embers still crackling, La Radieuse was flanked by two tall reservoirs, each holding a good ten litres of water which, when it evaporated under the effect of the heat, kept the air in the room from getting too dry. The female face in the middle—a classical effigy in the manner of La République—was the reason for the feminine name La Radieuse, and turned this utile object into a personification of the domestic hearth ... When I draped myself on my mother's knees near La Radieuse, the stove did not strike me as a monster, but a warm, benevolent animal with a reassuring breath. My mother, who is very short, must have been wearing an old bathrobe over her nightgown with her braided hair hanging down her back. My father, in a smoking jacket, held in his hand the medicine, a small bottle of brownish liquid which, he said, contained a feather that would tickle the back of my throat and make me vomit. I didn't want to take the emetic, but the idea of the feather intrigued me, as did the circumstance of being the lead part in the drama being played out in the middle of the night, with my mother seated like a Roman matron close to the blue metal of La Radieuse and my father searching for the ipecac among the wreathed ornaments of the Henri II sideboard.

THROAT CUT

At the age of five or six, I was the victim of an assault. What I mean is: I underwent an operation on my throat to remove some adenoidal growths; the operation took place in a very brutal way, without my being anaesthetized. My parents had first made the mistake of taking me to the surgeon without telling me where we were going. If I remember rightly, I thought we were off to the circus; I was therefore far from anticipating the nasty trick about to be played on me by our old family doctor, who assisted the surgeon, as well as by the latter himself. The entire occasion unfolded, scene by scene, like a play that had been rehearsed, and I had the impression of having been lured into a frightful ambush. Matters proceeded as follows: leaving my parents behind in the waiting room, the old doctor led me into another room where the surgeon was waiting for me, sporting a huge black beard and a white gown (that at least is the image I have retained of the ogre); I saw various sharp instruments and must have looked scared, for the old doctor took me on his lap and to reassure me said: "Come here, *mon petit coco!* Now we're going to play kitchen." From this moment all I can remember is the sudden lunge of the surgeon, who rammed some sort of sharp instrument into my throat, the pain that I felt, and the scream—like that of a slaughtered animal—that I let out. My mother, who heard me from the next room, was terrified.

On the way home in the carriage, I didn't say a word; the shock had been so violent that for twenty-four hours it was impossible to get a word out of me; my mother, quite at a loss what to do, wondered if I had become a mute. All I can remember about the aftermath of the operation is the ride back in the carriage, my parents' vain attempts to cajole me to speak, and then, once home, my mother holding me in her arms in front of the fireplace in the living-room, the iced sherbets she had me swallow, the blood I spat out at various mouthfuls and which, for me, became indistinguishable from the strawberry dye of the sherbets.

This recollection is, I believe, the most painful of all my childhood memories. Not only did I not understand why I had been hurt, but I had a notion in my head of a confidence trick, a trap, a terrible act of treachery on the part of the adults who had indulged me only so as to be able to mount the most barbaric assault on my person. My whole image of life has been scarred by this incident: the world, full of traps and ruses, is nothing but a huge prison or operating theatre; I am on earth only to become a specimen for doctors, cannon fodder, food for worms; like the false promise to take me to the circus or to play kitchen, everything pleasant that can happen to me in the meantime is only a beguilement, a way of sugaring the pill to lure me more securely to the slaughterhouse where, sooner or later, I must be led.

Excerpt from "Le génie du foyer," "Gorge coupée," *L'Age d'homme,* 1939.

MIGUEL TORGA

Diary

Miguel Torga (1907–1995), kept a diary for most of his working life as otolaryngologist and GP in the poor hilly interior of Portugal between Lisbon and Porto: a period of sixty years. In his sharp, superbly executed and sometimes ruminative entries he describes some major changes in the nature and practice of medicine: the advent of penicillin, the disappearance of the last European peasants, reflexivity, and medical overconsumption. Torga understands his own need for roots, and though it chafes against the liberty of writing, he never considers ditching the ordinary traffic of empathy for the sirens of the city. The universal, he once wrote, is the local without walls.

Coimbra, 8 December 1933
So now I'm a doctor. As tradition demands, at the moment the master of ceremonies intoned yes and the professors and dean had authorised me to administer enemas to mankind, a group of strangers and familiars "plucked" me from top to toe. All they left me was my academic cape. And I had to walk through the town in this gear, as close as I could be to my own reality: a naked man wrapped up in three metres of darkness, and the body shaken by a deep fright, and nobody knows whence it comes and where it goes.

Vila Nova, 7 November 1934
Today it ended. And as always, there I was, completely at a loss. Even when it was no longer possible to have the least illusion, I still clung to it and … I hoped. It's something I've never been able to destroy in myself: the idea that a being, from the moment it is born, has the right (and the obligation) to live for sixty years on average. At least, the sixty years of the average. It often happened, when I was holidaying with my father, that I

helped out with the harvest. Then to see the corn, or the flax, growing. And even while knowing that these are fleeting lives to go and visit the furrows next holiday, and be upset to find out that instead of flax or corn there was a large square of potatoes.

"What about the flax that was growing here?"

"We gathered it in August, son!"

In August, it is true, the flax ripens. For the few months nature provides, it takes all the heat it can from the sun and gorges itself. Then it shows signs of fatigue and dies.

But this little child hadn't tasted the sun yet. He was in the first week of his life. He wasn't yet at the age where the stalk is perfectly fibrous, the flower a delicate blue, the grain a ripe brown. That's why, when I went into the bedroom, it was the most painful feeling I've had in my life. He was there, not yet replaced by the barley or the rye, but just about to be. The mother was in tears. And the child, white-faced, discreet, face to the wall, turned his back on the useless drugs scattered on the night table.

A doctor can't even weep. He can only take the thin little arm, still warm, hold his hand to the inert artery and clench his jaw for a few seconds. After, it only remains for him to go, without so much as a word.

Who knows the words that are needed in moments like that? Words that a doctor can say to a mother who has given the world a living son and who receives from the world a dead child.

Vila Nova, 10 February 1935

I can't anymore. I can't spend my life doing that—playing cards with the priest, getting up who knows when to see a patient at Gandramàs and the rest of the time lending an ear to some hunting story or even telling one myself. I'm worth what I'm worth, but this isn't the life I deserve.

Vila Nova, 15 July 1936

A delivery. By dint of needles, forceps, in the midst of cries and the tears of the entire village, but a delivery all the same.

An animal with big legs and blue eyes. One called Newton.

As soon as his son had been pulled into this fallen world his father, don't ask me why, decided to call him Newton. Newton and nothing else.

And the employee at the registry office—a colossus of erudition—thought the father was overdoing it. Newton! Well, well! But I confirmed it. Newton, what of it?

Spade in hand, this new little man will definitely not discover another law of universal gravitation. But he will certainly discover suffering and, in my opinion, that is enough to give him the right to carry, on this earth, any name at all.

Vila Nova, 5 February 1937

It's useless. Either education and hygiene will gain a foothold in the mountains or it's simply not worth a doctor's time and effort. When they fall ill the good folk in these parts take to bed like a fox to its terrier, and bide their time. If God performs a miracle, wonderful! they get back on their feet. If God doesn't perform a miracle, they call on the priest for the extreme unction, the doctor because it's the done thing, then they close their eyes and hold their peace for ever.

Coimbra, 11 November 1937

I wear civvies. Outside and in. But I recognise that it requires twice the amount of energy to impose any kind of truth without a uniform. And even in the practice of this confounded medicine. The doctor with or without white coat is not the same thing for his patient. And that has nothing to do with the impression of cleanliness suggested by the white. No. It is the simple prestige of the cowl which, in the end, makes the monk.

And it's the same for everything. There's no musician without a crazy hair-do, no apostle without a beard, no bishop without mitre, no clown without his eyebrows turned arsy-versy. No. Because the rest of us, poor humans, before seeing with our reason see with our eyes.

S. Martinho de Anta, 18 April 1938

She was seventy-eight years old. Breast cancer. Always her hand wanting to cover her chest. To draw her dirty blouse over what had once been a breast and now was nothing more than a gaping hole at the bottom of which the "beast" fattens itself. Did she feel the cold? No, she wasn't cold. She covered herself out of modesty. And she blushed for shame, this poor little old woman.

Coimbra, 19 January 1939
While I was operating, between two loud groans, Fonseca told me his life. His father died when he was ten; then his mother when he was fifteen. At nineteen, he broke his leg and three ribs after falling from a cart. At twenty, he had a double pneumonia. One of his sons died when he was twenty-four; his daughter when he was thirty. At thirty-two, he caught typhoid fever. He was thirty-five when his wife died. And now, in the space of five months, he is going through his fourth operation. At the end, he asked me:

"Tell me, doctor, is that a fit life for a man, that?"

"Well! yes."

Leiria, 2 August 1939
It is midnight. I have just finished my day with a round of cards (I will have to explain again to my friends why I play with the same seriousness as if I had celebrated mass). Next door, the daughter of the owner of the hotel is in the process of giving birth. I may be a doctor, but I continue to tremble at the mystery of a pregnant woman. She groans softly, but in a different way from normally. The serving girl who, this very moment, is serving me tea, says that the baby's head has just shown and I'm choked with emotion. The young woman's husband is walking like a madman in the corridor. How beautiful and profound it is!

Coimbra, 22 June 1942
Someone said to me today:

"Dear chap, if you could be in the literary life what you are in the medical life—conciliatory, tolerant, ready to forgive—it would be a marvel!"

The poor man had lost sight of the difference which exists between both these lives, both sacred for me. As a doctor, I look after suffering brothers who knock at my door, to whom I owe love and assistance; but as a writer I fight against hypocrites, fat and in good health, who consider art a means of reaching grubby and unacknowledged ends.

Coimbra, 25 July 1942
Here I am, in my surgery, seated, waiting for the first unhappy person who has need of me and who, for thirty ecus, will buy the right to have my hands placed on his wounds. I suffer knowing this—since being mercenary, in any form, has always been repugnant to me—but there is no doubt about it: if someone knocks on my door he will pay for the consultation. We know that shoes cause corns on the feet. It doesn't do any good to weep over it (and nevertheless I continue to weep ...): the cells which remain living, underneath the bunions, are not the true reality. All they do is make us suffer and even then, when we complain that it's not them, it's callus.

Coimbra, 18 December 1942
X-rays and more X-rays. The morbid and troubled visions of my own poor viscera, indecently exposed to the light of day. Discussions and interpretations about their tiniest fold. And nobody can understand the pain, despair and shame that grip me seeing myself reduced in this way to a film of celluloid.

Coimbra, 11 March 1943
She had made an effort, held herself proudly, rouged the pallor of her face with a little life which clearly did not belong to her anymore, and she said to me brusquely:
  "Don't you recognise me?"
  "Off the cuff, I must confess ..."
  "I'm Beatriz ..."
  "Excuse me but ..."
  A cloud of disappointment eclipsed my surgery. Then everything was clear again.
  "Beatriz Pitaça!"
  "Yes! You remember now!"
  "But of course!"

She could hardly hold herself erect but nevertheless stood standing there, and something adamantine in her pupils reflected her resolve.

"Well, well, have a chair ..."

She hadn't heard. What residual energy she possessed refused to capitulate without glory.

"Antonio Vilela's daughter. Gonçalo's wife ..."

"I know, I know. But you've lost a lot of weight ..."

"So it would seem ..."

The black cloud returned and this time stayed a little longer. With the flicker of life gone her bony face fled that very instant to the world that already claimed it. She staggered.

"Now, now! What's come over you, do have a seat ..."

She slumped down on the cushions like a marionette suddenly freed from its strings.

"Well?"

A weak groan emerged from the clothed cadaver.

"I'm very ill ..."

"Come on! It's just tiredness. Let me feel your pulse."

She shook her head sadly. Then she began to stare melancholically at the pale remains of the day that lingered in the room.

"I'm done for. But I don't want to die just yet ... I want to live a little while longer ..."

A new surge of energy caught her. Her eyes shone as they had when she came in and her entire being tautened with intent.

"I'm not forty yet ..."

"You'll live to be a hundred. What's troubling you?"

Now she was no more than renunciation.

"A terrible illness. I'm rotting away inside ... A devilish tumour. They opened me up, took away a kilo or two of flesh, but it's even worse than before ..."

Leaving to one side the accusation she had made against her illness, one would have said that it was the cancer itself talking in that thick, tired voice.

"But they'll operate on you again, and you'll be alright."

She replied with a strangled voice.

"I won't have the strength to go through with it ..."

"Of course you will! My word, one wouldn't think you're a woman from the mountains! You've come all the way from the deepest neck of the woods full of courage and now you're scared?"

"Yes..."

The silence of death chilled the room for a little while. But life returned with a light-hearted and quite ordinary bit of banter.

"Tell me, Beatriz, did you come by train?"

"Yes, I just slumped back in the seat and here I am ..."

And then, as if electrified:

"And why don't I want to die yet? There they were all saying to me: 'Don't go, you'll have to stop on the way; it's better to wait for it peacefully at home.' But I said to myself: I'm going to go all the same ..."

A flame, it seemed, was burning on its own.

"And your husband, why didn't he accompany you?"

She became even paler.

"He is dead. Don't you remember?"

"Oh yes ... True enough. But your father! ..."

Then her face hardened.

"We don't get on. I went through the operation there, and he never once asked me if I were any better or worse! He doesn't think any more of me than he would of a dog ... And he is going to inherit everything ..."

"You don't have any children?"

The furious expression was changed into a resigned sadness.

"Alas no ..."

"Well, don't talk any more, it's tiring you. I'll look after everything, and we'll see if things aren't better afterwards."

The ghost of a vague smile flitted over her hostile death's head for a moment. She murmured softly:

"If only that could be true ... What I have is like a stone. It's hard, hard ..."

She put her hand on her belly and once again the death's head took possession of her face. Two tears started down the creases.

"Come on now! Now that's right! You're crying! Come, come, gently now!"

"This time I'm not going to survive it ... I have a notion that I won't return to San Martinho ..."

"Don't be silly ..."

"Precisely. I'd like you to promise me something now, this minute ..."

"Whatever you like ..."

"Should I die, don't give my father this bracelet and this money I have with me ..."

"And what should I do with them?"

"Go to mass. Say mass for my soul and for my poor Gonçalo's. I picked quarrels with him a lot when he was alive. And even afterwards ... I thought it was his fault that we didn't have any children ... But no, the poor man. It was already this bloody cancer ..."

Coimbra, 18 March 1943

It happened in the operating room, while some poor man came to an end breathing his chloroform with the haste of someone who wants to get out of a place full of bad smells pronto in order to see if he'll find a good atmosphere further on in which he can rinse his lungs. It was one of my colleagues, of course, who told me that. He told me that a short while ago a little old lady on whom he had just operated asked him for "her" tumour in order to be able to take it with her in her coffin, beneath the earth ...

Coimbra, 28 April 1943

If the roof of the old hospital building hasn't collapsed it's because old things are more resistant than one imagines.

It was the admission period. The form required short, concise replies.

"Profession?"

"Prostitute."

"Children?"

"Eight."

"How many?"

"Eight."

"And all since ...?"

"All of them."

As serene as if she had said something of no account, she remained standing, leaning against the wall.

"Have a seat."

"Thank you."

She took her swollen abdomen between her hands, found a place on the bench and continued to answer the questions.

"Abortions?"

"None."

"None!"

"That's right, sir."

"With the life that you have, it's ..."

"No. I never wanted an abortion."

"And your children? Alive or dead?"

"All living and in good health."

"Raised by yourself!"

"Of course!"

The writing on the registration form wobbled, uncertain. But this unfortunate woman was calm and steady, with her admission form for the maternity ward properly and duly completed.

"Very well, please go up."

And number nine was born, like the child of any honest mother. The mother in confinement left her bed this morning.

"I'll send you some business", promised a colleague, confused in the face of such grandeur. Then he added, addressing himself to me: "I want to help her. All that is a life of misery, but in the face of such purity one has to bow and admit defeat."

"I find it good that you want to be her protector", I said to him, looking him squarely in the eyes. "But if you really want to help her, follow her example and, even defeated, you won't bow down."

Coimbra, 1 February 1945

Penicillin. I too want to try out the latest panacea invented by science. On a young boy burning up with fever, pus running out of his ears and terrible pain. In the old days, the tympanic membrane would be doused with milk from a wet nurse which cured it radically. Now it's penicillin. When I went to look for it in the house of a patient who had some left over the father didn't want to let go of his treasure. He was in possession of a talisman of health, and he didn't want to sell it or to give it to anyone at all. He was drunk: perhaps that was why he believed with a supernatural force in the magic of this drug. His wife, who was steadier, intervened and they finally gave me the holy viaticum. At my other patient's house they were waiting for the miracle treatment in their prayers. And I gave the injection, both in humility and in humiliation. On one hand I knew that the yeast in question would have become ridiculous fifty years hence; on the other I knew that it represented the highest point so far reached by the ingenuity and hope of man.

What would you say about that, you Greek philosophers, who didn't believe in achievements! you who restricted yourselves to speculation, comprehension, beauty and natural health!

Coimbra, 13 October 1947
Here I am again for my consultations. Yesterday, only yesterday, I was clambering among the rocks, free as the day, and I've spent all today in this hell, smelling these foetid nasal discharges. I'm the only one who knows what it all counts for in my life as writer. It's like being sterilised in boiling water. I'm out of inspiration, the will to create is gone. I was born to be a falcon, not a farmyard bantam. In the pure air of the mountains, everything stimulates me, and the poetry comes in floods. Here, my poems are born with forceps, like those monstrous foetuses that don't want to be born.

"What long holidays you've taken!" my friends comment, with an air of disapproval.

And not one of them understands that these are my vacations, that I spend them here, the entire year, waiting for two months of prolific work. Because I'm a writer not a doctor. Any honest and halfway decent colleague could operate the way I operate, diagnose as I diagnose, write prescriptions that resemble mine. But to write what I write, whether good or bad, there's only me. Nevertheless, I don't react to provocations. What could I say to those who've never known who I am? Truth is, if they have any respect for me it's a grudging one for the practitioner who, now and again, treats their cold or their liver attacks. The writer has never interested them, either because they don't like what I write or because in Portugal we've never had time for artists. Not once has a charitable soul among them said the following to me:

"Come on, old chap! give up this filthy profession and become a writer, a fully-fledged writer!"

Not one of the persons whom I've known and thought highly of has ever encouraged me to follow my true path. What they say is:

"Patience, old chap! in Portugal nobody has ever been able to earn a living as a writer ..."

And here I am again busy attending to them, or attending to what they think my destiny.

Coimbra, 18 November 1947
For an artist, the wish to be applauded is more a need than mere vanity. It is the feeling that he is necessary, that he is loved. What could be more paralysing than to spend the entire day in the surgery, waiting for patients who pass before my door on their way to consult my neighbour. To write for posterity has never stimulated or consoled anyone. The legitimate prayer of every artist, whether he admits it or not, is: give me, Lord, a little glory while I'm still alive.

Coimbra, 18 March 1949
The last client has just left. It is six o'clock in the evening and since nine this morning I've been floundering in other people's misfortunes. But now I'm free: I'm watching the sun set on an avenue full of life, and smoking a cigarette that has a good taste of life, even if it isn't doing me any good. I have the time to go to a lecture but I'm going to skip it! Who cares right now what happened in Florence at the end of the Middle Ages? As far as human misery goes I had my share today. I have dried tears, relieved pain, treated what I could, by direct help, without philosophy, without ulterior motives, of no historical import. Blood welled up and I stilled the haemorrhage, that's all.

In a moment, when night falls (and it's almost here) and I've returned home, it may happen that out of force of habit I shall forget the reality of what I've lived today and sit down to read about culture and the past. But first I make a point of smoking my cigarette.

Montesinho, 28 September 1951
I've been called to the bedside of João Gata who is the oldest and most gnarled human stock in this community. He's ready for death, and he's dying in his bed. Just under the room in which his death agonies are taking place two cows provide a heavenly music for him with their cattle bells.

Caldelas, 16 August 1952
The old proverb says: "whoever treats himself with water won't last long." And here I am, searching for health from one fountainhead to the next. My bag is full of drugs, but I finish by swallowing only a couple of homeopathic doses of spring water, since I still tremble at the memory of the scalpel and Hippocrates' remedies, which I've experienced to my cost. I'm one of the Master's mediocre disciples, an interventionist where others are concerned but a sceptic when it comes to myself. Among the vines and the rocks, health seems to me to be something simple and spontaneous. And I, who get on so badly with today's science, I go over instinctively to the empirical knowledge of the past, which is more poetic anyway.

This treatment, however, has a major drawback: it always takes place in the same setting. The countryside has only three or four changes of clothes, and repeats itself incessantly. The devotees of these places, besides, are always the same, creditors of the same old conversations and the same old complaints that never get cured but only attenuated. What saves me is the species of cosmic tolerance which seizes hold of my mind as soon as I get here. Since I come here to cajole mercy from the gods, at the same time I'm prepared to accept, for a while, the lack of imagination.

Coimbra, 16 December 1952
The unholy pact that grows unbidden between patient and doctor drives me to despair. I try to elude it, to free myself from it, but I can't do it.

My poor patients insist on it, deliver themselves to it, trust me implicitly, and I'm obliged to take their life in my clumsy, powerless, human hands. "You, you know the answer, doctor! So, please, tell me!" Away with you! Can a black sheep like me really assume the responsibility of preserving for them a life continually under threat? "It's nothing really; of no importance. Rest easy!" Do I know if it's important or not, if it can be treated or not, if the poor patient is going to die or not!

I don't have the force to get used to the routine, to sleepwalk under the professional mantle; each consultation, even though I'm already an old hand at the job, is still an initiation rite, a smiling martyrdom. Yes, I smile, and inside I eat my heart out. Unable to stick the standard treatment stamp on the envelope of symptoms, I stop, indecisive, at harm's crossroads; puzzled by its fatality which, in the best of cases, is only ever deferred.

For twenty years I've been earning my daily bread this way; I practise medicine. The white coat, an ersatz surplice, makes me look as driven white as a deacon. But inside myself, sceptical, more and more sceptical, I'm like an atheist leading the mass.

Coimbra, 2 March 1953
A full day. From nine o'clock this morning to seven this evening, I've strewn reassuring words! My throat is sore, but I'm going to close my practice with a clear mind. The depressed young man ought to fight back, the girl in love ought to find her lover again, and the man with the ringing in the ears ought to feel better with a little bit of resignation and the pills I've prescribed.

It's good to be doctor and writer at the same time. One can give twice over. Young people come to see me because I write poetry, older people come because I can treat them, and we all benefit. They cease feeling alone in the world, and so, too, do I, ultimately. That's how I get through my day, doing things devoid of any dramatic heroism, things that are useful and modest; and which suit my natural shyness, which tends to camouflage itself behind intellectual and physical violence of a compensatory type.

I've even got to the point of wondering if I could exist just as a writer, and live without this commitment of the body, without this communion in pus and tears that my poems try to sublimate. When I open my bazaar in the morning two voices inside me argue the toss. One speaks bad of my lot, the other good. But when I've succeeded, like today, in rekindling a few vital sparks, then in the evening both my voices are reconciled.

S. Martinho de Anta, 13 December 1953
Here I am fighting for the life of the last root left to me. My father has had a cerebral haemorrhage and I've come to help him. But lying there unresponsive, his mouth twisted, my old man looks as if he's smiling ironically at my distress and my drugs. It even seems as if, already arrived on the other side of the river, he's confining himself to observing, whether I like it or not, the tragicomic spectacle of the human being in action. A kind of black passivity which makes me think of a watch that has stopped although it still seems to be telling the time.

But I act as if nothing was amiss and, with all the serenity I can muster, I weep inside and press on outside. What can a son do other than stay faithful to his roots; and what can a doctor do but look after others? Anyway, when a watch stops the only thing to do is wind it up. Even if it continues not to work, it takes on our energy and that protects us from its rude inertia.

Coimbra, 30 April 1954
What secrets are sunk in the four walls of a surgery! And what a human responsibility I took on the day I opened this confessional! Modest and careworn servant of a temporal religion, I have had to greet the most insistent pains, the most secret intimate details, the most unsettling doubts. And I've had to find a way of prescribing hope for all that! From the empty sack of my individual poverty, I've had to draw miracle remedies: of optimism, faith, illusions. The miraculously treated persons, in exchange, have left my office lumbered with ghosts. Skins of the unhappy beings they have, in this very place, sloughed off.

Coimbra, 4 April 1956
That was a solace for me. I gave her no indication of it, but it was a moment of plenitude. The bearing and style with which she entered the surgery

pleased me immediately. What she told me then can't be retold. And when, at the end of the consultation, she covered her retreat by invoking her artist's privilege at the Fornos de Algodres cabaret, I let her go without paying, smiling within myself, an admirer. Toothless, old before her time, dressed in rather suspect tawdry, she faced the world at the back of the stalls with the insolence of a star of the first order. And if I didn't applaud at the end of the performance, I, a man who has spent his life apologising for being a poet, who intimately desires the artist's condition but is publicly ashamed of showing it, it was only not to discredit Hippocrates' white coat and parchments.

S. Martinho de Anta, 21 April 1956
Four o'clock in the morning. I have just given extreme unction to my old man—the extreme unction that a doctor can give to a dying person: a cardiac tonic and the habitual panaceas. He is lost. Nonetheless I promised to cure him and to bring him to see his youngest daughter a few days from now. I lied to him for the first time in my life and precisely on that occasion I had the sense that he was trusting me blindly. Fate has imposed this pious last-minute lie on me, though I've done so much, over so many years, to prove to him I'm worthy of his candour.

"My son will come ..." he used to say, to intimidate death and give resolve to those who let themselves be beaten.

I arrive, and come to his aid with useless drugs and false promises! I know that he'll forgive me if he notices that I've deceived him. But he'll retain a sadness equal in measure to that which I experience: that of not having been capable of a miracle, at the decisive hour.

Coimbra, 10 December 1958
Twenty-five years now I've been battling death professionally, and I feel more incapable than ever of understanding and accepting it. Halfway between the peasant in the pure state and pure intellect, when death comes calling I find neither the peace of the credulous person who regards the slow decline of his existence as a cycle of nature, nor that of the intellectual who interprets life in terms of mental categories. Whenever I spy death at a patient's bedside, I always react in an instinctive, abrupt way. Without

waiting to hear more, I set about combating it tooth and nail, with all the means at my disposal. I exhaust the arsenal of the pharmacopoeia and of hope. And in putting myself almost physiologically in the patient's skin, and in making use of all the treatments science puts in my hands, I fight until I'm exhausted. And when it's death that triumphs, I accept my defeat—but only pragmatically. Conquered but not convinced, I steady my knowledge and my resolve, and prepare myself for the next combat. And that'll be the end of me, saying no to death.

Coimbra, 21 April 1959
So many insecticides have been discovered, and not one able to act against ambiguity—this parasite of human relations. It is true that to be effective the remedy, in most cases, has to kill the poisoner and the poisoned ... The fact is most people are ambiguous by nature. Unequivocal on the surface, equivocal inside. And when, in the face of an unwonted and tricky situation, we conclude that there has been a misunderstanding, in reality it is the fact that we fail to read the true character of the other person. Instead of a mutual superficial confusion, what we have is a unilateral error in depth.

S. Martinho de Anta, 26 December 1960
Consultations and yet more consultations. These poor people seem to have put their miseries on the side, for the entire year, so as to be able to tell me them when I come. I auscultate, I palpate, I give medications and I promise recovery. But I finish up feeling I've been the true beneficiary of this clinical largesse. At times like this, I rediscover the zest for my job which the big town has killed bit by bit. The one moment in the exercise of my profession that has always fascinated me is the history. The recitation of his woes the patient makes in response to the doctor's inquisitive cordiality. That is the great human moment of the medical transaction. The moment when abysses open or fail to, when truth comes to the surface or fails to, when distress and pity encounter each other or fail to. Civilisation has made it almost impossible, this rent in the darkness, this total, trusting surrender of the suffering soul to the solicitude of one of Hippocrates' disciples. A thousand inhibitory forces acting together hinder the instinctive

need to disclose one's pain to someone else. Every word says something different from what it means, every symptom is disguised. Social etiquette, fear, distrust and a solid rooting in everyday hypocrisy are sincerity's stumbling blocks. And between the four walls of his surgery the poor practitioner exhausts himself, destroys himself putting questions to patients who come in bad faith. No gift, no culture, no authority, no cunning have the power to disentangle the ambiguity of the confession, which always ends up as nothing more than a long premeditated lie. But with the peasant, everything takes place differently. Master only of a limited field of consciousness, still a virgin in his reactions, when he falls ill his entire being concentrates on observing the illness which is consuming him, and he subsequently describes it objectively, with the candour of a simple man and the precision of a scientist. Without false modesty, without reflexive overlay, he gives a honest and rigorous account of his disease. And it is an enriching and touching adventure to accompany him on the roads of anguish, supply and demand shaking hands, towards disillusion or hope.

Coimbra, 20 January 1961
The query is always the same, but the length of the reply depends on my available time and my self-possession.

"Medicine produces lots of writers! Do you know why?"

Patiently, I fold the prescription, take off my glasses, stand up and begin the sermon which, today, comes to me in fits and starts:

"It's not medicine which produces them. Medicine limits itself to maintaining the gift in those who're born with it, and that is no small thing. Unlike other professions which stifle in the individual the spirit that accepts and comprehends its kind, medicine does the contrary. The doctor *qua* doctor cannot close the doors of his soul, extinguish the glimmer of his understanding. All kinds of humans seek out his help, at all times of day: those who're suffering and those who're simulating, those who're afraid and those who're gone in their minds. A certain emotional and intellectual dimension is required to be able to respond effectively to so many types of calls. Now, this very dimension is implicit in the condition of the artist, the most receptive and the most perceptive of mortals. So when chance imposes a creative vocation on a condemnation to the clinic, there's no terrible conflict. The pen that writes and the pen that prescribes switch over harmoniously in the same hands."

Coimbra, 8 October 1963
My long experience as a doctor teaches me not to despair of the national lethargy. Collective bodies, like individual ones, give themselves over from time to time to a sort of aboulic voluptuousness, apparent death, for which there seems no cure. But, in the intimacy of the cells, metabolism continues. And at the most unexpected moment, the moribund opens his eyes, talks, reacts and resumes a normal life.

Nations, also, sometimes rise up from the tomb.

Coimbra, 14 October 1963
Humankind is still very far from wisdom. It may even be asked whether, in some fields, it wasn't closer to it in the past! In medicine, for example. All that the masters and manuals teach about reality to an Asclepius of our time is never more than poor appearance. I've spent years learning to observe and to treat patients. But I have learned to observe and treat them only from the outside. A wound? Disinfectant and dressing. A nervous breakdown? Tranquillisers. Fever? Quinine. Well, things aren't as simple as that, as I'm finding out for the millionth time. I receive patients in my practice. One enters and the other leaves, and so on. Faces known and unknown, agreeable and disagreeable, young and old. As an attentive inquirer, I ask questions, I examine, I conclude. I go from symptom to symptom, suffering to suffering, life to life. I promise recovery, improvement, I prognose death and I give words of hope as an added extra to all my prescriptions. But even when I see myself as efficient, I feel frustrated. I'm fully aware that I'm swimming on the sand, two steps away from a vast ocean. I can see perfectly that I'm applying logical rules to an illogical game, that I ought to be on the other side, at the centre of the world in disorder—or so it appears to me—of illness. But there's no room there for my well-ordered reason, which tackles methodically what has no method, which knows before having learned. I respond to the claims of dramatic uncertainties with bits of well-established

evidence, I argue objectively against subjectivity, I fill with peremptory affirmations the intervals of doubt that two or three tiny failures of logic have left gaping in the conversation. And what saves me is the blindness of my patients who, in their desire for cure, mistake chalk for cheese. These souls in distress have knocked at the door of the great sorcerer and listen to him with complete confidence, piously convinced that all he says he has puzzled out at the bottom of the wells they're drowned in. They do not even suspect that the magical formula is invented, manufactured in panic, and that it makes me laugh when other sorcerers, trained in the same school as myself, charge it to my account.

Arganil, 16 July 1964
Medicine, literature and politics, in decreasing order. Obligation, vocation and mortification.

Arganil Hospital, 1 December 1966
I've just finished operating. I'm smoking a cigarette and thinking of the nuns whirling about me. Kind, obliging, patient, they do the injections, provide the care, undress the patients, attend to their basic needs. But one feels that, even present and functioning, they glide above the reality. That they act outside the game of life. It even seems as if they regard us with a certain dose of commiseration, for all the impatience with which we discharge our temporal acts. What inner force protects these women? What imperious voice has called them, compelling them to ditch everything to follow it, breaking their emotional bonds, subduing their instincts, leading them to scorn all honours and goods? Where does the peace come from that one sees on their faces, untroubled by any tempest? I know they would answer me if I asked. But I don't want to hear words that sound in their mouths like an obvious fact, and in my ears like a mystery. God, faith, vocation ... With three such substantives at his disposal, who knows what specious reasoning the quibbling devil who lives in me would be capable of! Presumption, naivety ... Nothing but that! And the worse is that the problem remains the same. That would only be to hide my perplexity without other, even more pedantic substantives.

Blessed sisters of mercy! They don't know, pure in body and soul, the good and the harm they do me. The good of their being what they are, the evil of my not being able to understand them.

Coimbra, 21 December 1966
Instead of the electric shock he was expecting, I gave him a kick in the backside and treated him in my own way:

"If you don't want to be in the despicable position of being a bourgeois with a clear mind, then have the courage to be a troubled man."

My medical miracles are very simple: I act in such a way that deserters rejoin their unit.

Coimbra, 25 February 1967
She barged into my practice like a madwoman, full of hate for her father and her mother, in the grip of a blind revolt against the tyranny of the family. I gave her to understand she was right ... and a pill. She calmed down and then I tried to help her in another way, by showing her that there is a fatality that affects young people just as there is one that affects adults. But, fortunately or unfortunately as the case may be, youth does not look ahead. It wants, full stop. And that is its force. It wants now what doesn't belong to it yet—the future—and since it doesn't really have a grip on things, it lives it in irresponsibility.

However that may be, I took care not to ask her if she was sure of understanding and accepting from her own child, later, the disdain she felt at that precise moment for her parents, the parents she didn't even want to speak to. She might have been capable of saying yes. And she would have lied sincerely.

Arganil, 7 November 1968
I've spent the entire morning excising tonsils and I was far removed from thinking that once the butchery was over I might feel the need, satisfied here, to write something about how aggressive an operation is. To speak of the strange rage that takes hold of the surgeon, as against the poor patient who tries in some way or other to deflect the aggression he is

victim of. Started out in the good conscience of someone doing a good turn to his kind, soon the surgical act imperceptibly slips into who knows what kind of offensive sadistic brutalization, which has almost nothing more to do with the initial brotherly solicitude. From a certain moment, the butcher goes for the nitty-gritty. Everything unfolds as if the mechanism for rechannelling aggression has gone awry in him, as if the instinctive nature he had dominated suddenly comes to the surface again, with an animal plenitude. And it happens often when the surgeon takes off his coat that he reads in the eyes of the person he has just operated upon not a painful recognition for the service rendered, but an impotent rage at the bandit who was louring on his path.

Coimbra, 25 March 1969
I didn't find any other symptom, but the sentence he came out with was all I needed to establish a diagnosis.

"The world ...", he said, "—seen it all."

And I concluded that he was at the end of the road.

Unable to come up with any treatment better adapted to this mortal satiety, at least I attempted to starve him with my own hunger:

"Oh really! Well I haven't finished seeing Portugal yet."

Chaves, 19 September 1970
In the company of a colleague and at his request, I've just come to a mountain village to help a woman in arrested labour. Stretched out on a bed, the placenta stuck in her uterus, the end of the umbilical cord extending from her vagina, she was, for all the villagers, the very picture of human impotence in the face of destiny. We delivered her, and the bright sun of confidence once again shone in the fatalistic eyes of the community. Once again, I experienced the joy of being a doctor. Thanks to the "queen of sciences" not only have I been able, throughout my life, to understand and accept my condition as a child of Nature, to see myself integrated into its laws, and to found on it all my values, but I've also known, from time to time, the legitimate pride of correcting or completing its works.

Coimbra, 20 March 1971

I shall never forget this wild cry of terror:

"There it's coming! It's coming! There! Now!"

I gave another injection of adrenalin to stimulate the heart, I did cardiac massage and mouth-to-mouth. In vain: the man was dead, irremediably. Now he was no more than a heavy cadaver, in the process of cooling, gradually stiffening, like so many others I'd not succeeded in keeping alive. All that was left was to forget this incident, to return to my papers; besides the patient was expecting another doctor and my intervention took place only by accident. But there was this disturbing fact: the vision and the panicky fear. The horror-stricken dread before a spectacle that no one could see. And that's all I continue to think of, moved, disturbed, the words of the dying man furred up in my ear. What did this man see? What does the face of Death look like?

Coimbra, 2 August 1972

Here I am again at anchor in the port of the quotidian, harshly chained up, from morning to evening, to the galley slave's bench of literature and the profession. And I feel, by means of these justifications, some kind of insipid peace. Nothing I do or write gives me satisfaction, but after having persisted in my efforts all day long, there is no doubt that I go to bed reconciled with myself in some way. There is "vileness" worse than that of earning one's bread with the sweat of one's brow as denounced by Sá Carneiro, and it consists in chaining one's body and soul day in day out to the bench of servitude, any servitude, without being compelled to do so by hunger. But mankind is afraid of freedom that is not in employment. And he spends his time decorating with pretty names—duty, responsibility, dignity—his refusal to face up to (courageously idle in this) the absurdity of life and death.

Coimbra, 6 November 1974

Entire day taking refuge in my surgery, progressively deserted by clients. The sun floods my office, outside the traffic rumbles by, and I read, edit, laze about, freeholder of my solitude. Life is taking leave from me and enlarging little by little the void that surrounds me. And I thank it within me for preparing me the sedative of dying gently in this hole, which started out as a place that was unambiguously businesslike and which is now visited only on occasion, by the faithful few. Which makes me think of those secret service agencies that put a commercial name on their door, but only as a front.

Castro Laboreiro, 17 July 1976
One of those doctors who stands helpless beside a dying person and feels the pulse slip away gently, with a troubled finger ... Over the years I've witnessed the gradual dilapidation of this place. For centuries, it knew how to preserve, unaltered, sacrosanct human and social values. Today all it can guarantee to its visitors is the purity and authenticity of the air they breathe and the water they drink. All the rest is degenerate. The character of the buildings and the costumes, the agricultural and pastoral practices. It is here—and at Vilarinho das Furnas and at Rio de Onor—that I saw for the first time God's creatures in their abundance, conjoined and free. And since Vilarinho das Furnas has disappeared from the map, submerged by a dam, my impenitent communitarianism has sunk new roots at Rio de Onor and Castro Laboreiro. I persist in making these visits, even if I'm more and more disenchanted. It's an article of faith for me that humankind will finish by reacting against the global massification we're heading towards. Reason and instinct will finally tell us that all the plastic flowers in the world aren't worth the lilies of the valley, that all the laboratory chemicals aren't worth a fermenting cartload of dung, that all the imperious whistles of progress aren't worth the cordial gong of a cattle bell. And at this hour of salvation—which shouldn't be a long time coming since the longer it takes the worse it'll be—we'll rediscover these sanctuaries, rebuild them and give them back their dignity. That's why I suffer without losing heart when I see them collapse. My hope is in their foundations.

Entries from *Diário I–XII*, Coimbra, 1941–76.

ALBERT CAMUS

The Fever Ward

The plague, as René Girard once observed, "is found everywhere in literature." Published just after the Second World War, Camus's great novel was read as a parable on Europe under the Nazis, or on the violence and social disorder that came in their wake. But Camus's sense of evil is more metaphysical: his doctor-hero is "fighting against Creation as he found it"—an attitude which becomes manifest in this harrowing description of the death of a child. Even though our conceptual tools for defusing the menace of evil are poor, Camus insists on putting individual moral choice and simple decency at the heart of public issues. For the elements of moral contagion, as the famous last line of his novel suggests, are always dormant, biding their time to infect some "happy city," even—or perhaps most especially—when our experience of actual plague and epidemics is vestigial.

As October came to an end, Castel's anti-plague serum was tried for the first time. Practically speaking, it was Rieux's last hope. Should it fail like everything else, the doctor was convinced the whole town would be at the whim of the disease: either the epidemic would continue to ravage the town for months on end or it would die out all of a sudden.

The day before Castel called on Rieux, Mr. Othon's son had been taken ill and the entire family was forced to go into quarantine. The mother, who had only recently come out of it, found herself back in isolation. In deference to the official regulations the magistrate had promptly sent for Dr. Rieux the moment he saw symptoms of the disease on his little boy's skin. Mother and father were standing at the foot of the bed when Rieux entered the room. Their little girl had been put in another room. The boy was extremely listless and submitted to the examination without a murmur. Lifting his head, Rieux caught the magistrate's intent gaze, and, behind him, the mother's pale face. She was masking her mouth with a handkerchief, and her wide-open eyes followed the doctor's movements.

"He has it, I suppose?" the magistrate asked in a dull voice.

"Yes." Rieux looked at the child again.

The mother's eyes widened even more, and still she said nothing. Mr. Othon, too, said nothing for a while before adding, in an even lower tone:

"Well, Doctor, we must follow the procedure laid down."

Rieux avoided looking at Mrs. Othon, who was still holding her handkerchief to her mouth.

"It won't take long," he said, stumbling over his words, "if you'll let me use your phone."

Mr. Othon said he would show him where the phone was. But before going, the doctor turned toward Mrs. Othon:

"I'm very sorry. You should get some things ready. You know what it entails."

Mrs. Othon seemed taken aback. She was staring at the floor.

"I understand," she murmured, nodding her head. "I'll get it done at once."

Just before leaving, Rieux couldn't stop himself asking if there wasn't anything he could do for them. The mother gazed at him without a word. And now the magistrate averted his eyes.

"No," he said, and then swallowed. "Apart from saving my son."

Having started out as a kind of routine, quarantine had now been organized by Rieux and Rambert along very strict lines. In particular they insisted that members of the same family should be kept apart. The infection ought not to have increased chances of spreading where one family member had been infected unawares. Rieux explained his rationale to the magistrate, who found it sound. Nevertheless, he and his wife exchanged a glance which made it plain to Rieux how distressed they were at the prospect of their imposed separation. Mrs. Othon and her little girl could be given rooms in Rambert's quarantine hospital. There was no room for the magistrate, however, except in an isolation camp the authorities were in the process of setting up in the municipal stadium, using tents supplied by the public works department. When Rieux apologized for this, Mr.

Othon replied that there was one rule for all, and it was only right to abide by it.

The boy was taken to the auxiliary hospital and put in a former classroom which had been turned into a ten-bedded ward. Twenty hours later, Rieux was convinced that the case was hopeless. The infection was spreading all over the little boy's body, which was putting up no resistance. Very small and immature but acutely painful buboes were turning the child's puny limbs quite rigid. The battle was lost in advance.

Rieux therefore had no qualms about testing Castel's serum on the boy. That night, after dinner, they performed the inoculation, a drawn-out procedure, without getting any reaction. At daybreak on the following day they gathered round the bed to assess the effects of this crucial trial inoculation.

The child had emerged from his torpor and was tossing about convulsively on the bed. From four in the morning Dr. Castel and Tarrou had been keeping vigil at the bedside, following every stage and turn in the disease. Tarrou, with his stocky figure, stood bending slightly at the head of the bed, while, at its foot, Castel was seated, reading an old book. He wore an expression of apparent calm. Rieux stood beside him. One by one, as daylight intensified in the former classroom, the others arrived. Paneloux, the first to come, leaned against the wall on the opposite side of the bed to Tarrou. His face was drawn with grief, and the accumulated weariness of all the days during which he had offered himself so unstintingly had lined his somewhat bulbous forehead. Grand came next. It was seven o'clock, and he apologized for being out of breath; he couldn't stay long, but wanted to know if anything substantial had been observed. Without speaking, Rieux pointed to the child. Eyes shut, face sunk in a grimace, teeth clenched, the boy was tossing his head from side to side on the uncovered bolster. The rest of his body was motionless. When just enough light had entered the room to pick out the traces of an equation chalked on a blackboard that still hung on the wall at the far end of the room, Rambert entered. Posting himself at the foot of the next bed, he took a package of cigarettes from his pocket. But after glancing at the child he put it back.

Still seated, Castel looked up over his spectacles at Rieux.

"Any news of his father?"

"No," said Rieux. "He's in the isolation camp."

The doctor's hands were gripping the rail of the bed, his eyes fixed on the small moaning child. Suddenly the boy stiffened, clenched his teeth again, and drawing in his waist stretched out his arms and legs. Naked beneath an army blanket, the body gave off a smell of wool and stale sweat. Then very gradually he relaxed, bringing his arms and legs back to the middle of the bed, still without speaking or opening his eyes, and seemed to breathe a little faster. Rieux's gaze caught Tarrou, who looked away.

They had already seen children die—for many months now death had selected its victims quite impartially—but they had yet to watch a child die minute by minute, as they had now been doing since daybreak. Needless to say, the pain inflicted on these innocent victims had always seemed to them to be what it was: a scandal. But until that moment it had shocked them only in an abstract kind of way; they had never had to witness face to face, over such a long period, the end of an innocent child's life.

Just then the boy went into spasm again, as if something had bitten him in the stomach, and he wailed thinly. For moments that seemed endless he stayed in that contorted position, his body racked by rigors and convulsive trembling; it was as if his frail frame were bending before the wild breath of the plague and crumbling under the repeated gusts of fever. There was a lull in the storm, and he relaxed a little; the fever seemed to ebb, leaving him breathless on a dank and dismal shore where languor was pretty much like death. When the fiery wave broke on him for the third time, lifting him a little, the child shrivelled into himself and shrank to the edge of the bed in terror of the flames that were touching him, burning him. He shook his head wildly, and flung off the blanket. Big tears welled up between the inflamed eyelids and trickled down the grey, sunken cheeks. When the acute episode had passed, utterly exhausted, he extended his rigid legs and arms on which the flesh had melted to the bone in forty-eight hours and looked in his dishevelled bed like the grotesque parody of a crucifixion.

Tarrou leaned over him and gently stroked the small tear- and sweat-stained face with his big paw. Castel, who had closed his book a few moments before, had been observing the child. He began to speak, but had to cough before continuing, because his voice sounded so stentorian.

"There wasn't any remission this morning, was there, Rieux?"

Rieux shook his head, but said that the child was putting up more resistance than he would have expected. Paneloux, who was slumped against the wall, said in a monotone:

"If he has to die, he'll have suffered longer."

Light was swelling in the ward. The occupants of the other five beds were stirring and groaning, but at an orchestratedly subdued level. Only one patient cried out at the other end of the ward, emitting regular little exclamations which seemed closer to surprise rather than to pain. Even for the sufferers the terror of the early phase seemed to have passed, giving way to a kind of acceptance in the way they now confronted the disease. Only the child went on fighting with the strength he had. Now and then Rieux took his pulse—not because it was necessary but simply to do something instead of standing there helplessly—and when he closed his eyes, he could feel its tumult mingling with the unrest of his own blood. One body with the tortured child, he struggled to sustain him with all his remaining strength. Linked for a few moments, the rhythms of their heartbeats soon fell apart, the child escaped him, and his effort sank without a trace. Then he let go of the small, thin wrist and moved back to where he had been standing.

The light on the whitewashed walls was changing from pink to yellow. The heat of another day was starting to beat down on the windows. Grand turned to leave and they hardly heard him saying he would come back. They were all waiting. The child, his eyes still closed, seemed to grow a little calmer. His fingers, which had become like claws, were feebly working the edges of the bed. Then they moved upwards, and scratched at the blanket over his knees. Suddenly he doubled up his legs, lifting his thighs towards his stomach, and remained quite still. For the first time he opened his eyes and gazed at Rieux, who was standing right in front of him. The mouth opened in that small face, rigid as a mask of grey clay, and a long, unbroken scream emerged, hardly inflected by his breathing, and filled the ward with a protest that was droning, strident and so barely human that it seemed like a collective voice. Rieux clenched his teeth, and Tarrou looked away. Rambert went up to the bed and stood beside Castel, who closed the book lying on his knees. Paneloux looked at the child's small mouth, pocked with ulcers and bursting with the death-cry as old as humankind. He sank on his knees, and none of those present was in the least taken aback to hear him say, hoarsely but distinctly, in a voice that broke through that never-ending nameless wail:

"My God, spare this child's life!"

But the child continued to shriek, and around his bed the other sufferers began to get restive. The patient at the far end of the ward, who had been interjecting his staccato cries without a pause, now stepped up his tempo so that they merged in one long wail, while the others groaned more and more loudly. A burst of sobbing erupted in the room, over-whelming Paneloux's prayer, and Rieux, who still had his hands tightly gripped around the bed-rail, shut his eyes, dizzy with exhaustion and disgust.

When he opened them again, Tarrou was at his side.

"I must go," Rieux said. "I can't bear them any longer."

But all of a sudden the other sufferers fell silent. Now the doctor noticed that the child's wail, which had been getting weaker and weaker, had fallen silent. Around him the groans began again, but like a dull refrain, a distant echo of the combat that had come to an end. It was all over. Castel had gone around to the other side of the bed and said that it was finished. Mouth wide-open but mute, the child lay among the tumbled blankets, suddenly shrunken, with the tears still glistening on his cheeks.

Paneloux went up to the bed and made the sign of benediction. Then gathering up his cassock, he walked out by the passage between the beds.

"Will you have to try it all over again?" Tarrou asked Castel.

The old doctor nodded slowly.

"Perhaps," he said, and then added, with a bitter smile: "after all, he put up a surprisingly long fight."

Rieux was already walking out of the room, striding so rapidly and with such an odd look on his face that Paneloux put out an arm to hold him back as he passed by.

"Come on, Doctor," he began.

Rieux rounded on him fiercely in the same movement.

"Ah! That child, at least, was innocent, and you know it as well as I do!"

He turned away and, opening the classroom doors before Paneloux, strode across the school playground. Seated on a bench beneath the dusty, stunted trees, he wiped away the sweat that was beginning to run into his eyes. He felt like shouting—anything to loosen the stranglehold that had seized his heart. Heat was slowly pounding down between the branches of the fig trees. A white haze, which was rapidly obscuring the blue of the morning sky, made the air even more stifling. Rieux slumped back on the bench. He looked up at the branches and the sky, and his breath came slowly back. Bit by bit he choked down his fatigue.

He heard a voice behind him. "Why did you talk to me so angrily just now? It was just as unbearable for me as it was for you."

Rieux turned toward Paneloux.

"You're right. I'm sorry. But tiredness is next to madness. And there are times in this town when the only thing that moves me is a feeling of mad revolt."

"I understand," said Paneloux softly. "We find that kind of thing revolting because it exceeds our understanding. But perhaps we should love what we can't understand."

Rieux straightened up straightaway. He looked at Paneloux with all the conviction and feeling he could muster, and shook his head.

"No, Father, I've a very different idea of love. And until my last day I shall refuse to love a universe in which children are tortured."

A stricken look darted across the priest's face. "Ah, doctor," he said sadly, "I've just understood what is meant by the word 'grace'."

Once again Rieux slumped back on the bench. His tiredness had returned. This time he spoke from its depths, more gently.

"I know it's something I don't possess. But this isn't the moment to discuss it with you. We're working side by side for something which brings us together—beyond blasphemy and prayer. That's all that counts."

Paneloux sat down beside Rieux. He was clearly moved.

"Yes," he said, "you, too, are working for humankind's salvation."

Rieux ventured a smile.

"Salvation is much too grand a word for me. I don't aim that far: it's just human health that interests me. For me health comes first."

Paneloux wavered. "Doctor …" he commenced; but then he stopped. The sweat was running down his forehead too. Then he quietly said good-bye, and his eyes were moist when he got up. As he turned to go, Rieux, who had been deep in thought, got up too and took a step towards him.

"Please forgive me, once again," he said. "I won't make another outburst of that kind."

Paneloux held out his hand and added, regretfully: "Even so, I didn't manage to bring you round to my side."

"What does it matter?" said Rieux. "What I detest is death and disease—as you well know. And whether you wish it or not, we are partners in the enduring battle against them."

Rieux was still holding Paneloux's hand.

"And so you see," he added, although he avoided meeting the priest's eyes, "even God Himself can't sunder us now."

Chapter 3, Part Four, *La Peste*, 1947.

PETER BAMM

Treatment as a Moral Problem

It used to be fashionable to suggest that people get the diseases they deserve, although it is surely more important to point out that people also get the diseases they don't deserve. But do they get the doctors they deserve? Written in the 1950s, after the collective disaster of the Nazi period, Peter Bamm is wary about medicine's claims to bring about a perfect society, or even to understand the mechanisms of social justice. Bamm takes a cue from Nietzsche when he points out that illness, for many people, is not the negative event it is assumed to be: it may be meaning itself. "There is a degree of poor health that makes us happy" wrote Joseph Joubert, in 1809. But it is noteworthy that medical thinking has rarely given much heed to the intelligence and capacity for coping in the demeanour of patients themselves.

The history of medicine is the history of a field campaign mounted by human intelligence against illness, the bane of human existence ever since man was first obliged to eat his bread in the sweat of his face.

While theologians constructed the house of scholasticism in order to reconcile man with death through divine science, while preachers attempted to console him with the old tradition of the immortal soul, while the philosophers taught him resignation and wisdom, the life sciences made death their enemy.

This project seems plausible enough. But a few assumptions were made. They are not quite so self-evident that we can overlook them. Disease is fate. Insofar as medicine undertakes to heal diseases, it makes decisions over which hardly a word is ever uttered.

Human curiosity is enough to drive biology. Everything we find out about the chemical structure of the cell, about the soul of the white ant, about the physics of our sense organs, expands our knowledge and understanding of the world. We could be satisfied with what we know. Its practical use is something haphazard. It depends on man. It has no direct connection with the nature of knowledge itself.

This can be shown by looking at gunpowder. Gunpowder was initially discovered in the twelfth century, and discovered again in the thirteenth century, the first time by someone in China, the second time by a Franciscan monk. The fact that, in Europe, piety led to the discovery of gunpowder did not prevent it, in terms of progress, from ultimately being far more drastic than the old plague epidemics. But in China the technician was a Confucian. Accordingly the discovery of gunpowder did not lead the Chinese to kill men, but instead to emblazon the Emperor's garden party with rockets and fireworks. Chemically, the Franciscan powder was absolutely identical to the Confucian powder. What differed was solely the use to which the West and East put their discovery.

In scientific medicine knowledge is coupled to its appraisal. Diseases lead, or rather oblige the doctor to focus research methods on practical results, towards therapeutic success, in a word *cure*.

Medical research cannot be satisfied with what it knows. Knowledge is what it seeks, most certainly, just as every science seeks knowledge. Medicine, however, has to put its scientific insights into practice. With its practical successes it intervenes directly in human life.

What in fact is its justification for doing so?

It would seem self-evident that curing a disease is a gain. Here doctors and patients are entirely of one mind—in a kind of open conspiracy. But it's not that self-evident at all. It can't be denied, for instance, that many a disease has the property of being an excellent fit for the patient who suffers from it.

The picture of a retired minister of state is just as harmonically rounded off by him having gout as it is by the title "Excellency". For a retired minister of state to be cured of his gout is as satisfying for his doctor as for the patient himself. But is there any satisfaction in modifying a condition which seems earmarked for the patient? It would make the world a little bit less unfair. There is indubitably some justice in the fact that the price of the ticket for the many good dinners washed down with so many fine clarets enjoyed by His Excellency in the service of his country is a painful large toe. But then, if medicine seeks to lay claims to intrinsic philosophical dignity, it must at least uphold the principle according to which curing a retired minister of state of gout is justified under all circumstances.

How might this principle look?

It must also be said that rheumatism suits a cleaning lady well. What else would she have to complain about, sipping her afternoon coffee with the concierge, if not her rheumatics? Her son turned out well in the end. But she needs *something* to complain about. It's definitely easier to complain about pains in the shoulder and the inadequacy of bee poison as a treatment than about the inconsiderateness of her son and the trouble with the Fourth Commandment. In this case there may even be, philosophically speaking, some consolation in the fact that rheumatics in cleaning ladies cannot be cured.

At least once in his career, every intelligent doctor makes the stupendous discovery that after a great deal of effort he has brought about an outcome he did not want to attain. He lists the tricky differential diagnosis for a perforated right-sided renal stone. He carries out a brilliant operation. He gives up sleep for several nights in order to see his case through. Eventually he wins out; only then to discover that he has saved the life of a particularly repulsive character, let's say a loan shark. Had the loan shark died, his clients would have been saved, one of them from suicide. As it stands, through his exorbitant interest rates, the grateful patient is able to settle punctually the fee demanded by the famous surgeon, mankind's benefactor, whose good deed has ruined the existence of a score of ordinary folk and the life of a poor man.

It is generally accepted that when an important man has syphilis his important business will get done in spite of his illness. This assumption is naive. There is no evidence to support it. With a dose of Salvarsan it is possible to eradicate not only rashes from the skin but in some circumstances a whole symphony from the patient's imagination.

Medical science makes decisions in its combat with death without thinking at all about the consequences which its decisions bring in their wake. Medical science has only cursory ideas of the role which disease plays in the economy of life. It cannot really avail itself of the possibility that a disease may improve a person, bring him enlightenment, reform his character, or teach his biologically so poorly functioning heart the nature of goodness, something his healthy heart could never do. Scientific medicine has a concept of the normal functioning of the biological individual and its teachings are about how normal functioning can be restored. Science is interested in the causes for the disturbance of normal biological functioning only insofar they fit within its very narrowly defined concept. That a disease is a perturbation in the harmony of a whole person is not a problem for scientific medicine, but a problem for the doctor, who has to deal not with the biological individual but with the human being in the fullness of his humanity.

Medicine is therefore unable to contemplate with equanimity the prospect of a world full of petty tyrants, all of them fighting fit, emerging from under its hands; just as it is possible that one day it will be able to keep alive every fragile bit of Creation with a single dose of an effective serum, one of which might become the Descartes of our time.

If you start to ponder this issue, it will become apparent that it is not simple. It may happen, too, that, once liberated from the pain in his big toe, our retired minister of state puts together an excellent work on statesmanship that proves to be the crucial book in mankind's militant way to perpetual peace. Moreover, it can never be entirely ruled out that the camel will at least squeeze its head through the eye of the needle; and the loan shark, with eternity's breath on his face, reduce his interest rates from twenty to fifteen percent. The surgeon cannot tell in advance.

When thinking about health, even theology is lacking in zeal. The man from Nazareth didn't just forgive sins, he also cured illnesses.

The church, humanity's venerable matron, has kept sins within her purview. As far as diseases are concerned, medicine has snatched the Church's old power away. The doctor may still gladly shake hands with the priest at the patient's bedside, but only because the priest still knows how to go on when the doctor's art has ended.

The Church believes in the effective healing of infirmities through the power of saints, relics and prayers. Many of her miracles are miracles of healing. No doctor who knows anything at all about the secrets of the human soul would want to argue against them, as little as a cardinal with diabetes would want to doubt the necessity of insulin. But the way scientific medicine pursues cures has not yet been considered thoroughly enough by theology.

At this point the anarchy of our time reveals itself in the very destructive beauty of its torn crimson. Every one of us lives in many worlds, and we have no Descartes to draw a sky over them that might have brought them all into some kind of harmony.

The field campaign which research mounts against death has led to tremendous successes. One of its tasks, for which a solution is not even in sight, is to fit these successes in an order that gives them meaning. The advances made by research every passing year are not only admirable victories over death, but also a continual exhortation to human society to prove itself worthy of its own accomplishments.

"Therapie als moralisches Problem," *Essays*, 1960.

GUIDO CERONETTI

The Silence of the Body

Guido Ceronetti is an Italian philologist, bible scholar, critic, vegetarian and self-confessed hypochondriac whose book of aphorisms about the body cobbles together folk wisdom, occult legend, medical history and literary commentary. He writes likes an old-fashioned moralist, and some of his specular observations on the materials of life and medical history resemble fantastic literature: he may be delving into the silence of the body (the phrase comes from René Leriche) but he is clearly just as preoccupied by the noisy city. Like the old Roman physician Galen, whose teachings dominated medicine for fifteen hundred years, he seems to be scouring medicine for a kind of master logic. Five hundred years ago he would probably have written an ars moriendi—*a book on the art of dying well.*

Famous mistakes of Greek medicine, later adopted and disseminated by Arab physicians: the birfurcated uterus, the existence of growths to nourish the uterine mucous membrane, the migration of the uterus inside the body (Meyerhof, *La Gynécologie et l'obstétrique chez Avicenne et leurs rapports avec celles des Grecs*, 1938). Both the imaginative Plato and Hippocrates believed in the migration of the uterus, an animal eager to mate, whose craving for semen made it travel from one part of the body to the other, provoking Hysteria; but this is only a way of saying that, like every other living creature, the female body travels inside the uterus.

★

Albert Camus said to Jean Guitton, "He never killed a fly." Guitton replied, "The fly he didn't kill carried the plague elsewhere." He should have said flea rather than fly, but the moral is the same.

★

For Littré, *panser* is the same as *penser*, because if you wish to panser (to medicate, to heal), first you have to think. Then, as Paré used to say, God will do the healing.

★

It is painful to discover that a doctor is not God, because we cannot abandon the idea of a friendly, healing God above us.

★

A beautiful thought from Le Clézio: "Perhaps one day we will realize there was no art but only Medicine."

★

Karl Jaspers to Rudolf Bultmann: "By applying the method of technology to actions and behaviour that technology cannot dominate, scientific superstition leads to a specific activity, analogous to magic's aberrations, which have never been overcome."

★

"True doctors are few and little known, for almost all physicians are true invalids" (Giordano Bruno, *Ash Wednesday Supper*).

★

Do you want to become a medical specialist? Then specialize, as did the most subtle Egyptians, in Unknown Illnesses.

★

"We are more sensitive to the Surgeon's incision than to ten slashes of the sword in the thick of battle" (Montaigne, "That the Taste of Good and Evil ..."). The scalpel is awaited, but the sword arrives unexpectedly. We have stopped fighting but are forever waiting to enter the operating room.

★

I never experienced any kind of pain, said Montesquieu, that could not be eased by an hour of reading. Now there's a true man of letters.

★

Jünger says that even in Medicine, Tactics are variable and Strategy unchangeable. "The moving hand treats, the steady hand heals" (*Strahlungen*). This sounds like a Taoist maxim.

★

Goethe says that medicine must absorb a physician's total being, because his object is the total human organism.

★

Zola the naturalist denies moral responsibility; Zola the Dreyfusard is forced to defend it (as was Spinoza, after the massacre of the De Wytts). Theoretically, we can accept moral irresponsibility, but if we try to lead lives consistent with this principle we immediately gasp for air.

★

If we deprive loving feelings of the morbidity that lubricates them, we will become not *healthy* but sterile, atrophic, buffeted by the arid wind of cruelty.

★

Hippocrates says that a disease in which sleep is painful is fatal, while one in which sleep provides relief is not. With laudanum, morphine, and barbiturates, we have lost sight of this distinction.

★

In Seveso. Everything seems normal, yet there is a plague. On July 10 the chemical boil explodes. The forbidden zone is poorly guarded, and anyone can pass through by avoiding the main roads. The children play and ride their bikes to the edge of the most contaminated spot. In the stores a sign guarantees that the produce comes from elsewhere. Rain has fallen on the first posters put out by the Health Commission, which said not to be alarmed. ICMESA is a huge iron tumour over Meda, which borders on Seveso, a silent dragon at the centre of a meadow covered with its own slime. This is how, if our eyes were not sealed by a spell, we should see Industry, which everybody desperately, wretchedly adores. Industry is a mythological animal that deals out death, a Minotaur to which everything must be sacrificed. Tomatoes and lettuce ripen in the gardens, untouchable. The sky is heavy and filled with fumes. A region in the grip of industries, where disfigured lives persevere, in an almost unreal ugliness, chronically ill and bandaged. The power of Man: the toxic cloud killed the animals but (for the time being) only sprayed acne on the children of man (August 26, 1976).

★

Dr. Richard Blackmore asked Sydenham which authors he should read in order to become a good physician. Sydenham recommended Cervantes.

★

A struggle between two concepts. In 1917, the prevention of venereal disease among the troops was so important to the United States government and high command that they restricted individual freedom and interfered in the Allied countries. The British were more tolerant of *Treponema* and would not curtail the soldiers' freedom to get infected. The moralists in England did not want people even to talk about the fight against venereal disease: their enemy was vice. But not even the preachers demanded the suppression of brothels: the virtuous soldier was expected to refrain spontaneously.

★

Petronius' amazing maxim *Medicus enim nihil aliud est quam animi consolatio* (For a doctor is nothing more than consolation for the spirit) reduces medical practice to its essence—psychology—and equates medicine with landscape, poetry, perfumes, and love (Seleucus' speech, *Satyricon*, 42).

★

When the fatal illness appears I hope to be conscious and helped to see it clearly; the problem will be how to resist, how to avoid treatment without too much natural suffering. Disease is less frightening if one reflects on it. The endless exams, therapies, and the whole medical apparatus do not reassure me; they distress me. I will fight for power rather than calmly offer my flank to an ointment. The most urgent problem will be finding a doctor, not a cure.

★

Paul Valéry's response to the final disease—"Je suis foutu et je m'en fous"—I'm damned and I don't give a damn—remains the best possible (even a religious spirit can find it exemplary). To be perfectly wise without ceasing to be human, pronounce the first part firmly (realization of the ineluctable fact: "Je suis foutu!" Good! You're right!) and the second part with secret reluctance, a slight hesitation, to spare one's human reality from trembling at the prospect of a loss one fears complete—that of everything the unsaved person believes him or herself to be. On close reflection, Valéry's response also suits nations, empires, religions, civilizations, and the whole of human-kind—every apparition of matter.

★

Today medical school is attended by mobs, not students; a mob receives its degree, a Doctor-Mob practises the medical profession. We learn to distrust it immediately; this mob may even be armed, may even be equipped with powerful weapons. Whoever wishes to become a doctor should reflect before entering the profession; enter only if you are determined to be different and to adopt different principles and teachings. Otherwise do not enter. On the margins of omnipotent medicine, free spaces exist for Paracelsians and Neo-Mesmerics and for doctors armed only with Laennec's stethoscope or a few Chinese needles.

★

Leibniz referred to Spinoza as a *physician* because in those days whoever excelled in philosophy was considered a physician or honoured by the title. (Thus I will never be a physician.) Without attending the Anatomical Theatres and peering inside cadavers, a person was not really a philosopher. Rightfully so, because one must be a vulture before being an eagle, ready at every moment to turn into a worm, into an almost true demon, and turn back into an angel when the cock crows.

★

The crucifix in hospitals is not apotropaic; it is a symbol of the best Christian paradox. Through the obsessive presence of the crucifix, the Christians who invented the hospital attempted to deny radically its function as a place to restore patients to health and to normal life. The crucifix rejects medical therapy and surgery (although it shares a sympathy for the blood they spill), because surgery seeks to extirpate suffering and not to burn away, or even gnaw at, earthly pain. (Freed from a kidney stone or a fistula, a patient will seethe with even more sin than before.) Hence the sorrow, the profound misery of the hospital under that symbol for as long as hospitals were Christian.

The total secularization of life has made the hospital emerge as a place that can be calm and decent despite the negative presence of the crucified Christ, memento of the agony, the *Eli, Eli*, the *consummatum*, the ever-flowing haemorrhage. Now the symbol has almost completely disappeared except in hospitals run by religious orders, and its grand disappearance has left a void: the sense of death followed it into the bonfire, where it had *weakened* but not burned. A hospital filled with triumphant life and anti-Thanatos *pruderie* is no less gloomy (though much warmer and more pleasant) than a hospital dominated by chants of "dust to dust" and a bleeding rib cage. No hospital will ever be good.

★

When Disraeli was dying, the Queen's doctors refused him a consultation, since he had been under the care of a homeopathic doctor; their professional association rejected any contact with homeopathics. (On the Queen's insistence, they visited him.) The separation between the two medicines is still rigid. Today many patients have their illnesses diagnosed by ordinary doctors and then resort to homeopathic cures, an ark against the flood of poisonous therapies. This behaviour reveals a twin distrust of both schools of medicine.

From *Il silenzio del corpo: Materiali per studio di medicina*, 1979; translated from the Italian by Michael Moore.

SAMUEL BECKETT

A Testimonial Advertisement

This marvellous parody comes from Beckett's last novel written in English, Watt, *and brings the popular American tradition of selling snake-juice up to date. Beckett seems to be uncommonly knowledgeable about high fats.*

Have you tried Bando, Mr. Graves, said Arthur. A capsule, before and after meals, in a little warm milk, and again at night, before turning in. I had tried everything, and was thoroughly disgusted, when a friend spoke to me of Bando. Her husband was never without it, you understand. Try it, she said, and come back in five or six years. I tried it, Mr. Graves, and it changed my whole outlook on life. From being a moody, listless, constipated man, covered with squames, shunned by my fellows, my breath fetid and my appetite depraved (for years I had eaten nothing but high fat rashers), I became, after four years of Bando, vivacious, restless, a popular nudist, regular in my daily health, almost a father and a lover of boiled potatoes. Bando. Spelt as pronounced.

Excerpt from *Watt*, 1959.

KARL VALENTIN

Dialogue of the Deaf

According to a received idea in the British Isles, the Germans have no sense of humour. Not true; you simply need a licence to be funny in Germany. Karl Valentin, the great Munich cabarettist and model for some of Beckett's tramps, had a way of getting to the point by being beside it. In this sketch with his stage partner Liesl Karlstadt, he tries to find out what a doctor is for, within the purview of the Bismarckian health scheme. Tree frogs, placed in a bottle with a ladder, used to be employed as weather forecasters by German children.

Liesl Karlstadt: Next patient, please.

Karl Valentin: Good day, doctor.

L. K.: Good day, Herr Meyer. Now what seems to be the problem?

K. V.: Dear me, Doctor, my stomach is never right. Whenever I've eaten something it gets so bloated.

L. K.: Well, that's no illness, is it? That's logic: if you put something into your stomach, it will get full. What happens then if you don't eat at all?

K. V.: Quite the reverse. Then I get such a hollow feeling in my stomach.

L. K.: Well, there you are—your stomach is quite in order.

K. V.: Alright, but why is it that I pant so much climbing up the stairs?

L. K.: My dear patient, another person would be panting, too, climbing up your stairs, but that has nothing to do with your stomach: that's your lungs.

K. V.: Yes, my lungs are healthy, nothing wrong with them, but all the same I broke my foot two years ago.

L. K.: Oh, you broke your foot—how did that happen?

K. V.: I had one too many.

L. K.: But too much alcohol doesn't break your foot.

K. V.: True enough, I was sozzled, and then I went and slipped on a banana skin from foreign parts and broke my own foot.

L. K.: Yes, but it wasn't the alcohol that was to blame then but the banana skin.

K. V.: Of course the banana skin was to blame since I didn't see it, and while we're at it I wanted to say, Doctor, that my eyes don't ever seem to be quite right because, when I'm at home and reading the paper I get such a pain in the neck that I have to stop reading.

L. K.: But my dear Herr Meyer, bad eyesight never gives rise to pain in the neck.

K. V.: That's as may be, but there must be some kind of secret connection between the eyes and the spine, since you often hear old people complaining and saying: "It's a real pain in the neck not being able to see well."

L. K.: Well, Herr Meyer, you simply ought to read the newspaper less often and eat more fruit—fruit is good for you.

K. V.: Not for everyone, Doctor. I know someone who almost choked on a plum.

L. K.: How old are you then, Herr Meyer?

K. V.: Doctor, I'm nearly ten years older than my wife. Yes indeed.

L. K.: Well, well, well—and how old is your wife then?

K. V.: Ah, my wife, she's—I'm afraid I couldn't tell you that right now.

L. K.: Well, never mind, that's just a minor matter.—Are the bowels working?

K. V.: My wife's?

L. K.: No, no, yours.

K.V.: Ah, my bowels—yes, yes—of course, they are—well, strictly between you and me ... [*Valentin whispers into the doctor's ear.*]

L. K.: Well, well, well, ha ha ha ha ha—in that case perhaps not: I'll prescribe you opium tincture instead of castor oil.—By the way, what is it you do for a living, Herr Meyer?

K. V.: I make ladders.

L. K.: Oh, you make those telescopic ladders for the fire brigade?

K. V.: No, no, I make the really small ones for tree frogs.

L. K.: You don't say! Very interesting. Well, a ladder is a ladder, but to come back to what we were saying, Herr Meyer, as far as I can tell there's really nothing wrong with you apart from a touch of diarrhoea. You're in the best of health.

K. V.: What? Me—healthy? What on earth am I paying into the sickness fund for then?

"Beim Arzt," *Alles von Karl Valentin*, 1978.

JEAN STAFFORD

The Interior Castle

In this story, which is partly autobiographical, the patient internalizes the idea of theatre: strapped on the operating table, she conducts a kind of self-defensive back-biting dialogue with the medical staff and surgeon who are about to repair her nose after an accident that has left her with facial and head injuries. Her inner dialogue makes a sharp contrast with the military campaign described in Heart Suture, *her cocaine-fuelled imagery of snow sculptures relaying the strange experience of having bodily tissue manipulated and manhandled without any perception of it being painful.*

Dr. Nicholas came at nine o'clock to prepare her for the operation. With him came an entourage of white-frocked acolytes, and one of them wheeled in a wagon on which lay knives and scissors and pincers, cans of swabs and gauze. In the midst of these was a bowl of liquid whose rich purple color made it seem strange like the brew of an alchemist.

"All set?" the surgeon asked her, smiling. "A little nervous, what? I don't blame you. I've often said I'd rather break a leg than have a submucous resection." Pansy thought for a moment he was going to touch his nose. His approach to her was roundabout. He moved through the yellow light shed by the globe in the ceiling which gave his forehead a liquid gloss; he paused by the bureau and touched a blossom of the cyclamen; he looked out the window and said, to no one and to all, "I couldn't start my car this morning. Came in a cab." Then he came forward. As he came, he removed a speculum from the pocket of his short-sleeved coat and like a cat, inquiring of the nature of a surface with its paws, he put out his hand toward her and drew it back, gently murmuring, "You must not be afraid, my dear. There is no danger, you know. Do you think for a minute I would operate if there were?"

Dr. Nicholas, young, brilliant, and handsome, was an aristocrat, a husband, a father, a clubman, a Christian, a kind counselor, and a trustee of his preparatory school. Like many of the medical profession, even those whose specialty was centered on the organ of the basest sense, he interested himself in the psychology of his patients: in several instances, for example, he had found that severe attacks of sinusitis were coincident with emotional crises. Miss Vanneman more than ordinarily captured his fancy since her skull had been fractured and her behavior throughout had been so extraordinary that he felt he was observing at first hand some of the results of shock, that incommensurable element, which frequently were too subtle to see. There was, for example, the matter of her complete passivity during a lumbar puncture, reports of which were written down in her history and were enlarged upon for him by Dr. Rivers' interne who had been in charge. Except for a tremor in her throat and a deepening of pallor, there were no signs at all that she was aware of what was happening to her. She made no sound, did not close her eyes nor clench her fists. She had had several punctures; her only reaction had been to the very first one, the morning after she had been brought in. When the interne explained to her that he was going to drain off cerebrospinal fluid which was pressing against her brain, she exclaimed, "My God!" but it was not an exclamation of fear. The young man had been unable to name what it was he had heard in her voice; he could only say that it had not been fear as he had observed it in other patients.

Dr. Nicholas wondered about her. There was no way of guessing whether she had always had a nature of so tolerant and undemanding a complexion. It gave him a melancholy pleasure to think that before her accident she had been high-spirited and loquacious; he was moved to think that perhaps she had been a beauty and that when she had first seen her face in the looking glass she had lost all joy in herself. It was very difficult to tell what the face had been, for it was so bruised and swollen, so hacked-up and lopsided. The black stitches the length of the nose, across the saddle, across the cheekbone, showed that there would be unsightly scars. He had ventured once to give her the name of a plastic surgeon but she had only replied with a vague, refusing smile. He had hoisted a manly shoulder and said, "You're the doctor."

Much as he pondered, coming to no conclusions, about what went on inside that pitiable skull, he was, of course, far more interested in the nose, deranged so badly that it would require his topmost skill to restore its functions to it. He would be obliged not only to make a submucous resection, a simple run-of-the-mill operation, but to remove the vomer, always a delicate task but further complicated in this case by the proximity of the bone to the frontal fracture line which conceivably was not entirely closed. If it were not and he operated too soon and if a cold germ then found its way into the opening, his patient would be carried off by meningitis in the twinkling of an eye. He wondered if she knew in what potential danger she lay; he desired to assure her that he had brought his craft to its nearest perfection and that she had nothing to fear of him, but feeling that she was perhaps both ignorant and unimaginative and that such consolation would create a fear rather than dispel one, he held his tongue and came nearer to the bed.

Watching him, Pansy could already feel the prongs of his pliers opening her nostrils for the insertion of his fine probers. The pain he caused her with his instruments was of a different kind from that she felt unaided: it was a naked, clean, and vivid pain that made her faint and ill and made her wish to die. Once she had fainted as he ruthlessly explored and after she was brought around, he continued until he had finished his investigation. The memory of this outrage had afterward several times made her cry.

This morning she looked at him and listened to him with hatred. Fixing her eyes upon the middle of his high, protuberant brow, she imagined the clutter behind it and she despised its obtuse imperfection. In his bland unawareness, this nobody, this nose-bigot, was about to play with fire and she wished him ill.

He said, "I can't blame you. No, I expect you're not looking forward to our little party. But you'll be glad to be able to breathe again."

He stationed his lieutenants. The interne stood opposite him on the left side of the bed. The surgical nurse wheeled the wagon within easy reach of his hands and stood beside it. Another nurse stood at the foot of the bed. A third drew the shades at the windows and attached a blinding light that shone down on the patient hotly, and then she left the room, softly closing the door. Pansy stared at the silver ribbon tied in a great bow round the green crepe paper of one of the flowerpots. It made her realize for the first time that one of the days she had lain here had been Christmas, but she had no time to consider this strange and thrilling fact, for Dr. Nicholas was genially explaining his anesthetic. He would soak packs of gauze in the purple fluid, a cocaine solution, and he would place them then in her nostrils, leaving them there for an hour. He warned her that the packing would be disagreeable (he did not say "painful") but that it would be well worth a few minutes of discomfort not to be in the least sick after the operation. He asked her if she were ready and when she nodded her head, he adjusted the mirror on his forehead and began.

At the first touch of his speculum, Pansy's fingers mechanically bent to the palms of her hands and she stiffened. He said, "A pack, Miss Kennedy," and Pansy closed her eyes. There was a rush of plunging pain as he drove the sodden gobbet of gauze high up into her nose and something bitter burned in her throat so that she retched. The doctor paused a moment and the surgical nurse wiped Pansy's mouth. He returned to her with another pack, pushing it with his bodkin doggedly until it lodged against the first. Stop! Stop! Cried all her nerves, wailing along the surface of her skin. The coats that covered them were torn off and they shuddered like naked people screaming, Stop! Stop! But Dr. Nicholas did not hear. Time and again he came back with a fresh pack and did not pause at all until one nostril was finished. She opened her eyes and saw him wipe the sweat off his forehead and saw the dark interne bending over her, fascinated. Miss Kennedy bathed her temples in ice water and Dr. Nicholas said, "There. It won't be much longer. I'll tell them to send you some coffee, though I'm afraid you won't be able to use it. Ever drink coffee with chicory in it? I have no use for it."

She snatched at his irrelevancy and, though she had never tasted chicory, she said severely, "I love it."

Dr. Nicholas chuckled. "De gustibus. Ready? A pack, Miss Kennedy."

The second nostril was harder to pack since the other side was now distended and this passage was anyhow much narrower, as narrow, he had once remarked, as that in the nose of an infant. In such pain as passed all language and even the farthest fetched analogies, she turned her eyes inward, thinking that under the obscuring cloak of the surgeon's pain she could see her brain without the knowledge of its keeper. But Dr. Nicholas and his aides would give her no peace. They surrounded her with their murmuring and their foot-shuffling and the rustling of their starched uniforms, and her eyelids continually flew back in embarrassment and mistrust. She was claimed entirely by this present, meaningless pain and suddenly and sharply she forgot what she had meant to do. She was aware of nothing but her ascent to the summit of something; what it was she did not know, whether it was a tower or a peak or Jacob's ladder. Now she was an abstract word, now she was a theorem of geometry, now she was a kite flying, a top spinning, a prism flashing, a kaleidoscope turning.

But none of the others in the room could see inside and when the surgeon was finished, the nurse at the foot of the bed said, "Now you must take a look in the mirror. It's simply too comical." And they all laughed intimately like old, fast friends. She smiled politely and looked at her reflection: over the gruesomely fastened snout, her scarlet eyes stared in fixed reproach upon her upturned lips, gray with bruises. But even in its smile of betrayal, the mouth itself was puzzled: it reminded her that something had been left behind, but she could not recall what it was. She was hollowed out and was as dry as a white bone.

★

They strapped her ankles to the operating table and put leather nooses round her wrists. Over her head was a mirror with a thousand facets in which she saw a thousand travesties of her face. At her right side was the table, shrouded in white, where lay the glittering blades of the many knives, thrusting out fitful rays of light. All the cloth was frosty; everything was white or silver and as cold as snow. Dr. Nicholas, a tall snowman with silver eyes and silver fingernails, came into the room soundlessly, for he walked on layers and layers of snow that deadened his footsteps; behind him came the interne, a smaller snowman, less impressively proportioned. At the foot of the table, a snow figure put her frozen hands upon Pansy's helpless feet. The doctor plucked the packs from the cold, numb nose. His laugh was like a cry on a bitter, still night: "I will show you now," he called across the expanse of snow, "that you can feel nothing." The pincers bit at nothing, snapped at the air and cracked a nerveless icicle. Pansy called back and heard her own voice echo: "I feel nothing."

Here the walls were gray, not tan. Suddenly the face of the nurse at the foot of the table broke apart and Pansy first thought it was in grief. But it was a smile and she said, "Did you enjoy your coffee?" Down the gray corridors of the maze, the words rippled, ran like mice, birds, broken beads: Did you enjoy your coffee? Your coffee? Your coffee? Similarly once in another room that also had gray walls, the same voice had said, "Shall I give her some whisky?" She was overcome with gratitude that this young woman (how pretty she was with her white hair and her white face and her china-blue eyes!) had been with her that first night and was with her now.

In the great stillness of the winter, the operation began. The knives carved snow. Pansy was happy.

Excerpt from "The Interior Castle," *The Collected Stories*, 1973.

RICHARD HUELSENBECK
Why I Left America

"Blago Bung Blago Bung Bosso Fataka!"—that was one of the opening salvoes of dada. In 1916, a German medical student, Richard Heulsenbeck, came up with a magical word buried deep in the Indo-European subconscious. Out of a growing contempt at what was happening on the battlefields of Europe he loosed it on the stage at the famous Cabaret Voltaire in Zurich, hoping it would blow a defunct culture to smithereens. Half a century later, Dr Charles R. Hulbeck, distinguished psychoanalyst, changed his name back to Huelsenbeck and returned from New York to Switzerland, hoping to find what had charged him with creative energy in the middle of the First World War—and knowing he wouldn't.

The conflict between my existence as dadaist and as doctor has haunted my entire life; not surprisingly it has been with me during my time in America too. I'd even go so far as to say that, at least up till now, the Americans have never understood dadaism. Dada, in their eyes, is a kind of revolutionary brouhaha about art, not dissimilar to the way Williams S. Rubins conceived it when, in his position as director of the Museum of Modern Art, he organized the last big exhibition "Dada, surrealism and what came after." Throwing dada and surrealism together in one exhibition struck me as a perversity, but I couldn't stop it or do anything about it.

Here you have one of the motives for my leaving the States. I was never able to explain to anyone, to make it really clear, what dada wanted and what dada is, a revolutionarily reckless battle against the ideology of culture when it is used as a shield against social and political injustices. Dada fought for the freedom of the creative personality, against artistic snobbery and artistic lies. The problem is so complicated that the dadaists themselves could never quite explain it. Dada was thus the beginning of the revolution of the suppressed personality against the tyranny of technology, against the stereotyping of communication: it set free the feeling of being lost in an ocean of commercial superefficiency. Dada is a kind of humanism, not the humanism of the classic German writers but a fight for freedom and the right to be an individual.

I was never able to explain any of this to the Americans, and as a result I was a success as a doctor, but a failure as a dadaist (which was what was closer to my heart).

The feeling of being a failed dadaist filled my entire American existence and it had an effect—for good or bad—on my medical activities. After a certain time it therefore became impossible for me to feel comfortable in the group led by Karen Horney, although I never officially left it. I developed an interest in existential psychoanalysis, which although it had been founded years before by Binswanger was kept up by small groups in New York. We set up the New York Ontoanalytical Association, and—I take the risk of acknowledging it—its members awarded me a prize: the Binswanger Award for Outstanding Achievement.

What kind of achievement had I attained? I attempted to explain it to myself. I had never in my life written any kind of book about psychiatry, apart from the slim paperback that was published in German by Ullstein as "Sexuality and Personality." I was really very unhappy. I attempted to establish the nature of this unhappiness and to get it clear in my mind that it was the result of a conflict between medicine and dadaism. I couldn't help thinking about it more and more until, at the close of my life, something quite essential had to happen. I had to be either dadaist or doctor. I had to—the realization was overpowering—become a dadaist again. I had to go to a country where the problem of the creative personality had once existed and still existed.

I probably ought to make all that clearer. First I would like to repeat that I have absolutely nothing against America. I'm convinced that the matter of having to leave the States is to be laid entirely at my door. It is surely my shortcoming that I was unable to adapt, since I couldn't tear goddam dada out of my heart. That all sounds very fine, but it still doesn't explain why I had to leave America for ever. I've already said that many external circumstances played a role: my age, the fact that I wanted to retire and start writing again, and last but not least that I wanted to return to the place, country and situation in which my dadaist problem came into being. Let me put that in clearer terms: I hope that there is no dada conflict in America, something that still exists or at least existed until quite recently in Europe.

But is that really so? Isn't the world the same wherever you go? Under the influence of proud scientists who, however, are too stupid to grasp that something is not quite right with progress and that variability (in humans and things) is no less meaningful than blanket uniformity. You find the same nationalistic, depersonalized computer-thinking just as often among scientists in Europe as in America, don't you? What a joy it must have been for these people that we've managed to walk on the moon. But what will they say when it emerges that the piece of dirt scraped off the moon is the same piece of dirt that we find here on earth, and that we've offered up our billions more for the rocket dreams of Herr Wernher von Braun than for our own realities?

One or two facts about my life. Whenever I have to function like a machine I become deeply dismayed. And it has become clearer and clearer to me that precise functioning is the disease of American civilization, which is on the verge of throwing what's left of personal freedom and spontaneity on the garbage heap. In spite of all my love for American ideals and in spite of all my love for American reality I became more and more ill the more successful and orderly my life became. I was very close to becoming one of those handshaking "here's how" and "how are you?" types, whom I loathe with a vengeance. I had the longing to be a hippie again, a dadaist hippie, with my short hair and well-cut suit one of a kind—but a hippie nonetheless and nothing but a hippie. My desire to be unruly, my desire to identify myself with chaos and be, so to speak, a bug in the machine—all this overwhelmed me although the desire was continually counteracted by the official medical organisation and no less by the simple fact that I was surrounded by so many successful colleagues. I wanted to go back to a kind of chaos, not a chaos that kills, but a chaos which is the first step to creativity. I began to hate the doctor-businessman more and more, the type who makes use of every kind of test and trick but is incapable of giving his patient anything substantial to relieve his illness. I hated the attitude of doctors who put earning money, money, money before anything else, and ultimately I began to hate the fact that I was a doctor too.

There is my conflict. Since I'm not capable of resolving this conflict entirely, I'm attempting to resolve it through a change of scenery. I know it won't be successful.

I know it all too well but this anticipated failure may perhaps have healing effects. I have from my present residence in Switzerland a clear view of how things are: America is a tragic land and the Americans are a tragic people. Their grandiose attempt to found a free society has not come to pass, and now they find themselves in an inextricable conflict. The war in Vietnam, the black problem, the poverty and financial bankruptcy of the big cities—all of that while the weapons manufacturers increase their incomes many times over.

America is bankrupt. But I can't claim to be in a better situation. I'd like to be a hippie, and at the same time to be a doctor and a smart money-making citizen as well. All these things can't be reconciled.

Sometimes I try to help myself by taking in the famous panorama, the wonderful mountains, the more beautiful lakes, the palms and orange trees, the silent high forests. But after a little while it comes home to me that I'm a realist and not a romantic. My purpose can only be this: I have to get it clearer and clearer in my head why I left the United States, or on some memorable day I'll run to the station and buy myself a ticket to New York. I'll greet the Statue of Liberty with a melancholy smile, but I presume then I'll really understand that freedom has never really existed anywhere or time and that the American attempt to convert it into reality (although it did not succeed) was one of the most magnificent and compelling experiments in the history of humankind.

From *Reise bis ans Ende der Freiheit: Autobiographische Fragmente*, 1984.

RAYMOND QUENEAU
Instructions for the Use of Tranquillisers

Chlorpromazine was first synthesized in France in 1950; these short pieces by Queneau were written in that decade in response to a publicity campaign by the Laboratoires H. Baille, a French pharmaceutical firm. Queneau's texticules are a sly comment on the French medical profession's enthusiasm for new drugs. Arcole and Moscow are battles fought by Napoleon I, Magenta and Reichshoffen by Napoleon III; Marjolin and Nélaton were imperial surgeons. This invalid of the battlefield is humorously imagined as having the worst amputation in terms of disability claims: a wooden top.

I

Blistering blazes! Was this non-combatant going to make me wait any longer like this, a man like me who can go back to the days when they sawed legs off without anaesthetic. Indeed, my great longevity has allowed me to take the long road that goes from Arcole to Moscow and from Magenta to Reichshoffen ending up on the Avenue de Tourville; consulting on the way some of the hob-nobs from Marjolin to Nélaton. It was precisely one of these gents that I'd come to consult because of my headaches.

After a military salute, the doc stood to attention to garner information about my case, which I explained to him with the help of some drawings that I sketched on his wall; for, as our bald little Corsican said, one picture is worth a thousand words.

My explanations were clear as could be since he, taking a fretsaw, removed a shaving from my head which he examined carefully.

"Riddled with worms," he said, "better replace it with one in ebony."

"But I'll look like a negro," I squawked.

"Well, well," he replied, "I see what you need. You need tranquillisers."

II

"Da, what's the man going to do with me?"

"Nothing, son, nothing."

"If he's not going to do anything then why did you take me to see him?"

"Because you're not well, sonny, you're not well."

"How come you know that better than me?"

He was about to give me one around the ear when a man came in. Dad called him doctor.

"What seems to be the matter with the wee lad then?"

"He's got a sore head, doctor."

"Perhaps he's working too hard."

"Him? He's a blockhead!"

That was the giddy limit, and since I'm no blockhead I stuck my tongue out at my dad.

The doctor took a look at it and said:

"I see what the matter is, he needs some tranquillisers."

III

The doc gave me an appointment, I said to myself—Super! I'm not going to have to wait.

I get there: fifteen people. I wasn't pleased. Luckily there was a stack of weeklies. I take a look at the pictures. Twelve people. I fill in the crosswords. Eight people. I try the bridge problem, but since I don't know how to play bridge, it's a bit tricky.

At last it's my turn.

I go in. The doc says: "Take your trousers off."

"Oh, excuse me!" I inform him, "it's only for a headache."

"A-ha! A headache!" he says. "Do you have fixed ideas?"

"Yes. Fixed in my head."

"Can you localise where it hurts?"

Localise—what does he mean, localise? Another inkhorn term to frighten folk.

"I'm going to examine you," he says.

"That won't be difficult," I say and opening my mouth show him my wisdom tooth, the one that's in a bad way.

He looks at it and says to me:

"I see what the matter is. You need tranquillisers."

"Du bon emploi des tranquillisants," *Contes et Propos*, 1981.

JEAN REVERZY

The Doctor and Money

It has always amazed me that Napoleon is supposed to have referred, dismissively, to the British as a nation of shopkeepers: it is surely the French who merit this distinction. This piece, written in the 1950s by the French doctor and writer Jean Reverzy, most famous for his novel Le Passage, *raises what are almost taboo issues: exchange-value, slipped haloes, filthy lucre. In that decade general practitioners in the UK were already seeing patients without the need for money to distract them: they were operating within a social contract, whereas doctors in France were operating, as they always had, within a market. Recently a French colleague flatly told me it was "impossible" for a doctor to be financially disinterested. At which point, had I thought of it, a pithy observation by Robert Musil would have been apposite: "Today, although everybody is permitted to act as a trader, an old tradition demands that we talk as idealists."*

The consultation, patient and doctor alone together, resembles a tragedy in four acts. Act one: two beings size each other up and try to find common ground. Act two: the patient takes off his clothes, reveals his naked body to the person met ten minutes before who palpates and auscultates it. Act three: the patient gets dressed again. Mutual sympathy and confidence are obvious or implicit. The doctor explains, advises, assuages; but the drama isn't finished: the fourth and last act, decidedly short, is about to start; the consultation has to be paid for. Dread moment. And now the dialogue becomes flustered; the patient, however zealous he might be to pay his obol, is either slow in handing over the notes or does it with too much alacrity. And the physician, more than his interlocutor, is discomfited: he lowers or raises his tone of voice, he stumbles over his words. This embarrassment about asking for money does credit to the practitioner: if he feels ill at ease it is because he has suddenly switched his role; and that of the small businessman doesn't suit him at all. The small businessman is blithely unaware of this hesitancy in demanding his due; but the physician suffers from it. Before saying: "You owe me …", he has been party to a discussion behind closed doors and it pains him to have to convert sympathy, confidence and trust into cash.

This brief glimpse of the consultation, always brought to an end on a discord, sheds light on the psychology and behaviour of physicians: they might be compared at times to Ulysses' companions transformed by Circe into pigs but who, in their animal condition, still retained a mental image of their original humanity. And if evil money, as necessary for physicians as for all other human beings, has yet to metamorphose them, it would seem however to have shrunk them in a peculiar manner.

These thoughts are not intended as a polemic: their author, himself a physician, is subject to the law like everyone else, which allows him to talk about it all the more freely. Nobody has ever risen up against this law governing the medical world, the law of gain: that's why dissent against this state of things is even more keenly felt when the time comes to ask patients for money.

You become a doctor by vocation, in other words driven by common feelings or the desire for knowledge; a regard for wealth is almost always foreign to the choice of a profession which, after studies that are long and costly, but straightforward enough, elevates the person practising it above other people without freeing him materially from having to earn a living. Between twenty-five and thirty a doctor looks for a place to live; he buys some equipment; he screws a copper nameplate on his door and then he waits for patients. And from that day on, the day on which he opens shop, a new worry rears its head: he has to make a living, pay the bills; he needs money. Beyond medicine, he gets a glimpse of the looming trade; a little of the former ideal has already gone. At thirty-five, whether a big-shot doctor or not, he is usually a man who has "made it"; he can estimate his wealth. A good practitioner in a large city has a "turnover" of four to five million francs; the celebrated doctor or the famous surgeon make, depending on whether the year is good or bad, ten to fifteen. The reason for such disparities is evident when it is borne in mind that the cost of a consultation varies from five hundred to ten thousand francs. Rates are evaluated, not on the effectiveness of health care but on the basis of titles, age, fame; there is a doctor for every purse. A remarkable fact: the concern for money which tails the doctor never bothers his professional conscience; bad doctors crop up only rarely.

Embourgeoisement also becomes more apparent the higher you go in the hierarchy. Above the local or the country doctor, a modest investor who dies on the job after a life of hard work, the celebrated physician, worn down by the same tiredness as his humble colleague, is what people call a "grand bourgeois". And this state of things appears to be one of the profession's flagrant failings. Often the son of the celebrated physician follows on from his father: a faculty chair or a hospital department are inherited in the same way as business capital. That is astonishing, since, judged from the arts and sciences, it would appear quite rare for talent to be passed on hereditarily. But medicine is not a science, or will become one only tomorrow.

Yet money has never obsessed the physician to the extent of deflecting him from his true destiny. Many charitable acts fill the life of the most go-getting physician; nobody has refused his care to a patient because he was poor. Some physicians, after years of graft, die in need. But treatment without charge, which is daily becoming more difficult because of the new laws codifying and ratifying what doctors can do, is generally not provided wholeheartedly.

It is by dint of being definitively established in the bourgeois manner which guarantees the physician his intellectual and domestic comfort. The monotony of his occupation, the most demanding of all, is also a threat to his intelligence. The automatism of saying the same things and doing the same things over and over again has reduced him to this paradoxical situation: he is a man attached to the bourgeois values of fame and fortune who, nevertheless, in practising his profession, observes at every moment life escaping him, beyond capture.

This unmindfulness, while it never harms patients, is certainly detrimental to medicine and doctors themselves, the further they get from science and research. Worn out by fatigue, worrying about their wealth, hounded by the inland revenue, most, after their initial studies, acquire knowledge only through their personal experience. This should not to be gainsaid: it always stands him in good stead. But there was a time when the practitioner, by observing illnesses, contributed to research: a time far gone. Medical faculties have become places of instruction much like schools and colleges. Celebrated physicians, whom we readily mistake for men of learning, are subject to the law of maximum client servicing; they content themselves with their role as professors. In an era in which the life sciences are forging ahead, the physician, small-fry or big-shot, has lost his niche in research; nothing links him to the man in the laboratory whose discoveries he applies.

Accordingly, whatever their success, doctors are not satisfied; they are nostalgic for another kind of medicine, a medicine they once dreamed of. Overwhelmed by their clients, prisoners of their social status, they are too weary to want to change things. Nonetheless, at the end of the consultation, at the dread moment of payment, they always feel ill at ease. And their mute debate saves them and perhaps absolves them.

"Le Médecin et l'Argent," *Oeuvres*, 1977.

WELDON KEES

The Clinic

Weldon Kees was once described as the bleakest poet in America. "The Clinic,"
which is dedicated to Gregory Bateson, theorist of the double-bind, describes a
mysterious experiment, which might be animal or human (it all depends on how
"cats" is understood): a hot plate test in the former, some kind of neuropsychiatric
treatment in the latter.

Light in the cage like burning foil
At noon; and I am caught
With all the other cats that howl
And dance and spit, lashing their tails
When the doctors turn the current on.
The ceiling fries. Waves shimmer from the floor
Where hell spreads thin between the bars.
And then a switch snaps off and it is over
For another day. Close up. Go home.
Calcium chloride, a milligram
Or so, needled into the brain, close to
The infundibulum. Sometimes we sleep for weeks.
                                                    Report
From Doctor Edwards: sixteen tests (five women, fourteen men).
Results are far from positive. Static ataxia,
Blood pressure, tapping, visual acuity. A Mrs. Wax
Could not recall a long ride in a Chevrolet
From Jersey to her home in Forest Hills. Fatigue
Reported by a few. These smoky nights
My eyes feel dry and raw; I tire
After twenty hours without sleep. Performance

At a lower ebb.—The lights
Have flickered and gone out.
There is a sound like winter in the streets.
                                        Vide Master,
Muzie, Brown and Parker on the hypoplastic heart.
Culpin stressed the psychogenic origin. DaCosta
Ruled out syphilis. If we follow Raines and Kolb,
We follow Raines and Kolb.—It's only a sort of wound,
From one of the wars, that opens up occasionally.
Signs of dessication, but very little pain.

I followed Raines and Kolb, in that dark backward,
Seeking a clue; yet in that blackness, hardly a drop
Of blood within me did not shudder. Mouths without hands,
Eyes without light, my tongue dry, intolerable
Thirst. And then we came into that room
Where a world of cats danced, spat, and howled
Upon a burning plate.—And I was home.

Collected Poems, 1962.

W.H. AUDEN

The Art of Healing

W.H. Auden came from a medical family, and maintained a close interest throughout his busy poetic career in what poetry and medicine might contribute to the good life. This poem is written in memory of his own doctor, David Protetch, M.D.

Most patients believe
dying is something they do,
not their physician,
that white-coated sage,
never to be imagined
naked or married.

Begotten by one,
I should know better. "Healing,"
Papa would tell me,
"is not a science,
but the intuitive art
of wooing Nature.

Plants, beasts, may react
according to the common
whim of their species,
but all humans have
prejudices of their own
which can't be foreseen.

To some, ill–health is
a way to be important,
        others are stoics,
        a few fanatics,
who won't feel happy until
        they are cut open."

        Warned by him to shun
the sadist, the nod–crafty,
        and the fee-conscious,
        I knew when we met,
I had found a consultant
        who thought as he did,

        yourself a victim
of medical engineers
        and their arrogance,
        when they atom-bombed
your sick pituitary
        and over-killed it.

        "Every sickness
is a musical problem."
        So said Novalis,
        "and every cure
a musical solution":
        you knew that also.

Not that in my case
you heard any shattering
discords to resolve:
to date my organs
still seem pretty sure of their
self-identity.

For my small ailments
you, who were mortally sick,
prescribed with success:
my major vices,
my mad addictions, you left
to my own conscience.

Was it your very
predicament that made me
sure I could trust you,
if I were dying,
to say so, not insult me
with soothing fictions?

Must diabetics
all content with a nisus
to self-destruction?
One day you told me:
"It is only bad temper
that keeps me going."

But neither anger
nor lust are omnipotent,
    nor should we even
    want our friends to be
superhuman. Dear David,
    dead one, rest in peace,

    having been what all
doctors should be, but few are,
    and, even when most
    difficult, condign
of our biassed affection
    and objective praise.

Collected Poems, 1969.

R.D. LAING

Clinical Vignettes

For many years, R.D. Laing was one of the best-known psychiatrists in the world: he brought from his Calvinist upbringing in the south of Glasgow a rare empathy for the alienated and psychotic. This is the first part of an impressionistic short essay combining memoir, automatic writing and scraps of overheard speech: these "birds of paradise"(title of his essay) must be escapees from Hieronymus Bosch's Garden of Earthly Delights.

Each night I meet him. King with Crown. Each night we fight. Why must he kill me? No. I shall not die. I can be smaller than a pinhead, harder than a diamond. Suddenly, how gentle he is! One of his tricks. Off with his Crown! Strike. Bash in his skull. Face streams of blood. Tears? Perhaps. Too late! Off with his head! Pith the spine! Die now, O King!

Spider-crab moves slowly across bedroom wall. Not horrible, not evil. Acceptance. Another one appears and another. Ugh! No, too much. Kill.
Suddenly it was always a bird, so frail, so beautiful: now, twitching in death agony. What have I done? But why play such a game on me? Why appear so ugly. It's your fault, your fault.

Noon. Traffic jam. At first I can't make out why. Then I see. A large, magnificent dog is wandering in aimless circles across the road. It wanders closer to my car. I begin to realize that there is something terribly damaged about it. Yes, back broken, and as it veers round, the left face comes into view—bashed-in, bloody, formless, mess, on which its eye lies somehow intact, looking at me, with no socket, just by itself, alone, detached. A crowd has gathered, laughing, jeering, at the ridiculous behaviour of this distracted creature. Motorists hoot their horns and shout at it to get out of the way. Shop girls have come out of their shops and giggle together.

Can I be that dog and those angry motorists and those giggling shop girls? Is Christ forgiving me for crucifying Him?

> Glasgow.
> Grey street.
> Blank faceless tenements
> streaming with my drizzle. Red only in
> children's cheeks. Light fading from
> still laughing eyes ...

Glasgow repartee

FELLA [*to passing bird*]: Hey, hen—yi'll heat yir water.

BIRD: You're no going tae dip yir wick in it onyway.

Those termini of Glasgow tramcars in the 1930s in November Sunday afternoon. The end.

Flaking plaster. Broken window panes.

The smell of slum tenements. The dank "closes" on a Sunday morning. Impregnated with stale beer, vomit, fish and chips.

All that floral wallpaper and those borders, the curtains and the blinds. The three-piece uncut moquette.

The tiled fireplaces, the fireguards, the acres and acres of mock parquet linoleum.

The tiled close with banister and the stained glass window. The respectability. O the respectability.

Mrs Campbell was a nice young mother of two children. She had rather suddenly started to lose weight, and her abdomen had begun to swell. But she did not feel too ill in herself.

The medical student has to "take a history of the illness"—I made the mistake of chatting with her, learning about her little boy and her little girl, what she was knitting, and so on.

She came into our surgical ward on a Sunday. A mark was placed on her abdomen to show where the lower border of her liver was, because it was enlarged.

On Monday her liver had grown further down. Even cancer can't grow at that rate. She was evidently suffering from something very unusual.

Her liver continued to grow every day. By Thursday it was clear she was going to die. She did not know this—and no one dreamt of telling her.

"We've decided you don't need an operation."

"When will I be going home then?"

"Well perhaps in a little while, but we still have to keep you under observation."

"But will I be getting any treatment?"

"Don't worry, Mrs Campbell, leave it to us. We still have some investigations to do yet."

She probably had a haemorrhage going on inside her liver. But why? Secondary growths from a cancer some where? But where? Every part of her body had been probed, palpated, up her rectum, vagina—down her throat, X-rayed, urine, faeces, blood … It was an interesting clinical problem.

On Friday morning the students met with one of the young surgeons and her case was discussed. No one had seen such a case—we would find out at the post-mortem of course, but it would be nice if we could hit the diagnosis beforehand.

Someone suggested a small tumour in her retina. Her eyes had been looked into—but these tumours are sometimes very small indeed, easy to miss—when she had been first examined this wasn't being looked for specifically—perhaps—it was a long shot. It was almost lunchtime—at lunchtime over five hundred students ran from their classes all over the university buildings to the students' Refectory—where there was seating for two hundred. If you didn't get at the top of the queue you would have to wait an hour or more, and you only had an hour before the next lecture.

But we just had time to dash up to look into her eyes …

When we got to her the nurses were already laying her out, tying up her ankles.

Fuck it, she's dead! Still, quickly, before the cornea clouds over. We looked into the depths of her dead eyes. Dead only a few minutes after all. If you look into eyes at that time it's interesting anyway—you see the blood actually beginning to break up in the veins of the retina. But apart from that, nothing to see.

Fuck her, we've missed our fucking lunch.

Bookshop, Glasgow. Usual copy of *Horizon*. The last number!

"It is closing time now in the Gardens of the West. From now on a writer will be judged by the resonances of his silence and the quality of his despair."

All right—you did not have a circulation of more than eighty thousand. You ran out of money. But you bastard, speak for yourself. Write *Horizon* off and wish yourself off. Don't write me off. I'll be judged by my music not by my silence and by the quality of whatever pathetic shreds of faith, hope and charity still cling to me.

AMERICAN SAILOR [*to Glasgow Hairy*]: Baby, I'm going to give you something you've never had before.

GLASGOW HAIRY [*to friend*]: Hey, Maggie. There's a guy here with leprosy.

Fifty cadavers laid out on slabs. Before we are finished we shall each have got to know one of them intimately.

At the end of that term when they had all been dissected to bits—suddenly,—so it seemed—no one knew how it began—pieces of skin, muscle, penises, bits of liver, lung, heart, tongue, etc. etc. were all flying about, shouts, screams. Who was fighting whom? God knows.

The professor had been standing in the doorway for some while before his presence began to creep through the room. Silence.

"You should be ashamed of yourselves," he thundered; "how do you expect them to sort themselves out on the Day of Judgement?"

He was ten years of age and had hydrocephalus due to an inoperable tumour the size of a very small pea, just at the right place to stop his cerebrospinal fluid from getting out of his head, which is to say that he had water on the brain, that was bursting his head, so that the brain was becoming stretched out into a thinning rim, and his skull bones likewise. He was in excruciating and unremitting pain.

One of my jobs was to put a long needle into this ever-increasing fluid to let it out. I had to do this twice a day, and the so-clear fluid that was killing him would leap out at me from his massive ten-year-old head, rising in a brief column to several feet, sometimes hitting my face.

Cases like this are usually less distressing than they might be, because they are often heavily doped, they partially lose their faculties, sometimes an operation helps. He had had several, but the new canal that was made didn't work.

The condition can sometimes be stabilized at the level of being a chronic vegetable for indefinite years—so that the person finally does not seem to suffer. (Do not despair, the soul dies even before the body.)

But this little boy unmistakably endured agony. He would quietly cry in pain. If he would only have shrieked or complained ... And he knew he was going to die.

He had started reading *The Pickwick Papers*. The one thing he asked God for, he told me, was that he be allowed to finish this book before he died.

He died before it was half-finished.

I know so many bad jokes. At least I didn't invent them.
Jimmy McKenzie was a bloody pest at the mental hospital because he went around shouting back at his voices. We could only hear one end of the conversation, of course, but the other end could be inferred in general terms at least from:

"Away tae fuck, ye filthy-minded bastards ..."

It was decided at one and the same time to alleviate his distress and ours, by giving him the benefit of a leucotomy.

An improvement in his condition was noted.

After the operation he went around no longer shouting abuse at his voices, but: "What's that? Say that again! Speak up ye buggers, I cannae hear ye!"

We had been attending a childbirth and it had dragged on and off for sixteen hours. Finally it started to come—grey, slimy, cold—out it came—a large human frog—an anencephalic monster, no neck, no head, with eyes, nose, froggy mouth, long arms.

This creature was born at 9.10 a.m. on a clear August morning.

Maybe it was slightly alive. We didn't want to know. We wrapped it in newspaper—and with this bundle under my arm to take back to the pathology lab., that seemed to cry out for all the answerable answers that I ever asked, I walked along O'Connell Street two hours later.

I needed a drink. I went into a pub, put the bundle on the bar. Suddenly the desire, to unwrap it, hold it up for all to see, a ghastly Gorgon's head, to turn the world to stone.

I could show you the exact spot on the pavement to this day.

Fingertips, legs, lungs, genitals, all thinking. These people in the street are there, I see them. We are told they are something out there, that traverses space, hits eyes, goes to brain, then an event occurs whereby this event in my brain is experienced by me as those people out there in space.

The I that I am is not the me that I know, but the wherewith and whereby the *me* is known. But if this I that is the wherewith and whereby is not anything that I know, then it is no thing—nothing. Click—sluice gates open—body guts outside in.

Head with legs sings merrily in the streets, led along by a beggar. The head is an egg. A stupid old woman prises open the egg-head. Foetus. Its singing is its cries of unspeakable agony. The old woman sets fire to the foetus. It turns inside the egg-head as though in a frying pan. Commotion. Its agony and helplessness is indescribable. I am burning, I can't move. There are cries, 'It's dead!' But the doctor pronounces that it's still alive and orders it to be taken to a hospital.

Two men sit facing each other and both of them are me. Quietly, meticulously, systematically, they are blowing out each other's brains, with pistols. They look perfectly intact. Inside devastation.

I look round a New Town. What a pity about those viscera and abortions littering the new spick and span gutters. This one looks like a heart. It is pulsating. It starts to move on four little legs. It is disgusting and grotesque. Dog-like abortion of raw red flesh, and yet alive. Stupid, flayed, abortive dog still persisting in living. Yet all it asks after all is that I let it love me, and not even that.

Astonished heart, loving unloved heart, heart of a heartless world, crazy heart of a dying world.

Playing the game of reality with no real cards in one's hand.

Body mangled, torn into shreds, ground down to powder, limbs aching, heart lost, bones pulverized, empty nausea in dust. Wanting to vomit up my lungs. Everywhere blood, tissues, muscles, bones, are wild, frantic. Outwardly all is quiet, calm, as ever. Sleep. Death. I look all right.

That wild silent screech in the night. And what if I were to tear my hair and run naked and screaming through the suburban night. I would wake up a few tired people and get myself committed to a mental hospital. To what purpose?

5.00 a.m.: Vultures hover outside my window.

First part of "The Bird of Paradise," 1967.

JOHN BERGER

Clerk of Their Records

John Berger's study (with, in its original format, atmospheric photographs by Jean Mohr) of the life and times of a country GP, John Sassall, in what seems to be an island community (it is actually in the Forest of Dean) has been called one of the best books written about a doctor's life. Poised between social engagement and a phenomenology of medical practice, Berger's book follows earlier attempts (e.g. Georges Duhamel's essays of the 1930s) to register the effects of social and techno-logical change on the doctor's "apostolic" role. One or two changes have occurred since the 1960s: mobility has made us all islands circulating in a vast sea of money; everyone is a clerk of his own records; and government has developed a burning want for information, which it confuses with an understanding of reality.

In the village there is a medieval castle with a wide, deep moat round it. This moat was used as a kind of unofficial dump. It was overgrown with trees, bushes, weeds, and full of stones, old wood, muck, gravel. Five years ago Sassall had the idea of turning it into a garden for the village. Tens of thousands of man-hours of work would be involved. He formed a "society" to occupy itself with the task and he was elected chairman. The work was to be done in the summer evenings and at week-ends whenever the men of the village were free. Farmers lent their machinery and tractors; a roadmaker brought his bull-dozer along; somebody borrowed a crane.

Sassall himself worked hard on the project. If he was not in the surgery and not out on a call, he could be found in the moat most summer evenings. Now the moat is a lawned garden with a fountain, roses, shrubs and seats to sit on.

"Nearly all the planning of the work in the moat," says Sassall, "was done by Ted, Harry, Stan, John, etc., etc. I don't mean they were better at doing the work, better with their hands—they were that—but they also had better ideas."

Sassall was constantly involved in technical discussion of these ideas with the men of the village. The conversations over the weeks continued for hours. As a result a social—as distinct from medical—intimacy was established.

This might seem to be the obvious result of just getting on with a job together. But it is not as simple or as superficial as that. The job offers the possibility of talking together, and finally the talk transcends the job.

The inarticulateness of the English is the subject of many jokes and is often explained in terms of puritanism, shyness as a national characteristic, etc. This tends to obscure a more serious development. There are large sections of the English working and middle class who are inarticulate as the result of wholesale cultural deprivation. They are deprived of the means of translating what they know into thoughts which they can think. They have no examples to follow in which words clarify experience. Their spoken proverbial traditions have long been destroyed: and, although they are literate in the strictly technical sense, they have not had the opportunity of discovering the existence of a written cultural heritage.

Yet it is more than a question of literature. Any general culture acts as a mirror which enables the individual to recognize himself—or at least to recognize those parts of himself which are socially permissible. The culturally deprived have far fewer ways of recognizing themselves. A great deal of their experience—especially emotional and introspective experience—has to remain *unnamed* for them. Their chief means of self-expression is consequently through action: this is one of the reasons why the English have so many "do-it-yourself" hobbies. The garden or the work bench becomes the nearest they have to a means of satisfactory introspection.

The easiest—and sometimes the only possible—form of conversation is that which concerns or describes action: that is to say action considered as technique or as procedure. It is then not the experience of the speakers which is discussed but the nature of an entirely exterior mechanism or event—a motor-car engine, a football match, a draining system or the workings of some committee. Such subjects, which preclude anything directly personal, supply the content of most of the conversations being carried on by men over twenty-five at any given moment in England today. (In the case of the young, the force of their own appetites saves them from such depersonalization.)

Yet there is warmth in such conversation and friendships can be made and sustained by it. The very intricacy of the subjects seems to bring the speakers close together. It is as though the speakers bend over the subject to examine it in precise detail, until, bending over it, their heads touch. Their shared expertise becomes a symbol of shared experience. When friends recall another friend who is dead or absent, they recall how he always maintained that a front-wheel drive was safer: and in their memory this now acquires the value of an intimacy.

The area in which Sassall practises is one of extreme cultural deprivation, even by English standards. And it was only by working with many of the men of the village and coming to understand something of their techniques that he could qualify for their conversation. They then came to share a language which was a metaphor for the rest of their common experience.

Sassall would like to believe that the metaphor implies that they talk as equals: the more so because within the range of the language the villagers mostly know far more than he. Yet they do not talk as equals.

Sassall is accepted by the villagers and foresters as a man who, in the full sense of the term, lives with them. Face to face with him, whatever the circumstances, there is no need for shame or complex explanations: he will understand even when their own community as a whole will not or cannot. (Most unmarried girls who become pregnant come to him straightway without any prevarication.) Insofar as he is feared at all, it is by a few older patients in whom a little of the traditional fear of the doctor still persists. (This traditional fear, apart from being a rational fear of the consequences of illness, is also an irrational fear of the consequences of making their secret but outrageous and insistent demand for fraternity to doctors who always behave and are treated as their superiors.)

In general his patients think of Sassall as "belonging" to their community. He represents no outside interest—in such an area any outside interest suggests exploitation. He is trusted. Yet this is not the same thing as saying that he is thought of or treated as an equal.

It is evident to everybody that he is privileged. This is accepted as a matter of course: nobody resents or questions it. It is part of his being the kind of doctor he is. The privilege does not concern his income, his car or his house: these are merely amenities which make it possible for him to do his job. And if through them he enjoys a little more comfort than the average, it is still not a question of privilege, for certainly he has earned a right to that comfort.

He is privileged because of the way he can think and can talk! If the estimate of his privilege was strictly logical, it would include the fact of his education and his medical training. But that was a long time ago, whereas the evidence of the way he thinks—not purely medically but in general—is there every time he is there. It is why the villagers talk to him, why they tell him the local news, why they listen, why they wonder whether his unusual views are right, why some say "He's a wonderful doctor but not what you'd expect," and why some middle-class neighbours call him a crack-pot.

The villagers do not consider him privileged because they find his thinking so impressive. It is the style of his thinking which they immediately recognize as different from theirs. They depend upon common-sense and he does not.

It is generally thought that common-sense is practical. It is practical only in a short-term view. Common-sense declares that it is foolish to bite the hand that feeds you. But it is foolish only up to the moment when you realize that you might be fed very much better. In the long-term view common-sense is passive because it is based on the acceptance of an outdated view of the possible. The body of common-sense has to accrue too slowly. All its propositions have to be proved so many times before they can become unquestionable, i.e. traditional. When they become traditional they gain oracular authority. Hence the strong element of *superstition* always evident in "practical" common-sense.

Common-sense is part of the home-made ideology of those who have been deprived of fundamental learning, of those who have been kept ignorant. This ideology is compounded from different sources: items that have survived from religion, items of empirical knowledge, items of protective scepticism, items culled for comfort from the superficial learning that is supplied. But the point is that common-sense can never teach itself, can never advance beyond its own limits, for as soon as the lack of fundamental learning has been made good, all items become questionable and the whole function of common-sense is destroyed. Common-sense can only exist as a category insofar as it can be distinguished from the spirit of enquiry, from philosophy.

Common-sense is essentially *static*. It belongs to the ideology, of those who are socially passive, never understanding what or who has made their situation as it is. But it represents only a part—and often a small part—of their character. These same people say or do many things which are an affront to their own common-sense. And when they justify something by saying "It's only common-sense," this is frequently an apology for denying or betraying some of their deepest feelings or instincts.

Sassall accepts his innermost feelings and intuitions as clues. His own self is often his most promising starting-point. His aim is to find what may be hidden in others:

"I don't find it hard to express uncensored thoughts or sentiments but when I do, it keeps on occurring to me that this is a form of self-indulgence. That sounds somewhat pompous, but still. At least it makes me realize and understand why patients thank me so profusely for merely listening: they too are apologizing for what they think—wrongly—is their self-indulgence."

Using his own mortality as another starting-point he needs to find references of hope or possibility in an almost unimaginable future.

"I'm encouraged by the fact that the molecules of this table and glass and plant are rearranged to make you or me, and that the bad things are perhaps badly arranged molecules and therefore capable maybe of reorganization one day."

Yet however fanciful his speculations, he returns to measure them by the standards of actual knowledge to date. And then from this measurement begins to speculate again.

"You never know *for certain* about anything. This sounds falsely modest and trite, but it's the honest truth. Most of the time you are right and you do *appear* to know, but every now and then the rules seem to get broken and then you realize how lucky you have been on the occasions when *you think you have known* and have been proved correct."

He never stops speculating, testing, comparing. The more open the question the more it interests him.

Such a way of thinking demands the right to be theoretical and to be concerned with generalizations. Yet theory and generalizations belong by their nature to the cities or the distant capital where the big general decisions are always made. Furthermore, to arrive at general decisions and theories one needs to travel in order to gain experience. Nobody travels from the Forest. So nobody in the Forest has either the power or the means to theorize. They are "practical" people.

It may seem surprising to place so much emphasis on geographic isolation and distances when England is so small a country. Yet the subjective feeling of remoteness has little to do with mileage. It is a reaction to economic power. Monopoly—with its mounting tendency to centralization—has even turned what were once large, vital towns, like Bolton or Rochdale or Wigan, into remote backwaters. And in a country area, where the average level of political consciousness is very low, all decision-making which is not practical, all theory, seems to most of the local inhabitants to be the privilege and prerogative of distant policy-makers. The intellectual—and this is why they are so suspicious of him—seems to be part of the apparatus of the State which controls them. Sassall is trusted because he lives with them. But his way of thinking could only have been acquired elsewhere. All theory-makers have cast at least one eye on the seat of power. And that is a privilege the foresters have never known.

There is another reason why they sense that Sassall's way of thinking is a privilege, but as a reason it is less rational. Once it might have been considered magical. He confesses to fear without fear. He finds all impulses natural—or understandable. He remembers what it is like to be a child. He has no respect for any title as such. He can enter into other people's dreams or nightmares. He can lose his temper and then talk about the true reasons, as opposed to the excuse, for why he did so. His ability to do such things connects him with aspects of experience which have to be either ignored or denied by common-sense. Thus his "licence" challenges the prisoner in every one of his listeners.

There is probably only one other man in the area whose mode of thinking is comparable. But this man is a writer and a recluse. Nobody around him is aware of how he thinks. There are clergymen and school-masters and engineers, but they all use the syntax of common-sense: it is only their vocabulary which is different because they need to refer to God, O-levels, or stresses in metal. Sassall's privilege seems locally unique.

The attitude of the villagers and foresters to Sassall's privilege is complex. He has got a good brain, they say, why, with a brain like this— and then, remembering that he belongs to them, they realize that his choice of their remote country practice again implies a kind of privilege: the privilege of his indifference to success. But now his privilege becomes to some extent their privilege. They are proud of him and at the same time protective about him: as though his choice suggested that a good brain can also be a kind of weakness. They often look at him quite anxiously. Yet they are not, I think, so proud of him as a doctor—they know he is a good doctor but they do not know how rare or common that is—rather, they are proud of his way of thinking, of his mind, which has mysteriously allowed him to choose to stay with them. Without being directly influenced by it, they make his way of thinking theirs by giving it a local function.

He does more than treat them when they are ill; he is the objective witness of their lives. They seldom refer to him as a witness. They only think of him when some practical circumstance brings them together. He is in no way a final arbiter. That is why I chose the rather humble word *clerk*: the clerk of their records.

He is qualified to be this precisely because of his privilege. If the records are to be as complete as possible—and who does not at times dream of the impossible ideal of being totally recorded?—the records must be related to the world at large, and they must include what is hidden, even what is hidden within the protagonists themselves.

Some may now assume that he has taken over the role of the parish priest or vicar. Yet this is not so. He is not the representative of an all-knowing, all-powerful being. He is their own representative. His records will never be offered to any higher judge. He keeps the records so that, from time to time, they can consult them themselves. The most frequent opening to a conversation with him, if it is not a professional consultation, are the words "Do you remember when …?" He represents them, becomes their objective (as opposed to subjective) memory, because he represents their lost possibility of understanding and relating to the outside world, and because he also represents some of what they know but cannot think.

This is what I meant by his being the requested clerk of their records. It is an honorary position. He is seldom called upon to officiate. But it has its exact if unstated meaning.

Excerpt from *A Fortunate Man*, 1967.

PHILIP LARKIN

The Building

Philip Larkin was famous for his glumness, although on a good day, and especially when writing about jazz, he wrote like a Baudelairean dandy. This poem observes one of the new kind of cathedrals that sprang up in Britain in the 1960s and 70s—"disease palaces" as they were known a trifle dismissively by the 80s. The tone of dread which used to signal the presence of the divine ("error of a serious sort") now floats disembodied around Larkin's hospital, with an extra component thrown in for good measure, anxiety—perhaps occasioned by the ordeal of having to outbuild a cathedral.

Higher than the handsomest hotel
The lucent comb shows up for miles, but see,
All round it close-ribbed streets rise and fall
Like a great sigh out of the last century.
The porters are scruffy; what keeps drawing up
At the entrance are not taxis; and in the hall
As well as creepers hangs a frightening smell.

There are paperbacks, and tea at so much a cup,
Like an airport lounge, but those who tamely sit
On rows of steel chairs turning the ripped mags
Haven't come far. More like a local bus,
These outdoor clothes and half-filled shopping bags
And faces restless and resigned, although
Every few minutes comes a kind of nurse

To fetch someone away: the rest refit
Cups back to saucers, cough, or glance below
Seats for dropped gloves or cards. Humans, caught
On ground curiously neutral, homes and names
Suddenly in abeyance; some are young,
Some old, but most at that vague age that claims
The end of choice, the last of hope; and all

Here to confess that something has gone wrong.
It must be error of a serious sort,
For see how many floors it needs, how tall
It's grown by now, and how much money goes
In trying to correct it. See the time,
Half-past eleven on a working day,
And these picked out of it; see, as they climb

To their appointed levels, how their eyes
Go to each other, guessing; on the way
Someone's wheeled past, in washed-to-rags ward clothes:
They see him, too. They're quiet. To realise
This new thing held in common makes them quiet,
For past these doors are rooms, and rooms past those,
And more rooms yet, each one further off

And harder to return from; and who knows
Which he will see, and when? For the moment, wait,
Look down at the yard. Outside seems old enough:
Red brick, lagged pipes, and someone walking by it
Out to the car park, free. Then, past the gate,
Traffic; a locked church; short terraced streets
Where kids chalk games, and girls with hair-dos fetch

Their separates from the cleaners—O world,
Your loves, your chances, are beyond the stretch
Of any hand from here! And so, unreal,
A touching dream to which we all are lulled
But wake from separately. In it, conceits
And self-protecting ignorance congeal
To carry life, collapsing only when

Called to these corridors (for now once more
The nurse beckons—). Each gets up and goes
At last. Some will be out by lunch, or four;
Others, not knowing it, have come to join
The unseen congregations whose white rows
Lie set apart above—women, men;
Old, young; crude facets of the only coin

This place accepts. All know they are going to die.
Not yet, perhaps not here, but in the end,
And somewhere like this. That is what it means,
This clean-sliced cliff; a struggle to transcend
The thought of dying, for unless its powers
Outbuild cathedrals nothing contravenes
The coming dark, though crowds each evening try

With wasteful, weak, propitiatory flowers.

High Windows, 1972.

ANTHONY DANIELS
The Death of Ivan Illich

Ivan Illich is probably best described as a Christian anarchist. As his obituary writer points out, he was one of the most widely read authors of the 1970s, principally because he dared to call into question the good faith of the medical profession, at the time boosting its fees to remarkably high levels in the United States. Can a social thinker be a "radical radical" and "reactionary"? Perhaps it is best to think of Illich as bringing a premodern, Aristotelian intelligence to bear on the imperialism of Bacon's dream of science, of which modern medicine is undoubtedly both beneficiary and tributary.

Ivan Illich, the polyglot Austro-Croatian-Sephardic-Mexican-American philosopher and social theorist, died at the beginning of December last in Bremen, Germany. He had his hour of fame in the first half of the 1970s, when he appeared to be the most radical radical on the market, but afterwards went out of fashion and soon faded both from view and from the bookshops. Among the documents I found during a recent internet search was a plaintive request from an aging devotee for information about Illich's current whereabouts and activities. The person asking for this information sounded distraught, like a blind man who had lost his guide dog.

Illich was valued during his comparatively short period of fame for the destructive possibilities of his criticisms of almost all the institutions of industrial society, capitalist or communist, in books such as *Deschooling Society* (1971) and *Medical Nemesis* (1975). Since there was not the slightest likelihood of anyone in the Soviet Union giving him a platform or taking him seriously, his criticisms appeared de facto to be of the left: but, on reading him, one is never quite sure whether he was a follower of Trotsky or Joseph de Maistre. His training as a Catholic priest—he later broke from the Church, having applied to it the very same criticisms he applied to all other institutions—was evident in all his work.

Illich delighted the political activists of his day with statements such as "For most men the right to learn is curtailed by the obligation to attend school," and "The medical establishment has become a major threat to health." Could any sentiments be more revolutionary than those? Henceforth you could cheek a teacher, or challenge a doctor's diagnosis, secure in the knowledge that you were helping to bring about the deschooling or demedicalization that Illich advocated. He appeared to be against all forms of authority, even—or especially—those hitherto thought of as benign. For it was precisely in the seeming benignity of teachers and doctors that their danger lay.

And yet Illich was deeply conservative, or at least he would have been had he been born in the Middle Ages. The word reactionary fitted him quite well, insofar as he regarded pre-modern forms of existence as being in many ways superior to our own. He was an anti-Enlightenment figure: while he believed in the value of rational argument and of empirical evidence, and used them himself (as indeed did de Maistre), he certainly did not believe in a heaven on earth brought about by rational action on the part of benevolent governments and bureaucracies. He was completely unimpressed by supposed evidence of progress such as declining infant mortality rates, rising life expectancies, or increased levels of consumption. Indeed, he thought modern man was living in a hell of his own creation: the revolution of rising expectations was really the institutionalization of permanent disappointment and therefore of existential bitterness.

My attitude to Illich was composed half of admiration, half of irritation. He had a distinctly prophetic quality, but he could also be very silly, and some of the things he said were destructive of civilization itself. In *Deschooling Society*, for example, he stated that "The emerging counterculture reaffirms the values of semantic content above the efficiency of increased and more rigid syntax." This endorsement of poor grammar is a little rich coming from a man who studied at the Gregorian University, had a doctorate in history from the University of Salzburg, and was completely fluent in at least five languages, all of which he spoke grammatically as well as idiomatically. No doctrine, indeed, could have been better fitted in practice to enclose forever the poor of western nations in the restricted world in which they found themselves, and exclude them permanently from the worlds of culture, science, and philosophy, while at the same time persuading the self-indulgent scions of privilege that the merest of their spontaneous vaporings was of imperishable value.

And yet in the same book Illich was undoubtedly prescient about the effects of the relentless hypertrophy of formal education and its attendant bureaucracy: how such hypertrophy would inexorably widen the gap between formal schooling and real education. And I think he was one of the few men who would genuinely have understood why, after several years of residence in Africa, I came to the conclusion that mass formal education in the western style was catastrophic in its effects on the continent. Such education is, indeed, the fifth horseman of the African apocalypse.

Medical Nemesis was Illich's book that most affected me. It was published just after I qualified as a doctor, and I was not entirely pleased to discover that in his opinion the whole medical enterprise was harmful to humanity: I was on duty every second night, and one of the very slight compensations for this unhappy state of affairs was the illusion I might be doing some good to that tiny part of humanity that came within my purview. Soon I was to go to Africa, where I encountered many people who walked fifty or one hundred miles, despite being very ill, to the hospital in which I worked. Either they mistook their own interests, or Illich was wrong.

Still, Illich's arguments were not so easily disposed of. He argued first that the health of a population had very little to do with its access to doctors and to medical care, and that the tangible benefits that doctors conferred were more than outweighed by the tangible harm that they did. He argued second (and more importantly) that the medical enterprise gave rise to unrealistic expectations in the population it served, disguising from it the fact that suffering was an inevitable part of human life and thus deforming its entire personality. Furthermore, medicine as a profession had inbuilt imperialist pretensions: more and more of ordinary human life came under its jurisdiction.

In many respects, Illich was both right and prescient. It is undoubtedly true that the health of a nation (within quite wide limits) is not proportional either to the number of doctors, or to the amount spent per capita on health care. The principal effect of many screening procedures, practiced upon millions of people, is uselessly to raise their anxieties (they are generally entirely ignorant of the statistical reasoning upon which screening tests are performed). It is a moot point whether a technical triumph such as in vitro fertilization has increased the sum of human happiness by granting the dearest wish of a few, or decreased it by dashing the hopes of three times as many. Indeed, by raising the hopes in the first place, it has probably made the condition of childlessness, which might otherwise have been accepted with fortitude, worse than it was before. This was the kind of argument much favored by Illich, and it is far from completely irrational.

Moreover, the *Diagnostic and Statistical Manual of the American Psychiatric Association* renders so much of human behavior an illness that a satirical paper was once published in *The Lancet* suggesting that happiness, being outside the statistical norm, was a disease. This diagnostic expansionism would not have surprised Illich: on the contrary, he foresaw it and thought it was inevitable, once medicine was turned into a self-appointing profession with official powers. Nor would it have surprised him that the widespread prescription of allegedly powerful antidepressants has not lessened either human misery or dissatisfaction.

Illich was a modern opponent of the Promethean bargain, whose benefits the political right and left alike usually take for granted. According to Illich, modern man's fundamental error is to believe in the possibility of progress through advancing knowledge and technique, administered by others. This has led not only to a complete and alienating dependence on experts, but to a crudely materialist outlook, in which personal well-being is measured by physical possessions. I confess that whenever I see a crowd of shoppers, I think (as did Illich) of Sisyphus. Do the crowds really believe that the purchase of yet another unnecessary pair of jeans or piece of gadgetry, for the price of which they have labored, will afford them lasting satisfaction? Will they not be out shopping for even more equally unsatisfying items by the end of the week, because the former purchases disappointed, just as they always did in the past? And will they never learn from their own experience? Can novelty ever confer happiness upon them? Or are they on a treadmill, unable to get off for fear of understanding its futility?

In like manner, Illich saw pain as more than a mere technical problem to be solved by drugs and surgery. The medical profession, he said, holds out the false hope that pain (and other forms of suffering) can be eliminated by its ministrations. In the past, however, before the medical profession achieved its current importance and simulacrum of efficacy, pain and suffering were understood to be an intrinsic and unavoidable part of human life that had inevitably to be faced and given meaning. In practice, it was religion that gave cosmic meaning not only to pain and suffering, but to the rest of life. Not to accept pain and suffering, when in fact they are as ineluctable as ever, whatever the medical profession might claim or encourage its clientele to hope, is paradoxically to increase their dominion: for without meaning, they are either arbitrary and meaningless, or unjust. To fight against suffering is therefore to increase suffering.

This is not only a point of view that the medical profession generally rejects, but is an answer to a question that it refuses to ask. At the same time, Illich was also guilty of some serious evasion: he did not provide us with a guide as to how to distinguish avoidable from unavoidable pain and suffering. In the context of an entire life, pain and suffering may be inevitable, but surely not that consequent upon the inadequate treatment of a broken leg. To distinguish between the two types calls for judgment: precisely the quality that a good doctor should have.

It would be easy to condemn Illich as a hypocrite. He believed in bicycles and speed limits of fifteen miles an hour, yet jetted around the world, crossing the Atlantic innumerable times, and never by ecologically-friendly row-boat. He condemned formal education, yet spent much of his career teaching in universities. But the obituary in Le Monde mentioned that for the last twelve years of his life, from the ages of sixty-four to seventy-six, he suffered from a disfiguring tumour for which he refused to seek medical treatment. No doubt his desire to prove a point lent meaning to his suffering. For myself, I find something moving in his stubbornness.

He was a flawed figure as a man and as a thinker: but so, no doubt, are we all. And unlike the other radicals of the era such as Herbert Marcuse, he still repays reading. Being not easily pigeon-holed, he forces us to think.

"Ivan Illich: 1926–2002," *The New Criterion*, 2003.

GAEL TURNBULL

A Doctor's Month

From 19 October 1979 to 19 October 1980, the poet and GP Gael Turnbull kept a daily record of dealings in and around his surgery in a market town in Worcestershire. His observations, which offer a kind of involuntary surrealism and keen eye for the incongruous, both personal and historical, lend support to John Berger's contention that one important function of the general practitioner is to act as the scribe of his or her community.

May 1: 6.30 a.m., at just over 1,300 feet, wind driving the rain, anoraks flapping, six men, on highest point of the Malverns, with even the sheep looking miserable in the swirling clouds, dancing "The Rose".

2: Correction. Not testing. "When God made man, She was only jesting."

3: In the Birmingham Market, a drench on the air: vegetables and coffee, cheeses, pâtés, smoked fish, leather and vinegar, tobacco, onion, perfumes and deodorants, air conditioning and exhaust fumes; with the West Indian boys in their woolly caps, racing and scampering, urgent and proud, quick eyed, sons of Princes.

4: The Old Man, soaking up the attention like a well seasoned tom cat stretched in front of a gas fire. And then, as he finished reading and the audience kept on applauding, sitting on the stage with the half empty bottle on the table and some red wine still in the glass, peering around very slowly from one side, bit by bit, to the other, as if scanning some distant horizon, not an expression on his face. Completely intent, as if it were truly the strangest and most extraordinary thing he had ever examined, as if looking for some clue to explain it, as if mystified as to who we all were and why we were there at all.

5:   And that poem, written thirty years ago: something still troubles me about the first line, or the title, or both.

6:   "Don't know how it happened but my legs got taken from under me."

7:   Face of a potato, body lumpy and bulging as the crammed and tattered shopping bag in her hand, with half a dozen daffodils in a twitch of newspaper, upright in the other.

8:   Remembering, a week ago, in the church at Bromsgrove: "un' inferme d'Amore" of Monteverdi. The processional voices, light and refreshing as breezes after a hot day, down the avenues of the air.

9:   A motorbike, crimson and obsidian, with stainless steel ribs and horns, lying like a steer uncomfortably on its side upon a fresh fall of snow-pale, rose-tinted blossom.

10:   Chalk-white squiggle of a vapour trail, one edge tinted vermilion by the sunset, on the blue-board of the sky.

11:   Soaking up the light like a bleach and some remote damp cellar of my bones, finally rid of the dark, finally dry.

12:   The murdered man: "his clothes all in mooze."

13:   Thomas Dyer, as he went to the gallows at Worcester, 23 March 1823, protested vigorously that he had never stolen the horse for which he was about to be hung. But admitted, cheerfully enough, that he had stolen lots of others.

14:   Epitaph on John Mole, of Worcester, late 18th century:

> "His mind was as gross as his body was big.
> He drank like a fish and he ate like a pig.
> No cares of religion, of wedlock, of state
> Did e'er, for a moment, encumber John's pate."

15:   Letter: "Did God write this poem? If not, I suggest ..."

16:   Claw of mechanical digger, gutting a bank near Kidderminster, scooping out the red sand, clumped and thick, like dried blood.

17:   A tune: "Nipper," and the old sailor with "HMS Victory" on his flat brimmed straw hat, squeezing his concertina, grinning through his whiskers.

18:   Delirious in the heat, over the canal water, the gnats, racing back and forth in two layers, the lower ones in a downstream direction, the upper, upstream, almost skidding on the air, looping up at the corners and back over, as if on an invisible pulley, while an orange-tipped butterfly snipped and chipped its way along the tow-path, and cheerful songs of disastrous love came from the pub by the lock-gate, everyone and everything sozzled in the abandonment of early summer.

19:   Gunmetal clouds near Grimley and the may, on a line of trees, dense as a hoar frost.

20:   Dead at a little over six years but scarcely the size of a nine-month-old with puppet head, wax cheeks, ferret eyes, pointed fox nose, doll arms and twisted body, held together by tissue-paper skin, a crippled gnome, one of Mother Nature's jokes, like a changeling child, cursed from its birth, and even now, its real mother crying, real tears, disconsolate.

21:   "Surely to God there's something ... something can be done?"

22:   Head on one side, blowing a kazoo, one arm beating in time, with words from his mouth between and the audience clapping in amazed attention. Then laughing, as a poster slid off the wall, collapsed behind him.

23:   After arresting twice and being resuscitated (in the I.T.U. where they'd taken him, at his insistence, or he'd be dead), now grumbling cheerfully about his broken ribs and the nursing service.

24:   At the Colliery, sign in the entrance to the changing room: "Always use face sprags" and then "The number of brass riding tallies being lost recently is on the increase." Helmet. Light. Battery pack and mask. Down in the cage. A full half mile. Crawling through tunnels. No direction. Stooping and filthy. With mice for wild life and the sound of crickets. A "shot" fired. Grime in my lungs. Along a place called "The Gob Scower". At last, to see "The Face" and "The Face Machine". Under hydraulic roof supports. Another monster, with probing beak of tungsten steel blades, like stubby whiskers, rotating at 45 r.p.m., grinding into the rock, and swaying: "A Road Heading Machine." Then, testing for methane, carbon monoxide, and dioxide. The floors coming up more often than the roof coming down. Part way out in a little tram. Tin boxes with graffiti. "Huffin a mule is not sexually illegal" and "Charlie fucks spiders." Filthy in every pore. Pores I never knew I had. After just 3 hours. Up the cage again and to the showers. Another man, a miner, comes over, hands me his sponge to scrub his back and then scrubs mine. The two of us standing naked there together in the steaming drench. Our suds and dirt running off together. In simple necessity. In wordless ritual.

25:   Fearful with a grandeur that defies beauty.

26:   Old Indian in the documentary: "Well, sometimes the magic works. Sometimes it doesn't."

27:   Sign on car windshield, driving through Worcester: "I'm a satisfied young farmer."

28: "Been loo-ing all week and felt sick but haven't vomited. I'm what I call a dry-reacher."

29: In the Red Lion Annex: "How to glean for joy."

30: "Blood tadpoles in my phlegm."

31: Flaubert's mother: "Your mania for sentences has dried up your heart."

"May," from *A Year and a Day*, 1985.

DANNIE ABSE
Lunch with a Pathologist

Medicine is no stranger to black humour and a cynicism about the body that masks itself in the matter-of-fact. Dannie Abse's poem is an existential vampire act on the old Greek notion of the wandering uterus, and its special status within the (female) body. The pathologist, who is something of a mortuary romantic, vaguely suspects Abse, with his ability to exchange his "white coat" for the poet's "purple mantle," of trying to steal his show.

My colleague knows by heart the morbid verse
of facts—the dead weight of a man's liver,
a woman's lungs, a baby's kidneys.

At lunch he recited unforgettably,
"After death, of all soft tissues the brain's
the first to vanish, the uterus the last."

"Yes," I said, "at dawn I've seen silhouettes
hunched in a field against the skyline, each one
feasting, preoccupied, silent as gas.

Partial to women they've stripped women bare
and left behind only the taboo food,
the uterus, inside the skeleton."

My colleague wiped his mouth with a napkin,
hummed, picked, shredded meat from his canines,
said, "You're a peculiar fellow, Abse."

"Lunch with a Pathologist," *Collected Poems*, 1989.

OLIVER SACKS

An Interview

Stripped of his professorship by the Nazis, Kurt Goldstein (1878–1965), a pupil of Karl Wernicke, went to the United States where he became an influential figure at Columbia University. He brought with him what he called "holistic rationality," a line of Gestalt thinking that was opposed to what many doctors saw as the mechanistic thinking that dominated medicine. Years later, his ideas were developed and formatted in a quasi-literary form that made their author, the neurologist Oliver Sacks, famous across the world. This interview was conducted shortly after the publication of his book The Island of the Color Blind, *a travel essay and neurological field-trip to investigate patients on the Micronesian islands of Pinegelap, Guam, and Rot, who suffer from achromatopsia and lytico-bodig.*

You've been described as a neuroanthropologist, a neurobiologist, and a street neurologist. How do you see yourself?
I see myself in different ways. And I can't think of any one term which will cover them all, except possibly something like a naturalist, or an explorer, but in particular a naturalist or an explorer drawn to the varieties of human behaviour and in particular the impact of neurological disease and dementia. I certainly keep neurological eyes open in the street but I keep other sorts of eyes: I keep sexual eyes, I keep aesthetic eyes, I keep cultural eyes, I keep humerous eyes. So I don't know how I see myself, but I am struck by the affinity of anthropology to medicine and the need to see lives and diseases in context and not to isolate them as is often the case.

How did your early training bring you to the place that you're at?
I became a doctor rather slowly, with stops on the way in biology and physiology, which also seemed to offer a fascinating life. I finally went on to get my medical qualification. I think in retrospect it was less formal

teaching—either medical school or at school—than a habit of wandering about books, museums, libraries, and then hospitals that turned me into the sort of person I am.

I think that in England—and certainly the England of the 1950s—medicine may have been somewhat different from what it is now, here in America. In particular we seemed to have time, you could spend a lot of time with patients, so I can remember all the patients I saw as a medical student. I can hardly remember any of the lectures I was given, and I think that probably says something about their relative importance. We were encouraged to present a full narrative, which somehow brought the patient to life. And then before medical school I had been exposed to this by my parents who were doctors and also, I think, storytellers. So somehow doctoring and storytelling and listening to patients all went together.

What brought you to the United States?
Hunger for a new world. I felt, probably unfairly, that England was small and crowded and conservative, and that I might be able to make more of a life here in the States, which I imagined to be more spacious, in every way. I first went to California (in 1961) and somehow the physical spaciousness seemed to take on a moral and intellectual spaciousness as well.

Specifically, I thought of medicine as less tightly organised here. In England, there seemed to be a rather strict hierarchy in academic medicine. I thought it possible there might be interstices here, where someone like myself could survive. In a way, I have actually lived on the interstices.

How is neurology different in the UK and America?
I grew up in England with a feeling of medical history and of a medical tradition somehow steeped in nineteenth-century medicine and neurology. I remember that when I went to UCLA they had a journal club discussing the latest, and I said to them, why don't you talk about Hughlings Jackson, and they said, he's dead, what does he matter, he's been dead for 50 or 70 years or whatever. I think he matters very much and I fear for a neurology which forgets its historical roots. I think that's a little bit more likely to happen here. On the other hand, I would also fear for a neurology which

is not innovative, I would fear for a neurology which is too conservative. I think this is a very exciting time for neurology now all over the world, with everything from brain imaging to brain transplants.

Do you think that most practising neurologists have the kind of time that you're talking about to spend with patients and talk with patients?
Yes I do. Even if they say they don't. I don't think that time constraints alone can excuse clinical perfunctoriness or indifference or ignorance about the tradition. One can be a very busy neurologist seeing 50 patients a day and also have the rest as well. I'm obviously sort of pampered myself in that I see on a working day perhaps 8 or 9 patients and so I can take my time. Certainly it is economically difficult. My medical earnings have now become minus $7000 a year, if I subtract my malpractice insurance and other expenses from my medical earnings; fortunately I'm now not dependent on medical earnings alone. But I would like to think that one can earn a living as a doctor and at the same time have it be both a human enterprise and an intellectual adventure.

How does writing fit in with your work? Is it an essential part of what of you do?
I think I do find writing inseparable from my work. But it's not a double life. Chekhov once said that "literature is my mistress, medicine my lawful-wedded wife." But I don't have a feeling, as it were, of a wife and mistress, but of a single occupation in which the medicine and the writing are fused. And this involves listening and attending to patients and thinking about them and working with them and perhaps writing about them.

There's always writing about them, first in terms of my clinical notes, which are often long and read like some of my published case histories—but of course they're not seen by anybody unless someone looks through the hospital chart. But treating a patient and creating a clinical narrative go together very closely for me. And I think this closeness is part of medicine. In a way, the case history—which I didn't invent—is this intriguing blend of something which is both clinical and human, it's biologic. I think of it as being on the intersection of biology and biography, and the impact of a natural process on a human existence. So for me they very much go together.

Your books are filled with stunning metaphors. Do these come to you in the moment when you're with a patient, or later on, when you're writing up your notes?
Typically, I like to see my patients in the morning and then I need a gap. My Beth Abraham office is opposite the New York Botanical Garden. I go out for a walk and think about other things, nothing to do with neurology. But when I come back, narratives and metaphors have somehow formed inside me.

How is your work seen by your fellow neurologists?
You'd have to ask them. In brief, there's a range of opinions. Come to think of it, there always was. I remember that when I was a resident at UCLA I was thought of as partly an embarrassment, partly an ornament, but I think I'm sometimes seen as a spokesman, putting a human face on neurology, at other times having sold out to some sort of pop neurology. I don't particularly like either characterisation. But I do what I do. Some of my colleagues think I'm valuable and some think I'm rather odd, and they're probably both right. I would like to be seen as a sort of explorer, driven by, and trying to share, a strong sense of wonder.

Where do you get your sense of soul, of the complete person? It doesn't seem to derive from your having gone to medical school.
Well, for what it's worth, I had something of an orthodox religious upbringing. I remember that as a child that I used to have an odd mystical feeling about the Sabbath. Whenever the Sabbath came, I saw my mother light the candles. I would think this was an astronomical event. I would think that the peace of God was descending on remote star systems everywhere. I think it's a beautiful thought; I wish I could recapture it somehow.

Reading was very important for me, in particular Dickens and H.G. Wells, and novelists who talked about the wholeness of life. Although my parents were both doctors, they had met at the Ibsen Society in London, and so that was also an influence very early on.

Since you mention *Awakenings*, I named it after Ibsen's last play, *When We Dead Awaken*. It was for a partly guilty reason, because in that play the old sculptor Rubek is accused by his model of having taken her life to make it into his art. And I've occasionally had that sort of fear or guilt myself. I think it can inhibit me, and I've got to be sure that people do not feel bereft of their lives. I think if I felt they'd be hurt I wouldn't write about them, or if I would I wouldn't publish it.

Can you think of any particular moment in Dickens or other 19th-century novels that have the quality of those Sabbath candles?
There are so many H.G. Wells stories which fascinate me. One of them is *The Country of the Blind,* in which a lost traveler finds a secluded valley in South America where the houses are parti-colored. He thinks the people who built these must have been as blind as bats, and then he finds that, in fact, there has been for 300 years a community which lost their sight and has now lost even the memory, or the concept, of ever having seen.

That came to me overwhelmingly about 18 months ago when I visited an island of the color-blind. I love his story about the door on the wall, about a door which opens onto a sort of magical experience of childhood.

For some reason when you said Dickens I thought of an absurd thing— when Mrs. Gradgrind (in *Hard Times*) is dying, they say "Are you in pain, dear?" And she said, "There is a pain somewhere in the room, but I cannot be positive that I've got it." That's quite unimaginable, of course, because I think pain defines the self to some extent.

In your stories, the cure sometimes seems to be a destructive and frightening experience.
It solves the problem that was there in the first place, but brings worse things in its wake, which is a very familiar plot from fairy tales. I was struck by the fact that a deaf and dumb 13-year-old girl, after becoming fluent in American sign language, seemed to have become a little suspicious. She would often say, "You're lying." And one would say, "That's not a lie, it's a mistake."

But language carries the possibility of lying, and I'm not quite sure that gesture does in the same way. I wonder then, whether this is one of the fearful consequences.

I found myself thinking of language as the apple of the tree of knowledge, and the knowledge of good and evil and of truth and lies, and of some sort of innocence being gone. But this might also be a sort of silly, romantic notion.

You seem to shy away from the paranormal. How do you feel about inspiration ...
I'm all for it [laughter]. When I feel inspired, there certainly is a sense of a vehicle, and of passivity, and of entry, and even of taking over. But I would think of this entirely in terms of unconscious and preconscious thoughts and forces, pushing into what has been called the antechamber of consciousness. I don't think the thoughts come from out there, from the atmosphere, from the muses, from metapsychosis, from past souls, from Hades, from Heaven or wherever. Or to put it another way, I think all of these things are already inside one.

What do you read for pleasure, or do you prefer to see films or concerts?
I'm afraid I don't read much poetry now—it's an awful thing to say—nor too many novels, nor too many plays. In my old age I seem to read mostly history and biography.

I don't go to movies much. Concerts, yes, although I tend to take my notebooks to concerts and to sort of sit quietly at the back and write, but not about the music. But the music is important. You know Nietzsche used to do something similar. He was very fond of Bizet. He said, "Bizet makes me a better philosopher." So, Mozart makes me a better neurologist.

"Street neurologist with a sense of wonder": interview with
Sandee Brawarsky, *The Lancet*, 1997.

ROBERT PINSKY
Doctor Frolic

In his early career, Robert Pinsky brought his analytic talents to bear on the medical profession, writing a long poem called Essay on Psychiatrists, *which attempted to define the nature of those worker-bees after truth and money. In "Doctor Frolic" (a name which turns up, in corrupted form, as Docteur Frolichon in Céline's* Voyage*) he gives a character sketch of a more old-fashioned practitioner, a kind of honest grocer equally at ease doing slipshod minor surgery and gossiping with his patients. Dr Frolic has made his bundle, even as America eased itself from want, out of all his patients' "great depressions." The poem reminds me of those famous mass-circulated pictures of Norman Rockwell, an artist as well known in his day as that other kitschmeister Walt Disney.*

Felicity the healer isn't young
And you don't look him up unless you need him.
Clown's eyes, Pope's nose, a mouth for dirty stories,
He made his bundle in the Great Depression

And now, a jovial immigrant success
In baggy pinstripes, he winks and wheezes gossip,
Village stories that could lift your hair
Or lance a boil; the small town dirt, the dope,

The fishy deals and incestuous combinations,
The husband and the wife of his wife's brother,
The hospital contract, the certificate …
A realist, and hardy omnivore,

He strolls the jetties when the month is right
With a knife and lemons in his pocket, after
Live mussels from among the smelly rocks,
Preventative of impotence and goitre.

And as though the sight of tissue healing crooked
Pleased him, like the ocean's vaginal taste,
He'll stitch your thumb up so it shows for life.
And where he once was the only quack in town

We all have heard his half-lame joke, the one
About the operation that succeeded,
The tangy line that keeps the clever eye
So merry in the Punchinello face.

"Doctor Frolic," *Sadness and Happiness*, 1975.

ROBERTSON DAVIES

The Cunning Man

Robert Burton's Anatomy of Melancholy, *declares Dr Jonathan Hullah, a canny man indeed, is the greatest work of medicine written by a layman; he wishes to complete the greatest book of literary criticism by a doctor. This gives Robertson Davies ample licence to defend an old-fashioned humanism against its detractors, and his high-spirited and anecdotal novel comes, at times, close to frank autobiography. It is, however, a* Bildungsroman, *in which the ageing Hullah, brandishing phrases from Plato, Paracelsus and Jung, never stops, to the astonishment of his priest-friend Charlie Iredal, talking about the soul—"you, a doctor." Medicine's theatricality (not terribly welcome in these moralistic times) has never had a better advertisement, although Hullah's Toronto patients seem remarkably indulgent. Perhaps they stand in awe of his showmanship.*

IN WHICH OUR HERO ACQUIRES IRONY

When irony first makes itself known in a young man's life, it can be like his first experience of getting drunk; he has met with a powerful thing which he does not know how to handle. Of course I had been aware of irony in its superficial form, because Brocky made great use of it; but he was not a master, a subtle and gentle employer of mockery in almost every aspect of life, as was Dwyer; it was something Brocky had learned, not flesh of his flesh. Later, when I thought I had become wiser, I tried to find out what irony really is, and discovered that some ancient writer on poetry had spoken of "*Ironia*, which we call the *drye mock*," and I cannot think of a better term for it: the *drye mock*. Not sarcasm, which is like vinegar, or cynicism, which is so often the voice of disappointed idealism, but a delicate casting of a cool and illuminating light on life, and thus an enlargement. The ironist is not bitter, he does not seek to undercut everything that seems worthy or serious, he scorns the cheap scoring-off of the wisecracker. He stands, so to speak, somewhat at one side, observes and speaks with a moderation which is occasionally embellished with a flash of controlled exaggeration. He speaks from a certain depth, and thus he is not of the same nature as the wit, who so often speaks from the tongue and no deeper. The wit's desire is to be funny; the ironist is only funny as a secondary achievement.

One must have a disposition for irony, but it does not come without practice; like really good violin-playing, it must be practised every day. It seemed to me when I met Dwyer that I had the disposition, but I was an unpractised hand and, like a beginner on the fiddle, I suppose my squawks and screeches were painful to those around me.

IN WHICH OUR HERO DISCOVERS THE HEALING ART

I liked having the word there. It kept me on the track of my medical thinking. Because I was not devising a new notion of medicine; I was seeking a very old one, a sort of perennial philosophy of the healer's art, and fatality, or necessity was the element in life that kept me humble, for nothing I could ever do would defeat it. People must be ill, and they must die. If I could seem to postpone the dark day people thought me a good doctor, but I knew it was a postponement, never a victory and I could secure a postponement only if Fatality, the decision of my patient's *daimon*, so directed.

Of course I could not say that sort of thing to the anxious patient sitting in the chair opposite me. (I never sit behind a desk; always in a chair opposite to the patient and no greater in importance than his.) Who wants to hear his doctor saying that he must die sometime, and the doctor cannot say when, and that anything that can be done in the meantime will not change that fact? And in virtually all cases something could be done, some physical comfort assured, some assuagement of pain or disability, until the inevitable happened.

I certainly did not scorn what drugs could do for my patients, or the ministrations of Christofferson, who was a brilliant practitioner of all the manipulative arts, and intuitive in her application of her skills. I was not a convinced believer in anything the enthusiasts for psychosomatic medicine have to say though I was an intent listener. Of course the mind influences the body; but the body influences the mind, as well, and to take only one side in the argument is to miss much that is—in the true sense of the word—vital. Didn't Montaigne say, with that splendid wisdom that was so much his own that the close stitching of mind to body meant that each communicated its fortunes to the other? (And didn't he immediately afterward, like the seventeenth-century sage he was, plunge into the wildest rubbish about the Evil Eye, and women marking children in the womb by their thoughts? Even my dear old Robert Burton could not escape the influence of his time, any more than my contemporaries can escape the voodoo aspect of modern science.)

Mankind, it appears to me, seeks gloves with which to clothe the iron hand of Necessity, and these gloves he calls diseases. We doctors struggle against them, but no sooner have we got the better of tuberculosis than it appears again stronger than ever: cancer is unresting and who sees an end to AIDS? Mankind must have something upon which to hang its great Dread, which is Everyman's Fatality.

I think of my patient who has now been with me for almost three years, Prudence Vizard, who seems to have a travelling malady, for it has roamed from her back to her left leg, then soared upward to the back of her neck and is now bivouacking for a while in her right arm. The pain is real and gives her a lot of disfiguring physical distress for she hobbles, then hirples, then walks with her neck twisted toward the left, and is now unable to use her right arm for anything—cannot even lift a fork to her mouth. Christofferson cannot come to grips with her, for the pain darts off to another place as soon as it has begun to show improvement in the one under treatment. She doesn't like the saline baths and says they wear out her skin—which can't be true, for Christofferson rubs pots of emollient guck into her after every bath. My attempts to get below her symptoms and track down what is really gnawing at her are ineffective, and all I can do is give her sedatives as mild as she can be persuaded to use. If I were a well-informed physician of the nineteenth century—a pupil of Charcot, for instance—I should call her an hysteric and forget about her, but that is not my way. Why is she hysterical? There must be a cause, physical or mental.

Her trouble is not Nuns', Maids', and Widows' Melancholy, for she is none of those things and seems to have a pretty satisfactory sexual life, so long as Vizard does not jog the suffering place in his infrequently permitted visitations to her privy parts. She is indifferent to sex, but has long believed that "men like it" and so it is a duty to be performed. Has orgasms, but not always. Eats well. Is fond of wine. Has no money worries (Vizard is in investment banking). Gets on as well with her children as a chronic sufferer may be expected to do. Is not unattractive, dresses well, doesn't read much but likes the movies. I suggest that she make some investigation of religion, forgetting the nonsense she was taught as a child. She goes to St. Aidan's, for which I am sorry because she is likely to tackle me after Mass about her pain, or at least to signal to me, over the heads of other worshippers, that she is bearing up bravely and, by implication, when am I going to make her well?

It is useless to talk to Prudence Vizard about *Anangke*, and it is most unlikely to kill her with the mysterious ailment she complains of. She is a Sufferer—which is what Patient means, as I have rubbed into me every day of my life—and her suffering does not yield to anything I know. Is her pain in some way a complement to her character? For character lies deeper than any question of psychosomatic medicine, and contains the key to cure—or at least to courageous endurance. Mrs. Vizard is not very courageous and her endurance lays heavy burdens on her unfortunate husband and the one son who has not yet fled the nest.

IN WHICH OUR HERO DESCRIBES A MIRACULOUS CURE

She felt herself impelled to utter what she later described as "a mouthful of prayer," and then—!

And then a shooting pain of indescribable severity in her bad arm, followed by a glow of warmth of heat, really—and relief from the misery which had pursued her through her body for years, and which had defied every doctor she had consulted, and me the last of the list.

In the Bible women who were healed of diseases—issues, pains, fevers and the rest—rejoiced aloud, and so did Prudence Vizard. She howled her astonishment and delight, and flung herself face downward on the grave and wept uncontrollably. This hullabaloo roused Chips, who was weeding a bed of irises and enjoying the late spring sunshine. She hurried to the spot, which was just around the corner of her house, and hauled Mrs. Vizard to her feet, as she babbled forth the story of her miracle. She was determined that it was a miracle. The saint, of his great charity, had healed her, and though her arm was still hot—Chips felt it and it was indeed very hot—it was cured.

Chips summoned me, and fortunately I was not engaged with a patient. She appealed to Christofferson. Harry Hutchins, sensing something unusual afoot, dropped his laboratory work and came dashing to the scene in his white coat. We stood and gaped at Mrs. Vizard, and listened to her hymns of praise.

What does a physician feel when a patient over whom he has worked diligently for three years is suddenly cured by what she declares is a miracle? I felt some pique that a saint had done in a flash what I could not do in three years. I felt an unkind joy that my personal diagnosis of Mrs. Vizard, that she was an hysteric and that her roaming pain was a whim-wham of a disordered personality, had been suddenly confirmed. I was professionally interested in the flush that had come into her cheeks, and that she looked as if she had dropped ten weary years of age. I felt, well, here's a lark, and won't Charlie be pleased? And where is this likely to lead?

The immediate question was what to do with the emotionally over-charged woman? The sensible thing seemed to be to take her back into my consulting-room and give her a cup of tea, and that is what we did. Christofferson went off in search of Charlie, who was luckily in the vicarage, instructing a Confirmation class, which he was able to conclude immediately and come to the clinic. The sight of him set Mrs. Vizard going again at full steam. She repeated over and over the story of her depression, the cloud she felt over her mind and spirits—this was thickening with every repetition—and her prayer at the grave of the old priest.

"What form of prayer did you use?" asked Charlie.

"Oh, Father, the simplest. I just said, 'O God, be merciful to me, a sinner,' and then came this extraordinary feeling in my arm—like a very strong light being turned on—"

"Light? A light in your arm? How do you mean?"

"Not just in my arm. As if I were being bathed in very strong light all over—but especially in my arm, of course. Am I making myself clear? I don't suppose so. Because it was all terribly clear—wonderfully clear—but not in a way I can describe."

I had placed a thermometer in her armpit. I read it now. A surprisingly high reading. If Mrs. Vizard had not plainly been in good health I should call it a phenomenal one.

"My suggestion is that we take you home at once, and that you get as much rest as you can. We want to see if this astonishing cure persists. I'm not disparaging the power of your experience, but you understand that we must be as prudent as we can, before letting anyone else know what has happened."

"Yes, Father, I understand perfectly. But it will persist, I just know it will."

"Pray God it may be so. Dr Hutchins, would it be an imposition to ask you to drive Mrs. Vizard home?"

When they had gone Charlie said, "What do you think?"

"I think she's an hysteric, but who can really say what that means? Lots of miraculous cures happen to hysterics, but that doesn't change the fact that they are cured, for a while at least. This may be an unusual remission. But I wouldn't for an instant dismiss the truth of what has happened. She prayed at the grave of a man she believed was a saint. She is cured for the moment. What do *you* think?"

"I hardly dare to hope. It seems such an overwhelming wonderful thing to happen here and now. Who can say what might come of it? But we must be cautious, of course?"

"Very cautious indeed."

Excerpts from *The Cunning Man*, 1994.

MIROSLAV HOLUB

Suffering

The Czech immunologist (and expert on nude mice) Miroslav Holub was a poet so rational in his habits of mind he came to seem quite surrealist in his effects. This epic poem on some kind of dumb suffering laboratory tissue, for which death is only a relative term, shows Holub's laboratory carnivalesque style—a method of turning the microscope on society.

Ugly creatures, ugly grunting creatures,
Completely concealed under the point of the needle,
    behind the curve of the Research Task Graph,
Disgusting creatures with foam at the mouth,
    with bristles on their bottoms,
One after the other
They close their pink mouths
They open their pink mouths
They grow pale
Flutter their legs
    as if they were running a very
    long distance,

They close ugly blue eyes,
They open ugly blue eyes
    and
    they're
    dead.

But I ask no questions,
no one asks any questions.

And after their death we let the ugly creatures
  run in pieces along the white expanse
  of the paper electrophore
We let them graze in the greenish-blue pool
  of the chromatogram
And in pieces we drive them for a dip
  in alcohol
  and xylol
And the immense eye of the ugly animal god
  watches their every move
  through the tube of the microscope
And the bits of animals are satisfied
like flowers in a flower-pot
  like kittens at the bottom of a pond
  like cells before conception.
But I ask no questions,
  no one asks any questions,

Naturally no one asks
Whether these creatures wouldn't have preferred
  to live all in one piece,
  their disgusting life
  in bogs
  and canals,
Whether they wouldn't have preferred to eat
  one another alive,
Whether they wouldn't have preferred to make love
  in between horror and hunger,
Whether they wouldn't have preferred to use
  all their eyes and pores to perceive
  their muddy stinking little world
Incredibly terrified,
Incredibly happy
In the way of matter which can do no more.

But I ask no questions,
      no one asks any questions,
Because it's all quite useless,
Experiments succeed and experiments fail,
Like everything else in this world,
      in which the truth advances
      like some splendid silver bulldozer
      in the tumbling darkness,

Like everything else in this world,
      in which I met a lonely girl
      inside a shop selling bridal veils,
In which I met a general covered
      with oak leaves,
In which I met ambulance men who could find no
      wounded,
In which I met a man who had lost
      his name,
In which I met a glorious and famous, bronze,
      incredibly terrified rat,
In which I met people who wanted to lay down
      their lives and people who wanted to lay down
      their heads in sorrow,
In which, come to think of it, I keep meeting my
      own self at every step.

From *Selected Poems*, 1967; translated from the Czech
by George Theiner.

SUSAN SONTAG
Making it Literal

Immunologists took over a language saturated with military terms from germ theory in the 1960s. Now that these metaphors have been naturalized, their figurative origins go largely undetected. But as Susan Sontag shows, in her book Illness and its Metaphors, *allow metaphors their head and we end up in a city under siege, with permanent monitoring, demagogic recruitment and red alerts.*

The military metaphor in medicine first came into wide use in the 1880s, with the identification of bacteria as agents of disease. Bacteria were said to "invade" or "infiltrate." But talk of siege and war to describe disease now has, with cancer, a striking literalness and authority. Not only is the clinical course of the disease and its medical treatment thus described, but the disease itself is conceived as the enemy on which society wages war. More recently, the fight against cancer has sounded like a colonial war— with similarly vast appropriations of government money—and in a decade when colonial wars haven't gone too well, this militarized rhetoric seems to be backfiring. Pessimism among doctors about the efficacy of treatment is growing, in spite of the strong advances in chemotherapy and immunotherapy made since 1970. Reporters covering "the war on cancer" frequently caution the public to distinguish between official fictions and harsh facts; a few years ago, one science writer found American Cancer Society proclamations that cancer is curable and progress has been made "reminiscent of Vietnam optimism prior to the deluge." Still, it is one thing to be skeptical about the rhetoric that surrounds cancer, another to give support to many uninformed doctors who insist that no significant progress in treatment has been made, and that cancer is not really curable. The bromides of the American cancer establishment, tirelessly hailing the imminent victory over cancer; the professional pessimism of a large number of cancer specialists, talking like battle-weary officers mired down in an interminable colonial war—these are twin distortions in this military rhetoric about cancer.

Other distortions follow with the extension of cancer images in more grandiose schemes of warfare. As TB was represented as the spiritualizing of consciousness, cancer is understood as the overwhelming or obliterating of consciousness (by a mindless It). In TB, you are eating yourself up, being refined, getting down to the core, the real you. In cancer, non-intelligent ("primitive," "embryonic," "atavistic") cells are multiplying, and you are being replaced by the nonyou. Immunologists class the body's cancer cells as "nonself."

It is worth noting that Reich, who did more than anyone else to disseminate the psychological theory of cancer, also found something equivalent to cancer in the biosphere.

> There is a deadly orgone energy. It is in the atmosphere. You can demonstrate it on devices such as the Geiger counter. It's a swampy quality … Stagnant, deadly water which doesn't flow, doesn't metabolize. Cancer, too, is due to the stagnation of the flow of the life energy of the organism.

Reich's language has its own inimitable coherence. And more and more—as its metaphoric uses gain in credibility—cancer is felt to be what he thought it was, a cosmic disease, the emblem of all the destructive, alien powers to which the organism is host.

As TB was the disease of the sick self, cancer is the disease of the Other. Cancer proceeds by a science-fiction scenario: an invasion of "alien" or "mutant" cells, stronger than normal cells (*Invasion of the Body Snatchers, The Incredible Shrinking Man, The Blob, The Thing*). One standard science-fiction plot is mutation, either mutants arriving from outer space or accidental mutations among humans. Cancer could be described as a triumphant mutation, and mutation is now mainly an image for cancer. As a theory of the psychological genesis of cancer, the Reichian imagery of energy checked, not allowed to move outward, then turned back on itself, driving cells berserk, is already the stuff of science fiction. And Reich's image of death in the air—of deadly energy that registers on a Geiger counter—suggests how much the science-fiction images about cancer (a disease that comes from deadly rays, and is treated by deadly rays) echo the collective nightmare. The original fear about exposure to atomic radiation was genetic deformities in the next generation; that was replaced by another fear, as statistics started to show much higher cancer rates among Hiroshima and Nagasaki survivors and their descendants.

Cancer is a metaphor for what is most ferociously energetic; and these energies constitute the ultimate insult to natural order. In a science-fiction tale by Tommaso Landolfi, the spaceship is called "Cancerqueen." (It is hardly within the range of the tuberculosis metaphor that a writer could have imagined an intrepid vessel named "Consumptionqueen.") When not being explained away as something psychological, buried in the recesses of the self, cancer is being magnified and projected into a metaphor for the biggest enemy, the furthest goal. Thus, Nixon's bid to match Kennedy's promise to put Americans on the moon was, appropriately enough, the promise to "conquer" cancer. Both were science-fiction ventures. The equivalent of the legislation establishing the space program was the National Cancer Act of 1971, which did not envisage the near-to-hand decisions that could bring under control the industrial economy that pollutes—only the great destination: the cure.

TB was a disease in the service of a romantic view of the world. Cancer is now in the service of a simplistic view of the world that can turn paranoid. The disease is often experienced as a form of demonic possession—tumors are "malignant" or "benign," like forces—and many terrified cancer patients are disposed to seek out faith healers, to be exorcized. The main organized support for dangerous nostrums like Laetrile comes from far-right groups to whose politics of paranoia the fantasy of a miracle cure for cancer makes a serviceable addition, along with a belief in UFOs. (The John Birch Society distributes a forty-five-minute film called *World Without Cancer.*) For the more sophisticated, cancer signifies the rebellion of the injured ecosphere: Nature taking revenge on a wicked technocratic world. False hopes and simplified terrors are raised by crude statistics brandished for the general public, such as that 90 percent of all cancers are "environ-mentally caused," or that imprudent diet and tobacco smoking alone account for 75 percent of all cancer deaths. To the accompaniment of this numbers game (it is difficult to see how any statistics about "all cancers" or "all cancer deaths" could be defended), cigarettes, hair dyes, bacon, saccharine, hormone-fed poultry, pesticides, low-sulphur coal—a length-ening roll call of products we take for granted have been found to cause cancer. X-rays give cancer (the treatment meant to cure kills); so do emanations from the television set and the microwave oven and the fluorescent clock face. As with syphilis, an innocent or trivial act—or exposure—in the present can have dire consequences far in the future. It is also known that cancer rates are high for workers in a large number of industrial occupations. Though the exact processes of causation lying behind the statistics remain unknown, it seems clear that many cancers are preventable. But cancer is not just a disease ushered in by the Industrial Revolution (there was cancer in Arcadia) and certainly more than the sin of capitalism (within their more limited industrial capacities, the Russians pollute worse than we do). The widespread current view of cancer as a disease of industrial civilization is as unsound scientifically as the right-wing fantasy of a "world without cancer" (like a world without sub-versives). Both rest on the mistaken feeling that cancer is a distinctively "modern" disease.

The medieval experience of the plague was firmly tied to notions of moral pollution, and people invariably looked for a scapegoat external to the stricken community. (Massacres of Jews in unprecedented numbers took place everywhere in plague-stricken Europe of 1347–48, then stopped as soon as the plague receded.) With the modern diseases, the scapegoat is not so easily separated from the patient. But much as these diseases individualize, they also pick up some of the metaphors of epidemic diseases. (Diseases understood to be simply epidemic have become less useful as metaphors, as evidenced by the near-total historical amnesia about the influenza pandemic of 1918–19, in which more people died than in the four years of World War I.) Presently, it is as much a cliché to say that cancer is "environmentally" caused as it was—and still is—to say that it is caused by mismanaged emotions. TB was associated with pollution (Florence Nightingale thought it was "induced by the foul air of houses"), and now cancer is thought of as a disease of the contamination of the whole world. TB was "the white plague." With awareness of environmental pollution, people have started saying that there is an "epidemic" or "plague" of cancer.

From Chapter 8, *Illness as a Metaphor*, 1978.

PETER GOLDSWORTHY

A Statistician to his Love

Many doctors end up as fact-bores—as the Australian doctor and poet Peter Goldsworthy suggests in this acerbic little poem—sedating their friends (and lovers) and even scaring their patients with the scraps of learning that fall from the tables of epidemiologists.

Men kill women in bedrooms, usually
by hand, or gun. Women kill men,
less often, in kitchens, with knives.
Don't be alarmed, there is understanding
to be sucked from all such hard
and bony facts, or at least a sense
of symmetry. Drowned men—an
instance—float face down, women up.
But women, ignited, burn more fiercely.
The death camp pyres were therefore,
sensibly, women and children first,
an oily kind of kindling. The men
were stacked in rows on top. Yes,
there is always logic in the world.
And neatness. And the comfort
of fact. Did I mention that suicides
outnumber homicides? Recent figures
are reliable. So stay awhile yet
with me: the person to avoid, alone,
is mostly you yourself.

This Goes with That, 1991.

THOM GUNN

Save the Word

Gunn's fierce little poem (which is addressed to a student not a doctor) comments on the romantic ideal of empathy (feeling into someone), and its presumption, in our therapeutic society, that licensed experts are more likely to know "us" than we ourselves. Medical students are instructed in how to delve down into their patients' hidden agendas and empathize with their fears. It sounds like reading their mail. At best, it may be a delusion: it projects the doctor as infinitely pliable, emotionally correct and, frankly, a bit of a know-all.

Save the word
empathy, sweetheart,
for your freshman essays.
Doesn't it make
a rather large
claim? Think you can
syphon yourself
into another human
as, in the movie,
the lively boy-ghosts
pour themselves
down the ear-holes
of pompous older men?
Don't try it. Only
Jesus could do it and he
probably didn't exist.
Try "sympathy". With that
your isolated self may

split a cloak with a beggar,
slip a pillow under the head
of the arrested man, hold tight
the snag-toothed hustler with red hair.

"Save the Word," *Boss Cupid*, 2000.

BERT KEIZER

My Father's Death

Bert Keizer is a doctor working in a nursing home in Amsterdam. His mildly lugubrious meditations on his working life, in which he recounts his patients' deaths against a number of literary and philosophical reflections, were collected into a very successful book Dancing with Mister D, *which he translated himself into English. In this piece, originally delivered in front of an audience of doctors, he examines a question patients often ask doctors: well, what would you do if it were your relative? His article touches on the contentious issue of euthanasia which, as he sees it (and the Dutch lawmakers too), is less an act of violence against the person than a means of protecting patients from the intrusion of technology in the waning of their lives. Technology may well be no more than a fantastically elaborate apparatus to obscure medicine's inability to define what help really is.*

I wish to consider the subject of living well and dying well, with particular reference to the role of medicine in or around these activities. It is my uncomfortable belief that medicine, as it is practised today in western Europe, hardly contributes to dying well. And the contribution of medicine to living well is on the whole grossly overrated, by doctors and patients alike.

Let us first try to say something about medicine's contribution to living well. Looking back into history, it would appear that people have always been pretty good at the simpler tasks of medicine. I'm not so sure about obstetrics—I've read some horrendous accounts there—but I'm thinking of how to deal with fractures and wounds. As to the many other ailments, please don't press me for a definition. There was an extensive use of herbs and less pleasant concoctions, which occasionally hit a target people didn't even know existed, and apart from that there was a lot of vomiting, purging, cupping, praying, blessing, sacrificing, laying on of hands, going on a pilgrimage, smoking it out, burning it away, giving it to the neighbours, passing it to an animal, scaring it away, showing it to the moon, magnetising, electrifying, mesmerising or hypnotising—and then all of a sudden we've arrived in the nineteenth century.

Every reasonably educated doctor would like to say that it wasn't until the nineteenth century that our profession gained a solid footing. What we describe as scientific medicine, rational medicine, is a view of the body and its functioning and malfunctioning that developed in the first half of the nineteenth century, a development which quickly gathered momentum and turned into one of the most remarkable upheavals of our social and physical lives.

One could speak after 1850 of the rise and rise and rise of modern medicine. Three discoveries were the most important initial steps:

- firstly, the advances in the study of the anatomical basis of the symptoms of disease
- secondly, the discovery of the bacterial causes of diseases, and the methods developed to avoid bacterial contamination
- thirdly, the discovery of anaesthesia, giving the surgeon time to perform an operation instead of having to hack his way through the panic of a struggling patient.

Many steps were to follow: antibiotics, insulin, increasing surgical sophistication, psychotropic medication, vaccination programmes against childhood diseases, open-heart surgery, kidney transplants, hip replacement, oral contraception, traumatology, intensive care techniques, and so on, but not *ad infinitum*. I cannot enumerate all that has come our way, but I would like to point out to you one or two consequences.

Because medicine has become so clever, as it might seem, at removing so much suffering, the many kinds of suffering against which it is powerless have fallen into disregard.

We are so intoxicated by the marvellous successes of medicine in certain situations that we believe this to be applicable to all the other situations as well. And if not now, then certainly in the future. So we think that a patient's complaint will, after diagnostic procedures, always be traced to a diagnosis and thus a treatment will ensue—the cough, the chest X-ray, the pneumonia and then the penicillin. What we don't want to know is that in many situations, far more than we usually guess, this sequence doesn't occur at all. In fact in many cases we get stuck after diagnosis, for there is no treatment. We cannot cure a stroke, or Alzheimer's disease, or Parkinson's disease, or multiple sclerosis, or motor neurone disease, or schizophrenia, or nicotine addiction, or osteoporosis, or, most famously, and least believed of all, we cannot cure cancer.

The war on cancer, as it is fondly called, is one of the most fascinating aspects of medicine in the second half of the twentieth century. The best brains in the best laboratories all over the western world have spent five decades now at the cost of billions and billions on research into the cure for cancer. The great breakthrough has for 50 years been "just around the corner."

The cure for cancer resembles the coming of "true socialism," which had been about to occur in the late Soviet Union for more than seven decades, but never made its actual appearance. Oncology seems to be in much the same position.

This is so fascinating, because it offers an insight into the nature of medicine: medicine doesn't always have to deliver the goods, but can still send the bill. In that respect it resembles prayer: you ask for something but you don't blame your method if you don't obtain a result.

When we consider the whole area of medical practice we will discern a small bright circle at the centre where a number of treatments are gathered that have been proved to be efficacious. Beyond this centre we stumble into a twilight zone, where we find a number of treatments that might some day justifiably be placed in the bright centre but have as yet not *earned that place*. Beyond this zone again, darkness reigns. Here we find a vast array of doing things with people who are ill. These approaches are silly, cruel, dishonest, innocent, cynical, harmless or unhealthy, both in intent and in their effects. Doctors place many more of their doings in the hallowed centre than is scientifically justifiable. Patients are hardly aware of the murkier zones at all. They reckon all is in the centre, or almost there anyway.

Why this overestimation? The clear and simple answer is that we don't want to die. Because of this mythical demand for eternal life that medicine is to satisfy, I believe it is impossible to take the myth out of medicine, just as impossible as taking the glamour out of war. And while war shouldn't be glamorous, nor medicine mythical, it cannot be helped as we are so helpless in the face of disease, incapacity, decay, old age, death. When threatened by adversity on a sufficiently crushing scale, it is impossible to keep your wits about you, whatever philosophers tell you.

The actual contribution of medicine to living well is of course impossible to assess. But what doctors and patients *think* about this contribution is beyond reason and unfounded.

A second cause of the overestimation of medicine and what it can achieve lies in a misconception of science. Ludwig Wittgenstein said in the *Tractatus*: "We feel that even when all possible scientific questions have been answered, the problems of life remain completely untouched." I think what Wittgenstein means is this: around suffering there's always the question *why*. So when a patient asks "Why am I to die?," and the doctor responds with a lengthy disquisition on the insufficiency of her coronaries, the leak in her mitral valve, the accumulation of fluids in the lungs, the faltering oxygenation of her blood and so on, going into the resulting mitochondrial changes in her cortical tissue if you like, the patient will interrupt all this physiology and will ask: "Never mind all that, I meant why me?"

This is the point where the doctor breaks off and holds his tongue, ideally, because he realises the difference between a physiological and an existential question. Usually nothing of all this happens of course: the patient is dismissed, the why-me question is buried under a deluge of diagnostic moves. The sad misunderstanding being that a blood test, an X-ray, a scan, can ever tell us anything about why we are here. Since God left the premises, also somewhere in the nineteenth century, we have been lumbered with a certain ignorance about the purpose of life. It seems to me that this ignorance is eagerly buried underneath a pile of tests, none of which can show us why we suffer.

Why does this matter? First of all: it hurts. It hurts when you get faceless biochemistry offered while you are trying to digest your suffering religiously, metaphysically or psychologically. The doctor as priest is the man or woman who succeeds not so much in curing a disease as in explaining the disease in such terms as to make it credible and palatable— metaphysically digestible one could say.

Secondly, this matters because this misguided chase after scientific answers ("Can't you see I'm busy?") seems to absolve the doctor from what I take to be precisely one-half of our duty: to stand by your patient in his suffering. Doctors are very keen on taking away misery, well who isn't, and it is in this role that they like to shine. The silly reverence for scientific questions and their answers ignores the suffering that cannot be taken away.

Thirdly, the overestimation of the importance of scientific responses adds insult to injury: offering chemotherapy in certain stages of cancer, where its application is plainly cruel; admitting demented elderly patients to intensive care units, where they die unnecessarily painful deaths. There's a whole host of procedures that flaunt the Hippocratic dictum: don't make it worse. Ignoring a person's suffering because all the attention is focused on biochemical parameters is a daily sin in medical practice.

To some of you all this may sound unlikely, irresponsible, exaggerated, unfounded, hysterical even, but I assure you a certain shrillness in statement is necessary in order to rise above the horrendous din that the opposite view is usually making, and has been making for some 150 years now. I am not scoffing at medicine; I am merely trying to state what it can and cannot do.

So much for medicine's contribution to living well. Next we move on to the subject of dying well.

All patients must die. Doctors are so keen on statistics these days that I will gladly serve their interest: the percentage here is 100!

I would like to compare two deaths, that of Byron and of my own father, to show that ignorance can be just as awful as knowledge in its effect on a patient's suffering.

In 1824, Byron was 36 and found himself in Greece fighting for their independence against the Turks. The military scene was outrageously corrupt and he fell dangerously ill in the swamps of Missolonghi. He told his doctor, Julius Millingen, that he was heartily sick of life, "but the apprehension of two things now haunt my mind". He added: "I picture myself slowly expiring on a bed of torture, or terminating my days like Swift—a grinning idiot." Bed of torture it was to be. In the words of his biographer, Leslie Marchand, Byron had a healthy dread of the remedies of his medical men, the doctors Bruno and Millingen, who knew of only one way out of medical trouble: bleeding. On the morning of the 10th of April Bruno recommended this procedure, but Byron refused. The doctor gave him castor oil instead and put him in a hot bath. Three days later Bruno prescribed antimony powder against the fever, as Byron absolutely refused bleeding and the application of leeches. On the fifth day Dr Millingen was called in and together they tried to convince him to submit to bleeding. Byron became irritated, saying that "he knew well that the lancet had killed more people than the lance." They kept on administering pills and cathartics, and at noon the next day they returned again to demand his blood, but Byron refused, as annoyed as before. He told them that: "Drawing blood from a nervous patient is like loosening the cords of a musical instrument, the tones of which are already defective for want of sufficient tension."

In spite of this beautiful phrasing, Dr Bruno continued to plead for permission to bleed him, but Byron steadfastly refused and asked for the company of Parry, a rough old soldier with whom he felt more at ease than with the menacing doctors. When Parry left late in the evening, Byron was seized by a violent spasmodic coughing that caused him to vomit. Dr Bruno threatened him with inflammation of the lungs if he did not allow himself to be bled, and Byron at last gave in and promised his veins to Bruno the following day. But in the morning Byron felt better and retracted his promise, which set off a violent altercation between him and his doctors that ended in his throwing out his arm to them and exclaiming: "Come; you are, I see, a damned set of butchers. Take away as much blood as you will, but have done with it." They removed a pound, but the relief obtained did not correspond, noted Dr Millingen, "to the hopes we had anticipated." Two hours later they took another pound, after which he felt alleviated or exhausted. Anyway, he fell asleep. The quality of his pulse remaining the same, they proposed a third bleeding on the basis of Byron's complaint of a numbness in the fingers. In his lucid moments Byron resisted their further efforts. This did not mean that he was rid of his tormentors for now they gave him purgatives instead.

On the seventh day of his troubles he was continuously delirious and two more physicians were called in. They, for once, did not bleed him but gave him some China bark, water and wine, and applied two blisters on the inside of his thighs. On the eighth day it was clear to all that Byron was going down rapidly and Dr Bruno again came up with his favourite remedy: he applied 12 leeches to the temples of his dying patient and extricated two pounds of blood. From now on Byron was intermittently delirious. The doctors had decided on another purgation: "a clyster of senna, castor oil and three ounces of Epsom salts." Incredibly Byron got out of bed at six in the evening to relieve himself. "Damned doctors," he muttered, "I can scarcely stand." Back in bed he lost consciousness and the doctors again applied leeches to his temples. The blood flowed freely all night and he died at six in the evening of the following day.

This harrowing account of adding medical insult to physical injury seems so absurd that one might wonder what on earth these people thought they were doing. I think the doctors Bruno and Millingen meant no harm. And yet they did cause harm, by ignoring their patient and sticking to their textbooks.

This same thing still occurs, and not rarely. One hundred-and-seventy years later, in May 1994, my father was 87 years old, a dedicated smoker of roll-ups all his life and in recent years increasingly short of breath on account of emphysema. One of the most ill-starred meetings in modern medicine is that between a frail, defenceless old man nearing the end of his life, and an agile young intern at the beginning of his career.

Soon after my father's admission into hospital, chest X-rays were taken and he was seen by a chest physician. He prescribed oxygen, mucolytics, anti-biotics and physiotherapy. My father did not improve. A pulmonary embolism could not with all certainty be excluded and so he was put on anticoagulants. He was very feverish and anxious, and at night he was delirious.

The doctor suspected an element of cardiac failure so he called in the cardiologist. After another set of X-rays and an ECG had duly been performed, this colleague added diuretics to the medication, and went his way. The patient however did not improve at all; on the contrary, he seemed to be slipping away from us.

On his sixth day in hospital he passed a bloody stool, probably caused by impacted faecal matter damaging the intestinal mucosa on its way out. Now the gastroenterologist was called in. Of course he advised a colonoscopy, to exclude the possibility of cancer. In order for a colonoscopy to be possible my father was given about the same amount of purgatives as Lord Byron had had to sustain, and on the evening before the procedure my mother found him drenched in his own mess. He had totally lost his bearings at this stage and was restless at nights, trying to climb out of bed, forgetting he had a catheter. In order to prevent these hazardous nocturnal excursions he was given a tranquilliser, haloperidol.

On the seventh day he could hardly speak because of the tremor induced by the haloperidol, which made him all shaky and tremulous. He was taken for the colonoscopy, nevertheless, and the doctor found a polyp in his colon, which he proceeded to remove with a cauteriser, almost burning a hole in the intestinal wall, as he told me excitedly later, and certainly causing considerable blood loss.

On the ninth day one of the nurses came with the suggestion that my father was probably an Alzheimer patient. The thought being, if there was a thought behind this suggestion, that if they mutter incomprehensibly, they're probably demented. A psychiatrist and a neurologist were called in to evaluate this possibility, a brain scan was arranged, and admission to a nursing home was put on the agenda.

He had hardly been eating and was lying passively in bed, and now severe bedsores were threatening. In order to do something about this the dermatologist was called in. During these ten days my father had been seen by an internist consultant, a pulmonary physician, a cardiologist, a gastroenterologist, a psychiatrist, a neurologist and a dermatologist. He had been subjected to four X-rays, uncomfortable but not unsettling, many blood tests, and the gruesome procedure of bowel cleaning prior to the colonoscopy. Even if he had not been feverish and sedated he would have been completely baffled after so many encounters.

The net outcome of all this high-flown medical expertise was that he had turned from a very ill old man into a physical and mental wreck with whom it was almost impossible to communicate. When, to top it all, the consultant wanted to call in a nephrologist because of a touch of renal failure that was now showing up in his blood tests, we finally called a halt to all this and asked his GP to intervene.

The family doctor put in his dentures, then looked for and thoroughly cleaned his glasses, and after a lot of fumbling managed to get his hearing-aid properly positioned. He then sat down with him and they spoke for about half an hour. When asked what he really wanted, my father said he wanted to be left alone in order to die in peace. He was moved to a geriatric ward in a neighbouring hospital, was given some morphine, and died peacefully three days later. A week after his death, the pathologist called me to report on the benignant aspect of the polyp removed.

I believe that a death-bed like my father's is so annoying to the internal medicine consultant, because all his knowledge, all his knowledge, doesn't show the way to a cure here. There is no blood test that tells you when to stop calling in other doctors, hoping they have a cure. The point is, as Beckett would say: "You're human, and there's no cure for that."

You might say that Byron was as pestered with what we now call ignorance, as many a present-day patient with what we now regard as knowledge, and the contribution of modern medicine to dying well is, I would say, disastrous. We should be ashamed of the way we seize on the dying in their frailty, blinded as we are by the fatal notion that a man's potassium level is more telling than his innermost thoughts about life and death.

To sum up, then, in the nineteenth century scientific medicine was born. Its success in alleviating suffering was so immense as to leave us all over-impressed. However, not all physical suffering can or ever will be taken away by medicine, and yet we act as if medicine can do this, or will soon be capable of doing this. Paradoxically, this leads to increased suffering, especially in the hour of death, when the scientific analysis of bodily events ignores the sadness of parting from life. Our real questions, in Wittgenstein's sense, are not scientific. And we would do well, when talking about choices around death, to be aware of the understandable but therefore no less harmful blindness of one of the principal actors in the last act of life—the doctor with his scientific obsession.

"Living well, dying well," in *Medicine and Humanity*, 2001.

JEFF ARONSON

Patient-Centred Verbs

For years, Jeff Aronson has been writing an erudite column for the British Medical Journal *on the provenance of words, especially the obscure ones doctors like to use. Here he chronicles a change in usage which while it reflects a growing subjectivism ("patient-centredness") also testifies to a worrying confusion about the very nature of agents and objects.*

It is not surprising, in these patient-centred days, that some verbs that refer to inanimate objects associated with the patient, are used to refer to the patient instead. I have come across the following uses:

- The patient was diagnosed with the disease
- She was explained the seriousness of the diagnosis
- She was prescribed a course of chemotherapy
- She was administered vincristine.

However, it was not the patient but the disease that was diagnosed, the seriousness that was explained, the chemotherapy that was prescribed, and the vincristine that was administered.

The problem lies in the misuse of the construction known as the indirect passive. Verbs can be either transitive or intransitive—a transitive verb governs an object, whereas an intransitive verb does not. Now some transitive verbs have the luxury of governing two objects, a direct object and an indirect object; let's call them ditransitive. For example, in the sentence "The nurse gave her vincristine" the verb "gave" governs the direct object "vincristine" and the indirect object "her". Ditransitive verbs can be converted from the active to the passive voice in two ways, with either the direct or the indirect object as the subject of the new sentence:

"Vincristine was given to her" or "She was given vincristine". Since in the latter the indirect object has become the subject of the sentence, the construction is called the indirect passive.

However, some transitive verbs take a prepositional phrase instead of an indirect object. Thus, although you can say "He gave her vincristine", you cannot say "He administered her vincristine". Instead you have to say "He administered vincristine to her", where "to her" is a prepositional phrase. And verbs that do this cannot be part of an indirect passive construction. In other words you cannot say "She was administered vincristine."

Diagnosing and explaining also take prepositional phrases that deny the use of the indirect passive:

- The disease was diagnosed in her
- The diagnosis was explained to her.

Those who use these incorrect forms may take heart from the fact that Shakespeare once did so too: "His ancient knot of dangerous adversaries / Tomorrow are let blood at Pomfret Castle" (*Richard III*, act 3: scene I: line 179).

However, some verbs (including prescribe) can take a direct object and either an indirect object ("He prescribed her a drug") or a prepositional phrase ("He prescribed a drug for her"). Examples of the indirect passive construction with prescribe include "He was … prescribed a … Ptisan" (1758, from John Sparrow's translation *Le Dran's Observations in Surgery*) and a couplet from Robert Browning's poem "Ned Bratts" (1879):

> And ten were prescribed the whip, and ten a brand on the cheek,
> And five a slit of the nose—just leaving enough to tweak.

So, grudgingly, I concede that "She was prescribed vincristine" is acceptable. And no doubt in time we shall come to accept the ditransitivity of diagnose, explain, and administer, and hence, ugly though they are, their indirect passive forms; but not yet.

Recently, a different type of passive transformation has been rearing its ugly head. First, the intransitive verb consent ("She consented [to the operation]") has been tortured into transitivity ("The surgeon consented her") and then the direct passive has been applied ("She was consented"). I haven't yet heard the even uglier quasi-indirect passive form of this—"The operation was consented"—but I expect to before long.

This stresses, were stress necessary, that in the use of language, as in so many other walks of life, it is better to be active rather than passive.

"Patient-Centred Verbs," *British Medical Journal*, 2002.

MARTIN WINCKLER

A Little Medical Afflictionary

La Maladie de Sachs, Martin Winckler's second novel, found a huge public when it was published in France in 1998. It turned on the brilliantly simple expedient of having patients describe what goes on in the four walls of the consulting room rather than the person with the white coat. Winckler is a man with a mission, and he makes no bones about his dislike of the French medical establishment: "doctors," he roundly declares, "are cowards." His amusing "afflictionary" is revealing of the intense French preoccupation with reading the body personal—the more readings the better.

AIDS: in the western world, historical successor to the plague, TB and cancer at the top of the hit-parade (or Top 50) of sacred diseases. It may be noted that this distinction has nothing to do with the real number of affected individuals. In Africa, for example, malaria, TB and Aids are so frequent that they are considered not so much as threats, but as aspects of civilisation.

Alternative medicine(s): medical practices based on principles radically opposed to those of conventional medicine. While the latter is founded on respect for the symptom (see *Pain*), terror and ignorance, the bases of alternative medicine(s) tend to be enhancement of the symptom (see *Homeopathy*), anxiety and credulity.

Antibiotics: medications for lowering fever. Always a source of tiredness, they should never be taken with milk (it makes them curdle). Very common cause of allergy.

Appendicitis: benign childhood disease which is invariably diagnosed by mothers. Becomes serious when it occurs in an adult (and is then referred to as "peritonitis/septicaemia complicating atypical gangrenous perforated appendicitis").

Auscultation:
1. (outdated) technique involving listening to the internal sounds of the body using the ear (immediate auscultation) or with a stethoscope (mediate auscultation) placed on the patient's body.
2. (modern) examination of the patient by the doctor. Ex.: "I was really afraid of having cancer of the testicles but he auscultated me all over and it's just a fungal infection of the privates." (See *Consult*.)

Blood pressure (measurement of): objective reflection of the doctor–patient relationship (e.g.: "He didn't even take my blood pressure!") but differently assessed depending on the observer:
1. for the physician, "normal" blood pressure is greater than 155— the figure above which the occasional patient becomes a "patient on permanent treatment"—or less than 80—the figure below which hospitalisation becomes a must. Between these two values, French doctors say that the patient has "no tension" (i.e. normal blood pressure).
2. for the patient, the blood pressure is "normal" if, and only if, the figures obtained are strictly identical to those previously measured, even if the reading was three years beforehand. (Ex.: "How can that be, 120 on 80? Last year, I measured 130 on 90. It's not normal!")

Cholesterol: modern equivalent of the ancient gods. When it climbs, sacrifices have to be made (no more butter, meat, sugar); when it falls, one indulges (no more medication).

Clinical examination: mystical ritual (not to be confused with auscultation) during which the doctor examines a patient. The crowning act of the clinical examination is measurement of the blood pressure.

Consult, to: this term may be applied equally to patient or physician depending on whether:
1. the first asks the second to explain a complex problem, or;
2. the second examines the first (see *Auscultation*) and;
3. flicks through the telephone directory to find the number of a specialist (who is then referred to as a "consultant").

Consultation: friendly visit paid by the patient to the doctor. By extension: time of the day during which the doctor sees people he doesn't know drop in between two appointments.

Death: irremediable breakdown between a patient and doctor. Contrary to a received idea, death is not, as the physician sees it, an end in itself. It is only a stage—often inevitable—in the doctor-patient relationship which ought to be delayed as long as possible in order for it to be fully receipted.

Diagnosis 1: complex mental process at the end of which:
  (a) the doctor names the disease or
  (b) the patient dies without anyone understanding why. (These two propositions are not incompatible.)
This intellectual process is the product and conjunction of knowledge, intuition, hunches and sometimes amazing revelations, and may be compared to the resolution of a crossword puzzle in which symptoms are the horizontal definitions and signs the vertical definitions. The doctor is able to call upon three diagnostic tools: blood tests, appeals to specialists and hospitalisation.

Diagnosis 2: (by extension) capacity possessed by a physician to resolve crossword puzzles more or less reliably, i.e. to provide an explanation for everything including an inexplicable death (Ex.: "He has a good nose for diagnosis").

Diagnostic complex: this is applied to rare or poorly understood diseases (in other words, the most interesting) and calls upon a number of means which, depending on the rarity of the disease in question, enable the physician:

1. to prepare an article for publication in specialised periodicals;
2. to list the characteristics enabling him to spot, identify, detect or to drive out of hiding (for ethical purposes) patients suffering from the same disease entity;
3. to come up with possibilities for research and human vivisection with an aim to trying out new treatments, gruelling but promising;
4. to advance if not scientific knowledge then at least his own reputation.

Doctor: has a degree from the medical faculty or is just about to get one. Before 1945, his main function was to make diagnoses. From 1945 to 1975, spent most of his time prescribing antibiotics and measuring blood pressure. Since 1975, he has been wavering between the war against cholesterol and looking for more financially attractive gaps in the market. (See *Alternative medicine*.)

Euthanasia:

1. taboo subject (in hospitals).
2. hot topic (in the media).
3. method enabling a family to lose one of its members without risk ing legal pursuit, and enabling the family to arrange for burial or cremation at a set date.
4. last resort when a hospitalised patient, in spite of the (good or bad) care provided by the doctor(s), goes on filling a bed and getting up everybody's nose.

Family: universal pathogenic medium, resistant to antibiotics, vaccinations and to all therapeutic methods invented in the last six thousand years. (See *Family Doctor*.)

Family doctor: species currently disappearing. After rapid mutation in the last fifty years, the supposed focus of the family doctor's attentions has acquired a heightened resistance which makes it sometimes insensitive to this category of care provider. Today, it is not uncommon for a family to require multiple therapy involving GP + specialist + psychoanalyst + homeopathic doctor, which at least stabilises the general condition. Some authentic family doctors still subsist in remote regions, but it would seem that urbanization and the spread of parabolic antennae will soon have put paid to these last pockets of susceptibility. (See also *Family.*)

Fever: symptom which justifies:
1. wrapping babies in three pullovers and twin covers (to avoid them catching cold);
2. calling the doctor at night (in order to be sure of finding him at home);
3. prescribing antibiotics (in order to avoid a complication);
4. issuing a sick note for the mother (in order to ensure that baby doesn't develop an allergy to antibiotics).

History-taking: rambling conversation between the doctor and patient, sometimes in the presence of other participants. For the doctor, the point of history-taking is to transform the reason for consultation into an intelligible symptom (at least) or into a classified disease (at best). The patient sees it as an opportunity to ask the doctor all those questions his colleagues have so far refused to answer.

Homeopathy: method consisting of mixing undetectable amounts of various products in sweeties readily absorbed by children of all ages in order to treat numberless disorders of an indefinable nature. Homeopathic medication is defined by how it is manufactured and not by its effects on symptoms. It is therefore perfectly possible (and undoubtedly wise) to treat "life-buoys" with granules of "pneu 5CH." In any event, even if it doesn't help it won't harm.

Moreover, a fundamental concept distinguishes homeopathy from allopathy: "the principle of similitude" or like with like. This involves administering to a patient a toxic substance causing the same symptoms as the disease (but more pronounced), in order to convince him that the remedy is often worse than the disease. This is then referred to as "symptom enhancement." (Ex.: "With the trots these granules gave me just before I left, it's not surprising I didn't catch anything in Thailand!")

Home visit:
  1. change of location imposed on the physician by a bedbound patient (urgent visit), patient with car problems (comfort visit), or very generous patient (courtesy visit).
  2. in some circumstances, equivalent of a "gynaecological examination". (Ex.: "The doctor came for a long visit but he was unable to find why my fibroma hurts when Jules does his business.")

Hunting stories:
  1. (outdated) salacious, juicy, extraordinary or unlikely stories told by doctors to their colleagues to convince them that theirs are the more outstanding patients.
  2. (modern) waiting room conversations during which patients tell each other about the diagnostic errors made by their former physician(s).

Illness: the sum total of unpleasant phenomena which brutalise the body and mind of a patient, and whose cause, development and nature are codified, described and indexed in all good medical treatises. An illness is often a hydra with several heads. Whether it affects the body (physical diseases), psyche (psychiatric diseases), both (a real mess) or neither (psycho-somatic diseases), its origin is either external (measles, dysentery, malaria, chemical pollution, radioactivity, family conflict), internal (resentment, guilt, frustration, cancer) or mixed (that's life …).

Ill person: a patient with an illness (the doctor says so). Not all patients have diseases but in order to justify his standing and salary, the doctor prefers that they should. And he hates it if he gets word of the solution to the crossword puzzle before even seeing the grid. (See *Diagnosis 1*.)

Medical act: comedietta of variable length played out by at least two persons, at least one of whom is a physician.

Medical rep: person who gallantly camps in the waiting rooms in order to throw some light on the doctor's consultation and leaves him freebies to be used for treating his mother, wife and children. It is rare for reps to be patients, but is it not unheard of for reps to be completely sick. There are two types: the rep (male variety) generally sports a three-piece suit, an attaché case and a frosty smile. The rep (female variety) can be recognised by her portfolio, tailored suit, flat pumps and the gold chain (bearing her employer's arms) around her ankle. The characteristic common to both is frank hypocrisy. ("What! You haven't heard of my product yet?") and a tendency to treat physicians like imbeciles (they're only wrong about one in ten).

Medication:
1. object of profit.
2. instrument of power.
3. source of allergies. (Ex.: "I'm allergic to all drugs but especially to antibiotics.")

Morphine: illegal drug consumed solely by hopelessly dependent junkies and patients in terminal phase. Morphine is the doctor's worst enemy since, by denying the patient's sense of just how painful reality is, it makes him less dependent on the therapist.

My patients: term used by a doctor to suggest that a large number of patients are unable to suffer without him.

My doctor: outmoded term. Today, it has been replaced by various expressions: "my acupuncturist-iridologist," "my adolescent psychiatrist," "my plastic surgeon," etc.

Nurse:
1. person with the task of performing injections, blood tests and/or enemas ordered by the doctor (in hospital) or demanded by the patient (outside hospital).

2. senior registrar's mistress (in hospital); GP's skivvy (outside hospital).
3. sadistic torturer (in hospital); powerless confidante (outside hospital).
4. undervalued professional (in the media).

Orders: together with the diagnosis, which they may precede, follow or completely replace, doctors' orders are the other high point of the medical act; they are expressed as a written formalisation of the doctor's deep thinking, which is unintelligible to the patient. The purpose of doctors' orders may be diagnostic (ordering of further tests), therapeutic (prescription of several medications), administrative (completion of a certificate or work stoppage) or exorcal (request for a specialist consultation, hospitalisation or seclusion in a padded room). Orders are by convention handwritten, and thereafter remain legible only to a pharmacist (provided he's long in the tooth and the medications actually exist).

Pain: method of audiovisual communication used since the dawn of time by patients (of whom there are a great many) to draw the attention of doctors (of whom there are far fewer) to their person.

It required several thousand years before doctors understood that pain is a very common symptom which is found in very many diseases. Between 1880 and 1995, the reasonable attitude was to "respect the pain", i.e. to allow it to express itself freely in such a way as "not to mask the symptoms". (Otherwise how would one know the patient was suffering?)

Presently (since about 1995), pain is held to be a symptom which is absolutely unacceptable in a civilized society. As a result, the current attitude is pretty much to treat it with disdain.

Patient: an individual who consults a doctor. The word "patient" comes from the Latin *pati*, to put up with. The patient puts up with waiting, in the room of the same name, because he doesn't enjoy putting up with suffering. It may be deduced from the foregoing that a patient is usually (but not always) someone who suffers. At least, he is the one saying so. As a result, the doctor has to put up with—cost what it may!—listening to the patient suffer. (That is called "respecting the symptom".)

Pharmacist: medical auxiliary whose main field of competence, acquired through long experience, is to know how to decipher and translate prescriptions, and whose main function is to sell shampoos, toothpastes and slimming creams. In tubes.

Physiotherapist: a thug in hospital; a strongman outside. More often considered a masseur by patients than a colleague by doctors.

Prescription: sheet of headed paper on which the doctor writes—usually illegibly—the name of the medications he has been thinking of since the last medical rep visited, or recopies those which he manages to read on the out-of-date prescription presented to him by the patient on coming in. Now and again, the doctor may use these same sheets to write to a colleague, to certify the good health of a mother of four who is about to do a course in bungee jumping, or to ask the tax authorities to stagger the obligatory payments for the coming year.

"Rara avis" (rare bird): figurative term used by doctors to describe a patient lacking the decency to die of an identifiable disease.

Reason for consulting: pretext elegantly provided by the patient in order to allow the doctor to prostitute himself without having to tout for business.

Reimbursement: complex system for racketeering, laundering and recycling money between a producer (pharmaceutical laboratory), wholesaler (pharmacist), dealer (physician) and drug consumer (the insured person) under the supervision of two nationwide criminal organisations (the French State and pharmaceutical industry).

Sexuality:
   1. taboo subject (in consultation).
   2. conversational topic (on TV).
   3. main nutritive element of the pathogenic family milieu.

Sign: objective phenomenon which the doctor observes (coldly) on the body (still warm), in the behaviour or after further testing of a patient, whether ill or not. A sign is not necessarily pathognomic of a disease, but may often make the doctor worried and give rise to the extra-thorough diagnostic work-up. For doctors, the signs which are most exact, most trustworthy and which lend themselves best to teaching are of course best observed at autopsy.

Specialist: doctor who doesn't do home visits, and who looks after only a bit of the anatomy (eyes OR breasts OR haemorrhoids, but never all three at once).

Symptom: unpleasant sensation perceived by the patient and sometimes (but not always) observable by the physician. Not to be confused with sign. The symptom most frequently experienced by patients is pain. Many factors (physiological, psychological and cultural) are responsible for the fact that pain is described, acknowledged or expressed differently by each patient. Some weep and cry, others pull discreet faces beneath their pillows. The problem is complex because pain—unlike other physiological characteristics—is neither measurable nor comparable. Naturally, when patients openly give voice to their pain(s), doctors tend to think they're overdoing it a little. It's quite true that when this happens it's much more difficult to stay cool: the rooms are badly lagged.

Treatment:
1. fees paid to their physician by patients who come to consult him regularly: every five years for the tetanus booster; every year for the fitness certificate, vaccination or smear; every six months for allergies; every three months for the pill; every two months for hypertension (you just never know when it might go up again); every month for infants; every fortnight for "normal" pregnancies (the others have to be hospitalised); every ten days for alcohol withdrawal support sessions; every eight days for leg ulcers; every week for morphine; every third day for fevers that won't go

down; every second day for pains in the neck; twice daily for the dying.

2. attitude of most doctors with reference to their former patients. (Ex.: "Personally, I couldn't put up any longer with the way he treats us.")

3. drug-based or surgical methods sometimes used by doctors to put an end to their patient's sufferings.

(See also: *Antibiotics. Pain. Euthanasia. Morphine.*)

White coat: distinctive sign of the caring profession, the white coat is an article of clothing whose significance is as polymorphous as a military uniform. Curiously, it is less the shape of the white coat which counts than what it carries or encloses. Under their white coat, auxiliary nurses wear a vest (especially in summer), nurses a skirt, departmental heads a bow-tie, house officers are clad in operating greens, physiotherapists sport shirt-sleeves and the crash team sweat. And if it happens that the men in white have the blues, it's always the patient they get shirty at.

"Un petit afflictionaire médical," *En soignant, en écrivant*, 2000.

JONATHAN KAPLAN
Working Underground

Jonathan Kaplan's book The Dressing Station *relates his experiences as a medical vagabond, ship's doctor and field surgeon, before concluding, in a nice twist, in the corporate underworld, where Pluto has managed to turn time itself into money: here Kaplan finds that war, or at least the perpetual readiness for war we might call mobilization, has followed him from the battlefields of Eritrea. Now he works in a bunker which seems to have dispensed with the outside world. His self-appointed global masters (their characteristics are those of slaves) have forgotten about the origins of labour in physical subjugation: in an odd reversal of perspective, voluntary servitude has become freedom in action. And a kind of game is played at breakneck speed, until necks do break.*

For the present, I work underground. Not in a reeking bunker with shit on the stairs, but in the profound, air-conditioned calm of a medical practice in the centre of London's financial quarter. The suite of consulting rooms lies several levels below the street. The floors above, and the deep green carpets, muffle all sound. Sometimes a human voice leaks through the partition that separates my office from an adjoining one: the voice of a colleague, in consultation or consolation. There is no daylight, only the flat white of neon. There have been times when a shelter like this would have been an ideal treatment area, while artillery thumped above. Instead it has the hush of an isolation ward.

I am acquiring some clinical experience for a qualification in the specialist field of occupational medicine—an interest that began when I saw those first cases of industrial mercury poisoning—and my text-books lie open on my desk while I await the arrival of my next patient. From this subterranean room I can feel, through the surrounding earth, the thud of construction work as foundations are sunk nearby for another banking headquarters. Now and then there is a sudden change in air pressure as the ventilation system kicks on, like the barometric shock-waves of a far off barrage.

I'm accustomed by now to dealing with the victims of war and crisis; swept away by forces they cannot escape, or crushed by the realization of their own helplessness. But in this new conflict—perhaps the strangest I have seen—my patients are under an attack far more insidious: from the very elements of the lives they have constructed for themselves. These brokers, bankers and traders are hard-working, productive individuals trying to survive in a ruthless environment. They are driven relentlessly by the pressure to succeed, and are laid low by the diseases of success: heart attacks, ulcers, anxiety attacks, addiction. When the financial tides go against them they suffer the terrors of failure; the sleep disorders, depression, impotence and alcoholism. In advance or in retreat the threats are endless. Some will eventually crack under the strain.

I am asked to assess a man whose incandescent performance on the futures floor over the past few months has been rewarded with massive bonuses and growing responsibility. Deferred to by all, his eccentric behaviour has been taken as clear evidence of his genius. Sometimes after work he's done crazy things in the stockbrokers' bars, but this has only added to his aura of omnipotence. Recently, though, unease has spread among senior management after clients began to complain about this paragon's increasingly weird business decisions. Challenged, the man attempted to describe the complex, personal formula he used for anticipating market movements. When he revealed the subliminal signals he has been receiving from sell-by dates on soft-drink cans, he was sent to me.

"It's all coded, doctor," he explains, pacing the room with his overcoat half-shed. "You just have to listen for the clues. A month ago I was in Paris when I realized that the people there weren't really speaking French. They were talking in code, in a made-up language that I wasn't supposed to understand. I tried to act as though I hadn't noticed, but eventually one of them went too far. As he passed me in the street he said something about my dealing record. That's privileged information: confidential. I demanded to know how he'd got it. There was a lot of shouting and the police came and tried to arrest me. That's how they keep you quiet if you find out what's going on."

It is not difficult to make a diagnosis—the man is suffering from acute schizophrenia—but I wonder at the sort of environment he works in where no one has apparently found anything odd about his paranoid delusions. I arrange for him to receive psychiatric care. Then I try to explain the situation to his line manager.

"What do you mean, a psychiatrist?" she demands. "This guy isn't crazy. In fact he's one of the best traders we've got."

"At the moment he is clinically ill," I explain. "He needs treatment. But in all likelihood he'll recover fully. He seems to have been quite well adjusted until he was exposed to levels of stress that he couldn't deal with. It happens to soldiers in combat: some become psychotic, but recover quickly when they are taken out of the front line."

"What do you mean, 'front line'?" she counters. "He's just a futures trader. No matter how good he was at his job, we can't take him back if he can't work under stress."

In the 1930s the cutting edge of medical research lay in the hunt for new hormones. The discoverer of insulin received a Nobel prize, as did the scientist who'd first worked out how the thyroid was controlled. All over the world, researchers were subjecting laboratory rats to unpleasant stimuli designed to evoke the secretion and "capture" of new hormones. Professor Hans Selye, working in Canada, noticed a consistent experimental finding among his rodents. Whatever the type of discomfort— noise, pain, cold or immobilization—the same pathological picture appeared. The lymphatic system, necessary for fighting infection, became shrunken. The adrenal glands enlarged, pumping adrenalin into the circulation, and the stomach shed its protective mucosa and became a mass of raw erosions. The organism could survive for a while, trying to adapt to the new demands it had to face, but if the stress was maintained it would eventually succumb.

"Stress illness" became a subject of strategic importance during the Second World War. In the winter of 1942, doctors among the German forces trapped in Stalingrad reported soldiers dying suddenly, without having been wounded or suffering from any diagnosable illness. A senior army pathologist named Girgensohn was flown specially into the besieged enclave to investigate the phenomenon. With formidable efficiency he managed, under constant shellfire, to perform autopsies on the bodies of fifty men who had died of no obvious cause; precious fuel was used to thaw out the cadavers so that they could be dissected. In half he found signs of starvation. The rest of the deaths he attributed—polishing his theory during the seven years he spent subsequently in a Russian prison camp—to metabolic exhaustion, caused by inexorable physical and psychological pressure.

Now, the existence of stress-related illness—even in circumstances markedly less extreme—is well accepted, though not really any better understood. I meet its casualties, sent by their company personnel departments with obliquely worded letters suggesting that they are no longer functioning according to the needs of the organization. Perhaps these people are off with illness too often. They might be hyperactive, with difficulty in concentrating on their work. Some have developed stomach ulcers. Sometimes the letters carry a suggestion of betrayal: here is an employee, they imply, who has let us down; perhaps you could furnish us with the means to fire him. In such cases the responsibility of the clinician is oddly skewed. The consultation is being carried out for the corporate client, the Company. But compassion, and the contract of care, exist between the doctor and his patient. Issues are sometimes far more complex than "Human Resources" comprehend.

A man is referred to me because he has been too relaxed. In the afternoons, when the markets enter their closing frenzy, he has been observed sitting at his desk apparently lost in reverie. As I talk to him he seems somnolent, almost drugged. He tells me about a series of incidental symptoms: backache, neck stiffness, headaches. He admits to being tired, but blames it on the hours he spends commuting to and from the office. He cannot accept that the quality of his work has deteriorated, or that the institution to which he has given his commitment is preparing to scrap him. Finally, the man denies drinking too much, his bluff faltering only when faced with the laboratory confirmation of alcoholic liver damage.

How could he have reached this abject stage, after negotiating every step toward success? With financial foresight he'd married a colleague, another high-flyer, and their combined incomes had made it possible to buy a wonderful home; to start a model family. Yet he has found no fulfilment. He hardly sees his young children except when he is exhausted. He is too tired to do any exercise. No longer hungry, he eats great, artery-clogging business lunches. His weight has increased, with his cholesterol level climbing steadily through the danger zone. I remind him of his fitness level at a previous health check just three years before, when—slim and ambitious—he'd played football, jogged and swam. He offers a wry explanation for his plight.

"Success brings guilt," he explains. "I never thought it would happen, but when I was promoted out of the shark pool to executive level the money became easier to earn, and there's so much of it. It just flows in, but without the anxiety of earning it. I owe my company for making me what I am, and now I worry that I'm no longer doing the best I can for it. So I try to compensate. Someone has to wine and dine the clients, and I've taken that on. I've tried to become the company's ace corporate entertainer."

I carry out pre-employment medicals on those at the beginning of the process: the new recruits, ardent to enter the fray. Feeling like a doctor on an army medical board, I examine them—eye tests, urine tests, blood tests, physicals—knowing how these young bodies will thicken with age and the attrition of stress. Those who make it onto the trading floors will live in an environment of uncertainty. Isolated behind a desk, hemmed in by computer screens, communicating in ciphers down a neck-cradled telephone, they will seldom see daylight. Their meals are bolted sandwiches, their reactions geared to the overhead news-screens carrying the market fluctuations. The traders work on commission: the better they perform, the greater the money, prestige and power. But behind every achiever, gnawing at his heels, gallops his nemesis: another climber—sharper, hungrier, more ruthless—waiting to usurp him. And over each corporate structure hangs the scythe of the merger, the faceless disdain of remote chief executives who can cancel a company and dissolve its workforce in a switch of contracts.

One of my patients is undergoing a comprehensive health assessment—a privilege offered by employers to productive staff—that includes a cardiac stress test. In the laboratory, beside banks of recording equipment, he pedals a specialized exercise bike furiously at the wall. Webs of electro-cardiograph wires trail from electrodes stuck across his chest and a mouthpiece muzzles him, measuring concentrations of oxygen and carbon dioxide in the air he forces in and out. He blinks sweat from his eyes as he tracks the lines on the cardiac monitor; not so much in concern at his own fitness, but as to how it might compare with that of his colleagues.

"I know that Max Guano from the dealing room was in here earlier," he pants as he is released from the apparatus.

"How long did he go on the bike? How soon did he reach maximum heart rate?"

Hoping—in a sympathetic way—to invoke a little insight and avoid violating confidentiality, I tell him that his question reminds me of the joke about two walkers faced by a voracious cheetah. One abandons himself to terror. The other hastily dons a pair of running shoes.

"Are you crazy?" screams the first man. "You can't outrun a cheetah."

"I don't have to," says the other. "I just have to outrun you."

My patient, though still trying to catch his breath, laughs generously. I can see he's humouring me: someone who has chosen the unfashionable career of making people better, rather than making money. By the standards he uses to judge himself and his colleagues—market performance, affluence, consumption and style—I am a complete loser. Within their system the pressure to win is high. I recall one man's response when, after a similar exercise test, I'd said that I would refer him to a cardiac specialist: his electro-cardiograph recording suggested that he might be at risk of a heart attack.

"You don't have to tell my company, do you, doctor?" was his first concern. "They'll take me off the dealing floor if they know."

No levity had occurred to me on that occasion: how can one raise a laugh out of someone who finds failure more frightening than death?

But even for those who make it to the top—who are rewarded with success—there is no protection. My patients include company directors, the ones that make the choices that make others sweat. Their decisions affect thousands of people, millions of pounds. Their reach is worldwide: "global" is the term that they prefer. Some are powerful enough to influence the policies of governments. A percentage of them earn salaries that, with share options and bonuses, exceed the entire annual health budgets of some of the ragged countries in which I've worked. Money has made these men visible, given them form. Their corporate empires are based on the trading of stocks whose value bears no relation to the concrete assets—plant, products and order books—of the companies that issue them. But dealing in abstract wealth, how do these men define themselves? If money begets power, what does phantom money produce? The lavish lifestyle so wondrously acquired can become a source of doubt. The country house, the children's private schools, the ponies and the all-accessories four-wheel-drive vehicle become increasingly unreal. The stage is set for a disaster, a Great Depression.

Sitting opposite me is a powerful man. He is the director of an international investment banking group, and everything—from his firm, close-shaven cheeks to his conservatively stylish suit—indicates success. He makes decisions involving millions; he undoubtedly earns his salary and his limousine. But his assurance has abruptly cracked.

"A ghost?"

He nods, doggedly confused.

"I was asleep at my girlfriend's flat. Something woke me. I opened my eyes and I could see clearly, although it was dark. A figure stood at the foot of the bed, looking at me." He shakes his head sharply, as though trying to jog the image from his mind. "I tried to wake my girlfriend but a weight pressed me to the bed, so great that I couldn't move a finger. The duvet felt as if it was made of lead."

He runs his hands over his pinstriped knees. "I know that room is pitch dark when the lights are off. I shouldn't have been able to see a thing, but I could see its eyes. I couldn't move, and I knew that I was going to die. It was my death looking at me."

"It must have been very frightening," I say, "but there is a logical explanation. What you've just given me is a classic description of a phenomenon called sleep paralysis, right down to the fear and in the inability to move."

He dismisses my suggestion. "A psychiatrist tried to tell me that, but he doesn't know what I saw. Neither do you. It was my death."

He explains that his relationship with his mistress has ended, his marriage has collapsed. He has been to counsellors, to mediums, to crystal healers, even to a Catholic priest. All, he feels, have tried to fashion his experience to fit their own realities.

Outwardly he still resembles the essential City stormer, the sort that sweats through regular sessions with his personal trainer to keep his stomach tight and his cholesterol level manageable. But the experience has forced a great rift in the beliefs that formed him. Now that he has seen the certainty of his death, nothing else has any truth. The great desires—possessions, accolades, power—that once motivated him are withered away. All he can do is what he has always done: to play the global markets. He does so with a nerveless fascination, watching himself make decisions about millions without any longer seeing the point of it. I feel a great compassion for the man. I wonder how much longer he can continue.

I talk about life, about motivation and hope, but to no avail. The man's desolation is as complete as that of a conscript who has stepped on a land-mine and now stares endlessly at his stumps. I realize that, tucked away in a sidestreet near the Bank of England, I am seeing the same pathology, the same shock of dislocation that I have encountered on other battlefields. All the figures I have for him—the blood results, the cardiograph, the very wires of his life—are meaningless. He sits beside my desk, distracted, like a man with another appointment to keep.

"There is no rush," I tell him. "Some try to avoid their deaths, others go out to find it. All will reach it at the same time."

"What do you know about it?" he asks, perhaps forgetting my profession. "What do you know about death?"

"Epilogue," *The Dressing Station, A Surgeon's Odyssey*, 2001.

SOURCES
AND
ACKNOWLEDGEMENTS

CHARLES DICKENS The Black Veil, Sketches by Boz: First Series 1836, London 1839.

GEORG BÜCHNER Beim Doktor, Woyzeck (1836/7), Nachgelassenen Schriften, Frankfurt am Main, 1850. Translated by the editor.

FANNY BURNEY Letter of 1812, The Diary and Letters of Madame d'Arblay, ed. Austin Dobson, London, 1904–5.

RENÉ THÉOPHILE HYACINTHE LAËNNEC Excerpt from On Mediate Auscultation, 1819, translation by John Forbes of Traité de l'Auscultation médiate, London, 1834.

JOHANN PETER HEBEL Der geheilte Patient, Der Rheinländische Hausfreund oder Neuer Kalender, Karlsruhe, 1807–11. Translated by the editor.

GEORGE ELIOT Chapter 45, Middlemarch, London, 1871–2.

NIKOLAI GOGOL Excerpt from The Nose, Moscow, 1836. Translated by Marjorie Farquharson.

GUSTAVE FLAUBERT XI, II, Madame Bovary: Moeurs de Province, Paris, 1857. Translated by the editor.

SØREN KIERKEGAARD Extract from Angest for det Gode (Det Dæmoniske), Caput IV, §2, Begrabet Angest, Copenhagen, 1844. Translated by the editor.

EMILY DICKINSON Excerpt from Poem 443, Poem 47, Poem 19, Complete Poems of Emily Dickinson, ed. Thomas Johnson, 1890.

SAMUEL BUTLER Excerpt from Some Erewhonian Trials, Erewhon, London, 1872.

FRIEDRICH NIETZSCHE V, 243, Menschlich, all-zu-menschlich, Leipzig, 1878. Translated by the editor.

LYTTON STRACHEY Part II, Florence Nightingale, Eminent Victorians, London, 1918.

LÉON DAUDET Excerpt from Souvenirs des Milieux Littéraires, Politiques, Artistiques et Médicaux, Paris, 1913–22. Translated by the editor.

ANTON CHEKHOV Letter to Maria Chekhova, 14–17 May, 1890, Correspondence, Moscow, 1973–83, translated by Sidonie Lederer and published by The Ecco Press, edited and with an introduction by Lillian Hellman. Copyright © 1955, 1984 by Lillian Hellman.

WILLIAM OSLER   Excerpt from Chauvinism in Medicine (1902 address to the Canadian Medical Association), Aequanimitas, London, 1904.

ARTHUR CONAN DOYLE   The Curse of Eve, Round the Red Lamp, London, 1897.

HJALMAR SÖDERBERG   July 17, excerpt from Doctor Glas, Stockholm, 1905, translated by Paul Britten Austin and published by The Harvill Press. Used by permission of The Random House Group Limited.

JEROME K. JEROME   Chapter I, Three Men in a Boat, London, 1889.

MARCEL PROUST   Excerpt from A l'Ombre des Jeunes Filles en Fleur, volume II, A la Recherche du Temps Perdu, Paris, 1919.

G.K. CHESTERTON   The Medical Mistake, What's Wrong with the World?, London, 1910.

MIKHAIL BULGAKOV   The Killer, Meditsinsky Rabotnik, 1925. Translated by Marjorie Farquharson and the editor.

GOTTFRIED BENN   Schöne Jugend-Kreislauf-Nachtcafé, Gedichte in der Fassung der Erstdrucke, herausgegeben von Bruno Hillebrand, Fischer Taschenbuch Verlag GmbH, Frankfurt am Main, 1982. Gottfried Benn: Sämtliche Werke, Stuttgarter Ausgabe. Band I: Gedichte 1, Stuttgart 1986, Seiten 11, 12, 19. Translated by the editor. Used by permission of Verlagsgemeinschaft Klett-Cotta Stuttgart.

ALAIN   Médecine, Propos sur le Bonheur. Copyright © Editions Gallimard, Paris, 1928. Translated by the editor. Used by permission of Editions Gallimard.

FRANZ KAFKA   Ein Landarzt, Ein Landarzt: Kleine Erzählungen, Leipzig, 1919. Translated by the editor.

GEORGES DUHAMEL   Excerpt from L'Humaniste et l'Automate. Translated by the editor. Copyright © Paul Hartmann, Paris. 1933.

BERTOLT BRECHT   Rede eines Arbeiters an einen Arzt, Svendborger Gedichte, copyright 1939 by Malik Verlag, London. Copyright © Suhrkamp Verlag, Frankfurt am Main, 1960. Translated by the editor. Used by permission of Suhrkamp Verlag.

WILLIAM CARLOS WILLIAMS   Jean Beicke, from The Doctor Stories. Copyright © 1938 by William Carlos Williams. Reprinted by permission of New Directions Publishing Corp.

ALFRED DÖBLIN   Döblin über Döblin, Autobiographische Schriften und letzte Aufzeichnungen. Copyright © Walter-Verlag AG, Olten, 1980. Translated by the editor.

JULES ROMAINS   Acte III, scène VI, Knock ou La Triomphe de la Médecine, Paris, 1924. Translated by the editor.

ROBERT MUSIL Der Bedrohte Oedipus, Nachlass zu Lebzeiten, Zürich, 1936. Copyright © Rowohlt Verlag GmbH, Hamburg. Translated by the editor.

VIRGINIA WOOLF Illness—An Unexploited Mine, Forum, 1926. Reprinted by permission of The Society of Authors as the Literary Representatives of the Estate of Virginia Woolf.

GOTTFRIED BENN Irrationalismus und moderne Medizin, Essays und Reden in der Fassung der Erstdrucke, herausgegeben von Bruno Hillebrand, Fischer Taschenbuch Verlag, Frankfurt am Main, 1989. Gottfried Benn: Sämtliche Werke, Stuttgarter Ausgabe. Band III: Prosa 1, Stuttgart 1978, Seiten 340-349. Translated by the editor. Used by permission of Verlagsgemeinschaft Klett-Cotta Stuttgart.

KURT TUCHOLSKY (Kaspar Hauser) Befürchtung, 1929. Copyright © Rowohlt Verlag, Reinbek bei Hamburg. Translated by the editor.

GEORGE ORWELL How the Poor Die. Copyright © George Orwell, 1946, reprinted by kind permission of Bill Hamilton as the Literary Executor of the Estate of the late Sonia Brownell Orwell.

KARL KRAUS Aphorisms from Half-Truths and One-and-a-Half Truths, translated by Harry Zohn. Reprinted by permission of Carcanet Press Ltd., Manchester, 1985.

LOUIS-FERDINAND CÉLINE Excerpt from Voyage au Bout de la Nuit, 1933. Copyright © Editions Gallimard. Translated by the editor. Used by permission of Calder Publications.

DEZSÖ KOSZTOLÁNYI Az idegen, Hét Köver Esztendo (Seven Fat Years), Budapest, 1930. Translated by the editor. Copyright © Dezso Kosztolányi.

PAUL VALÉRY Socrate et son Médecin, Mélanges, Œuvres complètes. Copyright © Editions Gallimard, 1941. Translated by the editor. Used by permission of Editions Gallimard.

ERNST WEISS Die Herznaht, Gesammelte Werke: die Erzählungen, Suhrkamp, Frankfurt am Main, 1982. Translated by the editor.

MICHEL LEIRIS Excerpts from Manhood: A Journey from Childhood into the Fierce Order of Virility, Paris. Copyright © Editions Gallimard, 1939. Translated from the French by Richard Howard, © 1963, 1984. Reprinted by permission of Chicago University Press.

MIGUEL TORGA Extracts from Diário I–XII, Poesia e Prosa, Coimbra, 1941, 1943, 1946, 1949, 1951, 1953, 1956, 1959, 1964, 1968, 1973, 1977. Translated by the editor.

ALBERT CAMUS Excerpt from chapter IV, La Peste, Editions Gallimard, Paris, 1947. Translated by the editor.

PETER BAMM Therapie als moralisches Problem, Ex Ovo: Essays über die Medizin, Hamburg, 1948. Translated by the editor. Copyright © Peter Bamm, by permission of Dr. phil. Walter Stehli, Zürich.

GUIDO CERONETTI Excerpts from The Silence of the Body: Materials for the Study of Medicine, translated from the Italian by Michael Moore. Translation copyright © 1993 by Michael Moore. Reprinted by permission of Farrar, Straus and Giroux, LLC.

SAMUEL BECKETT Extract from Watt, London, 1959. Copyright © Samuel Beckett. Reprinted by permission of Calder Publications.

KARL VALENTIN Beim Arzt, Alles von Karl Valentin, Munich, 1978. Translated by the editor. With the kind permission of Piper Verlag. Copyright © Piper Verlag GmbH, München, 1985.

JEAN STAFFORD Excerpt from The Interior Castle, The Collected Stories by Jean Stafford. Copyright © 1969 by Jean Stafford. Reprinted by permission of Farrar, Straus and Giroux, LLC.

RICHARD HUELSENBECK Excerpt from Reise bis ans Ende der Freiheit: Autobiographische Fragmente, Heidelberg, 1984. Translated by the editor. Copyright © Richard Huelsenbeck 1984.

RAYMOND QUENEAU Du bon emploi des tranquillisants, Contes et Propos. Copyright © Editions Gallimard, Paris, 1981. Translated by the editor.

JEAN REVERZY Le Médecin et l'Argent, Œuvres, Flammarion, Paris, 1977. Copyright © Jean Reverzy. Translated by the editor.

WELDON KEES The Clinic, The Collected Poems of Weldon Kees, edited by Donald Justice, reprinted by permission of the University of Nebraska Press. Copyright © 1962, 1975, University of Nebraska Press.

W.H. AUDEN The Art of Healing, Collected Poems, Faber and Faber, London, 1976. Copyright © 1976 by Edward Mendelson, William Meredith and Monroe K. Spears, executors of the Estate of W.H. Auden.

R.D. LAING Excerpt from The Birds of Paradise, in The Politics of Experience, London, 1967. Copyright © R.D. Laing, 1967. Reprinted by permission of The Penguin Group (UK).

JOHN BERGER Excerpt from A Fortunate Man (with photographs by Jean Mohr), The Penguin Press, London, 1967. Copyright © 1967 John Berger & Jean Mohr.

PHILIP LARKIN The Building, Collected Poems, edited by Anthony Thwaite, Faber and Faber Limited and The Marvell Press, London, 1988. Copyright © the Estate of Philip Larkin.

ANTHONY DANIELS Ivan Illich: 1926–2002, The New Criterion 2003. Reprinted by kind permission of the author and The New Criterion.

GAEL TURNBULL May, A Year and A Day, Mariscat Press, Glasgow, 1985. Reprinted by kind permission of the author and Mariscat Press.

DANNIE ABSE Lunch with a Pathologist, White Coat, Purple Coat: Collected Poems 1948–1988, London, 1989. Copyright © 1977, 1989, 1991 by Dannie Abse.

OLIVER SACKS The Naturalist: An Interview with Sandee Brawarsky, The Lancet 1997, Vol. 350, 9084: 1092. Reprinted by permission of Elsevier.

ROBERT PINSKY Doctor Frolic, Sadness and Happiness, Princeton University Press. Copyright © 1975. Reprinted by permission of Princeton University Press.

ROBERTSON DAVIES Episodes from The Cunning Man. Copyright © 1994. Reprinted by permission of McClelland and Stewart Ltd, the Canadian Publisher.

MIROSLAV HOLUB Suffering, translated by George Theiner, Selected Poems, 1967. Copyright © Miroslav Holub, 1967. Translation copyright © Penguin Books, 1967.

SUSAN SONTAG Excerpt from Illness as Metaphor, Farrar, Straus and Giroux, New York, 1978. Copyright © Susan Sontag, 1977, 1978.

PETER GOLDSWORTHY A Statistician to his Love, This Goes with That: Selected Poems 1970–1990, Sydney, 1991. Reprinted with kind permission of the author.

THOM GUNN Save the Word, Boss Cupid, Faber and Faber Limited, London. Copyright © Thom Gunn, 2000.

BERT KEIZER Living well, dying well, Medicine and Humanity, edited by Marshall Marinker, King's Fund Publishing, London. Copyright © King's Fund 2001.

JEFF ARONSON Patient centred verbs, from British Medical Journal 2002, 325: 387. Reprinted by permission of the BMJ Publishing Group.

MARTIN WINCKLER Petit Afflictionnaire Médical, En soignant, en écrivant, Montpellier, 2000. Translated by the editor. Used by kind permission of the author and Indigène éditions.

JONATHAN KAPLAN Epilogue from: The Dressing Station: A Surgeon's Odyssey, 2001. Copyright © Jonathan Kaplan, 2001. Reprinted by kind permission of the author and A.M. Heath & Co. Ltd.